Market Consistency

For other titles in the Wiley Finance Series
please see www.wiley.com/finance

Market Consistency

Model Calibration in Imperfect Markets

Malcolm H.D. Kemp

WILEY

A John Wiley and Sons, Ltd., Publication

Registered office
John Wiley & Sons Ltd, The Atrium, Southern Gate, Chichester, West Sussex, PO19 8SQ, United Kingdom

For details of our global editorial offices, for customer services and for information about how to apply for permission to reuse the copyright material in this book please see our website at www.wiley.com.

Wiley also publishes its books in a variety of electronic formats. Some content that appears in print may not be available in electronic books.

Designations used by companies to distinguish their products are often claimed as trademarks. All brand names and product names used in this book are trade names, service marks, trademarks or registered trademarks of their respective owners. The publisher is not associated with any product or vendor mentioned in this book. This publication is designed to provide accurate and authoritative information in regard to the subject matter covered. It is sold on the understanding that the publisher is not engaged in rendering professional services. If professional advice or other expert assistance is required, the services of a competent professional should be sought.

Library of Congress Cataloging-in-Publication Data

Kemp, Malcolm H. D.
    Market consistency : model calibration in imperfect markets / Malcolm H. D. Kemp.
        p. cm. – (Wiley finance series)
    ISBN 978-0-470-77088-7 (cloth)
    1. Capital market.   2. Banks and banking.   3. Risk management.   I. Title.
    HG4523.K46 2009
    332′.0415–dc22

                                                                    2009021636

A catalogue record for this book is available from the British Library.

ISBN 978-0-470-77088-7 (H/B)

Typeset in 10/12pt Times by Aptara Inc., New Delhi, India
Printed in Great Britain by CPI Antony Rowe, Chippenham, Wiltshire

Contents

Preface

This book grew out of a desire on my part to offer constructive help to the many different individuals who need to take account of 'what the market has to say' in their day-to-day activities. It builds on several papers and talks that I have given that explore how risk management and related disciplines might develop as fair valuation principles become more entrenched in finance and regulatory practice.

The most obvious starting point for such a journey, and probably the one most focused on by previous authors, is the problem of how to place a *market* value on a financial instrument or other asset or liability. This process is typically known as *marking-to-market* in the banking, market making and asset management worlds. It is known as adopting a *market consistent* or *fair* valuation (if applied to less liquid assets and liabilities) within the insurance and accounting worlds.

Marking-to-market has become a core business discipline for many different types of financial organisation in recent years. Significant further growth in its use can be expected as a result of the implementation of the European Union's *Solvency II* proposals for EU insurance companies. The underlying conceptual framework of these proposals is similar to the framework underlying the Basel Capital Accords applicable to banks.

However, marking-to-market has also been blamed by some for exacerbating the worldwide recession that was developing as this book was being written. We call this economic event the '2007–09 credit crisis' throughout this book even though it was no longer just a 'credit' crisis by the time this book was completed in early 2009 and it did not then look particularly likely to have drawn to a close by the end of 2009.

In this book we therefore first explore the theoretical justifications for (and against) market consistency. This allows us to identify from first principles when such an approach might be of most relevance and what it might then look like. Special attention is given to how market consistency can be adopted in ways that do *not* result in undue pro-cyclicality in regulatory frameworks, given the importance of this to society at large.

Merely deciding that market consistency might be a useful concept doesn't actually make it easy to apply. For example, when implementing Solvency II, EU insurance companies will face the practical challenge of identifying suitable market consistent valuations to place on their insurance liabilities even though markets in such liabilities are typically poorly developed, if they exist at all. How can you in practice develop models for valuing such instruments in these circumstances?

Moreover, in today's interconnected world, the challenges that one financial sector might face are often mirrored in other sectors. At the time of writing, we were in the middle of one of the most severe credit crunches in recent times. Markets in many types of commercial paper, asset backed securities and collateralised debt obligations had largely dried up. Bid-offer spreads on even relatively straightforward bonds had reached historical wides. More complex instruments were being ascribed very different marks-to-market by different market makers.

Sometimes marking-to-market is explicitly contrasted with *marking-to-model*. Such an approach involves defining a model the output of which is then deemed to be the relevant (market) price to use for the asset or liability in question. Some of the challenges seen in some of the markets mentioned above seem in part to reflect inconsistent or inappropriate design of models used for these purposes. However, there is no clear dividing line between marking-to-market and marking-to-model. Indeed, it is unrealistic to expect to be able to avoid marking-to-model especially for less liquid and less fungible assets. For example, market prices used in the property, i.e. real estate, markets are typically the output from surveyors' 'models', based on rental income, etc., which have been 'calibrated' to market information by reference to recent market transactions on similar but not identical properties. When tested by actual market transactions they may prove unreliable.

I strongly believe in the merits of adopting a holistic perspective. The recent trend towards enterprise risk management suggests that others also think viewing things holistically has merit. So, it seems to me that limiting market consistency *merely* to the task of valuing assets and liabilities is to diminish its true worth. There are many other areas of financial practice that can benefit from better incorporation of information extracted from market prices or other market observables.

In particular, it seems to me that market consistency is of great importance in risk management and even provides some key insights that can enhance portfolio construction. Indeed, I would argue that this must be the case. When thinking about the process of managing assets and liabilities end to end, we must start where we currently are. However, it would be a poorly managed organisation that wasn't then interested in understanding what might happen going forwards. A natural follow-on question to ask is what might happen if we *changed* the asset and liability mix. By implication we are trying to identify what might be 'good' changes to make to the asset/liability profile. Of course, applying market consistency to these disciplines involves somewhat different techniques to those applicable to the valuation problem. However, the underlying philosophy is the same, i.e. to make appropriate use of whatever information can be inferred from market observables.

However sophisticated is the analysis, market consistency cannot answer all questions. The world in which we live includes 'unknown unknowns'. There are certain problems that cannot even in principle be fully addressed by reference to market observables. Irrespective of how well developed a market might be, it will not provide all the information that might be needed to tackle all of these problems. For example, over the last few decades there has been a huge growth in derivatives markets. Core to this has been the development of associated hedging algorithms. Indeed, one can argue that a key reason for the wide adoption of, say, the Black-Scholes option pricing formula is that it provides a framework for *hedging* risk, as well as for *pricing* risk. Less well appreciated is that it is intrinsically harder to ensure *hedging* metrics are market consistent than it is to ensure that *pricing* metrics are market consistent. The market observables that we would need for the former are more complex and therefore less prevalent than those needed for the latter.

Given the holistic perspective that I think market consistency deserves, I have tried to write this book bearing in mind the varying needs of the different types of practitioner who should be interested in market consistency. Actuaries, auditors and other professionals are being required as part of modern financial regulation to focus increasingly on market consistent valuations. They may find the earlier chapters and the suggestions in the final chapter on how to tackle less liquid instruments particularly helpful. Traders and investment managers (and quants working alongside them) may be most interested in the later chapters relating to portfolio construction and hedging. Risk managers are likely to be interested in both of the above but may be particularly interested in the chapters in the middle of the book dealing with the practical ramifications of market consistency on risk management activities and on regulatory capital frameworks. Structurers, salespeople and others developing or marketing products to financial services organisations may find helpful the entire spectrum of material covered in the book. Every part of it may help them help their clients better in the changing world in which we live. Back office professionals preparing mark-to-market valuations may be most interested in the sections on marking-to-market less liquid instruments. Regulators may value the insights and the principles that the book sets out when exploring whether and how to place greater focus on market pricing in regulatory frameworks. And I hope that students, academics and others will find the systematic treatment of all of this material interesting and helpful in their ongoing studies and research.

The actual structure of the book naturally reflects some preferences on my part. I appreciate that not all potential readers will have a strong mathematical background. More technical mathematical aspects of market consistency are therefore concentrated into a few chapters. They are developed in ways that I hope will prove relatively intuitive to follow even for those who are not 'rocket scientists' at heart. The book aims to blend together a systematic development of underlying principles with their practical application. Core principles are highlighted as they arise in the text. My hope is that clear articulation of these principles will lead to long and fruitful interactions that will enhance the work that we all do within the financial community.

Acknowledgements

I would like to thank Pete Baker, Aimee Dibbens and their colleagues at Wiley for encouraging me to embark on writing this book. Thanks are also due to Colin Wilson, Seamus Creedon, Stephen Bashforth and others who have read parts of this manuscript and provided helpful comments on how it might be improved. A special appreciation goes to my wife and family for supporting me as this book took shape. I would also like to record my thanks to colleagues at Threadneedle Asset Management for providing an environment in which its ideas could develop and take root.

However, whilst I am very grateful for the support I have received from various directions during the writing of this book, I still take sole responsibility for any errors and omissions that it contains.

Abbreviations

AFIC	Association Française des Investisseurs en Capital
ALCO	asset-liability committee
AMA	Advanced Measurement Approaches
APT	Arbitrage Pricing Theory
ASB	Accounting Standards Board (UK)
ASRF	Asymptotic Single Risk Factor model
BBA	British Bankers Association
BCBS	Basel Committee on Banking Supervision
BVCA	British Venture Capital Association
CAPM	Capital Asset Pricing Model
CAQ	Center for Audit Quality
CDO	collateralised debt obligation
CDS	credit default swap
CEIOPS	Committee of European Insurance and Occupational Pensions Supervisors
CESR	Committee of European Securities Regulators
CFO Forum	Chief Financial Officer Forum (of major European listed, and some non-listed, insurance companies)
CPPI	constant proportional portfolio insurance
CPDO	constant proportional debt obligation
CRDV01	credit DV01
CRMPG	Counterparty Risk Management Policy Group
CRO Forum	Chief Risk Officer Forum (of major European insurance companies and financial conglomerates)
DB	defined benefit
DC	defined contribution
DV01	dollar value change for a basis point move in interest rates
EBF	European Banking Federation
EEA	European Economic Area
EEV	European Embedded Value
EL	expected (credit) loss
Eonia	Euro OverNight Index Average
ETF	exchange traded fund

Euribor	Euro Interbank Offered Rate
EU	European Union
EVCA	European Private Equity and Venture Capital Association
FAS	Financial Accounting Standard (USA)
FASB	Financial Accounting Standards Board (USA)
FSA	Financial Services Authority (UK)
GAAP	Generally Accepted Accounting Principles
GARCH	generalised autoregressive conditional heteroscedasticity
GC (repo rate)	'general collateral' (repo rate)
GPPC	Global Public Policy Committee
IAA	International Actuarial Association
IASB	International Accounting Standards Board
ICA	Individual Capital Assessment
ICAAP	Internal Capital Adequacy Assessment Process
ICG	Individual Capital Guidance
IORP	Institutions for Occupational Retirement Provision Directive
IRB	Internal Ratings Based approach
IRDV01	interest rate DV01
LGD	loss given default
LHP	Large Homogeneous Portfolio (pricing model)
Libor	London Interbank Offered Rate
LTCM	Long-Term Capital Management
MCEV	market consistent embedded value
MCR	Minimum Capital Requirement
MMMF	money market mutual fund
MVA	market value adjustment
NNEG	no negative equity guarantee
OIS	overnight index swap
ORSA	Own Risk and Solvency Assessment
OTC	over-the-counter
PCA	principal components analysis
PCAOB	Public Company Accounting Oversight Board
PIT	point in time
PPFM	Principles and Practices of Financial Management
QIS	Quantitative Impact Study
SCR	Solvency Capital Requirement
SHIP	Safe Home Income Plans (code of practice)
SIV	structured investment vehicle
Sonia	Sterling OverNight Index Average
SPV	special purpose vehicle
SREP	Supervisory Review and Evaluation Process
SRI	socially responsible investment
SRP	Supervisory Review Process
TARP	Troubled Asset Relief Program
TCF	treating customers fairly
TTC	through the cycle

TVaR	tail Value-at-Risk (aka Expected Shortfall)
UCITS	Undertakings for Collective Investments in Transferable Securities
UK	United Kingdom of Great Britain and Northern Ireland
UL	unexpected (credit) loss
US and USA	United States of America
VaR	Value-at-Risk

Notation

$a = $ swap rate per annum
$A = $ number of units of underlying in hedging portfolio
$\alpha = $ confidence level, also autocorrelation parameter
$\hat{\alpha} = $ observed number of breaches of confidence level
$\alpha_i = $ alpha (implied or realised) from stock i
$\mathbf{b} = (b_1, \ldots, b_n)^T = $ benchmark weights
$B = $ amount of amount of 'cash' (i.e. risk-free) in hedging portfolio
$\beta_{i,j} = $ the beta of stock i to factor j
$c_d = $ 'pure' credit default risk element (in spread decomposition)
$c_i = $ contribution to tracking error from ith security
$c_s = $ (corporate bond) spread
$c_u = $ 'credit uncertainty' risk element (in spread decomposition)
$c_y = $ convenience yield adjustment in multiplicative liquidity model
$C(S,t) = $ price of a call option
$C(\ldots) = $ the copula of a multivariate distribution
$CQV(t) = $ cumulative quadratic variation
$d = $ down movement in a binomial lattice
$D(x) = $ value of digital call spread paying 1 if at maturity underlying is between $S(x)$ and $S(x) + dx$
$D(\mathbf{p},\mathbf{q}) = $ relative entropy of probability distribution $\mathbf{p}$ versus $\mathbf{q}$
$D(X_T, T) = $ deflator applicable to contingency X_T at time T
$Dur = $ duration (of bond)
$\Delta = $ option delta
$E(X/I) = $ expected value (now) of X given state of the world I using the risk-neutral measure (and suitable risk-free discount rate)
$E^*(XT) = $ expected value (now) of contingency X_T using 'real world' probabilities (and suitable risk-free discount rate)
$\varepsilon_i = $ random (Brownian motion) contribution to return for stock i
$f = $ number of units of the underlying invested in a hedging portfolio
$f(t) = $ value of a forward contract
$f_{fut} = $ 'market value' of a futures contract
$F = $ forward price

$\mathbf{F}$ = factor loadings matrix, f_{ij}, where return on ith security has 'exposures' $f_{i,j}$ to jth 'factor loading'

$F(\ldots)$ = cumulative distribution function of a multivariate distribution

F_C = credit rating factor in computation of RCM

g = number of times S invested in the risk-free security in a hedging portfolio

$\gamma = \sigma\sqrt{T-t}$ = cumulative volatility from time t to time T

γ_1 = skew of distribution

γ_2 = (excess) kurtosis of distribution

Γ = option gamma

h = (short) time step

I = discrete income payment

$I(t)$ = comparator index for extrapolation/interpolation purposes

$I_t(\alpha)$ = indicator indicating 'failure', taking value of 1 if the actual outcome for time period t is worse than the α-quantile VaR otherwise 0

$J_{i,p}$ = contribution to return from unpredictable changes to volatility

K = strike price, i.e. exercise price, of an option

κ = option vega

l_a = additional spread to compensate for illiquidity in additive liquidity model

l_m = liquidity multiplier applied to $(c_d + c_u)$ in multiplicative liquidity model

L_C = loss if the underlying were to crash instantaneously to zero

L_S = loss if the underlying were to jump instantaneously to (near) infinity

LGD = loss given default

λ = risk aversion factor, also option lambda

m = number of factors, also fitted mean drift versus risk-free rate in weighted Monte Carlo analysis

m_i = marginal contribution to tracking error from ith security

m_0 = 'forward' strike level = $V_K(0)$

m_1 = 'forward' spot level = $V_s(0)$

M^* = maturity adjustment in computation of RCC

$MCTVaR$ = market-consistent tail Value-at-Risk

$Mdur$ = modified duration (of bond)

μ = mean drift of underlying

$\mu(\mathrm{x}, \mathrm{t})$ = mean drift of a multivariate underlying

n = number of securities

$N(z)$ = cumulative Normal distribution function

$p = (p_1, \ldots, p_n)^T$ portfolio weights

p_d = risk-neutral probability of down movement in a binomial lattice

p_u = risk-neutral probability of up movement in a binomial lattice

p_i = adjusted sample probabilities in weighted Monte Carlo analysis

P = principal amount applicable to a swap transaction

$P(x)$ = probability of x occurring (usually referring to the risk-neutral probability distribution)

$P^*(x)$ = probability of x occurring (referring to the real world probability distribution)

$P(S, t)$ = price of a put option

PD = probability of default

POF = proportion of failures

$\Phi(x, t)$ = market price of risk vector

q = continuously compounded dividend rate

q_i = original sample probabilities in weighted Monte Carlo analysis

r = continuously compounded interest rate

r_i = return on stock i

r_t = return series indexed by time t

$\tilde{r}_t$ = underlying 'true' return series of an autocorrelated return series

$\mathbf{r}$ = vector of expected returns

$R(t)$ = path that the underlying might take

RCC = regulatory capital charge (for credit risk)

RCM = risk capital margin (credit element)

ρ = asset correlation or correlation between different series, also option rho

$\rho_{A,B}$ = correlation between random variables A and B

s = spread between different interest rates (particularly between the market implied yield on customer liabilities and the risk-free rate), also square root of fitted implied variance in weighted Monte Carlo analysis

$S(t)$ = spot price at time t of one unit of the underlying

σ = volatility in underlying

$\sigma(\mathbf{x}, t)$ = volatility (matrix) applicable to a multivariate underlying

σ_A = volatility (forward-looking tracking error) of returns A coming from positions $\mathbf{a}$

σ_i = idiosyncratic risk of the ith security

t = time (now)

T = time at maturity

$\mathbf{T}$ = matrix characterising a factor classification

$TVaR$ = tail Value-at-Risk, aka expected shortfall

u = up movement in a binomial lattice, also price of a generalised derivative

$U(\mathbf{x})$ = utility

$U_{i,k}$ = contributions to return from unpredictable changes to volatility

$v(t)$ = present value now of a payment of 1 at time t

$V(\mathbf{a})$ = (market) value or price of a pay-off $\mathbf{a}$

$V(S, t)$ = value of derivative at time t if underlying is S

$\mathbf{V}$ = covariance matrix of joint probability distribution

$\hat{V}$ = covariance matrix between 'factor' returns excluding idiosyncratic risk

$V_K(t)$ = price of a zero coupon bond delivering K and maturing at time T

$V_S(t)$ = price of a zero dividend contract delivering one unit of underlying at time T

$VaR(p)$ = Value-at-Risk at a pth confidence level

x_j = return from factor j

X_T = a contingency at time T

Y_C = contributions to return from transaction costs

Y_E = cross-contributions to return from joint interactions between $U_{i,k}$, $J_{i,p}$ and Y_c

$\mathbf{Y}$ = sparse $n \times n$ matrix characterising idiosyncratic risks

Z = value of a zero coupon bond

1

Introduction

1.1 MARKET CONSISTENCY

This book is about *market consistency*, a term that we use throughout this book as a catch-all for the activity of taking account of 'what the market has to say' in financial practice. We will explore, from first principles, when it is (and when it isn't) most appropriate to listen to what the market is saying. We will also explore how in practice we might extract information from 'the market' (and also what 'the market' is) in those circumstances where market consistency has merit.

We can characterise the incorporation of market consistency in a piece of financial analysis as involving the creation of a suitable model or idealised abstraction of how something works, which is then calibrated using appropriate market derived information. We focus in this book on models applicable to three core areas of financial practice, namely:

(a) *Valuation methodologies*, i.e. the placing of values or prices on positions in financial instruments or other sorts of assets or liabilities;
(b) *Risk management processes*, i.e. the assessment and management of the (financial) risks that are created by holding such positions; and
(c) *Portfolio construction techniques*, i.e. the selection of which sorts of such positions or risks it is most desirable to hold (or avoid), and in what quantities.

We do so because these three disciplines are closely allied, both in theory and in practice. We do not value something in complete isolation. Instead, there must be reasons for doing so. One key reason is to understand better the characteristics of the positions we currently have. But what is the point of gaining this understanding? Surely, it is to be better placed to understand the potential behaviour that the positions might exhibit in the future. We want to understand the *risks* and possible *rewards* attaching to them, i.e. how they might behave in adverse and favourable circumstances.[1] The natural next step is then to consider and take decisions about how best to manage the risks and potential rewards we face. This in turn naturally leads to the question of which exposures we should adopt in the first place.

---

[1] We focus in this book principally on activities that concentrate on the present and the future. Another reason for valuing things refers more to the past, namely, to enable owners of an entity to judge how well its managers have performed as custodians of the owners' assets. Using movements in 'fair' (i.e. market or market consistent) values for this purpose is a well-established technique in the context of performance measurement of investment portfolios (or unitised funds), see e.g. Kemp (2005). However, misuse of such techniques within bank management and trader remuneration structures can create systemic instabilities, as Turner (2009) points out when discussing the causes of the 2007–2009 credit crunch. He notes that such remuneration structures can encourage irrational exuberance and lead to excessive rewards being paid for financial innovation that delivers no fundamental economic benefit but merely exploits opacity and asymmetry of information and knowledge. Such rewards may then eventually turn out merely to have been based on 'illusory' market value gains.

1.2   THE PRIMACY OF THE 'MARKET'

Why might we care about what the market has to say? The world of finance is rarely far away from anyone these days. For some, life is a day-to-day struggle to make ends meet. Others, more fortunate, may have surplus funds deposited with banks or invested in the multitude of financial products now emanating from the world's financial centres. But even they will often have been in debt at some stage in their lives. Perhaps this will have been to finance the purchase of a car or house, or, for the more entrepreneurially minded, to support a new business venture. The same is true on a larger scale for companies, charities, even entire countries. For better or worse, money, as a means of storing and transferring value, has proved to be one of humankind's more important inventions. Indeed, it has been like this for many centuries, at least for the wealthier end of society. Julius Caesar built up huge debts (like several other Roman politicians of his day) and then amassed huge wealth on his way to seizing supreme power in the Roman Republic. Banking provided the wealth that enabled the Medici patronage of the Renaissance.

The last few decades have arguably seen a spurt in financial innovation. There has been huge growth in derivatives markets and in the range and sophistication of financial products and instruments now available to individuals, corporations and financial entities. In part, this reflects the technological innovation, economic growth and capital accumulation that large parts of the world have seen since the Second World War. It also, in my opinion, reflects the particular focus given during this period by financial theory and practice to the concept of *the market*. By this we mean some possibly hypothetical construct in which whatever we are interested in can be bought or sold without (too much) difficulty. Economic theory has always argued that properly functioning marketplaces are important for effective competition and hence efficient allocation of resources across an economy. The core innovation over the last few decades has been to apply this more general economic insight to finance itself.

We have seen, for example, changes in the underlying business models that many banks have adopted, away from a 'borrow and hold' business model (in which a bank would raise money from its depositors and then itself lend the proceeds, or some multiple of them, to some of its other customers) and towards an 'originate and sell' business model (in which the bank's assets are repackaged and sold to other capital markets participants). Some reversal of this trend is also now apparent as more straightened economic times loom ahead.

The 'sell' element of such a business model ultimately involves transfer of risk exposures to third parties. It is of course facilitated if there are ready markets in such exposures. It places particular importance on the (market) prices at which transfers of these exposures can take place. Many banks and bank-like entities have historically been involved to some extent in market making activities. Increasingly, they have become 'market makers' of their own core cash flow streams.

Other players in the financial markets, such as pension funds and insurance companies, have perhaps been less affected by this fundamental change in financial mindsets. However, they too do not operate in a vacuum. The mere possibility of transferring blocks of pension benefits or policyholder entitlements reminds (or ought to remind) them that they too live not only surrounded by markets but also, in some sense, *within* them. For better or for worse, a focus on 'what the market has to say' is likely to be here to stay.

This does not mean that enthusiasm for 'the market' will not wax and wane over time. As I wrote this book, a number of pillars of the financial services industry were revealing eye-watering sized losses. These were arguably a consequence of their overexuberant hope that markets would continue to operate in ways to which they had previously become accustomed. Some of these firms subsequently defaulted. Others had to be rescued in mammoth government sponsored bailouts as governments endeavoured to bring stability to their financial systems. Enthusiasm for listening to what the market has to say often diminishes when what it is saying is unpalatable!

1.3 CALIBRATING TO THE 'MARKET'

Merely observing that there may be useful information extractable from the 'market' doesn't actually help us extract this information. Nor does it help us work out when such information is of most use or how to use it in ways that do not exacerbate systemic, i.e. economy-wide, risks. This is particularly true when the 'market' does not have all of the characteristics of the perfectly behaved construct of economic theory. In this book we explore how market consistency can be applied in the world in which we actually live, where markets are imperfect.

As mentioned above we focus in this book on three interrelated disciplines, namely valuation, risk management and portfolio construction. In each case, we focus on practical ways of incorporating greater market consistency, whilst simultaneously providing a systematic treatment of the underlying theory. For example, when dealing with valuation, we explore the theory and regulatory drivers currently favouring greater use of *marking-to-market* (as well as describing some of the current countervailing drivers) and we explore the differences, or often the lack thereof, between mark-to-market and mark-to-model valuations. However, there are also sections offering more practical guidance on how to determine market consistent valuations for assets or liabilities where markets are limited, illiquid or even almost non-existent.

In the field of risk management, market consistency can mean different things to different people. In my view, we are likely in due course to see a paradigm shift towards greater use of market implied risk measures. The principles involved are explored in some detail, because of the important ramifications this would have for practitioners in this field. However, I accept that this view has yet to achieve wide acceptance (not least because of the practical challenges involved and the unpalatable answers it might generate). The book therefore also provides a full treatment of the more limited types of market consistency that are incorporated in current risk measurement and management paradigms. These might best be described as attempting to quantify (probabilistically or otherwise) the 'real world' likelihood of some risk materialising over a given timeframe.

The application of market consistency to portfolio construction is simultaneously both core and peripheral. Decisions about what to buy or sell should take account of how much they might cost to buy or sell. However, a world in which the 'market' is taken to be the sole arbiter of knowledge is not one that can be fully reconciled with the concept of active management. By this we mean taking views about when the market is right and when it is wrong and acting accordingly. The need here is to understand and take due notice of the market but not to let it be the sole input into your decision-making process.

1.4 STRUCTURE OF THE BOOK

For practical reasons, this book is, in the main, segmented between the interrelated disciplines described above. Most larger financial organisations segment their business by activity. The day-to-day working life of readers within the financial services industry will therefore tend to have a bias towards one of these three disciplines. For example, asset management and investment banking businesses are often subdivided into three parts, a *back office*, a *middle office* and a *front office*. Typically, individuals working in the back office have day-to-day responsibility for the processes used to administer and value relatively simple instruments. Those working in the front office are responsible for deciding what positions to buy or sell. Those working in the middle office may provide a bridge between back and front offices. It is also becoming the norm for risk management to be explicitly differentiated from the front (and back) office and thus to fall within the remit of the middle office function. Similar types of role distinctions do also apply to insurers and pension funds, but in many cases the activities in question are outsourced or given different names.

The structure adopted by this book is as follows.

Chapters 2 to 6 cover in the main core material applicable to all of the disciplines being considered. Chapter 2 focuses on when market consistency is and isn't appropriate, extrapolating from the properties of money to establish what sorts of properties we might expect *monetary values* to exhibit. From these properties it deduces when it is most and least relevant to be market consistent. It also explores at a high level some of the main drivers currently for and against market consistent approaches, and how this can influence what in practice is actually meant by 'market consistency'. Chapter 3 focuses more on valuation activities, and on how in practice different standards setters and commentators interpret market consistency and other similar terms. Chapter 4 provides a primer on derivative pricing theory. It cannot be claimed that it does so without reference to *any* mathematics. However, hopefully even those less welcoming of complex mathematical arguments will feel that they have gained some useful insights after reading it. In this context 'derivative pricing theory' is really a catch-all for virtually all of the financial theory that underpins the rest of the book (apart from the theory relating to the interaction of risk and return, which we introduce principally in Chapter 12). Chapter 5 explores a particularly important issue in practice when applying market consistent principles to less liquid instruments. This is how to understand and identify a suitable 'risk-free' interest rate or yield curve. For a book that is focused in part on how to handle less liquid markets it is also natural to include in this part of the book a chapter specifically on liquidity theory, i.e. Chapter 6.

Chapters 7 to 10 consider market consistency in the context of risk management. Chapter 7 covers the fundamental theory, such as the description of different sorts of risk measures and how they are typically calculated. Chapter 8 focuses on capital adequacy. It provides examples of how current regulatory frameworks try to identify the appropriate minimum capital that an organisation should hold to protect itself against risks that might lead to insolvency. Chapter 9 explores how to apply market consistency in what might be called the current risk management paradigm. It focuses principally on how market valuations might vary in the future, and hence how the risks being expressed in these positions might be best managed. Chapter 10 considers how these approaches would need further refinement if we want them to adopt a *fully* market consistent paradigm. This involves applying market consistency not merely to the valuations used within the risk assessment but also to the probability distributions ascribed to the future movement of these valuations. Reasons for adopting this paradigm are also covered in this chapter.

One claim some commentators made during the 2007–09 credit crisis was that inappropriate use of marking-to-market techniques can create a lack of confidence in the financial soundness of banks in stressed market conditions, which can then become a self-fulfilling prophecy. It behoves a book on market consistency to consider carefully this logic. We explore in Chapter 11 ways in which as a society we may best protect against system-wide concerns whilst not diluting other benefits that may come from a greater focus on 'what the market has to say'.

Chapter 12 focuses on portfolio construction techniques. As noted earlier, the application of market consistency to portfolio construction is less direct than for valuation and risk management, but arguably no less important. There are also several analogies that can be drawn out between market consistency as applied to portfolio construction and market consistency as applied to other financial disciplines.

Chapter 13 draws together many of the strands developed in earlier chapters. It provides case studies exploring how to incorporate market consistency in various types of computations relating to different types of assets and liabilities. It also explores questions like what to do when all available market observable prices relate to relatively illiquid instruments with relatively large or uncertain bid–offer spreads. There would be less need for this book if markets were always 'perfect'.[2]

Finally, Chapter 14 summarises and repeats in one place all of the market consistency principles highlighted elsewhere in the book.

Throughout the book we draw out principles, i.e. guidance to *practitioners*, that have relatively universal application, independent of any particular regulatory or current market practice drivers. Within the text these principles are indented and shown in bold, and are referenced by P1, P2, etc.

Each chapter contains at least one such principle, along with many other insights. Thus readers only interested in certain aspects of market consistency should still find this book worthwhile reading, even if they limit their attention just to those chapters particularly relevant to their own specialisms. Conversely, there are valuable insights throughout the book, including in the more mathematical sections (even for readers who don't wish to follow the mathematics in detail). I would therefore encourage all readers to consider exploring parts of the book that they might have assumed were only tangentially relevant to their own specialisms, because of the greater depth of understanding that this might bring.

1.5 TERMINOLOGY

In parts of the book focused on valuation, we use as essentially interchangeable terms such as market consistency and 'marking-to-market'. Another term with much the same meaning is the accounting concept of *fair value*. When financial services regulators use the term 'realistic valuation' they also normally have a similar concept in mind. We define the market consistent value of an asset or liability to mean:

(a) Its market value, if it is readily traded on a market at the point in time that the valuation is struck; or
(b) A reasoned[3] best estimate of what its market value would have been had such a market then existed, in all other situations.

---

[2] When practitioners talk about markets not being 'perfect' they typically have several different concepts in mind simultaneously. These include 'incompleteness' (i.e. markets not having as complete a range of instruments as we might like), 'market frictions' (i.e. markets being subject to transaction costs, etc.) and 'inconsistency' (i.e. the same exposures being priced at a particular point in time inconsistently in different parts of the market). There is sometimes a tendency to equate 'inconsistency' with 'irrationality', but as we will see in Section 2.10, markets do not need to be behaving rationally for market consistent principles to be applicable. This is fortunate since most practitioners seem to believe that markets do at times exhibit irrational behaviour.

[3] By 'reasoned' we here mean that the valuer has carefully thought through the sorts of principles set out later in this book, rather than (at the other extreme) merely plucking a number out of thin air. It would have been nice in this book to have been able to define a prescriptive approach that practitioners could follow in all circumstances to come up with a single 'right' answer. However, this just isn't possible in practice. As we shall see, market consistency, when applied to less liquid assets and liabilities, inevitably involves some subjectivity. The best that we can hope for is to place appropriate limits or constraints on this subjectivity and on the mindsets adopted by those who necessarily have to exercise this subjectivity.

Such a definition is similar to the more standard accounting definition of fair value as 'the value at which an arm's-length transaction involving willing, knowledgeable counterparties would take place'. However, explicit inclusion of the word 'market' within the terminology has the advantage of highlighting that for a non-traded asset or liability we are not wanting to focus on the valuer's *own* intrinsic assessment of its value. Rather we are interested in modelling how some actual or hypothetical market would be expected to value the asset or liability. By implication, we also demand that any such model should, if possible, be calibrated back to market prices of instruments that are more readily traded.[4]

More generally, choosing to use the term 'market consistency' has the advantage of not unwittingly guiding the reader towards an overly valuation centric focus, thus downplaying other disciplines to which market consistency may be applicable. Focusing too much on terms like marking-to-market (or indeed any other phrase involving the word 'mark') runs this risk because a 'mark' is typically associated with the price we place on an instrument in our books. As we have already noted (and we will stress subsequently), we do not value things in isolation. Valuations ultimately gain their wider meaning and context from the purposes to which they are put.

Given that this book covers risk management, it is also appropriate to include in this section terminology to help categorise the main sorts of risks faced by financial services entities. We shall explore in more detail later what we (and others) might mean by 'risk'. However, at this juncture, a helpful subdivision often used in practice is the following. It should be noted that it is not always easy (or even useful) to identify clear boundaries between some of these different types of risk.

(a) *Market risk*, i.e. the risk of loss due to adverse market movements. More generally, we might focus on adverse market movements affecting the entity's asset/liability position, although this might be called *asset-liability risk*. Market movements in this context would typically include movements in equity values and in interest rates.

(b) *Credit risk*, i.e. the risk that the creditworthiness of a name or counterparty to which an entity is exposed declines, causing the entity loss. At one extreme would be actual default of the counterparty. A subtlety here is whether credit risk should be deemed to include only *default risk* (i.e. some intrinsic assessment now of the risk that the counterparty or issuer might default in the future) or whether it should also include *ratings migration risk* or *spread risk*. The *spread* on a bond-like or cash-like instrument is the difference in the redemption yield available on the instrument versus the corresponding yield available on some standard reference instrument. For example, people refer to 'spread' versus government bond yields, as the difference between the yield on the instrument in question and the yield on government bonds of equivalent duration, type and currency.[5] However, spread could be measured versus Libor, see Section 5.2, or some other interest rate or yield measure, etc. The market price of a bond subject to default risk is influenced by likelihood of future default. We might attempt to proxy this by some statistic based on the credit rating that a credit rating agency or an internal credit ratings team ascribes to the instrument. However, the *market* price, and hence spread, will also be influenced by

---

[4] Another difference is that market consistency does not need to be limited to the special case where both sides are 'willing' participants in the trade. In some situations of practical importance (e.g. assessment of the amount of capital needed to withstand stressed conditions), such an assumption may be inappropriate.

[5] Yields (and hence spreads) can be quoted in a variety of ways, e.g. annualised, semi-annualised, etc. These are generically called 'annualisation conventions'. For further details see e.g. Kemp (2009).

the market's expectation of how likelihood of default might change over time. Even if one ignores market prices and focuses on some perceived 'intrinsic' likelihood of default derived from credit ratings, these can also change through time (even if the instrument has not defaulted). A rating ascribed to a particular instrument can migrate up or down. At issue is whether spread risk is a form of credit risk (i.e. defining credit risk as risks associated with 'credit' instruments) or whether it is a form of market risk (i.e. defining market risk as anything relating to movements in market prices whatever the instrument type).

(c) *Liquidity risk*, which the UK's Financial Services Authority (FSA) defines as the risk that a firm, although balance sheet-solvent, cannot maintain or generate sufficient cash resources to meet its payment obligations in full as they fall due, or can only do so at materially disadvantageous terms, see FSA (2007). Some view a part of the spread payable on non-default-free instruments as relating to their liquidity characteristics, again highlighting the difficulties in rigidly demarcating between different types of risk.

(d) *Insurance risk*, i.e. risks specific to insurance companies, typically relating to the uncertain outcome of insurance contingencies. These would typically include life contingencies, i.e. risks linked to mortality, morbidity or longevity.[6] They would also include property/casualty and other sorts of non-life insurance risk. Non-life insurance is called 'general' insurance in some jurisdictions. It is not always easy to differentiate what risks are 'insurance-related' and what are not, other than by falling back onto the practical but partly circular definition that insurance risks are ones that are carried by insurance companies.

(e) *Operational risk*, i.e. the risk of loss resulting from inadequate or failed internal processes, people and systems or from external events. In the six-way classification of risk described in this section a wide range of risks would be deemed to fall into this category, including *legal risk* and, possibly, *strategic risk* and *reputational risk*.[7]

(f) *Group risk*, i.e. the additional risk to a particular legal entity caused by it being within a larger group structure. For example, resources may be diverted from the entity in question to other group companies if the latter companies suffer a large loss, which can have adverse knock-on effects which would not have arisen had the entity been stand-alone.

For convenience, we also follow the convention, adopted by many other writers in this field, of using the term *firm* to encompass not just bodies with an explicit corporate form and purpose but also other entities that operate within the financial services arena, such as pension funds. Where the context demands, we clarify the specific type of 'firm' or 'entity' on which our attention is focused.

---

[6] 'Mortality' and 'longevity' risk are different facets of a single underlying risk, namely, that of uncertainty of when people might die. Mortality risk typically refers to the situation where the insurer is at risk if the person dies sooner than expected whilst longevity risk typically refers to the situation where the insurer is at risk if the person lives longer than expected (e.g. an annuity continues in payment longer than expected). Morbidity refers to ill-health rather than death.

[7] Strategic risk and reputational risk are excluded from the definition of Operational Risk in Basel II.

2

When is and when isn't Market Consistency Appropriate?

2.1 INTRODUCTION

In this chapter we seek to identify when focusing on market consistency is most relevant. There is little point in expending substantial effort on being market consistent when it is less relevant or even misguided to try to do so.

To do this, we start by formulating from first principles what we ought to understand by 'market consistency'. Any such logic needs to link back to the underlying economic theory underpinning the functioning of markets. So, we focus on intrinsic characteristics exhibited by money itself, since the existence of money is a necessary precursor to the placing of a *monetary* value on anything. This powerful analogy helps us identify how to place a (monetary) value on assets or liabilities, and how this value may vary depending on the purpose of the valuation.

However, we do not live in a world governed merely by economic theory. So, later on in this chapter we also look at some of the more practical drivers favouring greater (and in some instances lesser) adoption of market consistency. In particular we explore current regulatory and accounting pressures. Since these drivers will change from time to time, we also explore what are the underlying mindsets that have influenced and are likely to continue to influence these drivers.

Towards the end of the chapter we develop from these underlying principles a conceptual framework for valuation, risk management and capital adequacy to which we can refer whenever we need greater clarity on what we mean by 'market consistency'. This framework necessarily includes elements covering both valuation and risk management. The amount of assets that a financial entity needs to hold to demonstrate 'solvency' depends not just on the value of its liabilities but also on whatever additional capital is considered necessary by regulators, markets and others.

2.2 DRAWING LESSONS FROM THE CHARACTERISTICS OF MONEY ITSELF

2.2.1 The concept of 'value'

As humans, we value things that are worth something to us and, if we are altruistic, worth something to society (or life more generally). What we value can be many and varied, e.g. our relationships with others (particularly our family), the pleasure we get from a nice meal or seeing a beautiful sunset, the benefits we may get from the ownership or use of a good or provision of a service. Taking a utilitarian philosophical stance we might say that the value of such things depends on the utility that they provide to the recipient (or conversely the disutility they generate to the provider). Those with a more religious perspective, like me, might argue that some things like human life, a just and free society, etc. have an *intrinsic* value (or value to God) irrespective of the utility that they might bring to any specific individual.

> **Principle P1: 'Value' is a term that has many different meanings. Unless the context makes clear the intended meaning, it should be used with a qualifier.**

Early in the history of civilisation, humankind invented *money*. Individuals (or groups of individuals) can barter one good (or service, etc.) for another. Implicit in such bartering is some valuation process that each party is putting on the goods (or services) being swapped. It was found to be convenient to set aside special 'commodities' in restricted supply, i.e. 'money', which could provide a common means of exchange. Individuals no longer needed to 'sell' and 'buy' from the same person. They could disaggregate the barter into two separate transactions that could then be carried out with different parties.

Work relating to financial matters will typically involve placing *monetary* values on things. Strictly speaking, all such values must include a *numeraire* in which the value is expressed. We do not say that the monetary value of a loaf of bread is, say, 60 without some qualifier. Instead we might say that it costs £0.60 or $0.60, etc. Numeraires are often *currencies* (e.g. GBP, USD, EUR) but can also be, say, units in a fund, shares, barrels of oil, etc. In this context a currency would typically be the normal medium of exchange within a given economy, although occasionally bespoke currencies are created that are not in general circulation (e.g. the International Monetary Fund's Special Drawing Rights).

> **Principle P2: When value is expressed in monetary terms and is immediate in nature then people will expect it to correspond to the amount of money that would need to be exchanged to buy or sell the item being valued, because the most important characteristic of money is that it is a medium of exchange.**

2.2.2 The time value of money

Most of finance involves not just consideration of the present but also consideration of the future. As soon as money was invented, it actually became not just a medium of exchange but also a *store of value*. Rarely do we obtain money via one transaction and *instantaneously* use it up in another. The greater the time difference, the more money is being used as a store of value or wealth. This means that in practice the numeraire in which we express value needs to include a time dimension. This concept goes under various names, including the *time value of money*.

Most currencies exhibit a positive time value of money most of the time. This reflects the greater utility that people typically gain by consumption now versus consumption later, which typically works itself out economically in a positive interest rate being paid on whatever is the normal medium of exchange within a given economy. However, if an economy is undergoing sufficiently large negative inflation, the increase in purchasing power of a unit of its currency may provide a sufficient consumption deferral incentive without any positive interest rate. In some circumstances, it is even possible for interest rates on the normal medium of exchange to go negative. For example, if money is costly to store physically, then after taking these storage costs into account the net interest rate may be negative. This is one reason why societies typically now favour paper or electronically operated currencies that involve little if any physical storage costs.

It might be thought helpful to circumvent this issue by using a numeraire on which the relevant future 'interest rate' is set exactly equal to zero and then to re-express all future payments using this numeraire. This is the basic concept behind the *present value* of a future payment. It is the amount of money that you would need to set aside now to provide for a future payment, when compounded with interest in the meantime.

However, this basic concept is not by itself sufficient because it does not necessarily take fully into account the *risk characteristics* of the payments in question. Suppose that the 1 year interest rate on 1 year deposits is 10 % (for a given currency). Then the (current) market value of a payment of 110 in that currency in 1 year's time is 100 currency units (if we ignore the risk of default), since this is the amount that you would need to put into a bank now to receive the relevant payment in the future.

This does *not* mean that an asset that involves a payment in 1 year's time that we estimate to have a 50 % probability of being 100 and a 50 % probability of being 120 (and so currently to have an average or *expected* size in 1 year's time of 110) will necessarily also have a market value of 100. Baxter and Rennie (1996) make a particularly eloquent case for why this so-called strong law of expectations which we might expect to apply in these situations actually leads to erroneous conclusions. For example, the circumstances when the payment is lower might correspond with situations when the typical recipient of the payment is also worse off in other ways, and may therefore be given a higher weighting in the formation of the market price than 50 %. Moreover, we will rarely know with certainty the exact probabilities involved since in practice the payment will depend on the outcome of *contingent events* the characteristics of which are not fully predictable in advance. Any one individual's estimates of the probabilities involved may not correspond with others, again leading to a different price.

Properly taking into account the time value and risk characteristics of future payments requires the introduction of the concept of a *pay-off*. This is shorthand for the description of the complete tabulation of what the future payments might be (and when) in every possible outcome for the contingencies on which the payments depend. Any asset or liability can then be characterised by a suitable pay-off. Another equivalent term is a *(contingent) claim*.

2.2.3 Axioms of additivity, scalability and uniqueness

In this context, money has yet another characteristic that will strongly influence a lay person's understanding of (monetary) value, which is its *fungibility*. By this we mean that any two separate units of a currency are typically interchangeable with each other, and thus will be expected to have exactly equal value. More generally, the market value of money adheres to the mathematical axioms of *additivity* and *scalability* and hence lay people will generally expect (monetary) values to do likewise.

By these axioms we mean that if the 'value' we place on a pay-off $\mathbf{a}$ is $V(\mathbf{a})$ then the value of a pay-off $k(\mathbf{a} + \mathbf{b})$ (i.e. a pay-off which is k times as large as $\mathbf{a} + \mathbf{b}$ in all circumstances) satisfies the relationship:

$$V(k(\mathbf{a} - \mathbf{b})) = k(V(\mathbf{a}) + V(\mathbf{b})) \tag{2.1}$$

The market value of money exhibits these characteristics. If 1 unit of currency A is worth a in currency C, and 1 unit of currency B is worth b in currency C, then the combination of k units of currency A and k units of currency B will be worth $k(a + b)$ in currency C.

We note that implicitly we have also adopted an assumption of *uniqueness*, i.e. that $V(\mathbf{a})$ is single-valued.

> **Principle P3: Most recipients of advice from financial practitioners will take for granted that monetary value, however measured, adheres to the basic axioms of additivity and scalability unless the context clearly justifies otherwise, because money itself adheres to these axioms.**

Additivity and scalability are very powerful axioms. They, for example, imply that:

(a) The valuation framework needs to average away transaction costs, at least at the aggregate pay-off level, since: $V(\mathbf{a} + \mathbf{b} - \mathbf{b}) = V(\mathbf{a})$;
(b) If market prices exactly match the 'values' arising from a valuation framework satisfying additivity and scalability then the market in question will typically satisfy the so-called *principle of no arbitrage*, since for all k we would have $kV(0) = V(k.0) = V(0)$ and hence $V(0) = 0$ and so $V(\mathbf{a} - \mathbf{a}) = V(0) = 0$; and
(c) There exists a probability distribution, which we can call the valuation framework's *risk-neutral probability distribution*, using which it *is* possible to calculate present values of future pay-offs using expectations and discounting as per Section 2.2.2.

The existence of a suitable risk-neutral distribution as per (c) above follows if we decompose the overall pay-off into scalar multiples of many component parts. Each component involves a payment of unity only when the contingencies driving the original pay-off result in a particular outcome. There is one such component for each possible outcome. The risk-neutral distribution is then found by rescaling the values of these components in a manner that results in a unit payout in all circumstances being valued in a manner that corresponds with the time value of money for the particular currency in which the valuation framework is expressed.

Conversely, a valuation framework will satisfy additivity and scalability if:

(a) There exists a probability distribution covering all possible outcomes; and
(b) The values ascribed to pay-offs under a given valuation framework equal the expected value of these pay-offs calculated by reference to this probability distribution.

Of course, we do not actually need to express a valuation (even one within a framework that satisfies additivity and scalability) in the form of a discounted value of an expected outcome, with the expectation being based on risk-neutral probability distributions. A widely used alternative is to carry out the expectation using our own 'real world' estimates of the probabilities of occurrence of the different possible outcomes and to adjust the time value element, i.e. to use a suitable *risk discount rate*. More accurately, the risk discount rate would in this formulation be a risk discount yield curve, to reflect how the time value of money varies by term to payment. In some disciplines such a discount rate is also called a *deflator* or a *state price density*.

A potential weakness in such a presentation is that lay people (and even some experts) might be misled into assuming that use of the term 'risk discount' somehow implies that the resulting discount rate should be *higher* than the corresponding *risk-free discount rate*, since pay-offs involving uncertain payments might be expected in some sense to be riskier (i.e. less certain) than ones involving certain payments. The difference between the risk discount rate and the risk-free discount rate is typically referred to as the *risk premium*, a term which again might be thought to imply that risk premia should normally be positive.

However, if a valuation framework is to adhere fully to axioms of additivity and scalability then the appropriately averaged risk premium across all possible pay-offs must be zero. Thus, there will be some pay-offs the values of which when presented in this fashion need to incorporate negative risk premia, as well as some that will need to exhibit positive risk premia.[1] Perhaps this is why practitioners in this field may prefer to use more technical terms such as 'deflators' which are less easy to misinterpret in this manner (or perhaps use of such terms is merely an example of jargon creep).

Principle P4: Financial practitioners wishing to derive valuations of future cash flows by calculating the expected values of these cash flows using their own (or other people's) 'real world' probabilities of outcomes should carefully consider the risk adjustments that then need to be incorporated in the discount rates used in these computations. In particular they should bear in mind that the correct 'risk premium' to incorporate in the discounting computation (if they want their valuation framework to adhere to additivity and scalability axioms) may be negative and may bear no obvious link to the degree of uncertainty or 'risk' applicable to the cash flows being valued.

An important ramification of these axioms that we explore further in Section 3.3 is that they in effect force the focus to be on the 'marginal' trade.

2.2.4   Market consistent valuations

Principles P3 and P4 are generic to valuation frameworks that satisfy additivity and scalability. They do not by themselves place any requirement on the valuation framework to exhibit *market consistency*. However, they do guide us towards defining a *market consistent valuation framework* as one where:

(a) the (present) values of pay-offs that are actively traded in a deep and liquid market match (at all times) their observed market prices;
(b) the (present) values of pay-offs that are not actively and transparently traded in such a market are reasoned best estimates of the prices at which such pay-offs would trade in such a market, were such a market to exist; and
(c) valuations adhere to the basic axioms of additivity and scalability.

It is implicit in such a definition that the market must be suitably transparent, as otherwise the market prices would not be observable to those involved in preparing the relevant valuations. Also implicit is that any market to which (a) is applicable is sufficiently deep and liquid (and responds sufficiently rapidly to new information) to adhere to the principle of no arbitrage. Otherwise (a) and (c) are inconsistent with each other.

We note that in practice there will be subjectivity in (b). Indeed there will even be some potential subjectivity in (a), given the existence of bid–ask spreads and time delays in price formation within markets. The less the pay-offs can be decomposed into things that are actively

---

[1] Moreover, if some future cash flows are positive and some are negative then in general there may be more than one discount rate that equates the present value of the cash flows with whatever value we place on them. So, discount rate(s) in this context may also not always be well defined in a mathematical sense.

traded in deep and liquid markets the greater is this subjectivity, which might be expressed in terms of widened implied bid–ask spreads.

> **Principle P5: Whilst a core aim of market consistency is objectivity by being faithful to market prices, market consistent valuations will often still involve subjective input. The more material is this subjectivity the more important it becomes for practitioners preparing these valuations to explain the judgements involved. They should be careful to minimise the impact that their own biases might have in selection of these subjective inputs.**

2.2.5   Should financial practitioners always use market consistent valuations?

If market consistent values should ideally eliminate as far as possible subjective views, does this mean that financial practitioners should never express such views?

Of course not! Their 'work product' is wide and varied and there are several obvious situations in which use of market consistent valuations would be inappropriate.

An important example in practice is where the practitioner is in essence being asked to identify instances in which, in his or her opinion, the market is 'wrongly' valuing a particular asset or liability, to help in a decision linked to the purchase or sale of the relevant pay-off. Such a task naturally expects an answer that will, in normal circumstances, differ from the market value as it involves attempting to identify whether an investment represents 'good' or 'bad' value at its current market price. This situation can arise in a variety of circumstances including:

(a) *The practitioner might be employed as an investment analyst (or the equivalent) to identify which actively traded securities might at present be most 'incorrectly' valued by the market.* Unpicking this example, we note that in one sense the market always 'correctly' values such a security, if by 'value' we only ever mean 'market value'. What such an individual is actually being asked to do is not to repeat the market value but rather to express a subjective opinion (which the recipient hopes to profit from) about how the market value of the security might move in the future (relative to other investments that the recipient might otherwise hold).

(b) *The practitioner might be employed to advise on the price at which to offer to buy or sell an (unquoted) subsidiary.* This is similar to (a), but without a directly observable market price (normally) being available for comparison purposes.

(c) *The practitioner might be employed to identify arguments for one party in a proposed transaction for why a particular asset or liability might be 'worth' some figure to some other party in the transaction, to support the negotiating stance being adopted by the practitioner's client.* In concept at least, the practitioner might do this by considering the generality of arguments that might be put forward, and then selecting the ones that most favour his client.

All three of these examples share the same fundamental characteristic. The individual in question is acting for *just one side* of a possible transaction rather than for both sides simultaneously. This is not to say that even in these situations market values (or market consistent values) are irrelevant. We might, for example, expect an investment analyst to contrast his view with the market's view, since if the market price moved to the analyst's target price then presumably the analyst would no longer think that the security in question was 'misvalued'.

Anyone involved (or aspiring to be involved) in real-life business management will almost certainly come across such situations. Few shareholders would, for example, want a company to follow a strategy of passively following everyone else's prices and business models. More usually, they would want management to be actively trying to target the more profitable business opportunities.

Another example where undue focus on market consistency may be inappropriate is in setting the prices at which a firm might be prepared to offer a good or service to other firms (or to members of the general public).[2] A person acting for the first firm will no doubt wish to bear in mind the market clearing price level (if one exists) for the good or service in question (because if the offered price is too far above this level then sales may be negligible, whereas if it is too far below this level then the firm may be foregoing profit it could otherwise have obtained). But this is only one of several factors that in practice may drive the price the firm will wish to charge.

Principle P6: When a piece of work involves advising just one side of a commercial transaction then undue focus by practitioners on 'market consistency' with any previous ruling market price may not be considered the most desirable sort of advice by the client.

2.2.6 Equity between parties

There are many activities where a practitioner is in effect being asked to carry out an equitable apportionment of assets and liabilities between different parties. This is particularly true for some of the more important areas of work of professionals such as actuaries and accountants. For this type of activity, arguments in favour of use of market or market consistent valuations seem strong.

Sometimes achievement of equitable treatment might be an explicit goal. For example, in court sanctioned work on insurance company restructurings, there might be an explicit need for the outcome to be equitable between different policyholder interests. At other times, this goal might be more implicit, but not necessarily any less important. For example, one aim of a pension fund actuarial valuation might be to compute the size of any surplus or deficit within the fund and the proportion of liabilities attributable to different beneficiary types. The apportionment advised by the actuary might then affect actual payments ultimately received by different beneficiaries.

There are two related reasons why market consistent valuations would be favoured in these circumstances:

(a) *Additivity* (again!). Where the interests are monetary in nature, the parties concerned will expect the sum of the apportioned components to add to the whole (see Principle P3 above) and will expect to have apportioned to them their 'fair share' of the total. Where a market price is readily available, Principle P2 will favour the use of the market price, since the

---

[2] 'Pricing' is a term that has several meanings. Here is it being used in the context of one firm setting a price that it will charge for something. A different meaning (one to which Section 2.2.6 is more relevant) is where we 'price' an open-ended fund. Here, the pricing involves, in effect, a determination of the price at which ownership of the fund changes hands between different unit holders whenever there are inflows or outflows into or out of the fund.

apportionment is then a subdivision at the current point in time of the assets and liabilities; and

(b) *Objectivity*. The parties in question could, if they so wished, seek to have the apportionment replicated by some other financial expert. If the second apportionment differs too much from the first one then at least one of the parties involved may feel that the original advisor was unfairly favouring another party. If market prices are readily available, it will most probably be very difficult to argue that any particular practitioner's subjective opinions are more objective than 'the market'.

> **Principle P7: When a piece of work involves an equitable apportionment of assets or liabilities between different parties then the parties in question are likely to expect the practitioner preparing the apportionment to do so broadly in line with a 'fair' (i.e. 'market consistent') apportionment struck by reference to the prices at which the assets or liabilities in question might trade between a willing buyer and a willing seller.**

For some types of work the methodology to be used may be prescribed by a particular third party. For example, the methodology might be one imposed by the regulator, by the relevant tax authority or by relevant accountancy guidelines. However, even here Principles P1 and P2 are likely to be relevant. Quoting such figures without qualification may give a lay person the impression that the value being quoted does actually broadly correspond to a market or market consistent price. It may be better to use words such as 'the value as determined in accordance with Regulation xxx', etc., especially if the practitioner thinks that the prescribed methodology is *not* market consistent.

2.2.7   Embedded values and franchise values

Conceptually, one can split the total value of a business (or of its operating parts) into the following elements:

(a) The value of its 'current' net assets (i.e. current assets minus current liabilities[3]);

(b) The net value of any contracts it has in place, including income and outgo cash flow streams that are reasonably certain to be payable under existing contracts, and capital that may be needed to support these contracts not included in (a); and

(c) The value of any contracts it may enter into in the future (but which neither it nor its customers are obliged to enter into under other pre-existing contracts).

Some types of business, e.g. convenience stores, may have few if any contracts that extend over material lengths of time. At any point in time the proportion of the value of the business falling into category (b) may be small or nil. Essentially, they will have some current assets and liabilities as per (a) (much of which might be accounted for in stock), and they will have a franchise value (e.g. due to their location, reputation amongst local inhabitants, etc.) which could dwindle in value to very little if, for example, a competitor with a better reputation opens up nearby.

---

[3] Current here means assets and liabilities that are essentially unencumbered in any way and are readily realisable in a short time frame, e.g. cash on short-term deposit or payments to suppliers for goods and services already delivered (unless these payments are not expected to be honoured in the near future).

Other types of business (including life insurance and some other types of financial services companies) may have a much more extensive base of contracts entered into with customers that extend over long periods of time into the future. These contracts may also include commitments (or options available to one or other party) that relate to future cash flow payments to or from the customer. The value contribution from (b) (positive or negative) may be proportionately much larger for these sorts of businesses.

There is a key distinction between the first two elements and the third element. Elements (a) and (b) are in principle objective. By this we mean that if two unconnected people were asked to list all of the elements contributing to their value then after a sufficiently extensive examination of the books of the business at any particular point in time they should both arrive at the same list. In contrast, (c) is necessarily more subjective.[4]

Accountants and actuaries have recognised the greater objectivity applicable to (a) and (b) and have over the years developed methods for placing a value on these elements of business value. In the life insurance context they are together typically described as forming the *embedded value* of the existing (or 'in-force') business of the company.

If the contracts in question extend over material timeframes (as is typically the case with life insurance) then it becomes important to allow for the time value of money in computation of embedded value. A market consistent approach to such value computations should also ideally take into account options embedded within the in-force contracts (either exercisable by the company or by the customers).

2.2.8   Solvency calculations

We have already noted two areas in which the time value of money may have important ramifications, namely identification of appropriate prices to charge for long-term contracts and appropriate accounting values to place on such contracts. A final area where the time value of money has important consequences for financial services entities is in capital adequacy, i.e. solvency, computations.

The scenario implicitly tested in most solvency calculations assumes that no future profits or contributions will be forthcoming from third parties to make good any shortfalls that might have arisen. This is akin to the entity putting itself up for sale, see Kemp (2005). It implicitly involves placing a current monetary value on the entity, which Principle P2 would suggest ought therefore to be market consistent. Also implicit in such a scenario is that the entity is no longer in control of its own destiny. It would therefore seem inappropriate to take positive credit in such a scenario for potential future outright value creation by management. Irrespective of how skilled the current management team might believe itself to be, it may no longer have the authority to execute strategies that could be value enhancing.[5] Perhaps it would in some circumstances be appropriate to include allowance for some of the franchise value implicit in the business, but franchise values have a habit of dwindling at an alarming rate if a business

---

[4] A possible way of estimating the market consistent value of the goodwill is to identify market consistent valuations for all other aspects of business value and to subtract the sum of these from a market consistent valuation for the business as a whole (e.g. as derived from its share price, if the company is listed).

[5] However, there may be other sorts of management action, e.g. altering investment policy to reduce shortfalls, which it may be more reasonable to assume might occur in adverse circumstances (to the extent that the firm has suitable systems and procedures in place that make it likely that these actions would be implemented, and to the extent that to do so would not breach actual or implied terms within the contracts it has with its customers).

undergoes an extreme stress.[6] As we explore in Section 2.7, it also becomes questionable whether we should recognise in advance any future profits that depend on discretionary customer behaviour, if the underlying purpose of the market consistent computation is linked to consideration of what might happen in a stressed scenario.

Solvency calculations are akin to an equitable apportionment of the sort described in Section 2.2.6, but with one important caveat. If we were to apply a completely market consistent approach to an entity that had both assets and liabilities to its name (and there was no possibility of it receiving further contributions or profit streams) then a shortage of assets would be completely compensated for by a reduction in the 'market' value of the liabilities. This is because the market, if functioning properly, should recognise that not all of the liabilities were then likely to be honoured. This is sometimes referred to conceptually as the *solvency put option*.

Such an adjustment would, of course, render the computation less useful for assessing the amount of surplus capital that the entity might need to hold now to be likely to remain solvent in the future. Instead, regulatory solvency frameworks normally require computation of the value of the liabilities to exclude the entity's own credit risk.

Whilst it is easy to see the practical benefits of excluding own credit risk in solvency calculations, it is difficult to identify compelling theoretical arguments for why market consistency should *necessarily* involve such an exclusion *whatever* the underlying purpose of the valuation. Indeed, some commentators argue that market consistency necessarily requires the *non-exclusion* of own credit risk, on the grounds that, for better or worse, such liabilities do typically include an element of exposure to the company in question.[7] However, this logic seems questionable. Whilst it is true that the liabilities themselves carry this default risk, there is no reason why in principle we should not instead be seeking to identify the market consistent value of a *combination* of the firm's own liabilities and an instrument that if held in addition would pay out were such a default to occur. Instruments such as credit default swaps that provide just such protection do exist and indeed are now actively traded, see Section 4.8.

If own credit risk is to be excluded then it becomes necessary to define a substitute reference rate, or more generally a reference yield curve, to replace the own credit risk yield curve. We explore this topic further in Chapters 5 and 6. For example, should this reference rate be fully 'risk-free' or should it merely be 'free of risk of *credit* default or deterioration', to the extent that these two might differ? Should the reference rate exclude *all* credit risk, or just the credit risk that is idiosyncratic to the firm in question?

> **Principle P8: One might expect 'market consistent' valuations to be uniquely identifiable if the markets involved are sufficiently deep, liquid and transparent. However, different adjustments in relation to the deemed future creditworthiness of the firm in question may be appropriate depending on the purpose to which the valuation is to be put. The practical impact of these adjustments will depend on the substitute reference rates that are used instead of the firm's own market implied level of creditworthiness.**

---

[6] Conversely, when companies default or go into liquidation, there is often a 'recovery' that is eventually paid on any bonds that they may have issued, and there may even be enough money to provide some return to equity investors.

[7] Not all such default risk may ultimately be borne by customers, particularly smaller customers. Often, regulated entities such as financial services companies are subject to industry or government sponsored solvency protection schemes or other types of regulatory safety nets. Much of the losses that would otherwise be borne by smaller customers may end up being borne by these schemes instead.

2.2.9 Pension fund valuations

One valuation purpose that perhaps fits uneasily in any of the above categories is the valuation of a defined benefit (DB) pension fund for the purpose of determining an appropriate long-term contribution rate to be paid by the sponsor into the pension fund, in a situation where the fund has a healthy surplus on a solvency basis. Historically, this sort of calculation has been the preserve of actuaries. Some actuaries have in these calculations taken credit for assumed future excess returns on the assets held by the fund (relative to risk-free assets closely matching the liabilities), the magnitude of the excess return assumption being set by the actuary.

Suppose we re-express the calculation using market consistent values of assets and liabilities together with a balancing item that capitalises a 'value' (in this computation) derived from an assumed future management strategy of continuing to adopt (perhaps indefinitely) a mismatched investment strategy. We see that the quantification of this balancing item corresponds to an expression by the actuary of opinions about which assets are likely to perform best in the long term, by how much and, implicitly, how sustainable is the mismatched investment strategy over the longer term.

If the only party affected by this advice is the sponsor then this approach may be a mathematically sound way of identifying a smoothed contribution rate (if not necessarily the easiest methodology to justify or describe in practice), since in this situation the advice seems most akin to that covered by Principle P6. Suppose, however, the answer materially affects more than one party and the actuary is implicitly supposed to be advising equitably between these parties. For example, a low contribution rate might potentially make scheme members materially more exposed to the future creditworthiness of their sponsoring employer. Then, according to Principle P7, a greater focus on market consistency would appear to be preferable.

2.2.10 Bid–offer spreads

The above analysis does not address how to cater for market *bid–ask (or bid–offer) spreads* or any additional bid–ask element arising from transactional taxes.[8] The existence of such spreads is an indication of the existence of market frictions. The deeper, more liquid and more efficient a market is, the smaller typically are bid–ask spreads observed in that market.

By 'bid–ask characteristics' we here implicitly include all round-trip costs, including *market impact*, as explained in Section 6.5.

The analogy with the behaviour of money, which forms the basis for the rest of this section, is unfortunately not very helpful in this regard. For large transactions the bid–ask spread on

---

[8] The bid price of an asset is the price at which someone wishing to sell the asset could do so. The ask price, also known as offer price, is the price that would be incurred buying the asset. Hence, unless a pure arbitrage exists, the ask price should be at least as high as the bid price. The mid-price of an asset is half way between the bid and offer prices, although it is conventional in this context to strip out the impact of transactional taxes which can sometimes apply on purchase but not on sale (or vice versa). Some care is needed when interpreting such terms for pooled vehicles. The bid and offer prices quoted by the provider of a dual-priced fund on a day-by-day basis may be the prices at which units in the fund can be bought or sold, but they are not necessarily symmetrically positioned around a mid-price valuation of the fund's underlying assets (and liabilities). Instead they may include adjustments dependent on the then prevailing direction of investor flows into or out of the fund so that incoming or outgoing investors pay a fair proportion of the transaction costs the fund itself incurs when it subsequently buys or sells assets. Likewise, single-priced pooled funds may not always be valued at mid-price. Terminology in the money market typically refers to 'bid' and 'offer' *rates*, which one might argue is the opposite way round to a terminology relating to 'bid' and 'offer' *prices*.

buying and selling money[9] is typically small, which is not the case for transactions in many other asset or liability types.

Transactions can typically occur anywhere within the relevant market bid–ask range without disrupting the principle of no arbitrage. It is therefore unclear whether there are intrinsic reasons for favouring the *mid-price* over any other point within the bid–ask range, except perhaps if we argue that natural justice means that willing buyers paired with willing sellers will inherently favour a position half way between the bid price and the ask price. In any case, the scenario implicitly being analysed may include an assumption that there may be some element of distress applicable to the party for which the valuation is being prepared. The scenario may not therefore necessarily involve pairing of a willing buyer with a willing seller.

> **Principle P9: Market consistency may not just require a view to be formed about the price at which one might reasonably expect assets or liabilities to trade were markets to exist for them. It may also require assessment of the bid–offer characteristics of these hypothetical markets.**

Whilst one might think that the accounting principle of 'fair value' would favour use of mid-prices, some accounting contexts instead mandate use of 'exit value'.[10] This principle takes on greater importance when we start to consider liquidity, which as we note in Chapter 5 is a concept in part linked to bid–offer spreads.

2.3   REGULATORY DRIVERS FAVOURING MARKET CONSISTENT VALUATIONS

Two key external developments encouraging greater use of market consistent valuations are:

(a) developments in international accounting standards; and
(b) developments in international thinking regarding how financial services entities ought to be regulated.

The international nature of capital markets means that international accounting standards setters are keen to move towards carrying assets and liabilities in balance sheets at market consistent values (which accountants typically refer to as 'fair values'), because of the greater uniformity and standardisation that this should bring. The argument is strongest if the assets or liabilities are relatively easily traded financial instruments somewhat divorced from the rest of the organisation's business, since these are the ones where one might intrinsically expect accounts to exhibit the greatest harmonisation.

Globalisation has also led to a desire for harmonisation in the regulatory sphere. An example is the Basel II agreement on banking supervision, see BCBS (2006). Some of this harmonisation relates to the conceptual frameworks being adopted. For example, Basel II adopts a three pillar approach, with the first pillar relating to suitable capital adequacy rules, the second pillar relating to effective interaction between the firm and the regulator, and the third pillar relating to transparency and the extra disciplines then able to be imposed by the marketplace. This three pillar framework is becoming the regulatory norm across the whole of the financial services

---

[9] I.e. buying one sort of money and selling another, e.g. buying one currency with another.

[10] Exit value would value assets at bid price and liabilities at offer price.

industry. It has spawned a similar overarching Solvency II project within the European Union (EU) for insurance company regulation.

More important for our purposes is the desire for the results of such computations also to exhibit harmonisation. Whilst governments may be incentivised to encourage organisations to domicile within their own domains via lax regulation, regulators (called supervisors in some jurisdictions) may have the opposite incentive. Who wants to be the regulator that ends up with another BCCI[11] on its plate? A key advantage from a regulator's perspective of mandating the use of market consistent valuation techniques is their objective foundation. We explore practical examples of this tendency further in Chapter 8.

A factor that also seems to be correlated with speed of adoption of market consistent valuations is the extent to which the regulator in question is a unitary regulator. By this we mean that the regulator regulates a wide range of different types of financial services entities.

An example of a unitary regulatory regime is the one currently prevailing in the UK. The UK's Financial Services Authority (FSA) regulates nearly all types of UK financial firms. In broad terms, the FSA's overall framework for the whole financial services industry might be characterised as permitting more sophisticated players to use their own internally developed models (subject to vetting by the regulator), with less sophisticated players having to fall back on more broad-brush calculation methodologies. Over time, we might expect the more broad-brush calculations to involve higher capital requirements in the majority of cases, to provide an appropriate incentive to enhance the sophistication of internal risk systems.

The FSA introduced a new regulatory framework for UK life and non-life (i.e. property/casualty) insurers in 2004. The approach owes much to the one that it had already adopted for the banking sector. Significant elements of this regulatory framework are likely to be copied by other EU insurance regulators when Solvency II is finally agreed. The FSA's framework involved a greater focus than previously on 'realistic' reporting and capital adequacy computations. UK life insurers' assets had for many years typically been carried at market value. So the key change was that liabilities (for large with-profits funds) would also be 'realistically' valued, i.e. valued in a more market consistent fashion as if they were traded in an open market or hedged by purchasing broadly equivalent instruments from third parties. The new regulatory framework also introduced greater focus on systems and processes to measure and manage risk.

Another factor is the extent to which the sector concerned is relatively global. For example, firms in the asset management industry (which is relatively global) typically value their funds at market value (where practical). Trading desks within investment banks (also a relatively global industry) typically mark-to-market their assets and liabilities on, say, a daily basis (although the same is not necessarily the case for the loans that their loan departments hold). Conversely, pension fund practice often varies significantly by location and fair valuation is less entrenched within this sector. But even here, Cowling *et al.* (2004) amongst others suggest that, at least in the UK, fair valuation methodologies will in time become more standard practice.

---

[11] Bank of Credit and Commerce International (BCCI) was a major international bank set up in London in 1972 which was shut down in 1991 on charges of fraud and other malpractices. Its liquidators then filed a lawsuit against BCCI's auditors which was eventually settled for $175 million in 1996. Its liquidators also instituted a $1 billion lawsuit against the Bank of England as the relevant regulatory body. After a nine-year struggle due to the Bank's statutory immunity, the case eventually went to trial in January 2004, although the liquidators eventually dropped any action against the Bank in November 2005 as it was no longer considered in the best interests of the creditors after a High Court ruling.

Pensions provide a good example of how political factors can influence this debate. For example, Patel (2008) indicated that opinions in Europe were then polarised between those who viewed pension schemes as financial institutions not too dissimilar to insurance companies and those who viewed pension schemes as a cross between a financial product and a 'best endeavours' activity aiming to deliver certain social policy objectives. Different EU member states have different welfare arrangements and hence different mixes and structures underlying state and private pension provision. Hence, these opinions are partly dependent on country of domicile. Where private pension provision is principally in the hands of insurance-like entities then adoption of insurance-like regulation may be seen as natural. Conversely, where pension provision in the EU is principally in the hands of separate employer organised schemes, a wider variety of views seems to exist.

2.4   UNDERLYING THEORETICAL ATTRACTIONS OF MARKET CONSISTENT VALUATIONS

From a firm's own perspective, greater focus on market consistent valuations has some attractions, as long as its use does not hinder its competitive position. These include:

(a) It is conceptually the most appropriate way to value assets and liabilities for solvency purposes. If we had to sell off all our assets and liabilities because we were insolvent or in danger of becoming insolvent then the value of these assets and liabilities to us would ultimately be what we could get for them in the open market. Of course, this does not remove the challenge of what to do when markets appear to be dysfunctional and the fundamental axioms underlying market consistency set out in Section 2.2.3 seem to have broken down. In particular, liquidity may be insufficient for the axiom of scalability to apply. We explore this issue further in Section 2.10 and Chapter 6.

(b) Fair values are widely seen as more 'objective' than any other sorts of valuation. Conceptually, they should require less in the way of subjective input than other methodologies.

(c) Carrying assets and liabilities (or more precisely their difference) at anything other than fair value implicitly involves taking a view about the amount of value that will be added (or subtracted) by how they are managed (versus the market implied view of what others might achieve with the same portfolio).[12] It would seem prudent from a risk management perspective not to assume an ability to add value from a skill that we might not actually possess (or at least haven't demonstrated beyond reasonable doubt that we possess). Conversely, it would seem overly conservative to assume that we will systematically subtract more value than others in a similar position. Tax can complicate the picture (although if the difference is large enough then there may be a risk that the tax authorities take a different view to tax advisors on the matter in question!).

(d) Several other organisations, e.g. ratings agencies, analysts and regulators, would all like the same information. Many organisations are interested in the likelihood of default of the companies that they are reviewing. They should favour approaches to the valuation of assets and liabilities that aid comparability (both within and across business types). Fair valuation has a strong appeal to them. Arguably, if they cannot access fair valuations directly then

---

[12] This incidentally means that market consistent valuations may be particularly helpful in the context of assessment of value added being contributed by management, hence the relevance of market consistency to embedded value computations, see Sections 2.2.7, 3.4.5 and 13.5. In this context, it may also be important to bear in mind the potential systemic effects of different remuneration structures, see Section 11.8.

they will attempt to create their own harmonised views across different entities. It ought to be economically efficient for entities themselves to provide such harmonised information without having others attempting to second-guess what the numbers should be. By doing so, the entities should also be helping themselves understand better their own competitive positioning. Company managers might, of course, have less incentive to exhibit openness than shareholders might like.

More generic rationales also exist, e.g.:

(e) Financial markets in effect exist to promote the 'law of one price', i.e. the idea that for any financial instrument there should be, at any particular point in time, a single price at which the instrument should trade (defined by the interaction of market participants). If the relevant instrument is freely traded then this price will be the fair value of the instrument. To be more precise, there will actually be a range of prices, but one of the aims of a properly functioning market is to keep this dealing spread as narrow as possible, thereby providing as much liquidity as possible in the given instrument.

(f) Over the last 20 or 30 years there has been a huge amount of innovation in financial markets, particularly in relation to derivatives. Much of the financial theory underlying these instruments is based on how they can be hedged by transactions in physical instruments. Thus their valuation is intimately linked to the price at which we might expect to be able to carry out such hedging transactions in the relevant underlying financial markets. Moreover, derivatives can be used to create an extremely wide range of potential pay-off profiles including some where each individual derivative instrument within a portfolio may be quite complicated but where taken as a whole they have very simple pay-offs. Ensuring that the value placed on any potential combination of derivatives makes sense (not least that the value of a series of derivatives with zero pay-off is zero) becomes a real challenge if a market consistent valuation framework is not adopted.

2.5   REASONS WHY SOME PEOPLE REJECT MARKET CONSISTENCY

There are also drivers in the opposite direction. During the 2007–09 credit crisis, credit turbulence that started in the US sub-prime mortgage market spread more generally across the financial system. Some senior executives of various financial companies voiced concern that when markets become 'dysfunctional' then over-adoption of marking-to-market can exacerbate a crisis rather than calm it, see e.g. Financial Times (2008a). The thesis seems to be that if panic in some particular market becomes extreme enough then buyers may completely disappear. This can then make it extremely hard to identify a suitable market value for an asset. This leads to banks needing to post greater (regulatory) capital against such holdings, encouraging banks to reduce their exposure to such instruments or to lend less against them, creating further declines in value and even less liquidity. The technical term for such a feedback loop is *pro-cyclicality*. This is a topic that we consider in greater depth in Chapter 11.

These executives' concerns reached the ears of politicians. In late 2008 governments around the world announced a series of measures that aimed to foster greater confidence in their financial systems. In October 2008, apparently after some pressure from EU politicians, according to some newspaper reports, and to bring greater harmonisation with equivalent US practice, the IASB agreed to relax international accounting standard IAS39. This allowed some loans and debt instruments (but not derivatives) to be reclassified from being carried at fair value to being carried at amortised cost (i.e. at a 'hold-to-maturity' value), see IASB (2008). At the same time the IASB modified IFRS 7 to require the amounts so reclassified to be disclosed.

Some national insurance industries have apparently lobbied against fair valuation and few people seem prepared to get banks to mark-to-market fully their retail books. Other concerns seem to have been that:

(a) Introduction of fair valuation of assets and liabilities creates greater volatility in profits. Of course, arguably the volatility is there all along (just not readily apparent if you do not use marking-to-market), as accounting standards setters may argue, according to Financial Times (2008a);
(b) Fair values may be overly complex to calculate (and understand); and
(c) Introduction of new capital adequacy rules with which developments in fair valuation are linked may penalise specific sections of the economy. For example, new risk weighting rules may make it more onerous for banks to lend money to, say, medium-size corporates. Of course, if banks had sufficiently sophisticated risk management systems, then they might not focus on any specific regulatory capital adequacy rules, but would instead work out the 'true' risks inherent in such lending. If lending policies to such corporates had previously been too lax (or too stringent) then introduction of new capital adequacy rules may not ultimately alter the outcome as far as the affected corporates are concerned.

2.6   MARKET MAKING VERSUS POSITION TAKING

The only sensible valuation metric to use for some market participants, whom we might refer to as *market makers*, is the market price (adjusted in some suitable way to reflect current or potential dealing spreads). These participants seek a return on capital employed by providing liquidity to the market, carrying an inventory of financial assets (or liabilities) that they add to or subtract from on an opportunistic basis. The capital that they are employing is this inventory (plus IT and human capital) and the market price reflects the cost of replacing their existing inventory with a new one.

We might expect the other main sort of market participants, whom we might refer to as *position takers*, to be able to focus more on the 'intrinsic' value of a particular position, if this can be differentiated from its current market/fair value. Thus they might be better positioned to take idiosyncratic views regarding the value of particular assets and liabilities. Indeed, active investment managers acting as agents for these position takers are specifically paid to take such views.

However, even position takers cannot (or should not) ignore market prices. There is a risk that their views prove erroneous. How ought an organisation to control this risk? An obvious element is to monitor how assessments of these 'intrinsic' values compare with the value assessments that others ascribe to the instrument, as represented by its current market value.

Few market participants are exclusively market makers or exclusively position takers. Most participants have some elements of both, even if the vast majority of their activities can be categorised into one or other camp. Participants that might normally be firmly in one category can temporarily flip into the opposite category, or might need to consider what might happen if such a switch were involuntarily imposed on them.

This blurring of roles is of particular relevance to capital adequacy. Banks, insurers, pension schemes and other financial services entities maintain appropriate capital bases to protect their deposit holders, policyholders and beneficiaries against the risk that their assets might prove insufficient to meet their liabilities. An obvious question is whether, if they tried to transfer all of an entity's assets and liabilities to some other entity, they would be able to do so without further capital injection. Thus, the underlying premise of a capital adequacy calculation involves hypothetically 'market making' the entity itself. A natural starting metric for this purpose is some estimate of the combined fair value of its assets and liabilities.

2.7 CONTRACTS THAT INCLUDE DISCRETIONARY ELEMENTS

A significant complication that arises in practice with some sorts of financial contracts is that they may include some element of discretion. This can in principle relate to discretion that the firm can exercise or that the customer (or other party) can exercise, or potentially both.

Sheldon and Smith (2004) consider this point in some detail in relation to the discretion that a with-profits insurer has on what bonuses it might declare in the future on this type of business. The Solvency II Project's QIS3 and QIS4 included elements in their computations reflecting the impact that such discretion might have on required capital.

Discretion can also be the other way round. It is then often closely linked to the tricky question of profit recognition. Take, for example, a time deposit with a retail bank. The lower the interest rate the bank provides (relative to market norms), the more profitable the contract is likely to be to the bank. Or rather, the more profitable it may be *until* depositors exercise their discretion to take their money and deposit it somewhere else. Usually, the 'fair value' ascribed to such contracts for regulatory purposes excludes the value of future profits generated by what one might describe (depending on one's point of view) as customer goodwill or customer inertia. From time to time there are runs on banks. These indicate that a shock to a bank sufficiently large to imperil its solvency can invalidate persistency assumptions otherwise needed to justify capitalising future profits that might in normal times accrue from customer goodwill. However, in other contexts we may want to include some of these future profits, see e.g. Section 13.5.

A special form of 'discretion' available to an entity is the discretion not to honour its debts because it has gone insolvent, i.e. the 'solvency put option' mentioned in Section 2.2.8.

Principle P10: Part of the market consistent value of an asset or a liability may relate to how discretion might be exercised in the future. In these cases it is normally helpful to divide the overall market consistent value between the part that relates to the value placed on contractual obligations and the part that relates to the value placed on continued exercise or non-exercise of these discretions. The two have different economic characteristics and hence may react quite differently in different scenarios.

2.8 VALUATION AND REGULATION

In Chapter 3 we explore some of the variation that exists in practice in how different standards setters and commentators interpret the term 'market consistent valuation'. Some of this variation stems from a lack of a clear conceptual framework describing how capital adequacy operates (or ought to operate), which we can refer back to whenever we need to work out exactly how to interpret this concept.

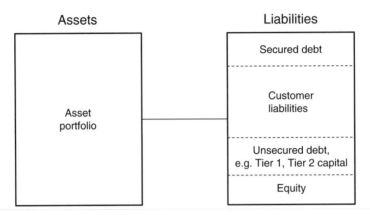

Figure 2.1 Schematic representation of a financial services firm

This point is hinted at in Wüthrich *et al.* (2007). In their book they argue that they have developed theoretical foundations for market consistent valuation, for use by insurance companies. However, they also indicate that their set of foundational principles 'is not the "full story" since it only gives the price for risk (the so-called (probably distorted) pure risk premium) for an insurance company. It does not tell how we have to organize the *risk bearing . . .*'

As noted in Kemp (2005) it *is* possible to construct a conceptual model that includes such 'risk bearing'. Kemp (2005) indicates that it is possible to re-express the balance sheet of essentially any sort of financial firm or entity (including an insurance company) into something akin to a Collateralised Debt Obligation (CDO).[13] In such a re-expression, a (proprietary) company's balance sheet includes both assets and liabilities, with the liability side consisting of (mainly) two parts, namely:[14]

(a) A 'senior' tranche corresponding to customer liabilities (i.e. viewing these liabilities as if they were a debt on the company); and
(b) A 'junior' or 'equity' tranche representing the shareholders' interests.

There may also in practice be other types of liabilities, some ranking above customers and some below them, depending on how the firm has financed itself. By customer we here mean policyholder for an insurance company, depositor for a bank, beneficiary for a pension scheme, etc. Visually, the balance sheet structure looks like Figure 2.1.

Kemp (2005) then argues that we can conceptually view capital adequacy assessment (at least if it is to be fully market consistent) as the process of:

(a) Working out the fair spread (versus a suitable 'risk-free' yield curve) applicable to the customer tranche; and

---

[13] For an explanation of the mechanics of CDOs, see Section 7.6.4.

[14] We here assume for simplicity that there is a single regulated entity, rather than a group of such entities with different sub-entities having differing claims over each other. Regulation of such groups usually focuses on the consolidated position, subject to the need for each individual regulated entity to be solvent in its own right. However, there are then issues about how to decide what to include in the consolidated picture, see e.g. BCBS (2006).

(b) Adjusting the size of the equity tranche or how the remainder of the balance sheet is structured (including the extent of any mismatch between assets and liabilities) so that the spread on the customer tranche is no greater than some level, say s.

In such a conceptual model we would typically view s as being set by the regulator. Where capital adequacy is enforced by market discipline then other bodies may be involved in setting s. For example, one might argue that analyst ratings or ratings awarded by credit rating agencies, etc. may influence an entity's external cost of capital and hence may enforce a level of capital adequacy without any explicit involvement by the regulator.

Kemp (2005) implicitly assumes that s might be constant. It is perhaps more likely that regulators might implicitly vary s through time (and that s might vary by term, like real life spreads), to mitigate the possible pro-cyclical impact of a fixed s, see Chapter 11.

Regulatory frameworks do not (currently) match this conceptual model, except if we adopt the circular logic that we can in theory solve for the s that corresponds to a particular level of capital mandated by a given regulatory framework for a given company. But there are still echoes of this conceptual model within current regulatory frameworks, not least the growing enthusiasm for market consistent valuations and for market disciplines more generally.

We will return to this conceptual model several times later on in this book. For example, we will use it to help clarify what should be understood by the 'risk-free' yield curve and to work out to what extent, if any, we should include allowance for liquidity or illiquidity in market consistent valuations.

At this juncture we shall merely draw out three key implications of this conceptual framework:

(a) If, at some deep level, capital adequacy is about ensuring that customers' liabilities carry a certain (maximum) level of market implied spread then *how* we build up this calculation is in some sense unimportant. Instead, the focus should be on getting the correct *total* (market consistent) size of the company's assets/liabilities (i.e. the total value of its customer and equity tranches combined) and then appropriately apportioning this value between the different liability tranches. In the alternative *best estimate plus risk margin* formulation this reflects the observation that the impact of greater or lesser prudence in any accounting standard or regulatory computation used to identify the *best estimate* (i.e. the value we place on the liabilities) can be unwound by an equal but opposite adjustment to the level of prudence included in the computation of the *risk margin* (i.e. the additional solvency capital that the company needs to hold in excess of this liability value).

(b) A significant theoretical challenge that most commentators in this field face at some stage in their deliberations is the need to decide on the extent to which the entity's own credit risk should be taken into account in the valuation of its liabilities. As we have noted in Section 2.2, we can in principle consider either inclusion or exclusion of own credit risk as being 'market consistent' (or indeed possibilities in between), but only if we carefully choose exactly what we are attempting to value in a market consistent manner. For example, exclusion of own credit risk theoretically requires our focus of attention to be on a package consisting both of the liability actually issued and of credit protection against the risk of default of the issuer. The above conceptual framework turns this problem on its head and instead constructs an approach in which this question becomes the centre of attention, rather than an intractable theoretical problem. The spread on the customer tranche, s, can be thought of as the risk-neutral measure of the credit risk exposure (and possibly liquidity risk exposure, see Chapter 5) that the customers (policyholders, depositors, beneficiaries, etc.) have to the entity in question.[15]

(c) Despite us having just concluded that there is no (single) theoretically right discount rate to use to value customer liabilities, our conceptual framework does provide a natural justification for one common approach used in this context. This is the special case where the liabilities are valued without *any* allowance for the credit risk of the entity itself. This can be thought of as corresponding to the situation where we have an infinitely well-capitalised company (or from the company that has an explicit guarantee from the issuer of the currency of the liabilities in question, as long as the currency issuer is itself of undoubted creditworthiness) and hence s can be expected to be zero.

Principle P11: Computation of market consistent valuations should not be viewed in isolation. Instead practitioners should bear in mind the wider purpose. In particular, where market consistent liability valuations are being carried out as part of a capital adequacy assessment, practitioners should appreciate that it is the overall balance sheet size and strength of the covenant being provided to customers that is important, rather than how this balance sheet is apportioned between values placed on customer liabilities and on other balance sheet elements.

A lack of conceptual clarity in exactly what might be the purpose of any market consistent valuation may explain the apparently diverse range of opinions that various parties provided on an IASB discussion paper on accounting for insurance contracts, see IASB (2007a) and IASB (2007b). Solvency assessment is only one of a number of possible uses of market consistent valuations. Regulators and other standards setters do seem to recognise that it is convenient and therefore economically beneficial to be able to reuse the same valuations in different contexts, but this may not always be feasible in practice.[16]

2.9 MARKING-TO-MARKET VERSUS MARKING-TO-MODEL

We mentioned earlier that the term 'market consistency' is less well entrenched within the banking world. Instead it would be more common to hear reference to the terms 'mark-to-market' and 'mark-to-model'.

In this context, a *mark-to-market* valuation is one derived from actual market transactions in the relevant instrument (which implicitly should therefore exhibit a certain minimum level of liquidity). In contrast, a *mark-to-model* valuation is one derived from a pricing model considered to be applicable to the instrument in question, into which suitable assumptions have been input.

---

[15] Own credit risk may be correlated with customer pay-off and this may influence the amount of regulatory capital required to achieve a given level of s. For example, suppose a fund was invested predominantly in cash but promised returns to customers predominantly in line with an equity market index. Situations in which the fund becomes insolvent would then be strongly correlated with ones where the relevant equity market index rises strongly, which in turn would be strongly correlated with situations in which customer payouts (if own credit risk could be ignored) would be highest. Thus computation of s in general involves pricing hybrid derivatives, i.e. ones that include several different elements simultaneously, including (in this instance) both credit risk and market risk elements.

[16] Even if it is not always feasible to use the same valuations in different contexts, it may still be possible to have building blocks that are capable of being used in more than one context.

Usually, the primary aim of any mark-to-model valuation is to come up with a reasoned best estimate (or prudent estimate, etc.) of what a mark-to-market valuation would have been had one been available at the relevant valuation point. A hierarchy is therefore established. If the instrument is sufficiently liquid we would refer directly to its market price, whilst if it is less liquid then we would typically need to include some element of modelling in the valuation process.

However, readers should be aware that sometimes the term 'mark-to-model' is specifically used in contradistinction to a 'market' valuation, e.g. the commentator may be contrasting 'reliable' market-derived valuations with inaccurate or 'unreliable' ones derived from models into which explicitly subjective (and biased) assumptions have been inserted.

Sometimes commentators express the view that 'mark-to-market' is intrinsically more reliable than 'mark-to-model'. In practice there is no clear dividing line between the two. For example, the market in straightforward interest rate swaps in most major currencies is typically highly liquid. If we wanted to enter into an interest rate swap then at any point in time we might know within, say, a basis point[17] or two what would be the interest rate that would be paid on the fixed leg of such a swap (in return for receiving a floating rate such as Libor). At any point in time rates for standard discrete period swaps (e.g. ones with terms of 1 year, 3 years, 5 years, etc.) might be directly accessible from market makers' quote systems. However, suppose we had entered into such a swap one week ago, or a day ago, or an hour ago (with an initial term of 5 years) and we now needed to identify its market value. Only a swap bought today would have a term exactly in line with the standardised ones that might be explicitly quoted on the relevant market maker quote systems. Even this swap may no longer have a rate payable on the fixed leg exactly in line with a current swap rate, i.e. the rate that exactly balances the present values of the fixed and floating rate legs. In practice, therefore, we are unlikely to be able to observe its exact market value *directly*. Instead, we would need to estimate its 'market' value using reference rates derived from swaps that we could actually then trade.

Is such a valuation a 'mark-to-market' or a 'mark-to-model'? A purist might argue that it is a mark-to-model, because a model is being used, however unimportant is the deviation from what can be observed live in the marketplace. A pragmatist might take the view that the market observables on which such a valuation is based are so close to what we are actually trading that the difference is irrelevant.

Suppose we ask a market maker to quote us a price for the instrument. Market makers' quotes in such circumstances are not always necessarily reliable (mid-market) estimates of the price at which we could have traded the instrument in question. For example, if a market maker can guess which side of the trade we are likely to be then it may adjust the bid and offer prices it quotes accordingly. Alternatively, we might be routed to the market makers' back office, and so may not get a price consistent with where its front office would actually trade. Even ignoring these niceties, market makers will typically need systems that ensure that the prices they quote on similar instruments are all consistent with each other. So, whenever

---

[17] A basis point is 0.01 %. When market makers quote bid–offer spreads and the like in basis points or percentages it is worth making sure that you know to what exactly the spread is being applied. In the context of a swap, typically it is applied to a per annum rate, i.e. if the swap rate were 4.00 % per annum then a bid–offer spread of ±1 basis point would typically mean a bid–offer range of 3.99 to 4.01 % per annum. Such a range can equate to much more than a ±0.01 % (of swap notional) spread in the mark-to-market price of the swap post set-up, for a long duration swap.

an instrument in question comes in a large range of slightly different variants (as is the case here), the market maker will almost certainly be using some sort of model to work out what prices to quote.

In any case, what we would normally be interested in is not a truly live price, but a price ruling at a particular point in time corresponding to that applicable to prices being used for other instruments in our portfolio. Again, for over-the-counter instruments (i.e. ones that are not standardised instruments traded on an organised exchange) and particularly for ones that come in a large number of variants, the market maker will typically be using pricing algorithms and models to provide 'market prices'.

Does the use of modelling by market makers somehow make the prices less reliable? We enter tricky territory here, indicating that the process of price discovery may not be quite as simple as it might first look, a topic we return to in Chapter 13.

2.10 RATIONAL BEHAVIOUR?

Physical scientists often lament the apparent inability of economics to predict things successfully. For example, Bouchard (2008) writes during the 2007–09 credit crisis: 'Rockets fly to the moon; energy is extracted from minute changes of atomic mass. What is the flagship achievement of economics? Only its recurrent inability to predict and avert crises, including the current worldwide credit crunch.' He does accept, paraphrasing Isaac Newton, that modelling the madness of people is more difficult than modelling the motion of the planets,[18] but thinks that 'statistical regularities should emerge in the behaviour of large populations, just as the law of ideal gases emerges from the chaotic motion of individual molecules'. His thesis is that classical economics is built on unwarranted assumptions that rapidly acquire the status of axioms, e.g. the rationality of economic agents and the efficiency of markets.

The 'theory' of market consistency set out above uses remarkably few mathematical axioms. The *only* ones used above are that market consistent valuations exhibit the axioms of additivity, scalability and uniqueness. In the next chapter we also introduce a final axiom, which we might call the *axiom of contemporaneous value continuity*, but which is more commonly called the *principle of no arbitrage*. The reason for using the first description here is to bring out the *point in time* nature of the axioms involved and to highlight that market consistent values assume very little about rational behaviour or market efficiency. They merely assume that at any particular point in time market participants rarely, if ever, deliberately sell something to a true third party at materially less than the price they can get in an open market for it, or buy it at more than they need to. We have not made any assumption about how market consistent values (and hence how market prices) might evolve through time, or whether, seen in the light of posterity, they will appear to have been rationally or 'efficiently' set by the market.

A corollary, as one reviewer of this chapter pointed out, is that if you seriously question the validity of these axioms as applying to value measurement then you will seriously question the applicability of market consistency at all. However, the challenge with this line of reasoning is that if you think that $2 + 2$ does not equal 4 or 1000×2 does not equal 2000 then what do you think they equal? Equivalent axioms underlie the mathematics of real numbers, so if you reject these axioms you make it very difficult to develop any theory of value that has an underpin that is expressible in conventional mathematical terms.

---

[18] Isaac Newton would have had personal experience to draw upon in this context, since he is said to have lost about £20,000 as a result of the South Sea bubble, a speculative excess described in depth in Mackay (1841).

One possible approach is, in effect, to incorporate additional factors that characterise the extent to which markets deviate from these axioms. For example, we might postulate a 'non-scalability' (i.e. 'liquidity'?) factor linked to the extent to which 1000 times something with a value of 2 doesn't then have a value of 2000. Indeed, this is exactly what is done in some circumstances, e.g. we talk of a bid 'premium' being the extra price an acquirer wishing to purchase a business would need to pay in excess of the current market value of the individual shares (or an equivalent sale 'discount' for a company wishing to exit from a business). In such a formulation, market consistent principles can be viewed as an abstraction or approximation to reality. In some sense, it is the exploration of deviations from these axioms that form the really 'interesting' elements of the theory of market consistency. This is because value creation/destruction within the financial services industry and transfers of value between economic agents operating within it ultimately occur through the medium of these discrepancies. For, at their most fundamental, financial assets and liabilities are otherwise merely proportionate claims on other 'more real' elements of economic activity.[19]

---

[19] Such a discussion again has echoes within the physical sciences. For example, the so-called Riemann tensor measures the extent to which the curved space–time equivalent of differentiation does not satisfy the axiom of commutativity, i.e. does not adhere to $A \times B = B \times A$. It is thus also intimately bound up with the extent to which space–time is curved. In Einstein's General Theory of Relativity, the Einstein tensor, which derives from the Riemann tensor, is proportional to the amount of matter or energy present. So in a sense we can view the force of gravity as being driven by the extent to which this particular 'axiom' does not in fact apply in the real world.

3

Different Meanings given to 'Market Consistent Valuations'

3.1 INTRODUCTION

In this chapter we explore different meanings that different standards setters and commentators give to the term 'market consistent valuation'. We explore intrinsic differences that can arise due to the underlying purpose of the valuation. We illustrate differences in practice that have arisen between different regulators or other standards setters. We also explore some of the different nuances that other commentators have placed on this term, and highlight some important practical points relevant when markets fail to come into existence or fail to remain functioning.

3.2 THE UNDERLYING PURPOSE OF A VALUATION

In Chapter 2 we saw that we could conceptually differentiate between several types of market consistent valuation, by reference to the purpose of the valuation. Each of the following type of valuation is potentially relevant in certain circumstances:

(a) A *fair mid-value* of an asset or liability at a particular instant in time. This would be the market price (or in the absence of a liquid market, the valuer's best estimate of the market price) at which marginal trades in either would occur between willing buyers and willing sellers (ignoring market frictions, e.g. bid–offer spreads in the underlying instruments, lack of liquidity, etc.).
(b) A *prudent fair value*. This might include a best estimate of how asset values might fall and liability values might rise because of market frictions, see Section 2.2.10.
(c) A *no goodwill fair value*. This would be a fair value (or prudent fair value) that excluded the valuation of future profits arising from contract persistency that was at the discretion of other parties (principally customers).
(d) An *entity credit spread eliminated fair value*. This would be what the fair value (mid, prudent or no goodwill, depending on its basis) would be were the default risk inherent in the entity itself to be removed from the market value of its liabilities, i.e. excluding any value placed on the 'solvency put option'.

3.3 THE IMPORTANCE OF THE 'MARGINAL' TRADE

It is worth highlighting that all of the above definitions ultimately derive from the prices at which *marginal* trades might be expected to occur. This is an inevitable consequence of a framework that seeks to adhere to the axioms of additivity and scalability, since the value placed on an asset or liability then needs to adhere to $(V(\mathbf{a})) = V(k\mathbf{a})/k$ for all $k \neq 0$, including small values of k.

A definitional issue arises here in relation to what constitutes the price at which a 'marginal' trade might occur. Typically, 'price' would be taken to mean a computation that strips out the impact of any per trade transaction costs, whether implicit or explicit. Market makers may not be prepared to quote for very small transactions (here 'very small' will depend on the market in question). Set-up costs for the market maker for such trades may be excessive relative to the economic characteristics of the trade including its likely profit margin to the market maker. As a result, we should expect that:

(a) Market consistent valuations of a business are unlikely to correspond directly to the price that another entity wishing to acquire the entire business would need to pay to gain control of it. This is analogous to the bid premium typically seen in corporate mergers and acquisitions.

(b) If trades in an asset or liability type occur only infrequently or only in large size then it may be difficult to extrapolate from market observations the price at which a marginal trade would take place.

An implicit assumption is that the willing buyer and willing seller involved in the hypothetical transaction that would set market valuations are both not so large as to dominate market dynamics. If either is particularly large then care may be needed to disentangle the quasi-monopolistic impact of this size.

Some interpretation is also needed if the transactions involved are not between 'professional' style market participants. For example, the prices at which individual members of the public might be prepared to buy a given financial product do provide 'market' information relevant for market consistent pricing purposes. There is, after all, a 'market' in such products. However, one needs to interpret such data carefully if one, say, wishes to extrapolate market consistent values of any assets or liabilities packaged within a product from the prices charged for the product in aggregate. There may be other service components included within the product that influenced the customer's choice of provider and hence willingness to pay the overall price being charged by the provider.[1] By 'professional' style market participants we here mean participants presumed to be dispassionately comparing the prices quoted by different market makers. We may not always expect the general public to behave in quite so rational a manner.[2]

Marginal transactions are not driven by the 'marginal views' of *every possible* market participant, but only by the views of the *subset* of all market participants actually interested in buying or selling a given asset or liability. It is impossible in practice for any one individual or even one company to articulate views on, or to develop the right infrastructure to be able to trade in, every possible asset or liability. This practical constraint is an example of how 'bounded rationality' can creep into markets. Even if each market participant rationally chooses between a range of different instruments, the fact that they choose only from within a subset of all possible instruments can have a discernible impact on market dynamics, see Chapter 9.

---

[1] Another way of interpreting this is that the market clearing prices of these products may also tell us something about the market consistent values to place on some of these additional services. For example, if explicit administration charge levels are included in such products then we might be able to infer what would be a market consistent value that customers would place on these services. The major challenge here is that these products do not typically come with unbundled rate cards. Even if they did, customers might not in practice be able (or willing) to pick and choose between different providers for each service component.

[2] Whether even market professionals necessarily actually act 'rationally' in their choice of price at which to trade is a topic that also generates some debate, and is included in the subject matter of the *behavioural finance* branch of financial theory (likewise 'behavioural economics').

3.4   DIFFERENT DEFINITIONS USED BY DIFFERENT STANDARDS SETTERS

3.4.1   Introduction

Another source of variation arises from the tendency of different standards setters to adopt slightly different definitions. Several examples of this tendency are highlighted below. We here consider different definitions of 'fair value' and 'mark-to-market' as well as 'market consistent' valuation.

3.4.2   US accounting – FAS 157

The standard framework for financial accounting in the USA is called US Generally Accepted Accounting Principles (US GAAP). These principles are now issued by the (US) Financial Accounting Standards Board (FASB). Its Financial Accounting Standard (FAS) 157 on 'Fair Value Measurements' defines fair value as the price that would be received for an asset or paid to transfer a liability in a transaction between market participants at the measurement date. FAS 157, which applies to financial statements issued for fiscal years beginning after 15 November 2007, requires that:

(a) 'Blockage' factors that might be based on the typical volume of the instrument that trades in an active market are not to be used, although it does appear to be possible to include a liquidity discount;

(b) Securities that are 'restricted' in the sense that a fund might only be able to hold such assets for certain of its unit holders or shareholders are to be valued using the quoted market price of an otherwise identical unrestricted security, adjusted for the effect of the restriction;

(c) The price is to be derived from the main market for the instrument, i.e. the market with the greatest volume or level of activity. If there are multiple markets in which the same instrument trades then the most advantageous market is to be used; and

(d) Transaction costs are excluded.

Under FAS 157, valuation techniques used to measure fair value should be consistent with one of the approaches set out in Table 3.1. FAS 157 has also introduced a three level fair value hierarchy that defines the priority applied to different inputs used to estimate fair value, set out in Table 3.2.

Financial statements drawn up in accordance with FAS 157 need to include disclosures indicating the proportion of the portfolio falling into each of the levels described in Table 3.2 and descriptions for each level present of the valuation techniques used.

Table 3.1   Acceptable valuation techniques under FAS 157

Approach	Description
Market	Uses observable prices generated from market transactions involving identical, similar or otherwise comparable assets or liabilities
Income	Uses valuation techniques to convert future amounts (e.g. cash flows or earnings) to a single (discounted) present value
Cost	Uses the amount currently required to replace the service capacity of the asset. This approach is not generally applicable for investment portfolios.

Table 3.2 Priority hierarchy for FAS 157 fair value estimation inputs

Level	Characteristics of inputs
1	observable market inputs that reflect quoted prices for identical securities in active markets (which the entity had the ability to access at the measurement date)[3]
2	observable market inputs other than Level 1 inputs, including: • Quoted prices for similar assets or liabilities in active markets • Quoted prices for identical or similar assets or liabilities in markets that are not active • Market inputs other than quoted prices (e.g. yield curves, volatility statistics, credit spreads, etc.)
3	unobservable market inputs, e.g. ones derived by extrapolation or interpolation not able to be corroborated by observable market data

3.4.3 Guidance on how to interpret FAS, IAS, IFRS, etc.

As derivation of fair value can involve subjectivity, a number of accounting firms (or bodies sponsored by the accountancy industry) have sought to clarify how to interpret relevant standards. Shortly before the end of 2007 there was a flurry of reports and letters attempting to provide added colour to some of the existing standards. These included PCAOB (2007), CAQ (2007a), CAQ (2007b), CAQ (2007c) on FAS 157 and GPPC (2007) on corresponding International Financial Reporting Standards (IFRS) and International Accounting Standards (IAS), as defined by the International Accounting Standards Board (IASB). In early 2008, auditors warned that they would apply extra scrutiny to a company's viability when auditing the company's accounts, including its access to credit for the coming year, see Financial Times (2008b).

These pronouncements have normally taken the form of a restatement of the relevant accounting standard and an attempt then to elaborate what it might mean in particular market conditions. For example, the Global Public Policy Committee (a committee of larger international accounting networks focused on public policy issues) noted in GPPC (2007) that:

(a) IAS 39.9 defines fair value as the amount for which an asset could be exchanged or a liability settled between knowledgeable, willing parties in an arm's-length transaction.
(b) IAS 39 contains a hierarchy for the determination of fair value, which in the absence of quoted prices involves the use of a 'valuation technique'.
(c) Under IAS 39.AG71, a financial instrument is regarded as quoted in an active market if quoted prices are readily and regularly available from an exchange, dealer, broker, industry group, pricing service or regulatory agency and those prices represent actual and regularly occurring market transactions on an arm's-length basis. A problem might then be whether regularly occurring market transactions are actually taking place, particularly if there is a suspicion that markets are not functioning properly.
(d) A significantly lower than normal volume of transactions does not necessarily provide sufficient evidence that there is not an active market. Also, an apparent imbalance between supply and demand is not the same as a forced transaction or distressed sale.
(e) If transactions are still occurring between willing buyers and sellers in a manner that is usual and customary for transactions then these can hardly be viewed as forced transactions or distressed sales. Merely because there are fewer of these trades than usual doesn't mean

---

[3] However, it is noted in FAS 157 that quoted prices may not necessarily be representative of fair values (e.g. if the prices are 'stale', i.e. out of date).

that information contained in the price at which these trades are struck should be ignored for fair valuation purposes.

(f) However, if observed transactions are no longer regularly occurring or the only observed transactions are forced transactions or distressed sales then the market should no longer be considered to be active, irrespective of whether prices are still available from it.

(g) Even if the relevant market is no longer considered active, the purpose of determining a fair value is independent of the means used to prepare the fair value. So even if the methodology used is a 'valuation technique', valuers should still take cognisance of market information that is available from transactions that do occur in that market (e.g. the size of liquidity premiums or credit spreads).

(h) IAS 39.AG76 requires any valuation technique to be calibrated periodically against market transactions in the same instrument or available observable market data for similar instruments.

Factors GPPC (2007) recommends should be taken into account when assessing the extent to which an entity may place reliance on a value supplied by a third party (e.g. a broker quote or pricing service) include:

(a) Whether it reflects a price at which the entity could be expected to transact (e.g. does the entity have access to the market from which the price was derived?);

(b) Whether and how the valuation incorporates recent market events (e.g. the extent to which it might include 'stale' prices);

(c) How frequently the valuation is updated to reflect changing market conditions;

(d) The number of sources from which the valuation is derived. A valuation that is derived from many quotes or data sources is generally considered preferable to one based on a small number of observations, although this would be less true if all of the quotes or data sources themselves ultimately relied on just one underlying data source;

(e) Whether the value reflects actual transactions or merely indicative prices; and

(f) Whether the value is consistent with available market information, including current market transactions in the same or similar instruments.

The length of this list of factors highlights again that carrying out fair (i.e. market consistent) valuations is potentially subjective, particularly for less liquid or less commonly traded instruments.

3.4.4   EU insurance regulation – 'Solvency II'

The Solvency II framework for life insurance regulation is due to come into force in late 2012 across the EU. In Chapter 8 we explore in more detail its likely capital adequacy implications. Here we focus principally on the emerging thinking it encapsulates on how market consistent valuations ought to be derived.

Typically, insurance companies have to file regulatory computations demonstrating solvency as well as preparing the sorts of statutory accounts required for any type of company. Traditionally, statutory accounts have been drawn up on a going concern basis, which is not necessarily the most helpful way to explore the likely position in the sort of winding-up scenario more relevant to demonstrating solvency. As a result, approaches used to value assets and liabilities in insurance company regulatory capital computations have not always exactly mirrored more general going concern accounting approaches.

Whilst the need for solvency specific calculations seems to be widely accepted, there is currently less agreement amongst stakeholders (supervisors, industry, professions, etc.) about exactly how these calculations should be carried out in practice, particularly for so-called *technical provisions* (i.e. valuations of policyholder liabilities[4]).

To prepare the industry for the changes that will occur with Solvency II, and to flush out and resolve points of disagreement, the Committee of European Insurance and Occupational Pensions Supervisors (CEIOPS) has organised several Quantitative Impact Studies (QISs). We focus below on QIS3 and QIS4.

3.4.4.1 QIS3

CEIOPS (2007a), when setting out instructions for participants in QIS3, gave an indication of its thoughts in April 2007 on how assets and liabilities should be valued for regulatory capital purposes under Solvency II. It indicated that assets should be valued at their market prices, as follows:

(a) Where reliable, observable market prices in deep and liquid markets exist, asset values should be set equal to these market prices. For long (asset) positions the appropriate quoted market price is the bid price taken at the valuation date, while for short positions it is the offer price;

(b) If a market price is observable but is not reliable (for example, due to illiquidity), reasonable proxies should be adopted, but they should still be consistent with any relevant market information. For tradable assets this should be an estimate of the realisable value;

(c) Illiquid or non-tradable assets should be valued on a prudent basis, fully taking into account the reduction in value due to the credit and liquidity risks attached; and

(d) If independent and reliable expert opinions are available these may be considered in the valuation.

CEIOPS (2007a) put forward the following principles for calculating technical provisions:

(a) Their value should take into account both hedgeable and non-hedgeable risks. Where it is unclear which applies, or where market consistent values cannot be derived, the non-hedgeable approach should be followed (i.e. a 'best estimate plus risk margin' approach). Where separable, the value of the hedgeable and the non-hedgeable risks should be separately disclosed. For non-hedgeable risks, the risk margin should be separately disclosed; and

(b) No reduction in technical provisions should be made on account of the creditworthiness of the undertaking itself.

CEIOPS viewed hedgeable risks as corresponding to risks that could be perfectly hedged or replicated in a sufficiently deep, liquid and transparent market, in which case the hedge

---

[4] Insurance accounting terminology includes several terms that may not be familiar to a wider audience. Typically their accounts are divided between 'non-technical' and 'technical' elements, the latter relating to their insurance activities and the former to everything else (usually just their shareholder account). 'Provision' is a term that has a defined accounting meaning. Liabilities to policyholders, being payable some way out into the future and often subject to uncertain contingencies, do not necessarily fall within the standard accounting meaning of the word. 'Technical provisions' are therefore a way of formulating accounting principles to circumvent such definitional challenges, since it is clearly desirable that insurance companies hold some assets to back commitments they may have given to policyholders for the future. In the actuarial world, 'technical provisions' are also known as 'mathematical reserves'.

or the replicating portfolio provides a directly observable price (i.e. a mark-to-market price). Reasonable interpolations and extrapolations from directly observable prices were permitted. Deep, liquid and transparent markets were defined as 'markets where participants can rapidly execute large-volume transactions with little impact on prices'.

For non-hedgeable risks 'the valuation should correspond to the explicit sum of a best estimate plus a risk margin, the latter being determined according to a cost-of-capital (CoC) approach. However for long-tailed non-life business alternative methods are envisaged.' It was envisaged that:

(a) Such risks might include risks that are of a financial nature (i.e. presumably not purely dependent on uncertainty in insurance claims occurrence), whenever there is no hedgeable price from deep, liquid and transparent markets. The valuation should then include an allowance for additional uncertainty;

(b) It might be possible to carve out from a non-hedgeable risk a hedgeable sub-risk which would be valued as above; and

(c) If a hedge is available but it is incomplete and will only to some extent eliminate the risks associated with a liability then the best estimate valuation could be done by 'reference to the market value of the incomplete hedge increased with an appropriate valuation of the expected basis risk'.

The same document proposed that 'cashflows should be discounted at the risk-free discount rate applicable for the relevant maturity at the valuation date. These should be derived from the risk-free interest rate term structure at the valuation date.' CEIOPS provided specimen term structures for different European Economic Area (EEA) currencies, together with ones for the US Dollar, Japanese Yen and Swiss Franc.[5] CEIOPS also indicated that the creditworthiness of the undertaking was not intended to influence the value of the technical provisions, and so term structures for other currencies should be derived adopting the principle that the risk-free interest rates relating to bullet maturities should be credit risk-free, with the suggestion that risk-free interest rates could be set by taking into account yields on government bonds, where available and appropriate.

CEIOPS did, however, consider that in some markets it could be more appropriate (due to illiquidity and/or insufficient selection of maturities) to derive risk-free rates from swap rates, but if so, appropriate thought should be given to the possible illiquidity or insufficient credit quality of swap rates in question. Use of risk-adjusted discount rates (i.e. 'deflators') was also permitted as long as the overall valuation process gave equivalent results to projections using risk-neutral probabilities and discounting at a risk-free interest rate term structure.

Subsequent clarification meant that yield curves derived from swap rates were generally used for the risk-free rate in the calculations.

3.4.4.2   QIS4

The corresponding QIS4 documentation[6] contained a rather more detailed elaboration of the framework that CEIOPS appeared to favour. It also used terminology more likely to be readily

---

[5] Although Switzerland has historically had close links to both the EU and the EEA, it was not at the time actually a member of either body.

[6] See CEIOPS (2007b) for the original draft and CEIOPS (2008) for the final version.

recognised by those outside the insurance industry. It involved some high-level principles, namely:

(a) Wherever possible, a firm must use marking-to-market in order to measure the economic value of assets and liabilities.
(b) Where this is not possible, marking-to-model should be used. CEIOPS (2007b) defined marking-to-model as 'any valuation that has to be benchmarked, extrapolated or otherwise calculated from a market input'. When marking to model, undertakings should use as much as possible observable and market consistent inputs.
(c) There was greater guidance offered when CEIOPS thought general purpose accounting figures might satisfy these principles and also a desire for participants in QIS4 to justify deviations from such figures.
(d) It was expected that undertakings would have appropriate verification processes in place to validate the accuracy and relevance of any market prices or model inputs used in marking-to-model. CEIOPS was expecting to receive additional information from undertakings on which assets were marked-to-market and which were marked-to-model, and on the characteristics of the models used in the latter cases, including the nature of their inputs.

On the topic of technical provisions, CEIOPS (2007b) indicated that:

(a) Participants should value technical provisions 'at the amount for which they could be transferred, or settled, between knowledgeable willing parties in an arm's length transaction' (i.e. a definition more in line with fair value accounting definitions);
(b) Their calculation should be based on their current exit value, and should make use of and be consistent with information provided by the financial markets and generally available data on insurance technical risk;
(c) Technical provisions should include all obligations towards policyholders and other beneficiaries of the insurance contracts of the undertaking;
(d) Technical provisions should be calculated in a prudent, reliable and objective manner. They should be set equal to the sum of a best estimate and a risk margin, with these two elements valued separately, except if the future cash flows associated with the insurance obligations could be replicated using financial instruments for which a market value is directly observable (in which case the value of the technical provisions should be determined on the basis of the market value of these financial instruments); and
(e) The best estimate element should be the value of the probability-weighted average of future cash flows, taking account of the time value of money, using the relevant risk-free interest rate term structure. It should be based on current and credible information and realistic assumptions, and be performed using adequate actuarial methods and statistical techniques.

Essentially the same hedgeable/non-hedgeable risk differentiation as per QIS3 was retained in QIS4, as was the requirement that there be no reduction in the technical provisions to reflect the creditworthiness of the undertaking itself. However, exactly what was to be understood by 'hedgeable' and 'unhedgeable' was elaborated upon. More explicit reference was made to no-arbitrage principles. A slight refinement was incorporated in what was understood by a market being 'deep, liquid and transparent', which was now defined as one that met the following requirements:

(a) Market participants can rapidly execute large volume transactions with little impact on prices;

(b) Current trade and quote information is readily available to the public;[7] and

(c) Both (a) and (b) are expected to be permanent.[8]

When estimating cash flows, CEIOPS (2007b) indicated that the 'expected cash-flows should be based on assumptions that are deemed to be realistic for the book of business in question . . . Assumptions should be based on a participant's experience for the probability distributions for each risk factor, but taking into consideration market or industry data where own experience is limited or not sufficiently credible. Such realistic assumptions should neither be deliberately overstated nor deliberately understated when performing professional judgements on factors where no credible information is available.'

The initial draft QIS4 instructions mandated discounting using risk-free yield curves that were derived from government debt, i.e. different to the swap rate basis typically used for QIS3. For cash flows denominated in Euro this was to be the Euro area yield curve published by the European Central Bank (ECB) derived from AAA rated Euro area Government debt.[9] CEIOPS expected to provide yield curves for other EEA and certain other currencies and undertakings were expected to use a similar approach for other currencies. However, participants were to be allowed to deviate from the prescribed term structures as long as they provided rationale (and didn't adjust for the creditworthiness of their own undertaking). This was perhaps again to allow CEIOPS to understand the impact of potential alternative definitions of 'risk-free'.

After some lobbying, the final QIS4 instructions reverted to use of a relatively prescriptive swap-based discount rate.[10] This about-turn perhaps reflects a lack of agreement between different interested parties about exactly how to define 'risk-free'.[11] At that time, in early 2008, spreads between swap rates and corresponding government debt rates were high relative to their historic levels (a symptom of the then challenging bank liquidity and credit market conditions). Even small spreads can have a significant impact on such liability valuations given the assumed long time to payment of many life insurance liabilities. One might therefore be

---

[7] A subtlety that is likely to need fleshing out over time is exactly what sort of information is 'readily available to the public' in this context. One can understand reluctance by insurance regulators to require firms to be suitably familiar with every possible source of market information, including ones that are private and may therefore incur material costs to access. However, one might also not want to limit the information that insurers should bear in mind merely to, say, information publicly available on websites or in newspapers. For example, data on longer-dated equity implied volatility is relevant to the market consistent pricing of many types of life insurance liabilities. However, derivatives expressing views on such volatility only in practice trade over-the-counter (OTC) rather than on listed exchanges. Information on longer-dated equity volatilities can therefore be accessed, at not particularly large cost, from market makers or from third party data vendors (or other intermediaries) who in turn collate such information from selected market makers.

[8] Whilst it is clear what sentiment is intended here, exactly what is meant by 'permanent' (and hence which markets should be deemed to exhibit these characteristics) could form an interesting debate at the time of writing, given the drying up of many markets many commentators might previously have expected to stay liquid in most market scenarios.

[9] The yield curve was specified as Geographic area: Euro area, Financial market instrument: Government bond, nominal, all triple A issuer companies, Financial market provider: Svensson model, continuous compounding, yield error minimisation, see ECB webpage www.ecb.eu/stats/money/yc/html/index.en.html

[10] The final QIS4 technical specifications mandated (for Euro denominated liabilities) use of 6 months' euro swaps against Euribor, as listed by Bloomberg. The interpolation approach used involves piecewise constant forward rates, which is consistent with the interpolation approach previously mandated by the Dutch National Bank in its supervision of Dutch insurers and pension schemes.

[11] Strictly speaking, the wording in QIS4 did not explicitly reject the notion of credit risk in liabilities, except by use of the term 'risk-free'. It stated that the 'creditworthiness of the undertaking should not have any influence on the interest rate term structure derived by the participant'. This could be interpreted as permitting a risky reference rate, provided this risky rate is not specific to the entity in question.

forgiven for surmising that the lobbying might be more focused on keeping liability valuations down than on identifying the theoretically correct 'risk-free' rate to use. Later on in 2008, this spread had become negative at the long end of the yield curve for many developed western currencies. We explore the topic of how best to define the 'risk-free' rate in Chapter 5.

3.4.5 Market consistent embedded values

We have noted in Section 2.2.7 that there may be reasons for trying to place embedded values on long-term contracts already entered into by insurance businesses and other sorts of financial services entities. The CFO Forum (2008a) published principles on how to determine market consistent embedded values (MCEVs), in an attempt to standardise the computation frameworks used in the European insurance industry. The MCEV principles attempted to standardise the earlier 'European Embedded Value' (EEV) computations. They included the requirement to project cash flows using economic assumptions that would result in them being valued in line with prices of similar cash flows traded in capital markets. The MCEV principles also included further guidance on what constitutes 'covered' business (i.e. the contracts that should be deemed to be in force at the relevant valuation date), how to cater for participating business (i.e. business in which payments to policyholders may depend on behaviour of the assets supporting the policies in question), etc.

The CFO Forum (2008a) also specified in some detail how to report on embedded values. The topic of how to report information is clearly relevant to any attempt to standardise accounting practice, but is not a topic that we explore further in this book.

In certain respects, CFO Forum (2008a) prescribes approaches that may not be fully market consistent. For example, they specify that the 'reference' rate to use for discounting purposes should be the swap yield curve appropriate to the currency of the cash flows. They also state that no adjustment should be made to the swap yield curve to allow for liquidity premiums or credit risk premiums. In their main paper they, unlike CEIOPS and the CRO Forum (2008a), refer merely to a reference rate rather than a 'risk-free' rate. However, CFO Forum (2008b) which gives justifications for the approaches proposed in CFO Forum (2008a) does appear to claim that such a reference rate should be regarded as a proxy for the risk-free rate. This implicitly seems to assume that swap curves do not themselves express credit risk. For some types of swap this may be largely true, but it is noticeably less true for others, see Chapter 5.

3.4.6 UK pension fund accounting and solvency computation

Changes also currently seem to be under way in the field of accounting for pension costs. These changes appear to be part of a more general harmonisation between approaches adopted for pension obligations and those for economically equivalent obligations that involve insurance contracts. For example, ASB (2008) proposed that '... the liability should be quantified for financial reporting purposes at an assessment of the cost of settling the benefit ... and so the cash flows should be discounted at a risk-free rate. The rate should not ... be increased to reflect the credit risk of the liability. This approach differs from practice ruling as at end 2007, under which the cash flows were typically discounted at a high quality corporate bond rate.'

As mentioned in Section 2.3.2, there is also a possibility that EU pension fund regulation will be increasingly harmonised with EU life insurance regulation and hence with the principles described in the section above covering Solvency II.

An evaluation of the potential impact that adoption of Solvency II style solvency tests might have on different types of EU pension funds was carried out by Peek *et al.* (2008). Their evaluation suggests that a funding ratio of assets to liabilities ('funding level') of 100 % as measured using a basis akin to that set out in the relevant international accounting standard (IAS 19) would often not be sufficient to fulfil QIS3 Solvency II requirements. Moreover, a fund's asset allocation stance can have a material impact on the Solvency Capital Requirement (SCR) element of a Solvency II type computation. There is no immediate equivalent market risk exposure element within more general purpose accounting standards such as IAS 19.

3.5 INTERPRETATIONS USED BY OTHER COMMENTATORS

3.5.1 Introduction

Terms like 'market consistency', 'market consistent valuation' and 'market consistent basis' are also now appearing more frequently in relevant professional literature. Use of the term (in a valuation context) is perhaps most common in the insurance and actuarial fields, because, as mentioned earlier, accountants typically seem to prefer to refer to 'fair value', and bankers typically seem more familiar with the term 'mark-to-market' or 'mark-to-model' (depending on the extent to which modelling is used in deriving a suitable value to place on the instrument).

In relevant professional literature, the terms and precise definitions used may be designed to stress some particular aspect of market consistency particularly important to the writer. We set out some examples below.

3.5.2 Contrasting 'market consistent' values with 'real world' values

Reference to market consistency may aim to contrast the valuation thus derived with some other way in which the valuation might be struck. A common contrast is with what is often called a 'real world' valuation basis.

For example, Hosty *et al.* (2007), when writing about the UK equity release market,[12] sought to quantify the cost of the *no negative equity guarantee* (NNEG) offered by most mortgage providers in this marketplace. Inclusion of an NNEG is compulsory for providers following the main UK code of practice, the Safe Home Income Plans (SHIP) code of practice. With NNEG, the provider guarantees the borrower that the redemption amount of the mortgage will be capped by the lesser of the face amount of the mortgage and the sale proceeds of the home, usually net of sale expenses. As the mortgage will often roll up with interest, negative equity claims are most likely to occur to the borrowers who live the longest.

Hosty *et al.* quantified the cost of the NNEG (to the NNEG provider) on two different bases, one of which they described as 'an approximate market consistent basis similar to the pricing of options on stocks' and the other they described as 'an insurance pricing basis using "real world" assumptions'. They noted that a challenge when trying to value the cost on a market consistent basis was the fact that there was no underlying market to speak of. They therefore postulated a proxy market in which the underlying property values were assumed to move in a log Normal fashion (akin to that implicit in a Black-Scholes world) assuming house volatility

---

[12] 'Equity release' typically refers to methods by which individuals can access wealth otherwise tied up in home ownership. It can take various forms, but here we concentrate on mortgages typically taken out by relatively elderly homeowners to fund the purchase of annuities at the expense of capital that might otherwise pass on their death to their estate.

Table 3.3   'Market consistent' versus 'real world' valuation bases: NNEG costs

Sample case	Value on an approximate *market consistent* basis as a percentage of initial mortgage	Value on an assumed *real world* basis as a percentage of initial mortgage
Male, aged 65	18 %	2.5 %
Female, aged 65	19 %	2.6 %
Joint life, both aged 65	29 %	4.1 %

Source: Hosty *et al.* (2007)

was 11 % pa, and the risk-neutral drift in house prices was the return on long-term risk-free instruments (taken to be government stocks) less an assumed rental income of 3.3 % pa (net of expenses), in line with the net rental yield on the IPD Residential Property Index for 2006. At the time current yields on long-term government stocks were around 4.75 % pa, implying a forward rate for house price inflation of 1.5 % pa. They contrasted the NNEG cost on this basis with the cost on an alternative 'real world' basis which involved the same assumed volatility but adopted a best estimate of 4.5 % pa for house price inflation going forwards (without any assumed mean reversionary characteristics).

The two sets of assumptions used in this example differ only in relation to the assumed rate of future house price growth, but nevertheless produce substantially different answers, see Table 3.3.

Even though equity release products are not a particularly important financial market (at present), the above comparison highlights many of the issues applicable to preparing market consistent valuations for any type of longer-term liability, namely:

(a) There is rarely a well-established market for the liabilities in question, so postulating how a market might operate in them is often non-trivial and therefore subject to uncertainty.
(b) Market consistent values often differ significantly from alternative 'real world' values. Often the market consistent ones are significantly larger (for reasons we explore further below). Indeed, the difference may be so large that it is not practical for organisations to compete in the underlying market if there are players who consider that (or who can account as if) the 'right' cost to ascribe to the liability is the one derived from 'real world' assumptions. This often makes market-based hedging of the liabilities seem expensive to the underlying market participants, discouraging the formation of a more liquid market in the relevant liabilities in the first place (and ensuring that valuations that are estimated on market consistent principles continue to be subject to a significant amount of uncertainty).
(c) The results can be quite sensitive to the assumed 'risk-free rate', i.e. how liabilities are discounted, and, for liabilities that incorporate option-like characteristics, by volatility assumptions.

There is no absolute prohibition of the opposite situation, in which market consistent valuations come up with answers *below* those that might typically be ascribed to a long-term liability using typical 'real world' assumptions. But typically, the liabilities involve the provision of protection against adverse economic developments by financial services providers to end clients. For example, in this instance the provider is protecting the end borrower against the value of the property not growing by as much as expected. Hence on average the whole of the financial services industry can be expected to be long the relevant risk, and therefore to price up protection against it occurring. Moreover, a ready market is more likely to form in the opposite situation where the price of hedging such risk is below what underlying market participants think it ought intrinsically to be. Once such a market has developed, this will over time then drive people's underlying expectations of what might happen in the 'real world'.

There is therefore likely to be a *selection effect* present. By this we mean that the more the typical investor believes (or wishes to believe) that market consistent valuations overstate the actual risks of adverse outcomes, the more likely it is that markets in such exposures will fail to get off the ground.

This assumes that there is no market present at outset. Equally, the greater the divergence between what people believe to be the 'true' value of an asset and the price ascribed to it in the marketplace, the greater is the risk that the underlying market dries up and becomes illiquid. This is regularly seen in property (i.e. real estate) markets, particularly the residential property market, where substantial falls in market values can lead to very considerable reductions in volumes, as individuals become unwilling to sell their own properties at what they view to be 'unreasonably low' prices, even if these prices are consistent with prices at which other transactions are occurring within the property market. It can also happen in other markets, e.g. the money markets during 2008.

This point is arguably an example of the wider adage that assets tend to end up with those investors who think they are worth the most, and liabilities with those who think that they are worth the least. The point here is that where a market exists then market consistency strips away such optimism. We should therefore bear in mind the need to mimic this effect when market observables are harder to come by.

> **Principle P12: Markets, when they exist, temper the impact that optimistic (or pessimistic) views about the intrinsic 'worth' of an asset or a liability have on its market price. Failure of a market to form (or to continue to exist) may indicate a collective bias in such assessments by practitioners most obviously associated with advising potential market participants. These practitioners may therefore need to temper their own (collective) views when estimating the (market consistent) price at which an asset or liability would trade were such a market to exist.**

Another example of a deliberate distinction being drawn between 'market consistent' and 'real world' valuations is the analysis of the variable annuity market described in Ledlie *et al.* (2008). Variable annuities are life insurance contracts that involve optional policy elements that policyholders can effect by paying an explicit additional premium, e.g. an optional maturity guarantee. Ledlie *et al.* (2008) indicate that there are two main types of stochastic valuation approaches that may be used to value these sorts of guarantees, either a traditional actuarial approach which uses a 'real world' projection methodology or a market consistent approach that typically uses a 'risk-neutral' projection.

Ledlie *et al.* (2008) note that pricing practice varies across different countries and companies but also indicate that they think that use of a market consistent approach is appropriate for actuaries and companies. The arguments that they put forward for doing so are that:

(a) Such a methodology is consistent with the market pricing of options;[13]

---

[13] The optional guarantees that policyholders can effect within a variable annuity contract are specific examples of options that may have been sold by a life insurance company to its policyholders.

(b) It can cater in a consistent way for most types of benefit and charging structures applicable to such contracts; and

(c) It facilitates the calculation of risk exposures that can be used to construct and manage a dynamic hedge portfolio.

The stochastic methodologies that Ledlie *et al.* (2008) describe in the paper include 'pure' market consistent methodologies. They also include 'mixed' methodologies that might be relevant for, say, profit testing purposes, in which valuations are carried out in a substantially market consistent manner but within a business projection framework in which economic outcomes are modelled using 'real world' probability distributions. They, for example, implicitly expect a life insurer's economic capital needs to be set principally using real world projections. This is the current life insurance industry paradigm but one that we question in Chapter 10.

3.5.3   Stressing the aim of avoiding subjectivity where possible

Kemp (2005) defines the *fair value* of an asset or liability to mean its market value, if it is readily traded on a market at the point in time that the valuation is struck, and, for any other asset or liability, a reasoned best estimate of what its market value would have been had it been readily traded at the relevant valuation point.

He noted that this definition was essentially the same as the more standard definition of fair value as 'the value at which an arms-length transaction involving willing, knowledgeable counterparties would take place' but aimed by choosing his particular definition to make clearer the link between fair values and market consistent valuation principles.

This was partly to stress that the fair value of a non-traded asset or liability *is not the same as the determination of the valuer's own intrinsic assessment of its value*. Rather, it involves *modelling how the market would value the asset or liability*, with the model by implication being calibrated in some suitable way back to market prices of instruments that are more readily traded. A corollary is that the fair value of a liability ought not to depend on how the entity incurring the liability might hedge or otherwise manage the liability (except to the extent that honouring the liability might depend on the non-default of the entity bearing the liability).

One can also see a direct interaction with Principle P12. If the aim is to estimate at what price the asset or liability might have traded on a market then one must also, in principle, reflect what impact the existence of a market might itself have on that price.

A potentially important example of this for life insurance companies involves longevity risk. At the time of writing the market for longevity risk is nascent. Application of this principle would caution against the common approach of valuing such exposures merely by reference to 'best estimates' of future mortality rates. It is implausible that a hedging market would develop for such exposures without some charge for risk being incorporated somehow in the prices at which such exposures would trade in such a market. Insurers may thus be systemically undervaluing (from a market consistent perspective) such exposures. By doing so they may be unintentionally hindering the development of a hedging market in such risks. We might view this as a sub-optimal outcome for society as a whole if we adopt the plausible premise that better hedging of such risks might result in more efficient pooling of insurance risks.

3.5.4 Extending 'market consistency' to other activities

Another core theme of Kemp (2005), and of large parts of this book, is the relevance of applying market consistent principles to activities other than purely valuing assets or liabilities.

For example, in this book we explicitly cover the application of market consistent ideas to the topics of risk management and portfolio construction. We also consider the implications of these ideas for regulatory framework design rather than merely taking these designs as 'given' for any particular type of regulated entity.

3.5.5 Application only if obvious market observables exist

Some authors use the term market consistency to mean use of what actually appears to be a mixture of 'market consistent' and 'real world' approaches, with the former being used for exposures where sufficient market data is available to make this practical, and the latter being used for everything else.

For example, Wüthrich *et al.* (2007) assume that you can 'factorise' the (market consistent actuarial) valuation problem into two parts, one part being driven by 'financial' events, and the other being driven by 'technical' events. In their formulation, 'financial' events involve expression within the portfolio of risks that can be hedged in the marketplace (which are valued using yield curves, implied volatilities, etc. as derived from market prices). 'Technical' events involve risks such as property/casualty insurance type risks, which they assume cannot be priced from market observables. Wüthrich *et al.* (2007) then implicitly assume that the right way to value risks relating to the 'technical' factors is to use traditional 'real world' valuation approaches, e.g. chain-ladder claims estimation techniques, based on the actuary's own assessment of what is a (prudent) likely outcome.

Such an approach also seems to be the one implicit in IAA (2008a). This research paper explores how one might come up with 'current estimates' and 'risk margins' to measure insurance liabilities.

It also can be argued that the 'best estimate plus risk margin' approach likely to be adopted for Solvency II and mandated by CEIOPS under QIS3 and QIS4 (see Section 3.4.4) also adopts such a framework.

Challenges that can arise with this philosophy are:

(a) What happens if a market develops in risks previously considered to be driven by 'technical factors'?[14] These may render inappropriate the valuer's subjective assessment of what might be (prudent) likely outcomes. And to what extent is there no market in these exposures anyway, given that there must have been a market of sorts, if only between the insurance company and its policyholders, for the policies to have been issued in the first place? To what extent should market observables used in market consistent valuations be limited to ones derived from transparent markets dominated by professional participants? How much price discovery should we infer from transactions in the reinsurance markets?

(b) Is it correct, when aiming to provide a market consistent valuation, to assume that the best way of estimating a 'market consistent' value for non-traded risk exposures is always to ascribe them (risk-neutral) probabilities in line with their assumed (real world) likelihoods of occurrence? We have already noted in Section 3.5.2 that in situations where both can be estimated, the two can differ quite materially. Typically, a 'real world' valuation

---

[14] An example might be the nascent market in longevity risk, see Section 3.5.3.

approach discounts a stream of expected future cash flows at a suitable discount rate, with the expectation taking into account the valuer's own subjective view of the likelihood of different outcomes. As noted in Section 2.2, a 'market consistent' approach can be re-expressed to involve exactly the same form of calculation, but using a risk-neutral rather than a 'real world' probability distribution for potential outcomes. The key issue is what relationship we should adopt, in the absence of any other market observables, between these two probability distributions. It is not clear why in principle the 'best' assumption to adopt in these circumstances ought to be that these two probability distributions are identical.

(c) Indeed, if it is true, as argued in Section 3.5.2, that markets are least likely to develop (or to continue to function) where there are the biggest inconsistencies between typical views on 'real world' values and 'market consistent' values, then we need to take due account of the selection effect mentioned there. Use of a 'real world' approach could easily then result in a biased answer, if the underlying aim of the exercise is actually to come up with a reasoned best estimate of the prices at which the asset or liability in question would trade were there to be a market in them.

Alternatively one can view a best estimate plus risk margin approach as a methodology that *is* aiming to be fully market consistent, merely providing additional guidance on how to estimate a 'market consistent' price on illiquid assets. From such a viewpoint, inclusion of a risk premium element (on top of a best estimate) can be thought of as a steer that encourages practitioners to recognise that any entity that might be prepared to take over such a liability is likely to want to do so only if the transfer price recognises the need to set up capital to support the liability. Thus, such an approach might be expected to be closer to a 'true' market consistent value than merely a best estimate computation in isolation. Use of a standardised approach may also facilitate comparison between firms, and may merely be reflective of whatever information is actually available for the task in hand.

However, the challenge with this line of reasoning is that the capital computation underlying the calculation of the risk premium element is often based on 'real world' economic capital-type computations. In the determination of the value to place on the risk premium the same discount rate may be applied for widely differing classes of business. It is thus difficult to work out whether the computation really is likely to give a reasonable estimate of the price at which the liability would actually change hands if a market did exist for the liability type in question. One could also question whether the value thus derived would be anywhere near as volatile as an actual market price, were one to be easily observable. A best estimate plus risk margin computation might therefore lead to false confidence about the efficacy of hedging that might be undertaken to mitigate the risks expressed by such liabilities.[15]

3.5.6   Hedgeable liabilities

A definition of 'market consistency' that is used in an actuarial context is that the market consistent value of a liability should be the market value of an asset (presumably trading on a

---

[15] This discussion does, of course, beg the question of why market prices are so volatile, which then leads us to consider the extent to which this volatility might be driven by a changing price of risk as well as a changing assessment of risk. Exploring these topics in any given instance may help to clarify the particular purpose of the valuation in question and whether it is helpful for this purpose to bring either or both of these sources of volatility onto the balance sheet.

deep, liquid and transparent market) that replicates the cash flows corresponding to the liability. This definition seems to have grown up to counter the use of valuations that are obviously inconsistent with how a perfect hedge might trade in situations where a ready and high quality hedge strategy exists to hedge the liability. It also fits well with the hedgeable/non-hedgeable distinction that is being explored in Solvency II consultations.

Unfortunately, this definition leaves less well explored what to do in practice when the liability contains risk exposures that do not readily correspond with assets that actually trade in deep, liquid and transparent markets.

One idea that some commentators focus on in this context is that the liabilities might be 'approximately hedgeable', see e.g. Creedon *et al.* (2008). This would apply where there is no perfect hedge available but market traded instruments do exist that can reasonably be expected to move approximately in line with the relevant liability.

The realisation that the world may not be black and white but is more likely to involve shades of grey is very important in the context of calibrating to market prices. The more hedgeable by a particular market traded instrument is the liability, the more 'credible' is the market value of that instrument in the determination of a market consistent valuation for the liability. Hence the greater the weighting that ought to be placed on that particular piece of market data when carrying out the valuation, see e.g. Section 4.13.

3.5.7   Fair valuation in an asset management context

Asset managers nearly always report to clients using market valuations (or other sorts of fair/market consistent valuations for less liquid assets such as property/real estate). The term 'fair valuation' (or fair value pricing) has a specific meaning for asset managers in the light of the market timing and late trading scandals that affected several US fund management houses a few years ago, see Investment Management Association (2004) and IMA and DATA (2004). It refers to the process of inferring a 'fair' price to place on units in a unitised fund at a point in time when some of the markets in which the fund invests are closed or in some other way the prices being used in the valuation are 'stale'.

In the UK context, the most obvious application is to retail funds invested in, say, US equities and priced at, say, 12 noon UK time, i.e. when the underlying market in which these assets are traded is closed. It might then involve taking prices that were ruling at last night's US close (c. 9 pm UK time) and inferring from them fair prices as at the fund's actual pricing point using movements in the interim in *market observables* that traded at both points in time. In this case, these observables might include the Globex S&P 500 future (which now trades almost around the clock) or foreign listed variants of US equities, exchange traded funds, etc. The aim is to stop arbitrageurs using the same sorts of calculations to exploit the otherwise stale nature of the fund's unit price to the detriment of other unit holders.

Such features, although often hidden, still exist in other contexts. We have here an example where the 'best' price to use for a particular purpose includes an element of marking securities (or in this case the entire portfolio) 'to model', in the sense that we take a variety of market observables and we do not use solely price feeds applicable to a particular security but we superimpose other mathematical calculations on top. If you delve deeper into how market values are determined you will find that inclusion of an element of marking-to-model is more prevalent than might appear at first sight. How do banks and market makers set the quotes at which they are prepared to trade, if not by consideration of a large number of interwoven factors? Marking-to-market and marking-to-model are not always as different as some might make out.

> **Principle P13: It is not correct to assume that there is a clear dividing line between marking-to-market and marking-to-model. Many examples of marking-to-market involve some element of modelling, albeit potentially hidden from the end-user. Even when the market in question appears to be deep, liquid and transparent, inclusion of some modelling element may result in a more accurate market consistent valuation, because the market may not be open continuously around the clock.**

4

Derivative Pricing Theory

4.1 INTRODUCTION

There are three main reasons for including a chapter on derivative pricing theory in a book such as this:

(a) Derivatives are instruments whose behaviour 'derives' from the behaviour of some more fundamental underlying instrument. In the special case where the behaviour of the derivative mimics in every respect the behaviour of the underlying instrument (such derivatives are called 'delta one' derivatives), then we should expect the price of the derivative to be very similar if not identical to the price of the underlying instrument (often shortened merely to the *underlying* in derivative market-speak). To put it another way, the underlying can be thought of as a special case of a derivative of itself, where the derivative pay-off function is merely the 'equality' or identity function. In this sense, derivative pricing theory can conceptually be thought of as incorporating any other part of economic theory relevant to the pricing of assets and liabilities (even if in practice the term is normally applied in a narrower context).

(b) We have already noted in Chapter 2 that application of market consistency to the valuation of uncertain future payments involves ascribing their likelihood of occurrence as coming from a risk-neutral probability distribution (identified by reference to prices of market observables) rather than coming from a 'real world' probability distribution (that the valuer might believe best represents probability of occurrence). The concept of a risk-neutral probability distribution (and the related idea of a pay-off structure) is a central theme of derivative pricing theory.

(c) Many instruments that are particularly challenging to value in a market consistent way are themselves derivatives or share strong similarities with them.

However, derivative pricing theory is notoriously mathematical in nature and this raises an important issue for an author of a book like this. Some potential readers may be very familiar and comfortable with the detailed expression of complicated mathematical ideas, whilst for others such expression can render the book largely unintelligible. For example, several of the papers referred to in Chapter 3, e.g. CAQ (2007a) on 'Measurements of Fair Value in Illiquid (or Less Liquid) Markets', provide only generic high-level guidance that ought to be accessible to most financially literate individuals, without recourse to any complicated mathematics. Conversely, a text such as Wüthrich *et al.* (2007), also referred to in Chapter 3, specifically aims to provide a more detailed mathematical treatment of some of the topics relevant to fair valuation of insurance liabilities.

My aim with this book is to adopt a middle ground in which mathematical ideas are explained in ways that are intelligible to those who do not have a strong mathematical bent, but also to provide a level of mathematical rigour and detail for those who may need to implement such ideas in practice. As a result, this chapter focuses more on core principles and on concepts in derivative pricing that illuminate the topic of market consistency, rather than on the precise details of how to price specific derivative instruments. It assumes some familiarity with the different types of derivative instruments now traded on such markets. However, it is worth emphasising that this chapter is still worth reading even for the non-mathematically inclined (or for those who wish to ignore the mathematics) because of the insights that analysis of the tenets of derivative pricing theory can shed on market consistency.

More mathematically inclined readers wanting a more detailed articulation of some of the mathematics underlying the ideas set out in this chapter or wanting access to software tools to help in such activities may find helpful the 'market consistency' section of the www.nematrian.com website set up by the author, referred to throughout this book as Kemp (2009). The www.marketconsistency.com website, also set up by the author, provides an alternative point of access to the same material. Alternatively, they may wish to refer to the numerous well-written texts that now exist that provide in-depth coverage of the application of derivative pricing theory to specific financial instruments, such as Hull (2003) and (for credit derivatives) Schönbucher (2003), or texts covering the underlying mathematical formalisms of derivative pricing, such as Baxter and Rennie (1996).

4.2   THE PRINCIPLE OF NO ARBITRAGE

4.2.1   No arbitrage

4.2.1.1   The principle of 'no arbitrage'

Arguably, the most important concept in derivative pricing theory is the so-called *principle of no arbitrage* (a phrase that is often in practice shortened merely to 'no arbitrage'). In Section 2.10 we also called this principle the axiom of 'contemporaneous value continuity', to bring out the point that it does not depend on markets operating rationally or efficiently (as conventionally understood by economists).

In this context, 'arbitrage' has a specific mathematical meaning that we set out below, which differs somewhat from its normal usage in day-to-day market parlance. However, it is easiest to appreciate the importance of this principle by first exploring its wider ramifications and only then seeking greater mathematical precision in its articulation.

If the whole economic world consisted of entirely discrete commodities or services ('goods'), each of which was in some sense completely distinct from any other, then any discussion on how to price them might be rather short. In practice, however, different sorts of goods can often be partially or even wholly substituted for one another.

For example, governments often issue fixed interest debt of varying terms. Usually, investors keen to buy government debt with a term of, say, 9 years (and a given coupon) are largely indifferent in terms of their overall economic thinking between buying just that issue or investing, say, one-half in an issue with a term of 8 years and one-half with a term of 10 years (with coupons set accordingly). These two alternatives are typically close substitutes for each other. We should therefore, all other things being equal, expect their prices to be similar, as otherwise buyers would tend to shun the most expensive approach to meeting their needs and favour the cheapest.

Exactly the same principle applies in the derivatives market (and indeed to other economic markets where substitution is possible). For example, all other things being equal we would expect a six-month put option with a strike price of 1000 to have a market price very similar to a six-month put option on the same underlying with a strike price of 1001 (or a corresponding six-month and a day put option).

We can extend this to the ultimate limit, where the two goods are economically identical. The two 'ought' then to have exactly the same price.

Essentially, this is the principle of no arbitrage. Strictly speaking, the absence of arbitrage in this context means that it is impossible to carry out a series of transactions which:

(a) Involve in aggregate no capital outlay; and
(b) In all circumstances will lead to no loss and in some circumstances will lead to some profit.

The principle of no arbitrage is most easily applied to idealised markets which are *frictionless*, i.e. have no transaction costs or other distortions, such as might arise from differential tax regimes, and where there are no restrictions on short sales. In such markets any deviation between the prices of identical goods can be expected to be arbitraged away by arbitrageurs. In such markets, if we assume that the price of the underlying is 'known', we should therefore expect derivatives on that underlying to trade at some unique 'fair price' relative to the mid-market price of the underlying.

In the presence of transaction costs, etc., we can still apply the concept of no arbitrage, but there will be a range of prices within which the market price of the derivative might lie. Only when the price approaches one or other limit of this range will arbitrageurs start to be active. In most circumstances we would expect the market to trade within this range. Market participants, by substituting one good for another in the determination of supply and demand, will typically drive a process similar to arbitrage, even if explicit arbitrage strategies are impractical.

It is sometimes assumed that application of no-arbitrage principles to derivative pricing needs the assumption that the price of the underlying drives the price of the derivative rather than vice versa. This is not an intrinsic part of the no-arbitrage assumption per se, which is really about the economic consequences of substitutability (and hence is relevant whichever way market pressures drive either price). It is also not necessarily how markets actually operate.

4.2.1.2   Other uses of the term 'arbitrage'

Identifying instances of arbitrage opportunities, as defined above, is actually quite difficult (not least because arbitrageurs would then typically rather rapidly arbitrage them away). Many that are presented as such confuse the concept of 'arbitrage-free' (as defined above) with market inefficiencies, i.e. anomalies in market prices that provide profitable investment opportunities, but which are not totally risk-free. For example, central banks intervene to stabilise currency markets. This ought to provide profitable investment opportunities, but they are not totally risk-free and are thus not 'pure' arbitrages as understood by the principle of no arbitrage, because the actions of central banks are not completely predictable in advance.

Common market parlance tends to describe such opportunities as 'arbitrages'. Characteristic of the usage of such terminology will be a belief by the commentator that the pricing in question is anomalous given plausible ways in which the future might evolve. However, for there to be a 'pure' arbitrage as per the principle of no arbitrage, the pricing must be anomalous *whatever* the future holds, even if the future evolves in implausible ways.

Even inside knowledge of what a central bank was about to do cannot really be considered 'risk-free', on the grounds that you might be prosecuted for insider trading or the equivalent if you attempted to take advantage of such knowledge. There is an echo of this in the formal mathematical application of no arbitrage, which generally includes assumptions that price processes are 'adapted', in the sense that the process depends only on the current position and past movements of the underlying driving process(es) and is unable to see into the future.

> **Principle P14: The term 'arbitrage' has several different meanings. Practitioners using this term should make clear what meaning(s) they are ascribing to this term, particularly if they may be perceived as providing both market consistent and non-market consistent advice at the same time, since the most natural meanings for this term are then inconsistent with each other.**

4.2.1.3   'On-the-run' versus 'off-the run' instruments

A more germane example of the difference between 'arbitrage' and 'inefficiency' is perhaps the distinction between 'on-the-run' and 'off-the-run' US Treasury bonds. It provides an example of how instruments that we might otherwise expect to be closely equivalent do not necessarily always trade at equivalent prices.

As explained in Fisher (2002), the US Treasury typically issues a new 10-year note every three months. The most recently issued 10-year Treasury security is referred to as the *on-the-run* issue. Once the US Treasury issues another (newer) 10-year note, the previously issued note is referred to as the *old* 10-year note (the one issued before that is the *old-old* note, etc.). Similar nomenclature is used for other Treasury securities of a given original benchmark maturity (e.g. 3-year, 30-year, etc.)

The on-the-run security is typically more actively traded than the old (or old-old, . . .) security, both in relation to the number of trades per day and in relation to the average size of the trades. In this sense the on-the-run security is more liquid[1] than the old, or off-the-run, security. We would therefore generally expect price discovery processes to result in price movements in the on-the-run security generally driving price movements in corresponding off-the-run securities rather than vice versa.

Dealers (and other organisations implicitly carrying out market making activities) must finance, or fund, every long and every short position they hold. A common way that this is done for Treasury securities is to *repo*[2] out the long positions and to *reverse repo* the short positions. In addition to financing their positions, dealers also need to decide how much economic exposure they wish to hedge; most pure market makers will want to hedge away most or all of these risk exposures. Suppose a dealer purchases from a customer an off-the-run Treasury security. The dealer might immediately be able to resell the security at a slightly higher price, thereby earning the bid–ask spread, but since the off-the-run instruments are less actively traded the dealer may have to wait some time before an appropriate purchaser arrives. An important way in which dealers hedge their positions in off-the-run securities in the meantime is to short sell corresponding on-the-run securities. This incidentally further drives liquidity towards the on-the-run securities.

---

[1] Higher liquidity in this context will typically translate into smaller bid–ask spreads for the relevant instrument.

[2] A repurchase agreement, or repo, can be thought of as a type of collateralised loan. At inception of the agreement, the borrower hands over the collateral to the lender in exchange for funds. When the loan matures, the funds are returned to the lender along with interest at the previously agreed-upon repo rate, and the collateral is returned to the borrower. Repo agreements can have any term. Most are for one business day, referred to as overnight repos. Ones for longer maturities are called term repos. A reverse repo is such a transaction but with the two parties swapped over. There are active repo markets for securities other than Treasury bonds. In equity markets, what is known as securities lending and borrowing plays an analogous role, although there are potential differences in the legal structures of such transactions which, for example, influence the counterparty risk exposures that the parties might incur when entering into such transactions.

The net effect of all of this activity typically results in there being some bid up of demand for on-the-run securities versus off-the-run securities (because the on-the-run securities are more effective ways of satisfying short-term dealer hedging requirements), which in turn typically leads to them carrying a slightly lower yield. We return to this point in Chapter 5 when we explore what should be meant by the term 'risk-free rate'.

Does this therefore mean that a strategy that is long the off-the-run instrument and short the on-the-run instrument is a sure 'arbitrage'? No. This was a strategy followed by an ill-fated hedge fund, Long-Term Capital Management (LTCM), see e.g. Lowenstein (2001). In 1998, there was a sustained loss of risk appetite across many markets. Amongst other things, this resulted in the spread between on-the-run and off-the-run Treasury notes rising to unprecedented levels. Whilst such positions might eventually have come good, the mark-to-market losses suffered in the meantime on these and other positions led to LTCM's collapse.

4.2.1.4   Closed-end mutual funds

Another (somewhat more historic) example where care is needed in differentiating between 'pure' arbitrages and market inefficiencies relates to closed-end mutual funds, see Lee *et al.* (1990). In the third quarter of 1929 just before the Great Crash, the median US closed-end fund sold at a premium of 47 % to its underlying net worth. In real terms levels of issuance of these sorts of funds far exceeded those seen today. During this wave of enthusiasm, theories explaining why closed-end funds should sell at discounts were not advanced. Even today, closed-end funds sold to retail investors often sell at a premium to net asset value but often then move to a discount for the sorts of reasons described in Mehta *et al.* (1996). Lee *et al.* (1990) conclude that such discrepancies reflect the existence of a pool of irrational investors, but also conclude that arbitrageurs may not operate to eliminate these inefficiencies, because it is unclear for how long the discrepancies might last.

4.2.1.5   Why is the principle of no arbitrage so important?

In a mathematical sense we have already, in effect, answered this question in Section 2.2. Assuming that the securities or instruments in question come in small fungible units,[3] and in the absence of market frictions, the principle of no arbitrage enforces the powerful axioms of additivity and scalability referred to there.

However, in another sense we haven't answered this question. If pure arbitrages seem to be so hard to identify and if arbitrageurs seem to be potentially so frustrated in their desire to profit from price anomalies because of potential for adverse mark-to-market movements in the meantime, how come the principle of no arbitrage really is so important?

Answering this question takes us into deeper territory, also hinted at in Section 2.2. When derivatives practitioners use the term 'value', they typically use it synonymously with the term 'price'. However, there is a whole branch of financial economics called *utility theory*, in which these two concepts differ. Utility theory is based on the concept that different goods and services (and by implication future cash flows) will differ in their attractiveness, i.e. their utility, to different people. At least in theory a person's 'utility' does not even need to

---

[3] This incidentally means that you can't easily apply no arbitrage principles to mergers and takeovers of entire companies.

be rationally set, although normally financial economics is developed in ways that include assumptions about some level of rational behaviour.[4]

Markets involve transactions between participants who in general have different utilities. But this does *not* mean that the value/price ascribed to a particular instrument by the market necessarily depends very much on the utilities ascribed to different pay-offs by individual market participants (or even, in some cases, on those of investors in aggregate). Even when prices do depend on investor utilities, we should still expect similar prices to rule for instruments that are close substitutes. We thus constrain the impact that we believe investor utility functions (or at least their transaction weighted averages) might have on the price formation processes for these instruments. Valuations that do not depend at all on investor preferences, i.e. investors' utility functions, are called *preference independent*. Some well-known derivative pricing formulae, such as the Black-Scholes option pricing formulae, have this characteristic, but in general derivative prices *are* preference dependent.

Perhaps it is best to view the principle of no arbitrage, amplified by the assumption that markets are frictionless, as an approximation to the underlying reality, around which you can construct a sound mathematical theory which then leads to a host of important corollaries. As always, there are times when approximations need to be handled with care. In the absence of market frictions it would seem unlikely that rational market participants would often miss the opportunity to profit from pure market arbitrages if they happen to come along. Hence, the focus in such circumstances is normally on exploring the impact of market frictions, i.e. attempting to understand what happens in real life markets and refining the mathematical framework accordingly.

> **Principle P15: The most important mathematical principle in derivative pricing theory is the so-called 'principle of no arbitrage'. In the absence of market frictions this principle results in market prices adhering to the axioms of additivity and scalability and might better be described as the axiom of 'contemporaneous value continuity' in the light of Principle P14.**

4.2.2 Valuation of symmetric derivatives

The principle of no arbitrage can be used directly to identify fair market prices for symmetric derivatives (such as forward contracts and swaps) in frictionless markets.

4.2.2.1 Forward contracts

Suppose the annualised (continuously compounded[5]) risk-free rate of interest (i.e. redemption yield) at time t for a zero coupon bond[6] maturing at time T is r. Suppose that the spot price

---

[4] An exception is 'behavioural finance' or 'behavioural economics', which explicitly explores how the innate workings of people's brains might lead them to behave in ways that are not purely 'rational' (rationality here typically being a slightly fuzzy concept equated with maximisation of expected wealth or, for evolutionists, expected numbers of progeny).

[5] By 'continuously compounded' we mean that an investment of 1 would accumulate to e^{rT} by time T. See Kemp (2009) for further details regarding annualisation conventions including continuous compounding.

[6] A zero coupon (or 'bullet') bond is a bond that provides merely a redemption sum at maturity but no income in the meantime.

of one unit of the underlying at time t is $S(t)$, and that the underlying generates an annualised income or interest yield (continuously compounded) of q between t and T. Then in the absence of arbitrage, the value, $f(t)$, of a *forward contract* with a delivery price of K at time T is given by:[7]

$$f = Se^{-q(T-t)} - Ke^{-r(T-t)} \tag{4.1}$$

The *forward price F* (at time t) is defined as the delivery price at which a forward contract for that maturity would have zero value. Thus it is the value of K for which $f = 0$. In this instance it would be:

$$F = Se^{(r-q)(T-t)} \tag{4.2}$$

We can justify this (preference independent) pricing formula by considering two portfolios:

(a) Portfolio A: consisting of one long forward contract plus $Ke^{-r(T-t)}$ of the risk-free asset (to be more precise, the risk-free leg involves K zero coupon bonds each maturing at time T each providing unity at that time, with the definition of r being the value which equates $e^{-r(T-t)}$ to the value of such zero coupon bonds); and
(b) Portfolio B: consisting of $e^{-q(T-t)}$ units of the underlying (each unit currently valued at S) with all income being reinvested in the underlying (or to be more precise an instrument consisting of the underlying but stripped of all income/interest payments prior to time T, but again the definition of q makes these equivalent).

Both of these portfolios provide exactly one unit of the underlying at time T, and hence by the principle of no-arbitrage must be of identical value (in the absence of market frictions).

Even if r and q are time dependent the above formula is still correct (if r and q are defined as the averages of instantaneous continuously compounded interest and dividend rates respectively), as can be determined by considering carefully the precise definitions of Portfolios A and B.

Equivalently, we can adopt the following argument. If we have sold a forward contract we can hedge it by investing in a *hedge portfolio* consisting of:

(a) Going short (i.e. borrowing) $Ke^{-r(T-t)}$ of the risk-free asset; and
(b) Going long (i.e. buying) $e^{-q(T-t)}$ units of the underlying (and reinvesting all income generated on the units in the underlying).

As the hedge portfolio mimics the effect of the forward contract, we can introduce the concept of the *associated economic exposure* of the contract. For a symmetric derivative, this is the equivalent amount of the underlying that an investor would need to hold to have the same economic effect as holding the forward, i.e. here $Se^{-q(T-t)}$. However, for a derivative that includes optionality, the term 'associated economic exposure' can take several different meanings (including the full notional value of the underlying). It is more usually helpful to concentrate on the contract *delta*. For equity derivatives it is defined as per Equation (4.3). For interest rate derivatives, the delta is usually calculated with respect to changes in the interest

---

[7] Here and elsewhere in the book e^x, also called exp x, is the exponential function, i.e. $e(= 2.718282\ldots)$ raised to the power of x.

rate, rather than the value of the investment equivalent to S, i.e. a zero coupon bond, and therefore has somewhat different characteristics.[8]

$$delta = \frac{\partial V}{\partial S} \text{ (in units of underlying) } or = S\frac{\partial V}{\partial S} \text{ (in value terms)} \qquad (4.3)$$

In some instances it may be more appropriate to assume that the income generated by a share is fixed in monetary terms rather than as a percentage yield. If the income is I (paid at the start of the life of the forward) then the value of the forward contract and the forward price become:

$$f = S - I - Ke^{-r(T-t)} \Rightarrow F = (S - I)e^{r(T-t)} \qquad (4.4)$$

The hedge portfolio also changes somewhat. It would be short $(I + K)e^{-r(T-t)}$ of the risk-free asset and long one unit in the underlying, so its associated economic exposure or delta would be S.

In either case, this sort of hedging could be described as *static hedging*, since we do not need to alter the hedge portfolio if the price of the underlying moves, except to reinvest dividend income (and to disinvest borrowing costs) in a suitable fashion. It may be contrasted with *dynamic hedging*, in which the structure of the hedge portfolio is altered in a suitable fashion depending on the movement in the price of the underlying.[9]

4.2.2.2   Futures contracts

The fair price of a futures contract (subject to daily margining) might appear to correspond to the forward price of a contract with the same maturity date. However, futures contracts are generally marked-to-market daily and therefore the quantity corresponding to the exercise price keeps being reset to the current futures price.

If the risk-free rate of return r is constant and the same for all maturities then the fair market price of the future would be the same as the forward price, see Hull (2003), i.e. (where there is a known continuously compounded dividend yield, q) it would be:

$$f = Se^{(r-q)(T-t)} \qquad (4.5)$$

---

[8] Here $\partial y/\partial x$ means the partial differential of y with respect to x, i.e. if y is a function of several variables, say, $x, u, v, \ldots$ then $\partial y/\partial x$ is determined by differentiating y with respect to x with all the other variables $u, v, \ldots$ deemed fixed. The logic behind this is that any suitably regular function of several variables (e.g. here three) can be approximated using a Taylor series expansion as follows $y(x, u, v) = y(x_0, u_0, v_0) + (x - x_0)\frac{\partial y}{\partial x} + (u - u_0)\frac{\partial y}{\partial u} + (v - v_0)\frac{\partial y}{\partial u} + O(\varepsilon^2)$ (where ε is the largest of $x - x_0$, $u - u_0$ and $v - v_0$). The delta of the contract, as defined above, is thus the sensitivity of the market value of the position to small movements in the price of the underlying. For a linear instrument, such as a forward, this sensitivity is a constant multiple of the position value and hence the term 'associated economic exposure' has an unambiguous meaning, since the same amount of the underlying is needed to hedge the position whatever the size of the postulated price movement in the underlying. For a non-linear instrument such as an option, the price of the instrument no longer behaves in a linear fashion whatever the size of the postulated price movement in the underlying, which leads to ambiguity in the definition of 'associated economic exposure'.

[9] In this chapter we focus mainly on the situation where we have an option or other asymmetric instrument that we want to hedge. A good way of hedging the risk exposures involved with such instruments may then be to use dynamic hedging. Conversely, we can reverse this process and design an instrument whose pay-off depends on the results of following some dynamic algorithm. The best known such instruments are ones that use constant proportional portfolio insurance (CPPI) or variants, in which a set proportion (or multiple) of the difference between the current value of the portfolio and the value of some guaranteed floor is invested in a 'risky' portfolio.

However, if the risk-free rate, r, varies then the two prices may differ. The hedge portfolio described above is then no longer perfect for a futures contract, since capital gains or losses credited daily must be reinvested at a rate which is not known in advance. For contracts lasting just a few months, the theoretical differences between say (equity) forwards and (equity) futures are usually small enough to be ignored, unless they differ in other ways (e.g. tax treatment, transaction costs or if the initial margin deposited with the clearing house is not credited with as high a rate of interest as other deposits).[10]

The associated economic exposure of a future is also more complicated, since any gains or losses are credited or debited immediately. However, if the price of the underlying doubled instantaneously or fell to zero instantaneously (and futures remained priced at their fair value) then a portfolio holding one futures contract would rise or fall in value by $Se^{(r-q)(T-t)}$ which may therefore be considered to be the associated economic exposure of a futures contract. Some futures (e.g. the LIFFE long gilt future) may be settled by delivery of stock from a range of alternatives (with delivery being possible on a range of dates). This element of optionality will also influence the fair price of the future.

4.2.2.3 Interest rate swaps

Exactly the same sorts of arguments can be used to value interest rate swaps and futures or forwards on bonds, but typically one then needs not just point parameters but information relating to the entire yield curve.

Take, for example, an interest rate swap involving a principal amount P, maturing at time T. For simplicity we assume the swap involves Party A paying floating rate interest payments to Party B in return for fixed interest payments of aP (i.e. the swap rate is a per annum) and that both the fixed and the floating rate payments are continuous (with the floating rate payments reset continuously). We also assume that the value of a zero coupon bond paying 1 at time t from now is worth $v(t) = 1/(1 + i(t))^t = \int_0^t e^{-r(x)} \, dx$ where $i(t)$ is the relevant (annualised) gross redemption yield of such a zero coupon bond, and $r(t)$ is the continuously compounded equivalent. In this simplified example we ignore the impact of credit risk, a topic that we return to in Section 4.8.

If we buy a zero coupon bond paying 1 at time x, sell a zero coupon bond paying 1 at time $y(>x)$, and put the amount we receive from the first bond on deposit (at floating rates) then we will receive floating rate interest on 1 between x and y. Thus the present value *now* of such floating rate payments is, by the principle of no arbitrage, $v(x) - v(y)$. The value *now* of (continuous) fixed rate payments of a between x and y is:

$$a \int_x^y v(t) \, dt \tag{4.6}$$

---

[10] The exception is in relation to credit risk, which is why clearing houses exist. In broad terms, the trades that different market participants have entered into are all novated so that market participants face just one single centralised entity, the clearing house, and so are exposed to the risk of default of that entity alone. The clearing house demands some collateral, i.e. margin, to be posted with it, to mitigate the exposure that it itself has to these investors. However, there can be subtleties in practice, e.g. the clearing mechanism may relate merely to members of the exchange, and end investors may therefore be exposed to counterparty risk relating to their clearing agent, the entity through whom they access this clearing mechanism.

Thus the value of the swap *now* to Party B is:

$$P \left(v(T) - 1 + a \int_0^T v(t)\,dt \right) \tag{4.7}$$

In practice interest rate swaps have discrete reset dates, at which the floating payments are recalculated and on which the fixed and floating rate payments are made. The value of the fixed rate payments would thus be discrete rather than continuous annuities, and there may be an adjustment for the period between the date of valuation and the date of the next reset date.

Although interest rate swaps typically involve regular payments through time, it is possible to enter into interest rate swaps in which any payments under the fixed and floating rate legs are rolled up until maturity of the swap contract. If such a swap contract is fully two-way *cash collateralised* then the economic impact of cash movements between the two parties may be little different to a fully cash collateralised swap involving fixed and floating interest payments being swapped through time. This is because any changes in the net present value of the swap would be reflected in day-by-day movements of collateral.[11] It can be valued in much the same way as a non-rolled-up swap. Application of the principle of no arbitrage means that the present value of a payment of 1 rolled up at a given rate to a set time in the future, and then discounted at the same rate back to the present time, is still 1 (as long as credit risk in the meantime can be ignored).

4.2.2.4 Inflation and other sorts of swaps

Roll-up of interest payments is more common with certain other types of swap. For example, inflation-linked swaps traded in practice typically involve a single (i.e. zero coupon) payment at some specified maturity date at which one party receives the swap notional compounded up in line with actual inflation experience (for a given inflation index) between inception and maturity, in return for paying the notional compounded up in line with a predefined growth rate as defined at outset in the swap contract. If the swap has zero net present value at outset then this predefined growth rate equates to the breakeven inflation rate.

The flexibility inherent in swap contract design has meant that many other types of economic exposure are also conventionally traded in swap form. Thus one can have credit default swaps (in which the 'floating' leg involves payments dependent on the default of a specified reference entity) or property swaps (in which the 'floating' leg involves the return achieved on a given property, i.e. real estate, index). The formulae for valuing such derivatives in a no-arbitrage world are similar to that set out above for a standard fixed-for-floating interest rate swap. However, it is important to bear in mind that such swap rates incorporate market implied

---

[11] If the collateralisation process involves movement of other types of collateral then one might think that the position is similar. However, normally there is some flexibility in choice of collateral that can be posted. Suppose a bank has two offsetting swap transactions with two different counterparties and can choose which sort of collateral is posted in each case. Then by receiving one sort of collateral (e.g. cash) and posting a different sort of collateral whenever the swaps have non-zero value, it in effect can achieve a result equivalent to borrowing cash against a particular sort of collateral or vice versa. Depending on what interest rate is deemed credited or paid on the cash under the relevant swap agreement, and depending on the liquidity needs of the bank in question, this could in principle prove to be an attractive way for the bank to borrow or lend secured funds.

views on future market clearing prices for the economic exposure in question. For less liquid underlyings, such as real estate, this can result in the swap rates appearing to be inconsistent with apparent mid-market prices in the corresponding physical market. Swap pricing may then be indicating that the mid-market prices quoted for the underlying physical markets are not representative of the current perceived balance between supply and demand.[12]

4.2.2.5 Deviations from fair value

Neither forwards nor futures are actually guaranteed to trade at the no-arbitrage fair prices described above. This is known as *basis risk* (or, if it refers to the impact when the contract is rolled forward, as *rollover risk*). If the difference between the actual price and the fair price is less than the bid–offer spread in the underlying market or if short-selling is difficult or impossible then arbitrageurs may not be able to profit from the difference. Usually, the deviation is modest, although still potentially important in some instances.

Very occasionally, the difference between the actual price and the fair price derived from no-arbitrage criteria can become much larger. This might only be expected to happen if a major shock prohibits the process of arbitrage from drawing the two prices closer together again. An example was the October 1987 Stock Market Crash, when for much of the day the physical and the futures markets appeared to be trading out of synchronisation with each other (in the USA, the deviation became so large that trading on the futures market was stopped).

4.2.3 Valuation of asymmetric derivatives

Pricing asymmetric contracts such as options is more complicated than pricing symmetric contracts. The reason is that the principle of no arbitrage *in isolation* no longer produces unique fair values for such contracts that all market participants will agree on, although it does introduce certain upper and lower limits.

4.2.3.1 Generic upper and lower valuation limits for vanilla options

For vanilla (equity) options, such as puts and calls, which never generate a liability for the purchaser, the lower limit must be at least equal to zero. However, we can sometimes do better than this. For American style options which are potentially exercisable immediately, the option must be worth at least its *intrinsic value*. This is:

$$\text{call option:} \quad \max(S - K, 0)$$
$$\text{put option:} \quad \max(K - S, 0) \tag{4.8}$$

For a European-style option these limits become the following, even though it is still usual to retain the American style formulae as the definitions of 'intrinsic value':

$$\text{call option:} \quad \max(Se^{-q(T-t)} - Ke^{-r(T-t)}, 0)$$
$$\text{put option:} \quad \max(Ke^{-r(T-t)} - Se^{-q(T-t)}, 0) \tag{4.9}$$

---

[12] Of course, there may also be bid–offer spreads on the swap contracts complicating the picture.

Upper limits are also relatively easy to establish. In the absence of transaction costs, a European call option giving the holder the right to buy a share for the price of K cannot be worth more than $Se^{-q(T-t)}$, whilst a put option giving the holder the right to sell the underlying for a price K cannot be worth more than $Ke^{-r(T-t)}$. For American put and call options, these limits become S and K respectively, since the option might possibly be exercised immediately. To achieve these limits, the underlying must rise in price infinitely much (for the call option) or fall to zero (for the put option).

The price of a vanilla (equity) option can in principle fall anywhere between these bounds. For example, suppose that S remains fixed until just before the maturity date of the option and then jumps in the instant before maturity to equal x with (risk-neutral) probability $P(x)$. Given an arbitrary probability density function $P(x)$, any European style option price between the lower and upper bounds stated above could be consistent with no arbitrage.

4.2.3.2   Decomposing option pay-offs into their (possibly infinitesimal) parts

To price options we therefore need something more than just the principle of no arbitrage. One way of tackling the pricing of European options might be to decompose the pay-off at maturity into lots of individual parts depending on the level the underlying reaches at maturity. Each of these parts pays out 1 if at maturity the underlying lies between $S(x)$ and $S(x) + dx$, but zero otherwise. Such contracts are technically known as *digital call spreads* (in this instance with infinitesimal spreads of width dx).

In the absence of market frictions (and credit risk), the no-arbitrage criterion places constraints on the values of these digital call spreads. Each must have a non-negative value. Also, if we purchase Sdx digital call spreads (relating to the spread $S(x)$ to $S(x) + dx$ for each possible x) then their combination is economically identical to a contract which provides one share at maturity, which we know how to value from Section 4.2.2. If we purchase dx of each such digital call spread then their combination is economically identical to a pay-off of 1 at maturity, i.e. the value of a zero coupon bond.

Thus in principle we must determine the value of an infinite number of digital call spreads, if we want to be able to value European options, i.e. we need to identify a function $D(x)$ defined such that $D(x)dx$ equals the value of a digital call spread between x and $x + dx$.

In derivative pricing theory this is done by identifying a hypothetical probability distribution, $p(x)$ called the *risk-neutral probability distribution* (or *risk-neutral probability measure*) which is defined so that $D(x) = Zp(x)$. Here Z is the present value of a payment of 1 at the maturity of the option, i.e. the value of a corresponding zero coupon bond. $p(x)$ is a probability distribution (or more precisely a probability 'measure') because $\int p(x)\,dx = 1$. The price of any European option can then be defined as the expected value of the pay-off of the option with respect to this risk-neutral probability distribution. In the continuous limit, we see that the value of a generalised pay-off $P(x)$ that depends merely on the value, x, that the underlying takes at maturity then takes the form:

$$V(P) = \int_{-\infty}^{+\infty} Zp(x)P(x)dx \qquad (4.10)$$

If the pay-off depends on multiple underlyings then the integral in question would be carried out over multiple variables describing the different values that each underlying might take.

> **Principle P16:** In the absence of market frictions, *symmetric* derivatives can be valued by reference only to the principle of no arbitrage, as long as suitable market observables exist to price the underlying building blocks. However, the valuation of *asymmetric* derivatives requires further assumptions, which can be encapsulated in the so-called *risk-neutral probability distribution* ascribed to future outcomes.

4.2.4 Valuation of path dependent derivatives

Usually, more complicated is the valuation of *path dependent options*. By these we mean options where the pay-off depends not just on the terminal value of the underlying but also on how the underlying gets there.

In the spirit of Section 4.2.3, we can in principle value any such pay-off by hypothetically identifying the value of a plethora of digital contingent call spreads, which pay out 1 if the underlying is between x and $x + dx$ at maturity *and* if the path taken to get there follows some particular path $R(t)$, but zero otherwise.

As long as $R(t)$ exhibits suitable regularity conditions[13] (e.g. there needs to be zero probability that there can be an infinite number of discontinuous jumps in any finite time period) then the entire set of these path-specific digital call options will span the complete range of derivatives possible to construct with this underlying. If there are multiple underlyings then the 'routes' incorporated in such a conceptual framework need to be deemed to incorporate all possible ways in which all possible underlyings can get to their end outcome. We can then use the same trick as in Section 4.2.3 to construct a risk-neutral probability distribution, which now refers not just to the risk-neutral likelihood of a given maturity level being reached but also the risk-neutral likelihood of each possible path by which it might be reached.

Path dependency of this sort does occur in some other mathematical or scientific disciplines, e.g. in quantum mechanics (or more precisely quantum field theory). One way of identifying how a quantum mechanical system will behave is to use the so-called *path integral formulation*. This involves determining the likelihood of finding the system in a given state by summing up the likelihood of every single path it might take to reach this state.

As with the path integral formulation in quantum mechanics, one rarely actually attempts to solve derivative pricing problems *analytically* using such a technique. However, the concept does illuminate and justify many of the more common *numerical* ways of calculating derivative prices. For example, a common approach to numerical valuation of more complicated derivatives is to construct a grid defining a wide range of paths that the underlying might take between its current (assumed known) value and its (as yet unknown) maturity value, and then by backwards (and sometimes also forwards) induction working out what the fair value of the derivative should be at each node of the grid, depending (in the case of a path dependent option) on how it has got there. If the grids are too large for it to be practical to compute the value of the derivative at all node points for all possible paths, then Monte Carlo simulation may be used to estimate the values, based on random choices of possible paths that might be taken, see Section 4.12. For such a grid to provide a suitably accurate approach to valuing the derivative the grid or lattice spacing must be fine enough to match closely the theoretically

---

[13] The term 'regularity' condition is the mathematical name given to a fundamental deep seated assumption that needs to be the case for some mathematical result to apply.

infinitely finely grained grid that characterises how the underlying (or underlyings) might actually move through time.

4.3   LATTICES, MARTINGALES AND ÎTO CALCULUS

Standard texts on option pricing theory generally develop option pricing theory using one of three approaches:

(a) *Lattices* (otherwise known as 'trees') that characterise how the underlying might move through time, where the timeline is discretised;
(b) *Stochastic calculus* (also known as Îto calculus), which can be viewed as the mathematically elegant way of characterising the continuous-time limit of a lattice approach as per (a); and/or
(c) *Martingales*, which are mathematical concepts arguably embracing the same underlying theory as (b) but re-expressed in a way that typically emphasises to a greater extent the importance of risk-neutral probability distributions.

4.3.1   Lattice valuation approaches

4.3.1.1   Single step binomial 'trees'

The lattice approach is perhaps the easiest to visualise. In it we assume that the paths that the underlying can take lie on a lattice or tree-type structure. The simplest such lattice is the binomial lattice, in which at each specified (discrete) time step, the underlying applicable to the option can only move in one of two ways, as per Figure 4.1.

Suppose we knew for certain that between time $t - h$ and t the price of the underlying could move from S to either Su or to Sd, where $d < u$ (as in Figure 4.1), that cash (or more precisely the appropriate risk-free asset) invested over that period would earn a continuously compounded rate of interest of r and that the underlying (here assumed to be an equity or an equity index) generates a continuously compounded dividend income of q.

Suppose that we also have a derivative (or indeed any other sort of security) which (at time t) is worth $A = V(Su, t)$ if the share price has moved to Su, and worth $B = V(Sd, t)$ if it has moved to Sd.

Starting at S at time $t - h$, we can (in the absence of transaction costs and in an arbitrage-free world) construct a hedge portfolio at time $t - h$ that is guaranteed to have the same value as the derivative at time t whichever outcome materialises. We do this by investing (at time

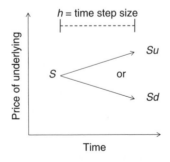

Figure 4.1   Diagram illustrating single step binomial option pricing

$t - h$) fS in f units of the underlying and investing gS in the risk-free security, where f and g satisfy the following two simultaneous equations:

$$fSue^{qh} + gSe^{rh} = A = V(Su, t) \quad \text{and} \quad fSde^{qh} + gSe^{rh} = B = V(Sd, t)$$

$$\Rightarrow fS = e^{-qh} \frac{V(Su, t) - V(Sd, t)}{u - d} \quad gS = e^{-rh} \frac{-dV(Su, t) + uV(sd, t)}{u - d} \quad (4.11)$$

The value of the hedge portfolio and hence, by the principle of no arbitrage, the value of the derivative at time $t - h$ can thus be derived by the following *backward equation*:

$$V(S, t - h) = fS + gS$$

$$\Rightarrow V(S, t - h) = \frac{e^{(r-q)h} - d}{u - d} e^{-rh} V(Su, t) + \frac{u - e^{(r-q)h}}{u - d} e^{-rh} V(Sd, t) \quad (4.12)$$

We can rewrite this equation as follows, where $p_u = (e^{(r-q)h} - d)/(u - d)$ and $p_d = (u - e^{(r-q)h})/(u - d)$ and hence $p_u + p_d = 1$.

$$V(S, t - h) = p_u e^{-rh} V(Su, t) + p_d e^{-rh} V(Sd, t) \quad (4.13)$$

Assuming that the two potential movements are chosen so that p_u and p_d are both non-negative, i.e. with $u > e^{(r-q)h} > d$ then p_u and p_d correspond to the relevant risk-neutral probabilities for the lattice element. It is not difficult in this instance to arrange for p_u and p_d to adhere to this constraint if we bear in mind that $e^{(r-q)h}$ is the forward price of the security at the start of the lattice. However, for more complicated sorts of options (e.g. where the volatility of the underlying price process is assumed to depend in part on its current value) then constructing lattices that have all their risk-neutral probabilities non-negative can be more tricky.

4.3.1.2   Multi-step binomial trees

One way of extending the one time period model described above is to build up a *binomial tree*, or *binomial lattice*, as in Figure 4.2. The price of the underlying is assumed to be able to move in the first period either up or down by a factor u or d, and in second and subsequent

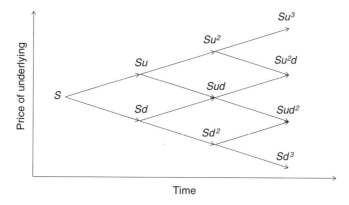

Figure 4.2   Diagram illustrating a binomial tree

periods up or down by a further u or d from where it had reached at the end of the preceding period.

More generally, u or d can vary depending on the time period (e.g. u might be size u_i in time step i, etc.) but it would then be usual to require the lattice to be *recombining*. In such a lattice an up movement in one time period followed by a down movement in the next leaves the price of the underlying at the same value as a down followed by an up. Non-recombining lattices are possible, but are more complicated to handle. It would also be common, but again not essential (and sometimes inappropriate), to have each time period of the same length, h.

By repeated application of Equation (4.12) we can derive the price n periods back, i.e. at $t = T - nh$, of a derivative with an arbitrary pay-off at time T. If u, d, p_u, p_d, r and q are the same for each period then:

$$V(S, T - nh) = e^{-rnh} \sum_{m=0}^{n} \binom{n}{m} p_u^m p_d^{n-m} V(Su^m d^{n-m}, T) \qquad (4.14)$$

where:

$$\binom{n}{m} = \frac{n!}{m!(n-m)!}$$

This can be re-expressed as an *expectation* under a risk-neutral probability distribution, i.e.:

$$V(S, t) = E(e^{-r(T-t)} V(S, T)|S_t) \qquad (4.15)$$

where $E(X|I)$ means the expected value of X given the risk-neutral measure, conditional on being in state I when the expectation is carried out.

> **Principle P17: In the risk-neutral formulation, the value of a derivative can be calculated by working out the expected value of future outcomes (conditional on where the world is currently), weighting these outcomes by the risk-neutral probability of occurrence and discounting at the risk-free rate.**

Equivalently, the value can be expressed as follows as the pay-off at time T weighted in line with composite factors (varying by outcome) that incorporate aspects of both the risk-neutral probability distribution and the risk-free discount rate. Such factors are called *deflators*.

$$V(S, t) = \sum_{m=0}^{n} D(Su^m d^{n-m}, T) V(Su^m d^{n-m}, T) \qquad (4.16)$$

4.3.1.3 *The lack of dependence on investor preferences, i.e. investor utilities, exhibited by binomial trees*

We note that p_u and p_d do not necessarily correspond to the probabilities that any given investor believes might be the actual probabilities of up or down movements. Indeed, in this particularly simple situation the pricing formula is preference independent; we do not need to know what anyone actually believes will be these probabilities. Instead we can think of the values of p_u and p_d as corresponding to the probabilities that would be assigned to up and down movements by a notional *risk-neutral investor*, who is an investor who assumes that the expected return on the underlying is the same as the risk-free rate (hence the derivation of the term 'risk-neutral' and the reason that p_u and p_d are called *risk-neutral* probabilities). It is relatively easy to show that if the price movement is as implied by such a binomial tree then this definition of risk-neutral probabilities is compatible with the more general definition given earlier.

As Neuberger (1990) notes, essentially the only examples of completely preference independent *option* pricing formulae are ones where the price movements in the underlying follow *a binomial tree known in advance* or *the limit of such a tree* in which the time interval becomes arbitrarily small (which as we see below therefore include the sorts of processes underlying the Black-Scholes formula).

The special behaviour in this respect of binomial trees is because if there are just two possible outcomes at any one time (known precisely in advance) then we have just enough flexibility to replicate the option behaviour exactly using dynamic hedging, by altering the mix of the hedge portfolio. If there are more than two possible outcomes, or if the two are not known with certainty, then we do not have sufficient flexibility, and dynamic hedging becomes intrinsically 'risky'. The presence of transaction costs also introduces preference dependence, see Section 4.5. It also makes dynamic hedging intrinsically 'risky'.

4.3.1.4 Deriving the Black-Scholes option pricing formulae as the limit of a suitable binomial tree

Suppose we have a European style put option with strike price K (assumed to be at a node of the lattice) maturing at time T and we want to identify its price, $P(S,t)$ prior to maturity in the framework described in Section 4.3.1.2. Suppose also that r and q are the same for each time period and so are u, d and h. Suppose we define the *volatility* of the lattice to be $\sigma = \log(u/d)/(2\sqrt{h})$. Then if we allow h to tend to zero, keeping σ, t, T, etc. fixed, with $u/d \to 1$ by, say, setting $\log(u) = \sigma\sqrt{h}$ and $\log(d) = -\sigma\sqrt{h}$, we find that the formula in Section 4.3.1.2 and hence the price of the put option tends to:

$$P(S,t) = Ke^{-r(T-t)}N(-d_2) - Se^{-q(T-t)}N(-d_1) \qquad (4.17)$$

where:

$$d_1 = \frac{\log(S/K) + (r - q + \sigma^2/2)(T - t)}{\sigma\sqrt{T - t}}$$

$$d_2 = d_1 - \sigma\sqrt{T - t}$$

and $N(z)$ is the cumulative Normal distribution function,[14] i.e.

$$N(z) = \frac{1}{\sqrt{2\pi}} \int_{-\infty}^{z} e^{-x^2/2}dx$$

The corresponding formula (in the limit) for the price, $C(S, t)$ of a European call option maturing at time T with a strike price of K can be derived in an equivalent manner as:

$$C(S,t) = Se^{-q(T-t)}N(d_1) - Ke^{-r(T-t)}N(d_2) \qquad (4.18)$$

---

[14] In more sophisticated mathematical texts and in symbolic algebra mathematics packages, readers may instead find reference to the 'error function' $erf(x)$ which is defined as $erf(x) = \frac{1}{\sqrt{2\pi}} \int_0^x e^{-t^2} dt$. Thus $N(z) = \frac{1}{2} + \frac{1}{2}erf(\frac{z}{\sqrt{2}})$.

This formula can also be justified on the grounds that the value of a combination of a European put option and a European call option with the same strike price should satisfy so-called put–call parity, if they are to satisfy the principle of no arbitrage, i.e. (after allowing for dividends and interest):

$$stock + put = cash + call$$
$$\Rightarrow Se^{-q(T-t)} + P = Ke^{-r(T-t)} + C \tag{4.19}$$

These formulae for European put and call options are the *Garman-Kohlhagen* formulae for dividend bearing securities. If q is set to zero then they become the celebrated *Black-Scholes* option pricing formulae. For simplicity in the remainder of this book we refer to them generically as the Black-Scholes formulae, and call a world satisfying the assumptions underlying these formulae as a 'Black-Scholes' world. The volatility σ used in their derivation has a natural correspondence with the volatility that the share price might be expected to exhibit in a Black-Scholes world.

4.3.1.5   Trinomial and other more complicated lattices

A necessary requirement of being able to derive a backwards equation of the sort described in Section 4.3.1.1 solely from no-arbitrage arguments is that at each node in the lattice there can only be two possible movements (since there are only two assets that exist in such a framework to construct the hedge portfolio). More complex lattices can be constructed and applied to the same underlying price processes, e.g. trinomial lattices at which the share price can go 'up', 'down' or 'sideways' at each node. The backwards equations that these lattices satisfy can no longer be deduced directly from arbitrage principles, but instead have greater degrees of freedom (and are consequently more complicated).

There are two ways in which the extra degrees of freedom introduced by trinomial and more complicated lattices can be useful:

(a) We can optimise the numerical properties of the lattice so that, for example, it converges much more rapidly as the step size becomes smaller to the same answer that a binomial lattice would give; or

(b) We can use the greater range of path types that we can model using such trees to model more complicated price processes. For example, we can identify fair prices of derivatives where the underlying price process includes the potential for large jumps. Because we cannot then derive risk-neutral probabilities directly from application of the principle of no arbitrage, these sorts of computations are in general preference dependent. For example, we might include in the pricing model a parameter that expresses the extent to which variability in the price of the underlying is coming from large one-off movements (i.e. jumps) rather than small continuous price adjustments (e.g. of the sort that might be modelled by a binomial tree as above). We might then calibrate this parameter by reference to market observables. We explore jump processes further in Section 4.5 and when discussing credit derivatives in Section 4.8. When an issuer defaults, the prices of instruments sensitive to the creditworthiness of that issuer typically undergo sudden jumps. Hence, it is natural to include the possibility of large jumps when modelling the underlying price processes of instruments sensitive to credit risk.

4.3.1.6 Comments on pricing algorithm complexity, applicability and calibration processes

In a situation where r, q and σ are constant through time, a trinomial lattice framework that seems to provide effective enhancements in convergence properties is as set out in Kemp (2009). However, the complexity of the mathematics involved rapidly ramps up. Whilst the principles are in some sense conceptually relatively easy to grasp, it rapidly becomes more challenging to apply such concepts in practice, particularly if you want to do so in ways that are computationally efficient.

It can be difficult to identify the most appropriate level of complexity to adopt for any given derivative pricing problem. For example:

(a) One might expect to be able to improve convergence still further by using quadrinomial or even more complicated lattices, but the effort involved in programming them becomes progressively more complicated, and it becomes less easy to ensure that the optimal lattice structure is recombining. For fast numerical computation of options using lattices, trinomial lattices are likely to be preferred over more complex lattices in most circumstances.

(b) There are actually two main sorts of errors arising with lattice pricing methods. The first sort of error relates to propagation errors via the backwards equation, which can be much reduced by using trinomial lattices rather than binomial ones. The second sort of error involves the approximation of a continuous pay-off at maturity with one involving discrete amounts at each maturity node. It can be reduced by setting the pay-off at each maturity node equal to the average of maturity pay-off for prices of the underlying closest to the node. This second sort of error is not improved merely by use of a trinomial lattice. A better approach may be to use a semi-analytic lattice integrator approach, see e.g. Hu *et al.* (2006) or Kemp (2009), if the pay-off function can be approximated by piecewise polynomials and the risk-neutral probability distribution is analytically tractable.

(c) Other ways exist of improving convergence of binomial lattices without (directly) using trinomial lattices or the like. Because the pricing formulae can be rewritten as expectations (under the risk-neutral probability distribution) and because expectations are merely specific instances of the mathematical process of *integration*, lattices can be thought of as approximate ways of carrying out integration. Various other mathematical tools and techniques exist that can be applied to this more general task, see e.g. Press *et al.* (1992). Some of these tools appear to be as good as if not better than using trinomial lattices, see e.g. Kemp (2009). Even if they are not actually better or intrinsically different mathematically, they may be rather simpler to understand and program reliably.

The mathematical and computational complexity of many types of derivative pricing problems results in major derivatives markets participants being extensive purchasers of relevant computer software and hardware. It also means that they employ many talented mathematicians and computer scientists to refine and speed up their pricing algorithms. Time is often of the essence in a market environment.

A danger that potentially exists with such a business model[15] is that senior management can end up taking false comfort from the amount of effort expended in such activities. Irrespective of how clever and computationally effective are the numerical algorithms being used, they are

---

[15] This is a danger that arguably a number of banks have fallen into in recent years.

all ultimately merely approximate ways of characterising how markets actually operate. If that characterisation is wrong then the whole edifice may ultimately prove to be built on sand.

Fortunately, as we shall see later, pricing algorithms are (or at least should be!) first *calibrated* to market prices. In other words, market participants do not actually use such tools to price instruments in splendid isolation. Instead, they use them as tools to *extrapolate* from observed market prices to derive prices they think ought to apply to other (often more complicated or otherwise over-the-counter) instruments. Unfortunately, this means that if markets cease to function then there may be little or no data to extrapolate from. The more complicated the instrument (and the more 'derivative' it is relative to the underlying) the more uncertainty there may be in these extrapolated prices.

The reliability of derivative pricing algorithms as pricing tools is therefore heavily dependent on:

(a) How close in economic terms are the instruments used for calibration purposes to the instruments being priced;
(b) How reliable are the prices from which any extrapolation is occurring; and
(c) How reliable and robust is the actual application of the calibration process.

Principle P18: However sophisticated are the models in question, the reliability of derivative pricing algorithms for deriving market consistent valuations depends heavily on the reliability of the calibration of these algorithms to market prices. This will depend not only on the computational robustness of the calibration process but also on how close in economic terms to the instrument being valued are the instruments whose prices are being used as inputs to the calibration process.

In the context of (c) it is worth appreciating some specific issues that can arise when using several input parameters sourced from several different providers, as can easily happen in practice. Each data provider may give their own interpretation to a particular parameter (based on how their own models operate). These may not be consistent with other providers' interpretations. For example, implied volatility is typically backed out of option prices, but the exact implied volatility thus derived will (for, say, the Black-Scholes formula) depend on other input assumptions such as interest and dividend assumptions. Who is to say that the choices one particular data provider makes in relation to these latter assumptions will be consistent with the choices that another one might make?

The only real way to test that there are no such inconsistencies is to see whether our pricing formula reproduces the price of the instrument off which the calibration is occurring, when we insert back into it the proposed implied volatility estimate (or whatever other market implied parameter we might be sourcing).

4.3.2 Stochastic (Îto) calculus

How might we best characterise the price movement dynamics (or price 'processes') of the underlying? We saw in Section 4.3.1 that lattices are typically treated as (discrete time) approximations to some more fundamental characterisation of (continuous time) price processes. The most usual way of developing pricing techniques in continuous time is by reference to the mathematical discipline of *stochastic calculus*. We here describe the basic theory mainly by reference to *partial differential equations* rather than by reference to *martingales*, as the concepts involved with the former may be more familiar to a wider range of readers than those involved with the latter. We show how to derive the Black-Scholes formulae using this approach, but again the focus is on the more general applicability of the concepts. We again assume no-arbitrage and frictionless markets.

4.3.2.1 Brownian motion

Although it is not an intrinsic requirement of stochastic calculus, it is often commonly assumed that the movement in the underlying follows a *Gauss-Weiner* or *Brownian* stochastic process. Mathematically this is written as:[16]

$$\frac{dS}{S} = \mu dt + \sigma dz \tag{4.20}$$

Here S_t = price of underlying at time t, μ = mean drift of price at time t, σ = instantaneous volatility of price of underlying at time t (which in general can itself be stochastic and thus not known in advance) and dz are (independent) normal random variables with zero mean and variance dt. Thus in each consecutive infinitesimal time period length dt the movement in the price of the underlying (relative to its mean drift) is, for a Brownian motion, a Normal random variable independent of that applicable in any subsequent or prior time period, with mean μdt and standard deviation $\sigma \sqrt{dt}$. The assumed form of the price process is thus similar to Brownian motion in the physical world, i.e. the observed behaviour of, say, very small smoke particles in a gas, which get jiggled around by random thermal movements of the molecules of the gas surrounding them.

The key tool to price derivatives in such a world is *Îto's formula*. This is effectively a Taylor series expansion but allowing for the stochastic nature of S. Alternatively, one can derive it as the continuous time limit, in a suitable sense, of the single time step backward equation given in Equation (4.12). Suppose that we have a derivative on S and that its price, at time t if at that time the price of the underlying is S, is $u(S, t)$. Îto's formula is that u evolves in the following way through time where dS is the change in S that occurs over time dt, etc.

$$du = \frac{\partial u}{\partial S}dS + \frac{\partial u}{\partial t}dt + \frac{\sigma^2 S^2}{2}\frac{\partial^2 u}{\partial S^2}dt \tag{4.21}$$

For economy of notation, we will use subscripts (when applied to u or the equivalent) to refer to partial derivatives. Thus u_t refers to the (first) partial derivative of u with respect to t, i.e. $u_t = \partial u/\partial t$, etc. Where two subscripts are used we refer to second partial derivatives, i.e. $u_{SS} = \partial^2 u/\partial S^2$, etc. In this notation Îto's formula becomes:

$$du = u_S dS + u_t\, dt + (\sigma^2 S^2/2)u_{SS}\, dt \tag{4.22}$$

4.3.2.2 Deriving the Black-Scholes pricing formulae using stochastic calculus

Suppose we assume that we have a *risk-free* (cash) asset (of constant nominal value), and that a holding H in this asset provides an income of $rHdt$ during time dt where r is constant (so r is the continuously compounded interest rate on the risk-free asset). Suppose that we also have a risky (e.g. equity) asset, characterised by a price process S, which provides an income

---

[16] Or sometimes more economically as $d(\log S) = \mu dt + \sigma dz$ since $\frac{d}{dx}(\log f(x)) = \frac{1}{f}\frac{df(x)}{dx}$, where $\log x$ is the natural logarithm of x.

(dividend) of $qSdt$ in time dt (so q is the continuously compounded dividend yield). The price of the derivative is $u(S, t)$.

We seek to construct a hedge portfolio which will at any instant in time rise or fall by the same amount as the value of the derivative. We therefore need the hedge portfolio to consist of:

$$A = \text{no. of units of underlying} = u_S$$
$$B = \text{balance} = \text{amount of 'cash' (i.e. risk} - \text{free)} = u - Su_S$$

The hedge portfolio therefore behaves as follows:

$$du = A(dS + qSdt) + Brdt = u_S dS + qSu_S dt + r(u - Su_S)dt \tag{4.23}$$

Subtracting this from Îto's formula, we derive the following partial differential equation satisfied by the price of *any* derivative on S, given the assumptions set out above:

$$-ru + u_t + (r - q)Su_S + \frac{\sigma^2 S^2}{2} u_{SS} = 0 \tag{4.24}$$

We immediately note that the mean drift in the price of the underlying, μ, does not appear anywhere in this formula, and hence does not directly affect the price of the derivative.

This partial differential equation is a second-order, linear partial differential equation of the *parabolic* type. This type of equation is the same as used by physicists to describe diffusion of heat. For this reason, Gauss-Weiner or Brownian processes are also often commonly called *diffusion* processes.

If r, q and σ are constant this equation can be solved as per Kemp (2009) by substituting for u, S and t new variables, w, x and y, say, that convert it into a 'standard' parabolic form, namely $w_y = c^2 w_{xx}$, where c is constant. We find that, say, the price of a call option takes the form:

$$C(S, t) = Q(1, K, S, T - t) - KQ(0, K, S, T - t) \tag{4.25}$$

where:

$$Q(k, K, S, y) = S^k e^{-kqy - r(1-k)y + \sigma^2 y(k^2 - k)/2} N(H) \tag{4.26}$$

$$H = \frac{\log(S/K) + (r - q - \sigma^2/2 + k\sigma^2)y}{\sigma\sqrt{y}} \tag{4.27}$$

Substituting $k = 0$ and $k = 1$ into the formula for $Q(k,K,S,y)$ then recovers the Black-Scholes formulae as per Section 4.3.1.4.

4.3.2.3   Closed form option pricing formulae

A solution to a mathematical problem that involves only 'elementary' mathematical terms, such as the ones appearing in the Black-Scholes formulae, is called a *closed form solution* or *analytical solution*. There is some flexibility here as to what constitutes 'elementary', since mathematicians have developed a number of functions over the years that are quite complicated to derive in practice. Generally speaking, the formulae have to appear in many different mathematical disciplines and to be amenable to relatively rapid accurate mathematical computation. Functions such as $\exp x$, $\log(x)$ and $N(z)$ easily fall within such terminology. There are even functions in standard spreadsheet programs like Microsoft Excel that compute such functions.

Most closed form option pricing formulae are derived using variants of the above approach and therefore also consist of terms that look vaguely like the expression derived for $Q(k,K,S,y)$ above.

4.3.2.4 Symmetries

It is notoriously easy to transcribe mathematical formulae incorrectly. It is therefore useful to have a mindset that seeks to ensure that whatever formulae are derived using complex mathematical manipulations exhibit characteristics that 'ought' to be expected for such formulae. Part of the skill is then to know what is reasonable for such formulae and what is not.

One useful approach is to identify underlying symmetries that the formulae ought to exhibit.[17] We have already seen one sort of symmetry that put options and call options exhibit, namely put–call parity. There is also a strong element of symmetry between the terms in S and the terms in K, which is typically called *spot-strike symmetry*. If $m_1 = Ke^{-r(T-t)}$ and $m_0 = Se^{-q(T-t)}$ and $\gamma = \sigma\sqrt{T-t}$ then the formulae for the value of a (European style) call option, C, and the value of a (European style) put option, P, are the same except that m_0 and m_1 are switched over, since:

$$C = m_1 N\left(\frac{\log(m_1/m_0)}{\gamma} + \frac{\gamma}{2}\right) - m_0 N\left(\frac{\log(m_1/m_0)}{\gamma} - \frac{\gamma}{2}\right) \tag{4.28}$$

$$P = m_0 N\left(\frac{\log(m_0/m_1)}{\gamma} + \frac{\gamma}{2}\right) - m_1 N\left(\frac{\log(m_0/m_1)}{\gamma} - \frac{\gamma}{2}\right) \tag{4.29}$$

We should expect such a symmetry to exist because a 'call' option giving the right to buy, say, equities at a certain predetermined rate for cash can also be expressed as a 'put' option giving the holder the right to 'sell' cash for equities at a predetermined rate. Indeed, in the FX options market it is conventional to refer to a currency option as, say, a 'USD put/GBP call with strike ...' or the like, since with a currency pair there is no particular reason to favour one or other currency in the nomenclature.

4.3.2.5 Time dependencies

If r or q are time dependent (or even stochastic in their own right) then more complicated substitutions are needed, but it is still possible to convert the partial differential equation governing the (no arbitrage) price of the derivative into the standard parabolic form referred to in Section 4.3.2.2, and this is still true even if σ is time dependent (but only on t and not on S).

Thus the Black-Scholes formulae, suitably understood, do not require interest (or dividend) rates to be constant. If the price at time t of a zero coupon bond delivering K and maturing at time T is $V_K(t)$ and the price at time t of a contract delivering one share at time T without dividend income in the meantime is $V_S(t)$ then we can rework the derivation of the Black-Scholes formula (either via a binomial lattice or via Îto's formula), and show that the price of, say, a put option will be given by:

$$P(S, t) = V_E(t)N(-d_2) - V_S(t)N(-d_1) \tag{4.30}$$

---

[17] As an aside, having an appreciation of modern theoretical physics can be helpful here since such theories are often developed in ways that highlight their underlying symmetries (or how such symmetries break down).

where σ is now the volatility of $\log(V_S(t)/V_E(t))$ and

$$d_1 = \frac{\log(V_S(t)/V_E(t)) + \sigma^2/2)(T-t)}{\sigma\sqrt{T-t}} \qquad d_2 = d_1 - \sigma\sqrt{T-t} \qquad (4.31)$$

Indeed it is not even necessary for the variability of the share price to be constant. If it is continuous and a function of time only (i.e. deterministic, not stochastic), then Equation (4.30) remains correct provided σ is taken as a suitable average volatility for the period between now and maturity. This result is usually attributed to Merton (1974).

Thus we may still use the Black-Scholes formulae even if interest rates and dividend yields vary stochastically and even if σ is a deterministic function of t, provided we use the appropriate rates applicable at the time of valuation for securities maturing at the same time as the option.

If σ is continuous (but not itself stochastic) *and* a function of both time and the price of the underlying then the option can still be found as the limit of an appropriate binomial tree or the solution to a partial differential equation which is preference independent, but the relevant differential equation can no longer be simplified into a form like $w_y = c^2 w_{xx}$ where c is constant. We might call such a pricing framework the *generalised Black-Scholes* or *generalised Brownian* framework.

Does Black-Scholes also require the share price to follow a Brownian motion, and hence the price of the underlying to be log-normally distributed at maturity? The above only requires the stochastic process followed by the price of the underlying to be the limit of a process involving just up and down jumps (with u/d tending to one). One might therefore think that more general processes might be possible. Somewhat remarkably, however, it is possible to prove that any continuous stochastic process (or to be more precise every continuous martingale, this concept being explained further in Section 4.3.3) is a sort of time-shifted Brownian motion, see Rogers and Williams (1994).

4.3.2.6 Options involving multiple underlying assets

Options involving combinations of two underlyings (which follow Brownian motions) can be derived as per Section 4.3.2.5 but replacing the σ shown there with one derived from the usual way of calculating the variance of the combination of different random variables, i.e.:

$$\sigma_{aX+bY} = Var(aX + bY) = a^2 Var(X) + 2ab Cov(X, Y) + b^2 Var(Y) \qquad (4.32)$$

More generally, for options dependent on multiple underlying price processes there is an equivalent equation to that given in Section 4.3.2.2. It can be developed using martingale theory, in which case the equation is known as the Feynman-Kac equation, see e.g. Duffie (1992). Equivalently, the equation can be developed in a partial differential equation framework, using no-arbitrage arguments, along the lines summarised in Vetzal (1994) or Kemp (2009).

In this sort of formulation, we assume that the state of the economy (or at least that part we are interested in) may be summarised by an n-dimensional vector, $\mathbf{x}$, of real-valued state variables, i.e. $\mathbf{x} = (x_1, \ldots, x_n)$, say. We assume that the movements of $\mathbf{x}$ through time are described by a (typically linked) system of stochastic differential equations (where $\mathbf{z}(t)$ is now a n-dimensional Brownian motion, i.e. with each sub-element independent, identically distributed) as follows. Here, $\sigma(\mathbf{x},t)$ is deterministic (but does not have to be fixed).

$$d\mathbf{x} = \boldsymbol{\mu}(\mathbf{x}, t)dt + \sigma(\mathbf{x}, t)dz \qquad (4.33)$$

If σ is not itself stochastic then we might call this a multi-dimensional generalised Brownian framework. In it, μ is an n-dimensional drift element.

This type of formulation is often essential when trying to value interest rate derivatives, since the state variables for such derivatives are not normally one dimensional, but will depend on the yield curve, which in general needs several factors to describe it fully. In an interest rate context and if $\mathbf{x}$ relates to zero coupon bonds, but we model the development of forward rates, then this approach would generally be known as the *Heath-Jarrow-Morton* framework, see Heath *et al.* (1992).

In general, the equation includes a vector (with one element for each underlying) called the *market price of risk vector*, the existence of which is a necessary condition for the absence of arbitrage. The different elements of this vector define the risk-neutral trade-offs between risk and return applicable to each underlying, see also Chapter 12. In such a multi-dimensional world the dependence on the market price of risk vector means that drift terms (or rather their differences) do not necessarily cancel out in the pricing formula. The resulting pricing formulae are therefore not as preference independent as those applicable in the equivalent uni-dimensional world.

4.3.3 The martingale formulation

The leap in mathematical complexity when moving to a multi-dimensional world can be daunting. An alternative way of simplifying the formalism is to express the results as an expected value under the risk-neutral distribution as per Equation (4.15), i.e. in the form:

$$u(\mathbf{x}, t) = E\left(e^{-\int_t^T r(\mathbf{x}, s)ds} u(x, T)|\mathbf{x}_t\right) \tag{4.34}$$

The multi-dimensional world now appears to be a simpler extrapolation from a uni-dimensional world. Most of the additional complexities introduced by the partial differential equation derivation are 'hidden' within the risk-neutral probabilities, i.e. within the function $E(Y|X)$, the expected value (under the risk-neutral probability distribution) of Y (some future event) given knowledge of X about the world (at the current time).

This expected value formulation naturally results if one develops option pricing theory using the concept of a *martingale*. A martingale is a process defined with respect to a probability distribution (technically a probability 'measure', i.e. a collection of probabilities on the set of all possible outcomes, describing how likely each one is) and an uncovering through time of information about the state of the world (technically a 'filtration', i.e. the history of a process, possibly multi-dimensional, and hence the information about the path taken by the process up to time t). It has the property that the expected value of all future values of that process (under the relevant probability distribution) is the same as its current value. Hence, for all $s > 0$ and for all t it exhibits the following, where the expectation $E(Y|X)$ is calculated by reference to the given probability measure:

$$E(Y_{t+s}|\mathbf{x}_t) = Y_t \tag{4.35}$$

In the derivatives literature, the use of a risk-neutral approach may thus be referred to as using an *equivalent martingale measure* since the discounted price process (under the risk-neutral probability measure) is a martingale.

This approach and the corresponding partial differential equation approach are formally equivalent (in the absence of jumps) and hence we have not attempted to summarise the martingale formalism any further. It is explained in detail in several standard textbooks on derivative pricing, e.g. Baxter and Rennie (1996).

4.3.4 Hedging

One of the beguiling features of derivative pricing theory is that it appears to provide a methodology for determining how to hedge derivatives as well as how to price them. This has been of fundamental importance in the development of derivatives markets. It has made market makers incrementally more willing to make markets where none might previously have existed, because it has indicated how positions entered into in the course of such activities might be hedged (at least in part) using more liquid instruments.

The word 'beguiling' is included at the start of the previous paragraph because in one sense derivative pricing theory does provide such a toolkit but in another sense it does not. As we have previously mentioned, derivative pricing algorithms are typically calibrated before they are used. This means that the price of an instrument 'close' to ones off of which the algorithm is being calibrated ought to be fairly accurately priced by the algorithm largely irrespective of the model of the world underlying that algorithm. But hedging typically concentrates on understanding the *sensitivity* that the derivative price might exhibit to movements in factors on which the price depends, which in mathematical terms are usually characterised by the so-called *greeks*[18] or partial differentials of the derivative price, u, with respect to different market drivers. It is less clear that these sensitivities will necessarily also be 'close' to the ones being exhibited by the instrument(s) which we use to calibrate the pricing model, since it is merely prices that we typically fit in such a context. Or to be more precise, what constitutes 'close' may not necessarily be the same.

Intrinsically, this is because two functions may be close to each other in some absolute sense, but their sensitivities may be substantially different. Take, for example, $f_0(x) = 0$ and $f_1(x) = x \sin(1/x)$ in the region close to (but not at) $x = 0$. $f_1(x) - f_0(x) = 0(x)$. So these two functions are arbitrarily close in value as $x \to 0$, but $\partial(f_1 - f_0)/\partial x = \sin(1/x) - \cos(1/x)/x$, so the difference in their sensitivity to small changes in x becomes arbitrarily large (and oscillatory) as $x \to 0$.

> **Principle P19: A pricing model that perfectly calibrates to a wide range of observed market prices will not necessarily correctly mimic the future or even current price sensitivities of these instruments or necessarily provide a reliable indication of how to hedge or mitigate the risks incurred with such exposures.**

We here merely reproduce hedging/sensitivity parameters, i.e. greeks, as if it is valid to assume that the underlying derivative pricing model is reliably calibrated in this respect.

The most important *greeks* are probably the option *delta*, Δ, and the option *gamma*, Γ. For an instrument with a single underlying, S, these are traditionally defined as:

$$\Delta \equiv \frac{\partial u}{\partial S} = u_S \tag{4.36}$$

$$\Gamma \equiv \frac{\partial^2 u}{\partial S^2} = u_{SS} \tag{4.37}$$

---

[18] These sensitivities are typically called 'greeks' because conventionally many of them are referred to by Greek letters.

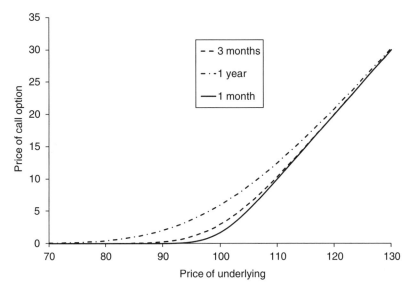

Figure 4.3 Variation of the price of a call option as the price of the underlying varies

Using this definition, formulae for these for a call option priced in a Black-Scholes world are $\Delta = e^{-q(T-t)}N(d_1)$ and $\Gamma = e^{-q(T-t)}f(d_1)/\left(S\sigma\sqrt{T-t}\right)$ respectively, where d_1 is as per Section 4.3.1.4 and $f(x)$ is the Normal probability density function. However, for practical hedging purposes it is often helpful to restate the formulae for delta and gamma to relate to the equivalent market exposures involved. This involves multiplying them by S and S^2 respectively, making them $\Delta = Se^{-q(T-t)}N(d_1)$ and $\Gamma = Se^{-q(T-t)}f(d_1)/\left(\sigma\sqrt{T-t}\right)$ respectively.

Graphically, we may interpret these sensitivities by reference to the way in which the price of the option varies as the price of the underlying varies. Figure 4.3 shows the form of this dependency for various times to maturity for a European call option, strike price of 100, assuming a constant volatility σ of 15 % pa, and constant (continuously compounded) risk-free interest rate r and dividend rate q of 0 % pa.[19]

The *delta* of an option, or indeed of any type of (equity) derivative, is the slope of such a curve, i.e. the rate of change of the price of the option with respect to the price of the underlying (multiplied by S if the aim is to express the answer in units of market value rather than units of stock). Deltas equivalent to the prices in Figure 4.3 (but without multiplying by S) are shown in Figure 4.4. Equivalent graphs for European put options are shown in Figures 4.5 and 4.6.

The option *gamma* is then the slope of the curve in Figure 4.4 or Figure 4.6, i.e. the rate of change of delta with respect to the price of the underlying. Gamma is important because:

(a) It is directly related to the level of turnover within the sort of portfolio that might be used to hedge dynamically the characteristics of the option; and
(b) The smaller the absolute size of the gamma the less, in effect, are the option-like characteristics of the derivative. If gamma (defined as above) is zero in all circumstances (and if certain other regularity conditions are met) then the derivative will have no asymmetric characteristics, and may be priced using merely the sorts of techniques described in Section 4.2.2.

---

[19] The spot and strike are thus expressed in 'forward' terms, so that the prices for options of different maturities have the same asymptotic behaviour for both small and large S.

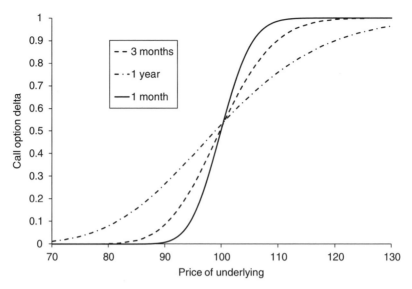

Figure 4.4   Variation of the option delta of a call option as the price of the underlying varies

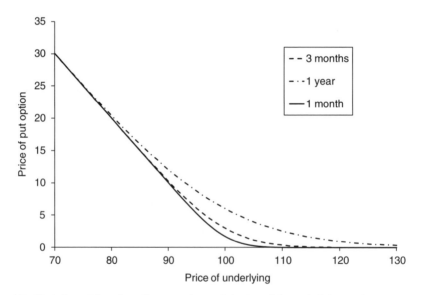

Figure 4.5   Variation of the price of a put option as the price of the underlying varies

Slightly different definitions of delta and gamma may be used for interest rate derivatives. Instead of relating to sensitivities with respect to movements in the price of some underlying they may instead relate to sensitivities to movements in the assumed interest rate drivers.[20]

---

[20] Sensitivities with respect to movements in yield curves can, of course, be expressed in terms of sensitivities to movements in suitably defined instruments given the link between the yield, modified duration and price of a bond, see Section 7.2.

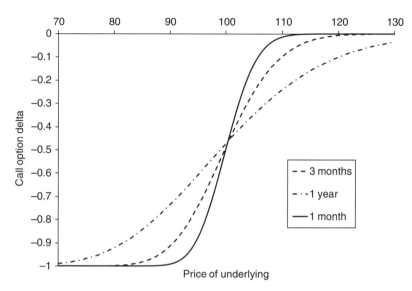

Figure 4.6   Variation of the option delta of a put option as the price of the underlying varies

The price of a call option also depends on σ, r, q and the time to maturity (and for pricing formulae which are more complicated than the Black-Scholes formulae on other relevant parameters). For example, the price of vanilla puts and calls will in general rise if σ rises. 'Greeks' capturing these sensitivities include *vega*, *rho* and *lambda* defined as follows[21] $\kappa \equiv vega \equiv u_\sigma$, $\rho \equiv rho \equiv u_r$ and $\lambda \equiv lambda \equiv u_q$.

$\Theta \equiv theta \equiv u_t$ is the sensitivity of the option price to changes in time. It can typically be derived from other sensitivities by referring back to the partial differential equations described earlier that the option price satisfies.

Analytical formulae for these (and other greeks) in the case of a Black-Scholes world are set out in Kemp (2009).

We mentioned above that instruments where gamma is zero whatever happens have no option-like characteristics. As we shall see later in this chapter this does not stop us constructing instruments that provide 'pure' exposure to volatility, interest rates or future dividend levels, such as variance swaps, interest rate swaps and dividend swaps.

Option gamma is also sometimes referred to within the equity derivatives industry by the term *convexity* (but readers should note that the way interest rate derivatives are usually described means that convexity has a different meaning for them, see Section 7.2). This is again highlighted graphically in Figure 4.3, e.g. the price of a call option relative to the price of the underlying is convex upwards. A purchaser of the option is thus said to have positive convexity, whilst the seller/writer of the option is said to have negative convexity.

If we attempt to replicate the effect of the option using dynamic hedging then the hedge portfolio would involve $S\,\partial V/\partial S$ in the underlying and $V - S\,\partial V/\partial S$ in cash. This would

---

[21] Greeks like vega, which involve partial differentials with respect to σ are in some sense 'invalid' in the context of Black-Scholes, since in its derivation we assumed that σ was constant. We might interpret it along the lines of applying to a model in which σ was slightly variable but otherwise was close to constant for all S,t, etc., and then it measures the sensitivity to changes in the mean level of σ.

change in value as per the tangent line to the graph. We might therefore infer that there should be a 'price' to convexity, and hence the price of the derivative 'ought' to adhere to the following equation, where *price(convexity)* is the price we place on the convexity, suitably defined (which might vary through time and depend on S) and *Amt(convexity)* is the amount of the convexity, suitably defined, exhibited by the derivative at that time (again it would in general also depend on S).

$$\frac{\partial V}{\partial t} = r \left(V - S \frac{\partial V}{\partial S} \right) + q S \frac{\partial S}{\partial S} + price(convexity) \times Amt(convexity) \tag{4.38}$$

A common mathematical measure of convexity is how rapidly the tangent angle changes, i.e. $\partial^2 V / \partial S^2$. To convert this to a monetary quantity we need to multiply by S^2. If we define the price of a unit of convexity per unit time as $\sigma^2/2$, we recover the Black-Scholes partial differential equation and hence the Black-Scholes option pricing formula. Indeed it is the simplest such example. If our measure of convexity includes the asymptotic behaviour of the option as S tends to $\pm\infty$ then we recover the cost of capital pricing model referred to in Section 4.5.2, if we price convexity appropriately. If our measure includes other types of aspects of 'convexity' (e.g. finite jumps) then more complicated pricing equations result.

4.3.5 Path dependent derivatives

The methodology described above can be extended to include path dependent options, since the risk-neutral probability distribution or equivalent martingale measure necessarily embeds within it probabilities for any particular path that the underlying might take.

However, this does not make computation of prices for such derivatives straightforward. For example, *American style* options are in general path dependent. These options are the same as European style options except that they can be exercisable at any time prior to maturity rather than just at maturity. Both European and American style options are traded on both sides of the Atlantic, so these names no longer have any geographical relevance. In a frictionless no-arbitrage world, the value of an American option is at least as much as the value of an equivalent European option. The American option provides the option purchaser with the right (but not the obligation) to exercise the option before maturity if he or she so wishes. This extra optionality must therefore (in a no-arbitrage world) have a non-negative value; its value is often called the *early exercise premium*. The 'path dependence' of American options arises because the optimal early exercise strategy on the part of the option purchaser generally depends on the price of the underlying during the lifetime of the option.

Producing analytical valuation formulae akin to the Black-Scholes formulae for American options (or equivalently valuing the early exercise premium) has to date proved impossible except in special cases. Every so often, however, clever derivative pricing theorists come up with approaches that provide ever more accurate quasi-analytic approximations. One special case where an analytic solution does exist is if the dividend yield is zero (for a call option) or the risk-free interest rate is zero (for a put option). In these circumstances it should never be optimal to exercise early, so the early exercise premium should be zero. Another special case is if the term of the option is infinite and r, q and σ are constant. The option can then be priced by identifying time independent solutions to the underlying partial differential equation and identifying the level of the boundary B as a function of K, etc. at which it should be optimal to exercise, this boundary being found by applying the so-called *smooth pasting condition* which is that $\partial u/\partial S = \partial I/\partial S$, where $I(S, t)$ is the 'intrinsic' value of the option, i.e. $S - K$ for an in-the-money call option.

More usually, American options (or just the corresponding early exercise premiums) are valued using lattice techniques, by placing a minimum on the value of the option (or early exercise premium) at each lattice point equal to what the purchaser would receive if the option were exercised immediately, i.e. based on its intrinsic value. As with European style options, the value thus derived should converge to the 'true' (continuous time) value as the spacing between different lattice points tends to zero.

However, there is a sense in which, as with hedging, a false sense of comfort can be drawn from such theorising.

Suppose, for example, we have a range of European style options with different strikes but all with the same *tenor*, i.e. time to maturity. We might find that we can fit all of their prices well using a single Black-Scholes style pricing formula. Does this mean that the same formula will also reliably price equivalent American style options given suitably well-designed lattices? No! We can think of a Black-Scholes world as evolving through time with varying r, q, σ, etc. whereas what we would in practice be feeding into the Black-Scholes equation in this instance would merely be some suitably *time averaged* values of these parameters. The problem is that the prices of European style options depend merely on these time averaged values but the prices of path dependent options such as American style options also depend on how these parameters might evolve *within* the averaging period in question. Our calibration may therefore prove less accurate than we might expect.

4.4   CALIBRATION OF PRICING ALGORITHMS

4.4.1   Market conventions versus underlying market beliefs

Professionals in all walks of life tend to develop language forms and conventions within their particular field of expertise. The derivatives markets are no different. Within the equity derivatives market, the Black-Scholes option pricing formulae have reached this level of language universality. Within interest rate derivatives the Black model (which can be thought of as a variant of Black-Scholes more suited to bond-land) has become widely adopted, as have other tools that together might be called the Heath-Jarrow-Morton framework. Within credit derivatives, the Gaussian Large Homogeneous Portfolio (LHP) approximation is approaching a similar level of usage.

It is, of course, well known by most practitioners that these formulae rely on a number of unrealistic assumptions that do not represent market reality. Despite this, they still remain very much in common market practice/parlance.

Why is this? External commentators sometimes misinterpret widespread market usage of a relatively small number of pricing algorithms as representing unwavering belief by market participants in the mathematical assumptions and models underlying these pricing formulae. Instead, in my view, market experts mostly refer to the Black-Scholes option pricing formulae they are using more as a price quotation convention than because they believe that they closely approximate reality.

By this we mean that the relevant formulae are being used to derive some market implied value for one or more of the input parameters that we cannot independently derive from other instruments. We do this by *calibrating* the model, i.e. identifying value(s) that these input parameter(s) need to take for the derived price(s) to match the actual observed market price(s).

Take, for example, the Black-Scholes[22] option pricing formulae as derived above:

$$\text{Call option:} \quad C = Se^{-qt}N(d_1) - Ke^{-rt}N(d_2)$$

$$\text{Put option:} \quad P = Ke^{-rt}N(-d_2) - Se^{-qt}N(-d_1) \tag{4.39}$$

The typical names given to the parameters involved are set out in Table 4.1.

For (European style) put and call options, the natural parameter for which to derive a market implied level is the volatility, σ. The result of this calibration of σ to market prices is called the option's *implied volatility*. It is 'natural' to concentrate on this parameter in such a calibration exercise because:

(a) The prices of 'simpler' instruments that might also be bought or sold, e.g. the underlying itself, do not depend on σ. Hence, implied volatility, in effect, represents the novelty created by inclusion of European style put and call options as instruments in which we might invest;

(b) Comparison of the Black-Scholes option pricing formulae with the generic upper and lower arbitrage-free price limits applicable to European style put and call options as noted in Section 4.2.1.3 indicates that any arbitrage-free frictionless-market price corresponds to *some* value of σ between 0 and ∞; and

(c) The Black-Scholes option pricing formulae are monotonic with respect to σ. Thus we can expect the resulting implied volatility to be *uniquely* determined from the observed option price, as long as the observed price is within the bounds referred to in (b).

It is not always correct to concentrate merely on the obvious calibration in this context. Only two of the six parameters in Table 4.1 are actually known with certainty, namely K and $T - t$. We do not typically infer market implied values for r using the Black-Scholes formulae because we typically expect to derive a more reliable value for this parameter from interest rate markets (and/or credit markets). However, this expectation might not be reliable if the option market in question was much more liquid than the corresponding interest rate market. We might also expect to derive q more easily from other sources, e.g. broker dividend estimates.

Table 4.1 Names typically given to different parameters used in the Black-Scholes option pricing formulae

Parameter	Name
S	Spot price, i.e. current price of underlying asset
K	Strike price
t	Tenor, i.e. outstanding term to maturity
r	'Risk-free' rate[23] (continuously compounded)
q	Dividend yield[24] (continuously compounded)
σ	(Implied) volatility

---

[22] As noted earlier, strictly speaking these are Garman-Kohlhagen formulae – the original Black-Scholes formulae related to dividend-free instruments, i.e. had $q = 0$.

[23] More generally, r may depend on t, i.e. have a *term structure*, in which case we might instead describe this parameter as referring to the risk-free yield curve rather than risk-free rate. The appropriate r to use in the formulae is then whatever value results in the value of a zero coupon bond of term t having a value e^{-rt}.

[24] Likewise the dividend yield can also in general be expected to exhibit a term structure.

However, we might not then be fully adopting market consistent principles. For longer term (equity) options we might instead reference the dividend swaps market, or we might derive the parameter by reference to put–call parity.

In principle, we might even calibrate S from a pricing formula such as Black-Scholes rather than obtaining it from quoted market data. Option markets are usually but not always less liquid[25] than the corresponding physical markets,[26] but the opposite is the case for the main equity index futures contracts and for several other types of derivative. For example, daily turnover in the main listed equity market index futures contracts is several times as large as volumes traded on the underlying physical markets.[27] Price formation at the market index level often first involves movements in derivative prices, which then lead to changes in the prices of securities in the underlying physical markets.

To put it another way, if a market maker takes on an unwanted exposure to a broadly based block of equities and wishes to hedge this exposure then he or she is most likely to implement the hedge using a market index futures contract. The same point is also relevant in terms of fair value pricing as applicable to asset managers, see Section 3.5.7. So, although we might not normally derive S from option prices, we might argue that the market often derives S from futures prices using formulae akin to those described in Section 4.2.2.

4.4.2   Why calculate market implied parameters such as implied volatility?

What then is the point of calculating the implied volatility? It isn't to help you calculate the price of the instrument used in its derivation – you know that already! Rather:

(a) It provides a price quotation convention that is more consistent across different related instruments than price in isolation;
(b) It aids in the derivation of 'fair' (i.e. market consistent) prices for less transparently traded instruments, by making potentially more accurate their interpolation or extrapolation from the observed prices of similar but more transparently traded instruments;
(c) It potentially helps you understand better the sensitivities that different instruments might exhibit to different economic factors, and hence how they might best be hedged; and
(d) It potentially helps you to understand better the differential likely future price behaviour that different instruments might exhibit and hence potentially helps you understand which out of a range of relatively similar instruments might prove particularly 'cheap' or 'dear' and hence particularly helpful (or unhelpful) for hedging (or position taking purposes).

In this list the word 'potentially' has been deliberately added at the start of (c) and (d). Generally speaking, the greater the range of transparently and liquidly priced instruments used in the calibration process, and the closer they span the range of instruments from which you are attempting to interpolate or extrapolate current *prices*, the more accurate is likely to be this interpolation/extrapolation process. However, increased instrument coverage does not necessarily guarantee more accurate interpolation or extrapolation of *hedging* or *future price*

---

[25] By 'less liquid' in this context we mean in relation to volumes of market exposures typically traded each day.

[26] I.e. markets in the instruments on which the options are based.

[27] This differential may, however, change over time, if volume continues to shift towards market index exchange traded funds.

behaviour characteristics, see Section 4.3.4. You may have a pricing model that is a perfect fit to current observed prices, but this does not necessarily make it a good descriptor of future price behaviour.

Principle P20: Market standard pricing models should be seen principally as providing price quotation conventions to make comparative value analysis between similar instruments easier or to facilitate extrapolation from one instrument to others that have similar characteristics. They provide little if any guide as to how any particular market practitioner might actually think markets might behave in the future. Market practitioner views on the applicability or otherwise of these assumptions will, however, influence the practitioner's views on how similar the instruments might need to be for these comparisons or extrapolations to be meaningful.

4.4.3   The volatility smile or skew

An example of how this calibration process operates in practice is given by the so-called volatility smile or skew. If the assumptions underlying the Black-Scholes formulae were correct then the implied volatility would be constant across all strike prices. In practice it is not. Instead it typically exhibits *smile* and/or *skew* effects. The smile effect is so called because the implied volatility is generally higher for far in-the-money and far out-of-the-money options than for options with strike prices closer to current levels. For equity options, an *in-the-money option* is one whose intrinsic value is greater than zero (e.g. for a call, $S > K$) whilst an *out-of-the-money option* is one whose intrinsic value is zero (and which is not at-the-money, i.e. on the boundary between the two, i.e. with $S = K$). Only one side of the smile may be noticeable (typically for equity markets the one involving low strikes), in which case the behaviour of implied volatility is said to exhibit a skew. Figure 4.7 illustrates how implied volatilities and their skews can vary by strike price (and term).

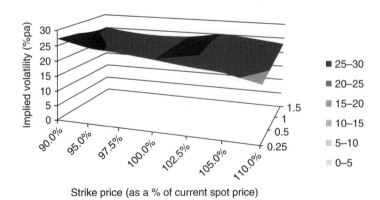

Figure 4.7   Variation in implied volatilities by strike price (and term) for FTSE 100 index options as at 26 June 2008
Source: Threadneedle, Bloomberg

4.5   JUMPS, STOCHASTIC VOLATILITY AND MARKET FRICTIONS

When deriving the Black-Scholes formula using a binomial lattice it is usual to adopt constant spacing (i.e. a constant u/d for a given time step) between lattice points, i.e. to have σ merely a deterministic function of t. However, we do not actually need to construct a binomial tree in this fashion. As soon as we permit arbitrary spacing, i.e. we allow σ to be a function of both S and t, it becomes possible to fit a much wider range of price processes.

Indeed, the flexibility is so wide that we can replicate exactly the price of any finite number of European option prices satisfying no arbitrage using a suitably chosen binomial tree, see e.g. Rubinstein (1996), although using this approach to replicate the prices of options with different maturities typically requires some care to implement. In a continuous time framework, and as long as the European option prices satisfy suitable regularity conditions (e.g. they are continuous functions of the price of the underlying and of time), then it is possible to price an entire term and strike structure of European option prices using a suitable $\sigma(S, t)$ which is a deterministic function of S and t, i.e. within the generalised Brownian framework introduced in Section 4.3.2.

However, not all price processes can be modelled using a binomial tree or limiting versions of it. The future price behaviour, i.e. the future sensitivity of the price of European options to inputs such as the then price of the underlying, will not necessarily be modelled correctly using some suitable $\sigma(S, t)$ as defined above.

To help us understand better this issue, we now explore the circumstances in which binomial lattices and their limit (i.e. the generalised Brownian motion framework) may fail to reflect reality.

4.5.1   Mileage options

A powerful conceptual tool for understanding the circumstances in which this might arise (and hence for understanding option pricing theory more generally) is a type of (total return) option called a 'mileage option' explored by Neuberger (1990), and referred to in Kemp (1997) and Kemp (2005). This is because it neatly encapsulates the different ways in which the fair value of a derivative instrument can diverge from the Black-Scholes option pricing formulae and their extensions. In Kemp (1997) and Kemp (2005) mileage options are described as hypothetical, but Deutsche Bank (2007) write as if these derivative instruments are now traded from time to time, with prices typically set based on the Black-Scholes formula applied with the target volatility and time to maturity.[28]

We concentrate here on 'total return' versions of mileage options, although price return equivalents are also possible. An example would be a European style put option which gives the holder the right to sell at time T an index, with gross income reinvested, represented by S_t, for a price set by reference to another index F_t, e.g. the total return on, say, cash. The pay-off of such an option at time T is thus $\max(KF_T/F_0 - S_T, 0)$ where K is the strike price of the option.

---

[28] It is understood by the author that it is also possible to trade such instruments with Société Générale, who refer to these types of instruments as 'timer' options. A sponsored statement in the October 2008 edition of *Risk Magazine* indicates that similar instruments can also be traded with Bank of America, who call them 'consumption' options.

The unusual feature of a mileage option is that it expires not at some fixed time T but when the *cumulative quadratic variation* of the option, $CQV(t)$ reaches a certain predetermined value, say, $CQVT$. The cumulative quadratic variation, $CQV(t)$ (if it exists!), is defined as the limit as $n \to \infty$ of the following (i.e. its value in the limit in which we partition time into infinitely small time steps):

$$\sum_{i=0,1/n,2/n,...}^{t-1/n} \left(\log \left(\frac{S_{i+1/n}/S_i}{F_{i+1/n}/F_i} \right) \right)^2 \tag{4.40}$$

The no-arbitrage pricing formula for this option is particularly simple, if we assume markets are arbitrage-free and are frictionless (i.e. no transaction costs, no limits on short-selling, borrowing, etc.). If $CQV(t)$ is continuous, however $S(t)$ moves, then the value of this option is as follows, see Neuberger (1990) or Kemp (1997):

$$P(S, t) = K N(-d_2) - S N(-d_1) \tag{4.41}$$

where:

$$d_1 = \frac{\log(S/K) + CQVT/2}{\sqrt{CQVT}} \quad d_2 = d_1 - \sqrt{CQVT} \tag{4.42}$$

This result can perhaps be most easily understood by remembering that the Black-Scholes formula can be derived as the limit of a binomial tree pricing approach, see Section 4.3.1. With a mileage option we merely redefine the rate at which 'time' passes, i.e. the step size, to match the rate at which the cumulative quadratic variation changes.

The important point about this analysis, as noted by Kemp (1997), is that there are only three possible ways that in a no-arbitrage world option prices may fundamentally diverge from a generalised Black-Scholes framework, namely:

(a) The price of the underlying might not be continuous, i.e. might exhibit jumps. $CQV(t)$ would not then be well defined because it would no longer be continuous;
(b) Volatility might itself be stochastic in some way. This then introduces uncertainty in when in 'real time' $CQV(t)$ will reach $CQVT$; and
(c) There might be market frictions, e.g. transaction costs.

Another way of reaching the same conclusion is to note that markets that consist merely of underlyings are, in these circumstances, *incomplete*[29] and can only be 'completed' by including extra 'underlyings' relating to volatility, jump costs and transaction costs.

We explore below each of these three possible ways of diverging from the generalised Black-Scholes framework.

4.5.2 Jump processes

The first potential deviation from the generalised Black-Scholes framework is the possibility of market jumps. If markets jump it is impossible to move the hedge portfolio fast enough in the fashion required to replicate the behaviour of the option by dynamic hedging.

---

[29] By 'completeness' we in essence mean that all possible economic exposure types can be decomposed into elements that are actually traded in the set of markets under consideration.

Perhaps the simplest way of incorporating jumps into option pricing formulae is the *cost of capital* model, see Smith (1995) or Kemp (1997). This model assumes that in any small instant the underlying may jump in price either infinitely upwards or down to zero. An option writer is putting his capital at risk from such jumps as they are not hedgeable by investing merely in the underlying and risk-free assets. It would therefore seem reasonable to assume that the option writer would demand an excess return on the 'risk capital' he thus needs, to reflect this risk. Of course, such risks can be hedged by buying suitable options, but this merely transfers the jump risk to someone else. Ultimately, someone must carry this risk.

The model assumes that writers of derivatives require some additional return on the cash/shares they need as risk capital to compensate them for putting their capital at risk. It therefore includes two extra parameters, r_a, the rate of interest (continuously compounded) required on the cash the writer would need to hold to make good the loss L_C that he would incur if there were an extreme downward jump in the price of the underlying shares and q_a, the dividend yield (continuously compounded) required on the shares the writer would need to hold to make good the loss L_S that he would incur if there were an extreme upward movement in the price of the underlying shares.

If the strike price is K then the formulae for the prices under this pricing model of European put options $P(S, t)$ and call options $C(S, t)$ are relatively similar to the Black-Scholes option pricing formulae, see Kemp (1997):

$$C(S, t) = Se^{(q_a - q)(T-t)} + Se^{-q_a(T-t)}N(d_1) - Ke^{-r_a(T-t)}N(d_2) \qquad (4.43)$$
$$P(S, t) = Ke^{(r_a - r)(T-t)} + Ke^{-r_a(T-t)}N(-d_2) - Se^{-q_a(T-t)}N(-d_1) \qquad (4.44)$$

In each case the first term can be thought of as corresponding to the jump element of the model, and the other two terms as corresponding to the diffusion element of the model. The model collapses to the Black-Scholes formula when the jumps are disregarded, i.e. when $q_a = q$ and $r_a = r$. Of course, markets do not in practice jump in the ways assumed in the model. Instead, we may view the cost of capital pricing model as the limiting case of more realistic models that include more modest jumps. As long as the option is not far in or out of the money (or of very long duration) then the losses incurred by more modest sized down or up jumps rapidly approach L_C or L_S as the sizes of the jumps become significant (if L_S is denominated in units of the underlying).

An unusual but informative feature of the cost of capital pricing model is that not all types of options have a well-defined price within such a model.[30] Suppose we tried to hedge an option position dynamically ignoring the possibility of jumps (so we would hold $S\,\partial V/\partial S$ in stock and $V - S\,\partial V/\partial S$ in cash). Then our loss (in units of cash) if the underlying were to crash instantaneously to zero is L_C and our loss (in units of the underlying) if the underlying were to jump instantaneously to infinity is L_S where:

$$L_C = \lim_{z \to 0} (V(z, t) - (V(S, t) - S\,\partial V/\partial S))$$
$$L_S = \lim_{z \to \infty} \frac{V(z, t) - (V(S, t) - S\,\partial V/\partial S)}{z} \qquad (4.45)$$

For vanilla puts and calls both L_C and L_S are finite, and so we can cover all losses by holding a suitable amount of cash or shares respectively. However, this is not so for power options, which have pay-offs expressed in terms of S^n where $n > 1$ and which therefore grow asymptotically

---

[30] A corollary is that market participants may want to be particularly careful when entering into such contracts.

faster than S as S becomes large. They also may not be finite for some sorts of quanto options (in which the pay-off is, say, \$1 for every one point rise in a Euro denominated index). In the presence of very large jumps, the values of these derivatives become unstable. We can interpret this as meaning that such options can exhibit systemic instability. This manifests itself as a situation where one of the counterparties is theoretically incentivised to drive the price of the underlying in one direction by an arbitrarily large amount, however much it costs to do so in the underlying market, because the gain on the mark-to-market of the option positions then theoretically exceeds any cost incurred in manipulating the underlying physical market in this manner.

The cost of capital model has two additional parameters and hence two additional degrees of freedom. This means that it can be used to fit an observed implied volatility smile with something akin to a quadratic curve. However, such a fit does not always necessarily correspond with financially reasonable values for the parameters, see e.g. Kemp (1997). In contrast, the Black-Scholes model fits an observed implied volatility smile/skew with just one degree of freedom (i.e. by a horizontal line).

A more common way of taking into account the possibility of market jumps is to assume that they might come from a specific size distribution, such as an exponential distribution and that they occur at a rate which is a Poisson process, with parameter λ (not necessarily constant through time). The probability that n jumps occur within time interval t is then $(\lambda t)^n$ (although it is not necessary to assume that λ is constant through time). It is then possible to develop a partial differential equation similar to Îto's formula but with extra terms incorporating a risk adjusted version of λ, as well as parameters describing the size distribution and the loss incurred were a jump of a given size to occur.

4.5.3 Stochastic volatility

The second source of discrepancy from the generalised Black-Scholes framework is the possibility that the volatility of the price movement of the underlying might change as time progresses in a way that is not predictable in advance.

Volatilities (both market and implied) often seem to rise when there is a downwards market shock, returning only over time to their previous levels. There are several different approaches that derivatives practitioners use in practice to cater for the dependency between implied volatility and strike price. For example, Ren *et al.* (2007) note how so-called 'local volatility' models as introduced by Dupire (1994) and Derman and Kani (1994) are widely used to price and manage risks in structured products that depend on such factors. The basic approach is to model the world using a formula along the lines of that described in Section 4.3.2.6, i.e. $dx = \mu(x, t)dt + \sigma(x, t)dz$, but making the $\sigma(x,t)$ explicitly stochastic rather than deterministic in nature.[31]

Equity derivative practitioners/modellers often seem to concentrate on this particular refinement when attempting to analyse deviations from the generalised Black-Scholes framework.

---

[31] An interesting theoretical question then becomes how implied volatility might move on an instantaneous time scale when the stock price moves. The most common theoretical constructs involve so-called sticky strike and sticky delta markets. With the former, the implied volatility of an option on S with cash strike K is deemed deterministic, whilst with the latter it is the implied volatility 'relative to the forward' that is deemed deterministic, see e.g. Overhaus *et al.* (2007).

This is despite, say, Kemp (1997) concluding that the main challenges in achieving good hedging appear to be jump risk and basis or rollover risk. Perhaps this reflects the relative mathematical tractability arising by incorporating such an assumption or an inherent belief that most deviations from 'Normality' (here to be equated with Brownian motion) come from time-varying volatility. Inconveniently, in Chapter 8 we will find that a significant proportion of such deviations actually appear to come from other sources, even for equity indices.

4.5.4 Non-zero dealing costs

The final[32] potential source of discrepancy from the generalised Black-Scholes framework is the existence of market frictions, principally transaction costs.[33]

Suppose we rebalanced our portfolio in accordance with a 'perfect' dynamic hedging programme at intervals separated by a short period h. Then as h tends to zero, it is possible to show that the total volume of transactions between now and maturity would tend to infinity. This is because Brownian motion has the characteristic that as the time interval becomes shorter and shorter, the observed variability of the price process reduces only by the square root of the time interval. In the presence of non-zero transaction costs, sufficiently frequent rebalancing will always completely extinguish the hedge portfolio.

One possibility would be to 'over-hedge', i.e. always hold more than enough to meet any level of transaction costs. Unfortunately, the characteristics of Brownian motion mean that to avoid completely the possibility of extinguishing the hedge portfolio we would need to hold the upper limit on the possible value of the option set out in Section 4.2.3.1 and then carry out no dynamic hedging whatsoever. This is overkill! Thus we need to accept some possibility of being unable to hedge fully an option pay-off, if there are transaction costs. There is a trade-off between the degree to which we rebalance (especially in terms of the frequency of rebalancing), thus incurring transaction costs, and the degree to which we replicate accurately the final option pay-off. The inherent uncertainty in the quality of replication this creates is explained in Davis *et al.* (1993). They borrow ideas from Hodges and Neuberger (1989). Using a utility maximisation approach, they show that the mathematics involved reduce to two stochastic optimal control problems, i.e. partial differential equations involving inequalities.

A simple asymptotic approximation to the solution to these equations is set out in Whalley and Wilmott (1993), if transaction costs are proportional to value traded. It involves rebalancing the portfolio if it moves outside a certain band, back to the nearest edge of the band, i.e. it

---

[32] Other factors less relevant to pricing algorithms that might also potentially disrupt dynamic hedging include:

    (a) Position risk, i.e. taking deliberate positions away from those required for pure dynamic hedging;

    (b) Credit risk, which could mean that the assets the dynamic hedger hoped would meet his liabilities do not actually do so, e.g. because of counterparty default, see Section 4.8;

    (c) Legal risk and taxation risk, which might cause the proceeds of the hedging instruments to be less than (or the payments on the written option to be more than) expected; and

    (d) Other operational risks, e.g. inadvertent position-taking and fraud.

[33] We use the term 'transaction costs' to include both directly visible costs, such as market maker bid–ask spreads, and less visible cost elements, such as 'market impact' (by which we understand the way in which seeking to execute a transaction will itself potentially move the price of the instrument in question).

defines 'buy', 'hold' and 'sell' regions.[34] The band is defined in terms of a factor Δ defining how much is invested in the underlying. It is like an option delta but given by:

$$\Delta = \frac{\partial V}{\partial S} \mp \left(\frac{3kSe^{-r(T-t)}}{2\lambda}\right)^{1/3} \left|\frac{\partial^2 V}{\partial S^2}\right|^{2/3} \tag{4.46}$$

The terms on the right-hand side relate to the actual delta and gamma of the option, ignoring transaction costs. The utility function assumed to apply in this analysis is an exponential one, with an index of risk aversion of λ. k is the cost of trading a unit value of the underlying. This approximation has the intuitively attractive characteristics that:

(a) The band (i.e. 'hold' region) becomes wider as transaction cost levels rise;
(b) The band tightens when the option becomes deep in-the-money, or deep out-of-the-money (i.e. when the rate of change of delta in the zero transaction cost case becomes small), but increases when the delta is liable to fluctuate more, i.e. where the option gamma is larger (although not as quickly as the change in the gamma, because of the trade-off between cost and quality of hedging); and
(c) In the limit of zero transaction costs (i.e. $k \to 0$), the band collapses to rebalancing in line with the standard Black-Scholes case, i.e. using $\Delta = \partial V/\partial S$.

4.5.5   Interpretation in the context of Modern Portfolio Theory

These three potential deviations from the generalised Black-Scholes framework can be interpreted in the context of Modern Portfolio Theory. Modern Portfolio Theory is an economic theory that aims to characterise how returns on different assets come about. The most common models used in Modern Portfolio Theory are the (single factor) *Capital Asset Pricing Model* (CAPM) and its multi-factor analogue, the *Arbitrage Pricing Theory* (APT). APT assumes that the (log) returns on any given investment can be decomposed into various factor components plus a residual (stock-specific) risk. It underpins the theory of much of modern portfolio risk analysis, see Chapter 7. CAPM is effectively the same as APT with a single factor, typically taken to be 'the market' (and with the exposure component of a particular stock to the market factor being the stock's 'beta').

In both CAPM and APT, the stock-specific return is typically assumed to be (log)-Normally distributed. Thus the APT and CAPM both assume that (log) returns on stock i can be decomposed in the following fashion:

$$r_i = \alpha_i + \beta_{i,j}x_j + \varepsilon_i \tag{4.47}$$

The mileage option analysis set out above indicates that in general we need to adopt a more complete decomposition which is conceptually along the following lines:

$$r_i = \alpha_i(t) + \beta_{i,j}(t)x_j(t) + \int U_{i,k}(t)d\sigma_k + \int J_{i,p}d\lambda_p + Y_C + Y_E + \varepsilon_i \tag{4.48}$$

---

[34] Whenever portfolio construction involves proportional transaction costs, it typically seems to be the case that you should rebalance back to the edge of some suitably defined band, rather than all the way back to the mid-point of the band, since this reduces the risk that you might then incur otherwise unnecessary dealing costs if you find that you have to trade the opposite way at some later point in time. Where fixed dealing costs apply then this effect may be moderated, since rebalancing back closer to the mid-point may then reduce the number of times you trade.

Here ε now relate to Brownian motions, U relate to contributions from unpredictable changes to volatility, J relate to market jumps, Y_C relate to transaction costs and Y_E relate to extra higher order cross-terms involving these additional elements.

In particular, we can think of economic quantities that we might call 'volatility' or jump/'gap' risk which can in principle be traded on derivatives markets. Derivatives practitioners often talk about trading volatility when they mean taking a position that will benefit or suffer if volatility changes. Just as there is a term structure to interest rates, there can also be a term structure to volatility.

An important corollary of standard Modern Portfolio Theory is that it is possible to diversify away non-systematic risk (i.e. the ε) by holding a sufficiently well-diversified portfolio. If we try to include other elements as above then diversification becomes a more complex topic. Diversification does not obviously apply at all to transaction costs (which presumably, other than for market makers, can on average be expected to deplete a portfolio over time). Care is also needed when considering diversification in the context of volatility and jump risk, because there may be systemic directional biases that on average apply to the entire market, i.e. the corresponding 'market' portfolio may itself express such exposures.

4.6 EQUITY, COMMODITY AND CURRENCY DERIVATIVES

In the next few sections we consider features specific to certain types of derivatives. Our focus is principally on the incorporation of options within the body of derivative pricing theory, since forwards and futures can typically be priced without introduction of risk-neutral probability distributions, see Section 4.2. We start with equity derivatives, given that we have developed the mathematical treatment above principally from an equity derivatives perspective.

The equity derivatives market is neither the largest financial derivatives market by volume nor by notional principal[35] but is perhaps the one that is most commonly in the public eye, because of its interaction with equity markets. Typical daily volume on the main index futures markets often exceeds the combined volumes of all corresponding individual equities, see Section 13.2.

The prices of individual equities can jump suddenly, both on the upside (perhaps because of short squeezes[36]) or on the downside (perhaps because of unexpected corporate events such as major frauds or bankruptcies), even relative to the significant level of ongoing volatility that such instruments often exhibit. However, extreme jumps at an entire market level are less obviously very large relative to the ongoing volatility such markets typically exhibit (although market indices still appear to display some 'fat-tailed' behaviour, see Chapter 8). As we have noted above, equity option pricing theory therefore tends to focus more on ongoing volatility than on jumps as the main sources of movement in underlyings, hence the focus on Brownian motion, stochastic calculus as characterised by Îto's formula, etc.

---

[35] The largest derivatives markets by volume and notional principal are generally considered to be the forward currency and interest rate derivatives markets respectively.

[36] A short squeeze is a situation where there are not enough owners willing to continue to lend securities as there are short sellers, forcing some short sellers involuntarily to unwind their positions. An extreme example of this was Volkswagen, a carmaker which according to Financial Times (2008f) briefly became on 28 October 2008 the world's largest company by market capitalisation. This followed extreme upward surges on two consecutive days triggered by the revelation a few days earlier that another carmaker, Porsche, had a much larger interest in Volkswagen than many traders had realised, 'squeezing' traders who had taken a view that Volkswagen shares would fall in value by short selling them.

Commodity prices can at times exhibit very considerable levels of volatility, even day by day. Indeed they are often more volatile than equity markets. Again, whilst more extreme one-off jumps can and do occur, they are not typically particularly 'extreme' relative to the level of these instruments' ongoing volatility.

Commodity derivatives do, however, involve particular subtleties relating to the interaction between physical settlement and investor interest, and consequently possess some industry-specific jargon. Most financial firms have relatively little interest in *physically* owning commodities or of taking actual physical delivery of commodities under a derivative contract. This means that such participants will nearly always close out their exposure under a commodity derivative prior to expiry. This interaction leads to effects such as *contango* and *backwardation* which introduce a term structure to commodity forward prices.[37] Commodity exposures, typically gained through derivative instruments, form only a small part, if any, of the asset base of most long-term investing institutions. However, over time their inclusion does seem to be increasing, as investors seek greater asset diversification.

We include currency derivatives with equity and commodity derivatives here because for many currencies option pricing theory used in practice also tends to focus on volatilities rather than jumps, at least in a post-Bretton Woods world in which many currencies freely float. A clear counter-example would be where one currency is formally or informally pegged to another. Firms in the countries involved can build up large exposures to assets in one currency and liabilities in another in the expectation that the peg will hold. They can therefore struggle if the currency peg comes unstuck. Relevant option prices, if available, can then provide some market implied guide as to the risk-neutral likelihood of such a decoupling occurring.

4.7 INTEREST RATE DERIVATIVES

Interest rate derivatives, including swaps, form the world's largest market involving long-term derivatives. The majority of these swaps involve exchanging fixed interest rates for floating rates. If credit risk is ignored then these instruments can be valued along the lines described in Section 4.2.2.3.

Such swaps can be for very long terms, e.g. 30 years or more. They are used by many different types of market participants, including corporates, banks and (typically in the guise of liability driven investment) life insurers, general insurers and pension funds.

Bonds issued in some bond markets (e.g. mortgage backed securities) often involve extensive use of option-like characteristics (e.g. putability and callability features) and may therefore need valuing using techniques borrowed from the interest rate derivatives market.

Particular characteristics of interest rate derivatives include:

(a) Nearly all options on any underlying have some exposure to interest rates (e.g. a one year vanilla European equity option is strictly speaking dependent on the prices of zero coupon bonds maturing at the same time as the option, as well as on equity orientated parameters). However, interest rate derivatives are often self-contained.

(b) We need to take explicit account of the stochastic nature of the interest rate, r. Its volatility is a key determinant of the value of interest rate options. Or more precisely, we need to

---

[37] If a commodity futures market is in contango then it has an upwardly sloping forward curve, i.e. the price of a commodity for future delivery is higher than the spot price (or a far future delivery price is higher than a nearer future delivery if the focus is on just one part of the forward curve). The opposite is the case if the commodity futures market is in backwardation.

take explicit account of how the entire yield curve might evolve, taking into account the correlation between different points along the yield curve, since the curve often but not always moves in a similar direction along its entire length.

(c) As time progresses, the duration/time to payment of every single fixed cash flow involved in the derivative will steadily fall. The volatility of the underlying will therefore also typically fall through time, if the derivative relates to bond instruments, rather than to some underlying interest rate itself (or to notional instruments with constant maturity). For example, suppose we have a European option on a zero coupon bond which will be redeemed at par shortly after the option matures. The price of the bond at the maturity of the option is then almost certain to be close to par, unless it is subject to significant credit risk. This effect is called *pull to par*.

What we therefore really need when tackling interest rate derivatives are models of how the whole yield curve might develop over time, rather than just how the price of some single underlying bond might vary.

Vetzal (1994) provides a useful summary of many such models. The first series of interest rate pricing models to reach prominence were *single factor* models, e.g. the *Vasicek* model and the original version of the *Cox, Ingersoll and Ross* model. These assumed that the single factor was the instantaneous risk-free interest rate, r, and that movements at other points on the yield curve could be derived from the short-end behaviour. The problem with such models is that they imply that the behaviour of the entire yield curve can be perfectly modelled by just one parameter. Experience teaches that this is not the case. For example, investment managers will often split the yield curve into two, three or more areas in order to understand its dynamics more completely. More complex *multiple factor* models were then developed to cater for such effects, e.g. the two factor *Brennan and Schwartz*, *Longstaff and Schwartz* and *Vetzal* models.

Early models also had the disadvantage that they were unable to fit the term structure of interest rates perfectly at outset. The argument in favour of models which perfectly replicate the opening term structure is that if a model cannot even price a straightforward bond correctly at outset, then little confidence may be placed in its ability to value other more complicated financial instruments. Calibration of a model becomes much easier if it can be arranged to fit the opening term structure exactly. Models with this characteristic include the *Black, Derman and Toy* and the *Hull and White* models, which are single factor models and, like most other interest rate models used nowadays, are special cases of the *Heath-Jarrow-Morton* framework mentioned in Section 4.3.2.

Relatively similar techniques can be used to price derivatives on inflation-linked bonds. They exhibit a term structure, but 'real' in nature (i.e. versus some relevant inflation index) rather than 'nominal'. The relevant derivatives markets are, however, smaller and less well developed, with wider bid–offer spreads.

4.8   CREDIT DERIVATIVES

The credit derivatives market has seen huge growth over the last few years. Indeed, in some respects it has become the market of choice for investors to express views on the creditworthiness of different entities.[38]

---

[38] This was true even in the depths of the 2007–09 credit crisis, when liquidity in large parts of the corporate bond market all but dried up, but there was still liquidity in parts of the credit derivatives markets, including index CDS.

The most important type of instrument by far in this market is the credit default swap (CDS).[39] In its usual form, one party (the 'protection buyer') commits to pay a regular, say quarterly, fixed premium (the 'fixed' leg of the swap) for a certain length of time, say 5 years, to another party (the 'protection seller'), in return for receiving protection against the risk that a particular named issuer (the 'reference entity' or 'reference issuer') defaults during that time. If default does actually occur then the protection buyer passes on whatever loss he or she might have incurred from holding some specified debt issued by the defaulted reference entity (the 'reference issue'). This can be achieved via 'physical' settlement in which the protection buyer hands over the defaulted reference bond and receives back par for it from the protection seller. Alternatively, the swap can be 'cash' settled, in which an equivalent monetary sum is transferred, derived from some suitably independent valuation of the defaulted issue (or from a predefined assumption about recovery value).[40]

Nowadays, there are loan CDS markets as well as 'normal' (i.e. bond debt) CDS markets.[41] The reference issues used in loan CDS contracts relate to loan capital that an issuer may have on its balance sheet. There are also index CDS markets for both normal and loan CDS, which allow trading of standardised baskets of single name CDS.

Market practice in such markets involves several subtleties, many of which are explained in Schönbucher (2003). For example, the regular premium payment structure described above is typically modified for high yield (i.e. 'junk bond') issuers where an upfront premium payment may also occur.

One factor behind the growth of the CDS market has been the impact of CDOs and other similar structures, see Section 7.6. However, in some sense a more fundamental factor is the intrinsic way in which CDSs unbundle credit risk from interest rate risk and therefore provide a 'purer' way for investors to take a view on the creditworthiness of particular entities. This factor seems likely to be here to stay. Even if CDOs and the like go out of favour as a result of the 2007–09 credit crisis, we should still expect to see the credit derivatives market remain vibrant, relative to other ways of expressing credit risk exposures.

The pricing of CDS is based on the observation that if you buy a bond and hedge away its interest rate exposure then you are in effect selling credit protection (on that issuer) to the person from whom you have bought the bond. Thus if 'default' affects the CDS in the same way as it affects the underlying (reference) bond holder, the two should have equivalent economic exposures and hence equivalent economic values.

The market implied default rate (bearing in mind potential recovery value) for the issuer (or more precisely the reference issue underlying the CDS) can thus be derived from the spread (versus risk-free) on the bond or from the premium rate payable on such CDS (which is therefore also typically called its 'spread'). In practice there is basis risk between these two spreads, so they do not necessarily trade fully in line with each other (e.g. impact of 'default' is not necessarily fully congruent, but more importantly there are bid–offer spreads

---

[39] Other types of credit derivatives, such as total return swaps, also trade.

[40] When a debt issuer defaults, the issuer is typically wound up and any residual business value achieved as a result of the wind-up is returned to the debt holders according to their stated priority position within the corporate structure. Thus in the event of default, bond holders often still receive some redemption proceeds from their bond holdings, but usually well below the par value of the bonds. As an aside, we note that settlement arrangements with derivatives are often quite complicated (for example, with credit derivatives a topic that has received much discussion in the past is exactly how to define 'default', particularly if the reference issue has been restructured, e.g. merged or demerged). It is ultimately how settlement is framed that defines the exact economic exposure to which a derivative relates.

[41] The development of the loan CDS market mirrors the growth in secondary trading of loans.

applicable in both markets). At times during the 2007–09 credit crisis volume was very much concentrated in the derivatives rather than the physical market and there could be significant apparent divergences between the two sets of spreads, probably because screen quoted prices on some of the bonds did not reflect the prices at which it might actually be possible to trade them.

It is possible to trade options on CDS, but more important refinements to the basic CDS building block are *basket CDS*, also called *tranche CDS*, e.g. an *n*th-to-default basket CDS. With such an instrument, the protection buyer only receives a payout if at least *n* of the underlying names in the basket default.[42] These types of derivatives are key building blocks when trying to price CDOs and other tranched structures. Generically, such derivatives involve payouts dependent on some contingency relating to the joint default behaviour of several credits in tandem. They are thus sensitive to correlation between the defaults of different credits. This complicates actual pricing of such instruments, see e.g. Schönbucher (2003). Correlation is typically quoted using the LHP pricing model, in which we adopt a 'firm model'[43] of each company's debt structure and assume that different credits within the portfolio all share a common correlation with each other (as well as each one exhibiting some idiosyncratic behaviour).

Index tranche CDSs are actively traded with the main index CDS as underlyings, but they do not necessarily provide accurate market implied views on the correlations between credits actually present within a non-index portfolio.

4.9 VOLATILITY DERIVATIVES

Volatility derivatives, most notably variance swaps (and corresponding futures such as the Vix futures), are also becoming more commonly traded. A variance swap provides a pay-off linked to the observed variance of an index.[44] Its underlying is, in effect, the cumulative quadratic variation introduced in Section 4.5, typically calculated using daily price or return movements.

Like a CDS it enables an investor to take as 'pure' a view as possible on some investment theme, here how volatile a particular index or security might be. In contrast a conventional put or call option also contains a market-beta component, namely the option delta, and has the further disadvantage for such purposes that its sensitivity to changes in volatility changes depending on how in- or out-of-the-money it is.

Originally, volatility derivatives had pay-offs relating to the *volatility* of the underlying, i.e. the observed standard deviation of movements over some set period in time after the inception of the contract. However, in due course it was realised that a better approach was to have the pay-off relate to the squared movement as per Section 4.5. With a not-squared computation

---

[42] Thus, a first-to-default basket CDS pays out as soon as any of the names in the basket default, a second-to-default as soon as the second one defaults, etc. Neither receives a payout if none of the names in the basket default during the lifetime of the derivative.

[43] The firm model of a corporate balance sheet is explained further in Schönbucher (2003). It involves assuming that there is some underlying driving variable (typically, Normally distributed) that characterises the evolution of the overall value of the firm, and default occurs if this value falls below some threshold level. One can use such a model to establish linkages between the (implied) volatility of a company's equity and the (implied) rate of default of a company's debt, i.e. between equity implied volatility and credit spreads.

[44] Variance swaps can be thought of as special cases of a more generalised type of derivative called an 'information derivative', see Soklakov (2008), which in some sense views information (in the case of volatility derivatives new information relevant to setting market prices) as arriving through time and attempts in a suitable sense to quantify its rate of emergence.

the pay-off cannot be replicated by a suitable basket of more vanilla options and forwards, whereas with a squared computation it can be.

Volumes in the variance swap market are surprisingly large for those not familiar with this market, although less than for vanilla options. This reflects variance swaps becoming the instrument of choice for hedge funds wishing to express volatility views,[45] and the overall importance in terms of trading volumes of hedge funds even though total hedge fund assets under management are still typically a small proportion of total market size in most physical markets.

The development of volatility derivatives has some potentially important consequences when considering what implied volatility to use in different sorts of instrument valuations. The theoretical replicating portfolio for a variance swap contains an infinite spectrum of vanilla options of different strikes. However, they are not uniformly weighted. Instead, ones with lower strikes have higher weights in the replicating portfolio, see e.g. Overhaus *et al.* (2007) or Kuenzi (2005). As option implied volatilities typically exhibit a volatility 'skew', this means that implied volatilities derived from variance swaps are typically higher than implied volatilities derived from at-the-money vanilla options of equivalent term. This does not make them better or worse value. It merely indicates that the two implied volatilities have slightly different meanings. As a generalisation, if a market consistent valuation requires market implied 'volatility' per se, rather than some particular strike dependent cut of the volatility skew curve, then variance swap implied volatility may be more appropriate for generic market consistency purposes than at-the-money option implied volatility. Using the latter may understate the cost/value of the optionality. Some commentators refer to the difference between the at-the-money option implied volatility and the implied volatility applicable to variance swaps as the *cost of skew*, see Figure 4.8. The costs of skew as at 5 December 2008 (here quoted in volatility points) were materially larger than the bid–offer spreads applicable to variance swaps, according to Société Générale.

4.10   HYBRID INSTRUMENTS

Hybrid derivatives, as their name implies, combine elements of more than one of the derivative types described above.[46] Usually, the chief risk elements are equity orientated, and hence hybrid derivatives are usually the responsibility of equity trading desks.

They present the interesting challenge of combining in an intellectually coherent manner the different modelling frameworks used in different derivative disciplines. In particular, such derivatives can have meaningful exposures to both equity and credit. The modelling used to price them often therefore involves a hybrid between the volatility-based diffusion approaches typical of equity derivatives and the jump-based approaches typical of credit derivatives.

A relatively sophisticated description of the modelling techniques used in this 'mixed' context is set out in Overhaus *et al.* (2007). As such mixed characteristics ultimately characterise problems in market consistency better than either discipline in isolation, we should expect such disciplines over time to become increasingly important building blocks in methodologies for applying market consistency to firm-wide portfolios.

---

[45] Kuenzi (2005) notes that even though variance swaps do provide 'pure' ways of expressing views on volatility, they can still be thought of as having two components, a gamma (convexity) component and a vega component, and uses this to propose further refinements that allow even 'purer' views to be expressed.

[46] As we have noted above, nearly all derivatives include some linkage to interest rates, so the contribution from this element needs to be more than 'normal' in terms of modelling complexity, for this to be a reason for characterising the instrument as 'hybrid'.

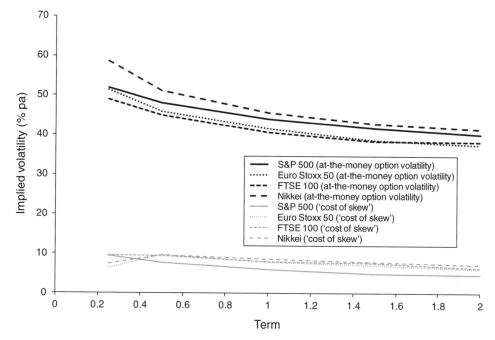

Figure 4.8 At-the-money and variance swap implied volatilities for different equity indices and different terms as at 5 December 2008
Source: Société Générale

4.11 MONTE CARLO TECHNIQUES

For more complex derivatives (or more complex prescriptions of how the underlying might behave) a fully analytical approach may be impractical. Instead a Monte Carlo, i.e. simulation-based, approach may be needed. This sort of approach involves:

(a) Defining a probability distribution that (as in the analytical case) describes the *risk-neutral* probabilities of paths that the underlying(s) might take between valuation date and maturity date;

(b) Randomly drawing from this probability distribution a large but finite sample of such paths, say n such paths;

(c) Calculating for each sample path the discounted present value of the pay-off at maturity (say g_i); and

(d) Estimating the present value of the derivative by averaging the g_i over the entire sample path, i.e. according to the following equation:[47]

$$V(\mathbf{g}) = \frac{1}{n} \sum_{i=i}^{n} g_i \equiv \sum_{i=1}^{n} q_i g_i \quad \text{where } q_i = \frac{1}{n} \tag{4.49}$$

---

[47] The q_i do not actually need to be the same. Instead, we might use 'importance sampling', in which we draw non-uniformly from the probability distribution with the aim of making the resulting computation more accurate. This would generally involve preferential selection of scenarios expected to involve large pay-offs, and then weighting these scenarios accordingly.

Mathematically, this process is akin to estimating the expected value of a function (given some underlying probability distribution) as the average of randomly selected evaluations of this function. As $n \to \infty$, the Central Limit Theorem implies that the average will tend to this expectation (as long as the expectation actually exists).

Unfortunately, convergence of the basic Monte Carlo approach can be relatively slow.[48] There are several ways of improving speed of convergence, e.g. using antithetic variables, stratified sampling and low discrepancy quasi-random numbers, see e.g. Press *et al.* (1992). Such methods can often be thought of as special cases of numerical integration techniques.

It is possible to calibrate a Monte Carlo pricing approach in a similar way to how we would calibrate an analytical price approach, i.e. by altering the parameters that characterise the distribution. This would involve including in the definition of the probability distribution in (a) some free parameters and then choosing the values of these free parameters so that the derived value of V (or strictly speaking its limiting value as $n \to \infty$) matches observed prices.

4.12   WEIGHTED MONTE CARLO AND ANALYTICAL ANALOGUES

4.12.1   Weighted Monte Carlo

An alternative way of calibrating a Monte Carlo calculation is the *Weighted Monte Carlo* approach described by Avellaneda *et al.* (2001) and Elices and Giménez (2006). In this approach we *directly* alter the probabilities ascribed to each sample path used in the Monte Carlo simulation (rather than only indirectly by altering free parameters describing the probability distribution from which the sample paths are drawn).

This involves altering the weights assigned to each path in Section 4.11(d), i.e. choosing a new set of probabilities p_i to ascribe to each sample (the p_i being in a certain sense as 'close' as possible to the original q_i). We therefore ascribe a price to the derivative as follows:

$$V(\mathbf{g}) = \sum_{i=1}^{n} p_i g_i \qquad (4.50)$$

To carry out this manipulation we need to have some measure of 'distance' between the two distributions $\mathbf{p}$ and $\mathbf{q}$. The most common approach used is a relative entropy measure $D(\mathbf{p},\mathbf{q})$ as follows even though strictly speaking relative entropy does not exhibit the usual metrical properties expected of a distance measure.[49]

$$D(\mathbf{p},\mathbf{q}) = \sum_{i=1}^{n} p_i \log(p_i/q_i) \qquad (4.51)$$

Weighted Monte Carlo is a *distribution-free* approach to pricing derivatives. By this we mean that, irrespective of the underlying distributional form used in the Monte Carlo sampling, it can always reproduce all observable market prices if the sample size is large enough (and therefore

---

[48] For a basic Monte Carlo simulation, convergence is generally $O(n^{-1})$, i.e. you generally need to double the number of simulations to double the accuracy, assuming that you have perfect knowledge of the underlying risk-neutral probability distribution, and that rounding errors can be ignored.

[49] It is also necessary to ensure that the adjusted probabilities do not permit arbitrage. This in practice involves choosing weights such that zero coupon bonds are correctly priced via such an approach, see Elices and Giménez (2006).

includes enough extreme outcomes). It is therefore an intrinsically attractive approach to focus on when calibrating to market observables.

4.12.2 Analytical weighted Monte Carlo

Monte Carlo approaches are merely convenient ways of carrying out the expectation computations needed to calculate derivative prices. As we have noted above, if $n \to \infty$ then the result tends to the same answer as would be produced by an equivalent analytical approach.

We can therefore use the same relative entropy type of approach to calibrate to market observables in effect for infinitely large Monte Carlo sample sizes, by considering the situation in the limit as $n \to \infty$. This can then result in an analytical or quasi-analytical pricing basis (which can then be calculated much more rapidly and accurately than a traditional Monte Carlo simulation). We might call this an *analytical weighted Monte Carlo* approach since it borrows from both an 'analytical' framework and a 'weighted Monte Carlo' framework.[50]

Such an approach can be thought of as being prototypical of the calibration problem that we will come across several times in this book, so we include here a somewhat more in-depth analysis of how calibration using this approach might work in practice.

The analytical weighted Monte Carlo approach involves identifying a (continuous) probability distribution $p(x)$ that is as close as possible (given a certain measure of distance between two distributions) to the original probability distribution $q(x)$ and that calibrates to market prices for specified pay-offs at maturity of $\mathbf{g}$, as per the following equation:

$$V(\mathbf{g}) = \int p(x)\mathbf{g}(x)dx \qquad (4.52)$$

In certain special cases, this calibration produces straightforward analytical results, including the situation where:

(a) The underlying model has the traditional multivariate Normal (i.e. covariance based) structure;

(b) The calibration refers to single strike (e.g. at-the-money) and common period market implied volatilities and correlations; and

(c) 'Distance' between probability distributions is measured using relative entropy as per Equation (4.51).

Consider, for example, the highly stylised example of a risk model that only involves a single instrument. The 'prior' probability distribution underlying such a model will then be a univariate Normal distribution $Q \equiv N(\mu, \sigma^2)$. Suppose we wish to calibrate this model (using analytical weighted Monte Carlo) to reproduce the market price of a one-period option on this instrument, with implied variance s^2 and a drift relative to the risk-free rate of m.

A Monte Carlo simulation would draw n paths from Q (with probabilities in each draw of drawing x_i being, say, $q(x_i) \equiv q_i$, typically $q_i = 1/n$). Using the analytical weighted Monte Carlo approach we seek to identify adjusted weights $p_i \equiv p(x_i)$, say, and we seek to understand the behaviour of p_i in the limit as $n \to \infty$. We note that in this limit, the p_i will form a probability distribution, say, P, i.e. $\int p(x)dx = 1$. We also note that for the mean of P to match our assumed mean drift relative to the risk-free rate of m and for the variance of P to match our assumed implied variance of s^2, we need $\int xp(x)dx = m$ and $\int (x - m)^2 p(x)dx = s^2$. Using Lagrange

---

[50] An alternative name would be 'analytical relative entropy'.

multipliers, P can thus be found by minimising L with respect to each p_i where L is defined as follows, subject to the constraints $\int pdx = 1$, $\int xpdx = m$ and $\int (x - m)^2 pdx = s^2$.

$$L = \int p \log(p/q)dx + \lambda_0 \left(\int pdx - 1 \right) + \lambda_1 \left(\int xpdx - m \right)$$
$$+ \lambda_2 \left(\int (x - m)^2 pdx - s^2 \right) \tag{4.53}$$

The solution to this minimisation problem satisfies $\partial L/\partial p_i = 0$ (for each i) and $\partial L/\partial \lambda_0 = 0$, $\partial L/\partial \lambda_1 = 0$ and $\partial L/\partial \lambda_2 = 0$. Hence the p_i satisfy:

$$\log(p_i) - \log(q_i) + 1 + \lambda_0 + \lambda_1 x_i + \lambda_2 (x_i - m)^2 = 0$$
$$\Rightarrow p_i = q_i e^{-1-\lambda_0-\lambda_2 x_i - \lambda_2 (x_i - m)^2} \tag{4.54}$$

However, the probability density function of a univariate Normal distribution is:

$$q(x) = \frac{e^{-\frac{(x-\mu)^2}{2\sigma^2}}}{\sqrt{2\pi}\sigma} = e^{a_0 + a_1 x + a_2 x^2} \tag{4.55}$$

where:

$$a_0 = -\frac{\mu^2}{2\sigma^2} + \log \left(\frac{1}{\sqrt{2\pi}\sigma} \right) \quad a_1 = \frac{\mu}{\sigma^2} \quad a_2 = -\frac{1}{2\sigma^2} \tag{4.56}$$

Indeed, *any* probability distribution with a probability density function expressible as an exponential of a quadratic polynomial, i.e. in the form $e^{a_0+a_2 x+a_2 x^2}$, corresponds to a univariate Normal distribution, since the term in a_0 is constrained by the need for the probability distribution to satisfy constraints $\int pdx = 1$ and a_2 must be negative for the integral to converge.

We therefore see that the calibrated probability distribution P is *also* a univariate Normal distribution, namely the $N(m,s^2)$ distribution, and thus happens to be analytically tractable.

We also note that:

(a) If we had no information at all to calibrate against (i.e. the terms in λ_1 and λ_2 do not exist) then, as we might expect, $\lambda_0 = -1$ and $p(x) = q(x)$, i.e. the 'calibrated' distribution is then identical to the prior uncalibrated distribution; and

(b) If we only calibrate to a given mean m (i.e. the term in λ_2 does not exist) then $a_2 = -1/(2\sigma^2)$ and $a_1 = 2m/\sigma^2$, i.e. the calibrated probability distribution is univariate Normal $N(m,\sigma^2)$, i.e. it has the same variance as the prior distribution but a different mean. Given our definition of m, the only possible market consistent value for m in a (univariate) no-arbitrage world is $m = 0$, i.e. a zero mean drift.[51]

---

[51] It can be argued that calibration of risk models using this methodology provides theoretical justification for the usual risk manager's approach of assuming a zero expected relative return between different assets. The risk manager is implicitly adopting a 'market consistent' approach to defining the distribution he is using to measure risk and is calibrating his views to some a priori set of assumptions, see Chapter 7. A possible flaw in this reasoning is that in a multivariate world there is the so-called market price of risk vector that might vary between economic drivers, see Section 4.3.2.7.

4.13 FURTHER COMMENTS ON CALIBRATION

The analysis in Section 4.12 indicates that we can think of calibration as involving a transformation that takes our starting 'guess' for the risk-neutral probability distribution and applies a *calibration transformation* to it, to result in a new 'calibrated' risk-neutral probability distribution.

In a *multivariate* world, the calibration transformation described in Section 4.12.2 would still convert or map an assumed prior multivariate Normal distribution into another fitted Normal distribution. The main difference is that we may have fewer calibration points than we have dimensions. The calibration transform then transforms the assumed prior distribution merely to the 'nearest' alternative multivariate Normal distribution that reproduces the calibration points, see e.g. Kemp (2009).

For example, we might be trying to calibrate a covariance matrix designed to characterise how every stock in a broad-based market index might move, and the only market observable to which we might have access is the implied variance level for the market index as a whole. The calibration would then, in the main, adjust upwards or downwards the variance assumed for each stock (with only second order adjustments to their correlations), depending on whether the overall market variance implicit within our assumed prior covariance matrix was below or above its actual market implied level.

We can also describe such a transformation using the language of Bayesian statistics. The original distribution is then called the *prior* distribution, and the calibrated distribution is called the *posterior* distribution. In the calibration example described above we had 100 % confidence in the reliability of the market derived data point which we used for calibration purposes.

An advantage of thinking in Bayesian terms is that it helps to identify how to cater for situations in which we have less than full confidence in the reliability of some piece of market data when trying to place a market consistent value on another less well-traded asset or liability. Bayesian theory indicates that we should then give *partial* weight to our own intrinsically justified prior distribution and *partial* weight to the observations, when coming up with the final posterior distribution. The greater the reliability ascribed to the observations (i.e. in statistical terms, the lower the uncertainty in the applicability of their values to the task in hand), the less weight is given to the prior distribution and the more weight is given to the market observable(s).

Principle P21: The determination of a market consistent value for an asset or liability not readily traded in a deep, liquid and transparent market will typically involve a *calibration* exercise incorporating market observable information. It therefore implicitly or explicitly includes subjective views about how relevant different market observables might be for the calibration in question.

In this sense, the incorporation of risk-neutral probability distributions can be viewed as use of a particular sort of calibration transform. The transform translates whatever 'real world' prior probability distribution we might have originally thought might be ascribed to the behaviour of the underlying into a probability distribution more consistent with observable prices.

Calibration to the market thus depends not only on the market prices themselves but also on:

(a) The credibility we place on any particular market observable. One example would be if the market observable in question is subject to wide bid–offer spreads. We might then give it less weight than if it was known with greater certainty. Another example might be if we wanted to fit a yield curve to observed prices for a range of bonds issued by a given issuer. If there are many such issues involved then an exact curve fit through all of these prices may be quite unsmooth, wobbling up and down to ensure that the curve goes through every point. We may think that application of no arbitrage and of principles of substitutability for closely similar instruments should force a smoother fit to the data (therefore involving fewer parameters, but each one more robustly estimated, etc.). However, by doing so we are necessarily incorporating a trade-off between accuracy of curve fit and credibility applied to the price of any single bond in the market consistent computation.

(b) Our choice for the prior distribution we have for market behaviour (typically implicit in the form of the pricing model we might use), if the credibility we place on market observable data is less than 100 %; and

(c) How we assess how far one probability distribution might be from another. This will implicitly underlie how we will interpolate or extrapolate from a finite number of market observables to an infinitely finely grained risk-neutral probability distribution. We have in the above example defined 'near' by reference to relative entropy (in part because it then leads to an analytically tractable result).

Another point highlighted by this Bayesian reformulation of the calibration problem is that as long as a market observable has *some* relevance to the market consistent pricing of an asset or liability then we should give it *some* weight in the calibration process. There is in principle no black and white dividing line between assets that can be market consistently valued and those that cannot.

> **Principle P22: Even if no market observables closely match the calibration needs in question, it will typically still be appropriate when carrying out market consistent valuations to give *some* weight to available market observables. Including *some* element of reference back to market data, however imperfect, is likely to be more objective than relying solely on the practitioner's own (uncorroborated) views about how a hypothetical market in the asset or liability in question might operate.**

5

The Risk-free Rate

5.1 INTRODUCTION

In Chapter 4 we proceeded as if it was clear what was the risk-free interest rate (or more generally the risk-free yield curve). In practice this is not necessarily the case. In this chapter we explore this topic further.

In the main we do so by referring to intrinsic principles. However, there may be pragmatic reasons for adopting simpler approaches in practice, particularly consideration of materiality. When calculating market consistent values of certain types of asset or liability there may be considerable uncertainty in *other* assumptions influencing the value computation. These uncertainties may affect the answer more than relatively modest disagreements about what risk-free rate to use (but may be questioned less because they are more uncertain or more subtle). Focusing too much on identifying the 'right' discount rate to use may be counterproductive if it distracts attention from more important issues.

5.2 WHAT DO WE MEAN BY 'RISK-FREE'?

As noted in Chapter 2, regulatory solvency frameworks often nowadays require liabilities to be valued using a 'risk-free' interest rate (or more precisely, if the liability payments are spread out over time, a risk-free yield curve). However, different commentators have different views on what exactly 'risk-free' then means.

> **Principle P23: The term 'risk-free' means different things to different people. As a result there may be a variety of observable rates all of which might be described by some as 'risk-free'. Practitioners should be careful to ensure that they choose the most appropriate rate when carrying out market consistent valuations, depending on the purpose to which the valuation will be put.**

For example:

(1) *The 'risk-free rate' might merely be the conventional name given to an assumption that is fed into a pricing algorithm*

As explained in Section 4.4 it is conventional with, say, the Black-Scholes option pricing formulae to call the input assumption r the 'risk-free rate'. The price derived using this formula depends on all of the assumptions including the implied volatility. Within suitable limits *any* choice of 'risk-free rate' is viable as long as a corresponding adjustment is made to the implied volatility.

To put it another way, the Black-Scholes implied volatility is ultimately merely a convention for expressing the price of an option. As long as everyone is agreed about how to derive r (etc.) when attempting to calculate the implied volatility, everyone will come up with the same value for the implied volatility (given the same input price). The label 'risk-free' in this context merely serves to distinguish r from other input parameters. Other market standard option pricing formulae typically have similar input parameters.

(2) *The 'risk-free rate' might be shorthand for what might more accurately be described as a 'reference rate', i.e. a convenient interest rate that can be used for a wide range of purposes, but which is not strictly free of all risk*

Examples would be Libor and Euribor. Libor stands for 'London Interbank Offered Rate'.[1] It is a daily reference rate based on the interest rates at which banks offer to lend unsecured funds to other banks in the London wholesale money market (or 'interbank market'). It is typically slightly higher than Libid (the 'London Interbank Bid Rate'), the reference rate designed to measure the interest rates at which banks are prepared to accept 'interbank' deposits. One occasionally also sees reference to Libmid (i.e. the corresponding mid-market rate). Investors depositing money in such a way in the interbank market would become exposed to the risk of default of the bank with which they have deposited their money (because Libor relates to *unsecured* funds). Hence, Libor is *not* free of credit risk.

Libor rates differ by currency. A Euro Libor rate does exist but mainly for continuity purposes in swap contracts dating from before the establishment of the European Monetary Union. For the Euro, the corresponding reference rates usually used are the Euribor rates compiled by the European Banking Federation. Libor rates are compiled by the British Bankers Association.

Libor rates for different currencies and Euribor also differ by term and thus have a term structure (typically available out to c. 5 years), even if in common parlance Libor is normally associated mainly with 7 day, 1 month, 3 month or 6 month deposit rates. Beyond 5 years attention would normally switch to Libor or Euribor *swap rates*. In the absence of any qualifier, a swap rate would generally be understood to relate to a standard fixed for floating interest rate swap in which one party agrees to pay a fixed rate of interest (on some fixed nominal sum) in return for receiving a floating rate payment based on a standard Libor or Euribor rate for the applicable currency. The stream of fixed payments is called the 'fixed leg' of the swap, whilst the floating payments are called the 'floating leg' of the swap. Typically, the 'swap rate' for a given term would then be taken to be whatever fixed leg rate was needed for the two legs to have equal market value at outset. It is thus the rate at which the swap would be entered into fairly without any initial premium payment by either party to the other.

Creedon *et al.* (2008) suggest that desirable characteristics for reference yield curves include:

(a) Price data used to derive the reference rate is readily available for a wide range of underlying instruments, with dates of cash flows conveniently spaced and in some cases extending far into the future to aid interpolation and extrapolation;
(b) The underlying market is typically subject to narrow bid–offer spreads, can absorb relatively large trades without these typically significantly moving prices and is subject to relatively few institutional limits on supply and demand, so that a wide range of institutions can (and do) buy, sell, borrow and lend the relevant instruments;

---

[1] The term 'Libor' is also commonly used as shorthand for the floating rate of interest earned by wholesale funds (for a given maturity and currency), where 'wholesale' means rates applicable between sizeable financial entities, as contrasted with 'retail', which would mean the rates that private individuals might get on deposit accounts with such organisations.

(c) The reference rates are widely used for pricing and for instrument definition, making it likely that the rates will be permanently available and inaccuracies or inconsistencies in their computation or definition are likely to be subject to extensive external scrutiny; and

(d) Contracts used to calibrate the reference rates are homogeneous, minimising distortions due to special contract conditions.

For a reference yield curve to be 'risk-free', it presumably also needs to be calibrated off instruments that carry little if any default risk.

It is not generally possible for any one set of instruments to satisfy perfectly all of these criteria simultaneously. For example, the broader the market is, the more likely it is that it will contain a range of credit qualities.

One reason why some commentators put forward swap rates as suitable discount rates to use when valuing liabilities for market consistent purposes is that swap rates appear to exhibit many of these characteristics. Swaps markets in most major currencies are often now large relative to other markets in other plausible types of instruments that might be used to define 'risk-free' (e.g. government debt) and are also typically more homogeneous. Swaps markets in many currencies also now typically extend a long way out into the future.[2]

(3) *The 'risk-free rate' might be deemed to be the interest rate available by investing in debt that is considered to be truly risk-free for the currency in question (typically, this involves debt issued by the government that controls the issuance of the relevant currency)*

Regulators amongst others may seek to define 'risk-free' by reference to yields available on relevant government debt. All other things being equal,[3] this typically results in a more prudent liability valuation than use of swap rates, since swap rates are typically somewhat higher than yields on government debt (at least for governments deemed to be subject to little likelihood of default).

One obvious justification for doing so is that government debt seems more naturally to fit the conventional meaning that one might expect to be ascribed to 'risk-free' for a given currency. If the government in question can issue as much of its own currency as it likes then it should be able to avoid defaulting on its own obligations in its own currency.[4] Countries do not always honour local obligations in their own currencies (e.g. Russia in the 1990s) and currencies can be devalued to nil (e.g. if there is a revolution or the country in question ceases to exist because it loses a war). But such risks are intrinsic to the currency itself (and governments can always expropriate assets denominated in their own currencies in other ways). So, as long as we understand 'risk-free' to mean as free as possible of risk of default then referring to yields on government debt is a natural way of defining 'risk-free'. However, see Section 5.3.3 for why it might not be the right way of doing so.

---

[2] However, at times during the 2007–09 credit crisis, banks largely stopped being prepared to lend to each other for as long as 3–6 months, i.e. the term interbank lending market largely dried up, raising questions about how reliable might be the 'fixings' used to derive the 3 or 6 month Libor/Euribor rates underlying the cash flows swapped in typical interest rate swaps.

[3] The 'all other things being equal' here needs to include no change to the (risk-neutral) probability distribution for the pay-off. As explained several times elsewhere in this book, one can typically compensate for any change in the assumed discount rate by a corresponding change in the risk-neutral probabilities (and vice versa), i.e. it is important to consider the two in combination rather than in isolation.

[4] The risk of default by a government (whether of their local or of their external debt) is called *sovereign risk*.

A potential disadvantage of using government debt as the reference point for defining the risk-free interest rate is that the relevant government debt market may not extend as far as is needed for valuation purposes, or may be too small to allow for reliable estimation of a yield curve.

The relevant government debt may also have been issued in forms that make extensive use of embedded options (e.g. including putability or callability elements). This can make it harder to extract a definitive yield curve from the relevant price data. This disadvantage can be circumvented if the relevant regulator prepares such a yield curve itself, which it declares to be the 'definitive' way of creating a yield curve from relevant observed market prices.[5]

Euro government debt (and debt issued by countries in other currency unions) introduces a further subtlety. Euro debt is issued by several different governments. Whilst it may not be politic to draw attention to the fact, the yields and spreads available (for the same term) differ somewhat according to the country of issuer, see Figure 5.1, part (b) of which focuses on selected Euro-zone countries. Presumably, this is in part because the market has different views on the creditworthiness of the relevant governments (although some of the differential may be linked to liquidity premia or 'convenience' yields, see below). In the event that one of the Euro governments defaulted, presumably the agreement establishing the Euro would unravel. One might expect the debt issued by that government to be redenominated into a new local currency (to the extent that it was honoured at all). It is unclear whether other Euro governments would stand behind their defaulting colleagues. Some commentators (particularly one might suspect from countries whose Euro government debt yields are higher than average) have argued that you should refer to the yield on your own government's Euro debt in such circumstances, on the assumption that your own liabilities would (in the event of unwind of the Euro) be redenominated into your own new local currency.

> **Principle P24: Debt issued by governments, even ones overseeing well-established and robust economies, is not necessarily free of risk of issuer default. Exactly how this observation should be taken into account by firms within that government's jurisdiction in relation to market consistency poses tricky business and regulatory questions.**

(4) *The 'risk-free rate' might be taken to be the interest rate available by investing in debt that is considered to be truly risk-free for the currency in question as per (3), added to which is any additional 'convenience' yield available from such debt*

In Section 4.2.1.3 we referred to the existence of a yield differential between on-the-run and off-the-run treasury bonds. Even if we wished to use government debt to define a 'risk-free' yield curve, we may therefore in principle need to work out which particular issues to consider and exactly how to interpolate/extrapolate to intermediate time points.[6]

---

[5] It can also be reduced by standardisation of technical features. This does seem to be occurring naturally. For example, inflation-linked bonds issued by different states typically nowadays adopt similar ways of incorporating inflation uplifts in coupon and principal payments.

[6] In practice, computation of yield curves is something that most market participants do not actually do themselves. Instead they implicitly contract this work out to a small number of data providers, such as Bloomberg, and merely then lift the information they need from standardised data feeds provided by such data vendors. Alternatively, they may be required to use figures specified and calculated centrally, e.g. by central banks or other regulators. The subtleties mentioned here are then implicit in the algorithms that such organisations use to calculate quoted yield curves. If these subtleties are considered likely to have a material impact on the overall answer then it behoves a user of such data feeds to understand how they are being derived and to adjust where appropriate.

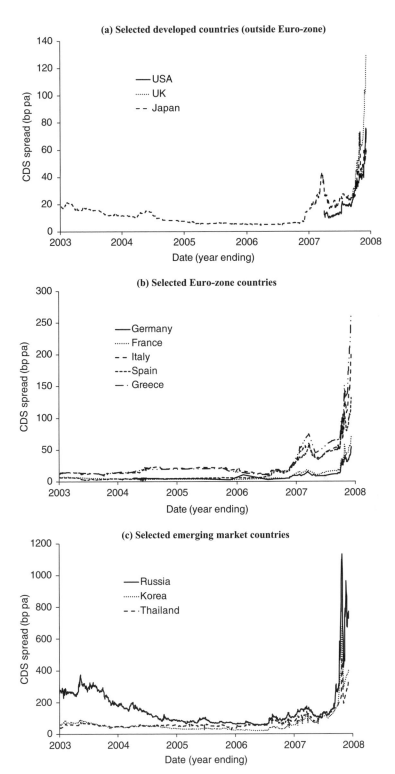

Figure 5.1 Ten year (external currency) Sovereign CDS spreads on external debt (end 2003 to 5 December 2008)
Source: Bloomberg

There is a more general point, however, which is perhaps best introduced by considering the concept of a *convenience yield*. The idea is that the mere holding or interim use of the pay-off, rather than the cash flows it ultimately generates, may have some utility in the hands of an investor. Take, for example, gold bullion. At any point in time it has a specific spot price. The majority of gold bullion in the world is closely held. However, there is also an active *stocklending* market for gold bullion. A long-term holder of gold can therefore enter into a contract with a counterparty involving the loan for a certain length of time of the gold to the counterparty, in return for which the counterparty pays the original owner a fee dependent on the length of the loan. To protect the lender against the counterparty defaulting, the counterparty must also typically pledge collateral (usually of somewhat more value than the gold originally lent). The lender can claim this collateral if the counterparty fails to honour the contract. Ignoring credit risk, if we compare the situation of a long-term investor who holds onto the gold and does nothing at all with it versus one who temporarily lends it out, we see that (ex credit risk) both involve the same ultimate pay-off (i.e. ultimate sale of the gold at some future date). However, in the meantime, the one who has lent the gold out should have picked up an additional return. The return a market participant taking advantage of this uplift can obtain by holding gold bullion can thus be decomposed into the pure price movement exhibited by the bullion plus any such stocklending fees earned (less any physical costs of actually holding/storing the bullion and losses, if any, due to the default of the entity to whom the bullion has been lent).

Most other commodities and many other financial markets have corresponding stocklending or repo markets. Active use of these markets is not merely the preserve of traditional dealers. A hedge fund may want to short a particular security, believing that it is overvalued. To do so, it would need to borrow the security from someone so that it could then sell it in the open market, buying the security back at a later date when it needs to return the security to its original owner. Or, it may ask a bank to provide it with a derivative that has an equivalent economic effect, with the bank then carrying out the same series of steps (or possibly netting off some of the steps with other transactions it is carrying out to synthesise exposures for other clients).

The differential in yield between on-the-run and off-the-run US Treasuries is an example where the concept of convenience yield is applicable even to large markets that one might otherwise think of as very liquid. Because the on-the-run treasuries are particularly liquid and particularly useful for hedging transactions, they command a premium price, and potentially carry a yield below what might otherwise be expected in relation to off-the-run issues.

The clear evidence that there is a convenience yield available on at least some government bonds raises the further possibility that there might be convenience yields available on *all* of a particular government's bonds (that happens to be somewhat larger in magnitude on particularly liquid issues, if we adopt the convention of measuring convenience yields relative to hypothetical illiquid assets). If this were the case then we could achieve a completely risk-free return (in the sense that we should only fail to get the return if the government defaults) somewhat higher than the yield directly available from holding government debt, if we could also somehow capture the convenience yield other market participants might be willing to place on such instruments.

Such a market reference rate does exist and is called the *general collateral repo rate*. For example, in the USA this would be the repo rate available on less actively traded US Treasury securities. Such securities are then known as *general collateral*.[7] In contrast, the financing rate

---

[7] Usually, the term 'general collateral' is applied to the government debt repo market. However, the term can also be used in other secured lending fields, where it then means whatever is the standard sort of collateral that might be

for some Treasury securities, typically the on-the-run ones or others that have recently been issued, is somewhat lower. Such securities are said to be *on special*, and their financing rates are referred to as *specific collateral rates*, also known as *special repo rates*. The difference between the general collateral (GC) repo rate and the relevant special repo rate is called the *repo spread*. A dealer or (tax exempt) investor holding the instrument that is on special can capture this spread, which is then called a *repo dividend*, by simultaneously repoing out the holding that is 'on special' (paying away the special repo rate) and simultaneously reverse repoing in 'general collateral' (receiving the higher general repo rate), both repos being for identical terms.

Other government debt markets also have equivalent general and special repo rates, although the bonds that are most likely to go special may not be quite so obvious. The naming convention is again that the repo rate available on the generality of relevant government debt is the GC repo rate, whilst debt that is 'on special' incurs a lower repo rate. Eurepo, the GC repo rate for Euro denominated government debt, is published by the European Banking Federation. Acceptable general collateral for it includes a range of debt instruments issued by most or all of the governments of the countries in the Euro block.[8] Rates are published for a range of time periods such as overnight, 1, 2 and 3 weeks and 1, 2, 3, 6, 9 and 12 months.

Several organisations that might be expected to be experts in such matters appear to view the GC repo rate as the closest interest rate that one can observe in the marketplace that is 'risk-free' in this sense.[9] Fisher (2002) certainly considers that the 'general collateral rate ... can be thought of as the risk free interest rate'. This also appears to be the view of the Bank of England which has apparently argued that GC repo rates should, in principle, be close to true risk-free rates. It has also noted that repo contracts are actively traded for maturities out to 1 year and the rates prevailing on these contracts are very similar to the yields on comparable-maturity conventional government bonds.

The lack of an active market in GC repo extending much beyond 1 year (at least for the Euro) does limit the practicality of using GC repo rates as a primary means of defining 'risk-free' discount rates for longer-term liabilities. It is not necessarily sound to extrapolate any spread between GC repo rates and corresponding government bond yields out into the future. The LTCM example mentioned in Section 4.2.1.3 highlights that the convenience yield differential between on-the-run and off-the-run treasuries is not necessarily stable through time. Hence, the convenience yield on either in isolation is probably not stable either. Stated central bank policy may, however, give some clues as to which other sorts of rates that do extend further out might be most likely to remain close to GC repo rates.

---

used to back the activity in question. For example, in the equity lending business the term might refer to collateral that consisted of large cap stocks that might typically be pledged when borrowing such securities, other than those where special terms applied because demand for that particular type of collateral was temporarily bid up, e.g. because of a forthcoming shareholder vote, or some dividend situation.

[8] See www.eurepo.org for further details. The European Banking Federation also publishes the Euribor rate (Euro Interbank Offered Rate), which is the rate at which Euro interbank term deposits within the Euro-zone are offered by one prime bank to another prime bank, and the Eonia (Euro OverNight Index Average) rate which is an effective overnight rate computed as a weighted average of all overnight unsecured lending transactions in the interbank market, initiated within the euro area by the contributing panel of banks.

[9] We are here and in the previous section focusing on GC (and special) repo rates relating to government debt, rather than the potentially wider range of instruments that may at any point in time be accepted as collateral by the relevant central bank (which will vary depending on the central bank in question). Once again, the Euro area presents some further subtleties here, since the general collateral in question in this instance can be issued by any one of a number of different governments, whose sovereign creditworthiness standings can and do differ.

Longer-term GC repo rates were they to exist might also not be as free from counterparty credit risk as shorter-term ones. A repo contract legally involves a sale and repurchase. At outset, the investor repoing out the bond receives cash from the dealer to whom the bond is repoed. At maturity, the cash and bond are returned to their original owners. In the meantime, if either side defaults, the other merely has the cash or bond in their possession plus an uncertain potential recovery of anything else owed to them. The credit risk exposure either party has to the other in this interim period is likely to be relatively modest for short-dated contracts. The investor repoing out the bond would acquire a credit risk exposure to its counterparty if the bond rose in value (relative to the amount of cash the investor is due to return under the repo contract), whilst the credit risk exposure would be reversed if the bond fell in value (relative to this cash amount), but for shorter-term repos the potential swings in market value are likely to be modest. However, the swings could be larger for longer-term repos, increasing the possibility that the credit exposure could be unbalanced, possibly influencing the market rate available for such GC repos. Such risks could be mitigated by use of further collateralisation techniques, see Section 4.2.2.

(5) *The 'risk-free rate' might be taken to be the interest rate available by investing in corporate/bank debt (in a given currency) less the cost of buying protection against default (in relation to obligations in that currency) of that corporate/bank (less the cost of buying protection against the provider of this protection, . . .) plus an additional 'convenience' yield available from such debt*

A possible alternative way of identifying the level at which longer-term GC repo rates 'ought' to trade would be to fall back on the principle of no arbitrage. Kemp (2005) argues that one way of identifying a hypothetical (illiquid) 'risk-free' yield curve should be to buy an (illiquid) bond of suitable maturity and at the same time to buy credit protection for the lifetime of the bond (e.g. via a credit default swap) against the risk of default of the bond issuer. To cover the possibility of the issuer and the provider of the protection defaulting together, Kemp (2005) proposes hypothetically buying further protection against just such an event from a third (unrelated) entity, etc. The risk of multiple simultaneous default should tend to zero quite quickly as this chain builds up, as long as the entities in question really are independent of each other. So, in the limit such a strategy should have zero credit risk (other than perhaps one relating to the issuer of the currency itself altering the legal standing of the currency). If the original bond potentially provided a convenience yield then we could access this by repoing out the original bond.

We might expect such a hypothetical structure to offer an exactly economically equivalent pay-off to the one described in (4), since in both cases there is no further convenience yield able to be extracted (the asset carrying the postulated convenience yield now being in the hands of the dealer to whom it has been repoed). By the principle of no arbitrage, the two should therefore have the same value.

In practice, there may be some residual risks that one might have to worry about in this type of construction, e.g. tax risk or legal or basis risk, such as the possibility that the credit default swap wouldn't actually pay out the same amount as the loss incurred when the original bond defaulted. There is also the possibility that every available protection provider defaults simultaneously. Conversely, such a computation may be 'too' risk-free to be comparable with a local currency obligation of a government. CDS spreads available in practice in the market might refer to any of a bank's obligations, not just those in a particular currency. However, governments are not deemed by the market to be risk-free in relation to their external debt, see Figure 5.1. This again highlights just how difficult it is to construct absolutely perfect arbitrages. However, if the risk exposure differentials can be kept vanishingly small then the price differential should be small too.

(6) The benchmark interest rate used to value liabilities might be associated with a deemed credit status for those particular obligations

In some areas it has become common to discount liabilities using an interest rate derived from yields on corporate bonds (typically of a particular credit rating). We should hesitate to call this anything other than a benchmark rate, because corporate bonds can hardly be called 'risk-free' given the exposure to risk of default that they carry.

For example, as at end 2007, yields available on AA rated corporate bonds provided the reference rate mandated by the UK's Accounting Standards Board (ASB) for use in valuing pension obligations for corporate financial reporting purposes in the UK.

The main rationale for discounting such liabilities at yields derived from corporate bond prices is not that corporate bonds are risk-free per se but rather that discounting at such rates reflects the economic reality that pension scheme obligations are akin to corporate debt. Indeed, in the UK they become debt obligations in the event of the sponsor winding up the pension scheme. It is then argued that they should express corporate bond style credit risk. To achieve standardisation the AA rate was chosen.

Conversely, it is less clear that individual pension scheme members, if they understood the concepts involved, would expect their future pension benefits to be no more free of default risk than AA-rated corporate bonds. They might expect a more prudent approach to be followed.

In ASB (2008) the ASB proposed abandoning the approach ruling as at end 2007 in favour of discounting using a rate that did not take into account the credit risk of the entity itself. The ASB recognised that this would increase reported liabilities. ASB (2008) contains an analysis of the pros and cons of such an approach. One particular problem that the ASB noted with the approach ruling as at end 2007 was that allowance in the calculation for some risk of default by the pension sponsor sat uncomfortably with the 'going concern' assumption that typically formed the basis of other elements of the accounts. This issue is in many ways analogous to the problem of how to place a value on the publicly traded debt of a company within that company's own statutory accounts balance sheet or to the discussion of the solvency put option in Chapter 2. However, a possible distinction is that current practice with pensions typically refers to a reference yield curve that although not risk-free is only obliquely related to the company in question rather than to a yield curve explicitly derived from the market valuations of the company's own debt.

Exactly how the ASB intended to define 'risk-free' going forwards was less clear from their document. However, it is clear that they thought that corporate bond yields could not realistically be considered to be 'risk-free' and that a 'risk-free' rate ought to be adopted for such purposes.

(7) The 'risk-free rate' might be derived by applying regression techniques to a range of instruments carrying different levels of credit risk to derive a hypothetical estimate of the yield on corresponding zero credit risk instruments

A 'puzzle' that has taxed the minds of many commentators in the context of (6) is that average spreads on instruments subject to credit risk actually observed in the marketplace appear to overcompensate for average likely future default experience (if the past is a reasonable guide as to what might happen in the future).

We might therefore postulate that the credit spreads (versus government debt) exhibited by instruments carrying different credit exposures can be decomposed into several components only one of which relates to 'real' credit risk as such. If so, we can then seek to estimate this component in isolation using, say, regression techniques. By excluding it we might then be able to derive a benchmark rate believed to be free of just credit risk.

For example, the spread on a suitable reference corporate bond (or index) might be decomposed into the following components:

(a) *Credit risk.* This might be considered to refer to just the actual likelihood of default of the issuer (probably averaged over an appropriate credit rating bucket, and probably derived from historic default rates, perhaps adjusted somewhat for where we might be in the economic cycle, particularly if the bond in question had a term not likely to span a complete economic cycle).

(b) *The yield premium that appears to be credited to investors willing to bear the risk of uncertainty in (a).* The existence of such a hypothetical reward to investors might be inferred from the extent to which yields typically exceeded reasonable best estimates of actual levels of default that a diversified basket of credits of equivalent rating might be expected to experience.

(c) *Liquidity.* This might merely be a catch-all name given to whatever is left over that we cannot explain in such a regression analysis. Or, it might be an explicit component whose existence is postulated because government bonds are typically far more liquid than most corporate bonds, in the sense that the market for them is much larger and deeper. In essence, it would be argued that part of the yield premium available on corporate bonds is due to their relative illiquidity. A further subtlety with this line of argument is that many types of liabilities for which we might wish to calculate market consistent valuations might be viewed as even less liquid than a typical corporate bond (in the sense that there may be little if any way in which individual policyholders or pension scheme beneficiaries can 'trade' their benefits), and so we might hypothecate an even higher illiquidity 'premium' to apply to such liabilities. Whether this approach is intrinsically logical is explored further in Chapter 6.

(d) *A residual element,* unless this is included in (c), to cater for, say, the extra costs of managing corporate bonds.

Examples of such analyses are given in Webber and Churm (2007), updated in Bank of England (2008b) and Bank of England (2008d), see Figure 5.2(a), and in Wilson (2008), see Figure 5.2(b). Both of these analyses sought to identify the compensation for expected default losses using a 'firm value' (i.e. Merton style) model for credit spreads, see Section 4.8.

The Bank of England (and other commentators) drew the conclusion in mid-2008 from this and other analyses that market prices for some credit sensitive instruments had overshot prices that incorporated a 'reasonable' allowance for the 'intrinsic' likelihood of defaults applicable to such instruments. This is close to saying that they believed that the market had overreacted.

For the period of overlap between the two charts in Figure 5.2, the two studies appear to reveal similar spread decompositions. The precise methologies involved are described in Wilson (2008).[10] We note that the *percentage of the total spread* explained by the residual, i.e.

---

[10] Both analyses appear to involve estimating levels of debt consistent with bonds of various terms and credit rating to match expected (real world) default probabilities to historical data given observed historical volatilities. The Bank of England analysis uses the Leland and Toft extension of the Merton model (allowing for bond coupons and defaults prior to maturity), but the main differences between the two analyses appear to be that the Bank of England analysis assumes higher fixed bankruptcy costs and lower volatility parameters.

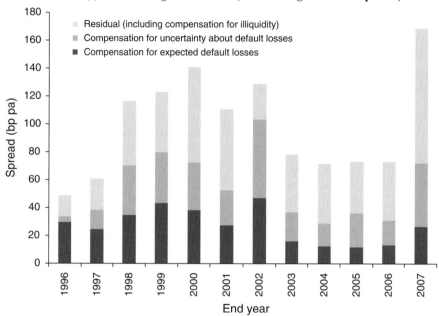

(a) Years ending 1996 to 2007 (investment grade credit spreads)

Legend:
- Residual (including compensation for illiquidity)
- Compensation for uncertainty about default losses
- Compensation for expected default losses

Y-axis: Spread (bp pa)
X-axis: End year (1996–2007)

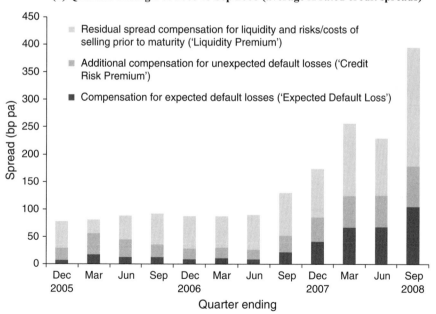

(b) Quarters ending Dec 2005 to Sep 2008 (average A rated credit spreads)

Legend:
- Residual spread compensation for liquidity and risks/costs of selling prior to maturity ('Liquidity Premium')
- Additional compensation for unexpected default losses ('Credit Risk Premium')
- Compensation for expected default losses ('Expected Default Loss')

Y-axis: Spread (bp pa)
X-axis: Quarter ending (Dec 2005 – Sep 2008)

Figure 5.2 Decomposition of average corporate bond spreads into different elements
Source: (a) Webber and Churm (2007), Bank of England (2008d); (b) Barrie & Hibbert

the element most commonly deemed to be the 'liquidity premium' element, is more stable (20 to 60 % in the Bank of England analysis, 30 to 70 % in the Barrie & Hibbert analysis) than its *size in absolute terms* (c. 15 to 100 basis points per annum in the Bank of England analysis, to end December 2007 and c. 25 to 216 basis points per annum in the Barrie & Hibbert analysis to end September 2008).

A slightly different type of analysis, but one seeking much the same end, is described in Jarrow *et al.* (2007). Their paper postulated a statistical or econometric style model for CDS spreads and then sought to model observed spreads (for the period 2 January 2004 to 3 November 2005) using regression techniques applied to a range of explanatory variables relating to estimated default probabilities and recovery rates. Their model appears to explain quite a high proportion of the variability in CDS spreads over that period. However, they conclude that a significant proportion of CDS credit spreads is not explained by the typical variables that are used to characterise default probabilities and recovery rates. They note that this omission is consistent with the importance of omitted liquidity issues and market microstructure effects in CDS markets.

Such approaches appear to offer a way of decomposing spreads into a number of different components. They are thus particularly favoured by commentators who believe that market consistent liability valuations should include equivalents relating to some but not all of these elements. For example, some commentators argue that it is reasonable to include in market consistent valuations of illiquid liabilities (such as annuities) an allowance for the illiquidity inherent in such liabilities. To do so in practice requires some way of quantifying in spread terms the impact of illiquidity. We explore this topic further in Chapter 6.

However, others note that what we are trying to do in such an analysis is to disaggregate elements that are most probably hopelessly and inevitably entangled,[11] because there is just one market observable (i.e. a bond's spread) that covers all of these contributory elements. If a bond was subject to zero default risk (i.e. (a) was zero) then there would also almost certainly be zero uncertainty in future default exposure (i.e. (b) would most probably also be zero) and probably little liquidity risk either, meaning that the elements in the above decomposition are very strongly co-integrated.[12] Novy-Marx (2004) notes that in such analyses any contribution ascribed to 'illiquidity' is normally merely a proxy for *any* unobserved risk. It may not therefore correspond to what we might consider 'ought' to be deemed to correspond to (il)liquidity in the context of the problem at hand, see Section 6.5.

---

[11] To be more precise, the complaint is that the spread cannot be 'objectively' decomposed into different elements in such a manner, at least not in the same sort of 'objective' manner exhibited by other sorts of market consistent valuation computations. Any analysis along the lines of Webber and Churm (2007), Bank of England (2008b) or Jarrow *et al.* (2007) is inevitably 'subjective', in the sense that the end answers are likely to depend on subjective choice of explanatory variables and on a number of other inputs needed in their definition (and/or on the past time period used within the analysis). In contrast, an option implied volatility is in principle objectively ascertainable (if the relevant market were deep, liquid and transparent enough). We don't in principle need to make any subjective assumptions in its determination; we merely need to agree a quotation convention.

[12] Commentators do occasionally try to identify liquidity premia directly, e.g. by comparing the yield on a standard government bond issue and one for a less liquid bond not issued by the government but carrying a government 'guarantee', in much the same way as we indicated when introducing the concept of convenience yields in Section 5.2(4). However, some (or all?) of this spread may reflect the possibility that the relevant government might honour some of its obligations but not others. For example, if the 'guarantee' is merely implicit, presumably there is a real risk that if the government were itself to run into financial trouble then it would only honour the debts that it really had to, to the extent that it honoured any at all.

(8) *Some variant of one or more of the above*

As at end 2007, the UK's FSA mandated in insurance company solvency calculations the use of government bond yields when discounting liabilities, but in practice seemed comfortable to allow insurers to increase these rates by c. 5–10 basis points per annum to reflect, inter alia, the increased liquidity of government bonds.

5.3 CHOOSING BETWEEN POSSIBLE MEANINGS OF 'RISK-FREE'

5.3.1 Real world or market consistent?

We can discount for this purpose the meaning ascribed to 'risk-free' in Section 5.2(1) (i.e. its use to differentiate one input assumption from another in a pricing formula). This usage does not by itself help to identify how to source any given rate. However, it does remind us that with more complicated instruments there may be subtleties regarding how to interpret different model input parameters.

The regression approach set out in Section 5.2(7) is a more interesting suggestion. My own view is that it is also *not* appropriate for market consistency (even if it is an approach worth exploring further as a potential source of ideas for profitable active investment management). The approach in essence involves decomposing the (current) observed spread into a part that is believed to reflect the correct 'real world' level of credit risk being expressed by the bond, i.e. (a) (or (a) plus (b)), plus a remainder.

My choice of terminology here, i.e. to describe the decomposition as ultimately akin to a 'real world' approach, is deliberate. In Section 3.5 we saw how inclusion of 'real world' elements within a pricing basis could give rise to answers that were far away from market consistent ones. There, the type of risk involved was market risk. It is not obvious why use of 'real world' approaches should be any more reliable when applied to credit (or liquidity) risk. In practice, commentators wishing to adopt such a decomposition within regulatory capital computations often want to do so because it reflects their view of how to incorporate liquidity premia in such computations. The implicit logic being adopted is that credit risk (or elements thereof) should be differentiated from liquidity risk in such computations. We discuss this topic in more depth in Chapter 6.

Principle P25: Different market participants may place different interpretations on what should be meant by 'risk-free' rates because they may be interested in rates that exclude some risks but not others. It is important that the underlying logic justifying selective inclusion of certain types of risk is soundly based, because it is often difficult to demarcate precisely between different types of risk.

5.3.2 Choice between different reference rates

The remaining ways of interpreting 'risk-free' all involve seeking to identify suitable market observables from which to extract more directly rates that are deemed risk-free. The most appropriate choice of market observable to use typically involves some interplay between theory and practice.

The theory can best be established by referring back to the conceptual model of regulation set out in Section 2.8. The model involved conceptually viewing any financial services entity as if it were a CDO with at least two liability tranches, namely an equity tranche and one belonging to customers. Computation of regulatory capital was then equated with assessing how big the equity tranche needed to be to ensure that the fair spread (versus the 'risk-free rate') on the customer tranche was no greater than a certain level.

Within such a framework, the discount rate is more the end product of, rather than an input into, the capital computation. However, the conceptual model does ascribe a natural meaning to the term 'risk-free rate', namely, the interest rate that one would expect to apply to the customer tranche of an infinitely well-capitalised entity. If the government responsible for issuing the currency in which the customer liability was denominated was of undoubted creditworthiness then this would presumably equate to the GC repo rate applicable to that government's debt, i.e. Section 5.2(4) or some no-arbitrage equivalent for longer terms, i.e. Section 5.2(5). As noted in Section 5.2(4), several central banks seem to share this view.

However, practicality might favour use of swap rates, for the sorts of reasons given in Section 5.2(2). It is therefore worth exploring briefly why swap rates might deviate from the 'risk-free' rate defined above, and whether the deviation in practice is sufficiently material to worry about.

Nowadays, swap contracts are typically collateralised, i.e. collateral flows between the two parties in a way that aims to reduce the credit exposure one party might build up to the other counterparty.[13] This means that there is typically relatively little *direct* credit risk *between* the two specific counterparties involved in the swap transaction.

However, this does *not* mean that swap rates are free of *all* credit risk. Typically, the floating rate payments involved in the swap contract derive from some short-term interest rate that is readily observable in the marketplace, e.g. 3 month or 6 month Libor (or in the case of Euro swaps, Euribor). Take, for example, two otherwise identical swaps, in one of which the floating rate payment is defined using 3 month Libor and in the other the floating rate payment is defined (somewhat unusually) as 3 month Libor $+ x\%$ pa. If the 'fair' swap rate on the former that equates the fixed and floating rate legs is $s\%$ pa then the corresponding fair rate for the latter will be $(s + x)\%$ pa (assuming suitable annualisation conventions, etc.). All other things being equal, the swap rate includes an *indirect* credit risk exposure relating to the credit exposure implicit in the reference floating rate used within the swap.

In the past, interbank deposit rates have often been assumed to express relatively little credit risk and might therefore have been viewed as a suitable approximation to a 'true' risk-free rate as expressed by, say, the GC repo rate. However, such an assumption became less sustainable during the 2007–09 credit crisis.

Consider, for example, the behaviour of several different types of Euro interest rates. In Figure 5.3 we show spreads between the 1 month Euro GC repo rate (Eurepo), the 1 month Eonia[14] swap rate and the 1 month Euribor rate. The Euribor rate is the rate for 1 month interbank unsecured loans and therefore we might expect the spread between it and Eurepo

---

[13] This form of collateralisation is called 'two-way' collateralisation. 'One-way' collateralisation involves only one side posting collateral to the other. It used to be more prevalent, particularly if at the time that the contract was initiated one side of the swap transaction was perceived to be much more creditworthy than the other side.

[14] Eonia is the effective overnight reference rate for the Euro. It is computed as a weighted average of all overnight unsecured lending transactions undertaken in the interbank market, initiated within the Euro area by relevant contributing banks. Eonia is published by the European Banking Federation. A similar overnight reference rate called Euronia is published by the Wholesale Markets Brokers' Association. On average, Eonia was c. 4 basis points per

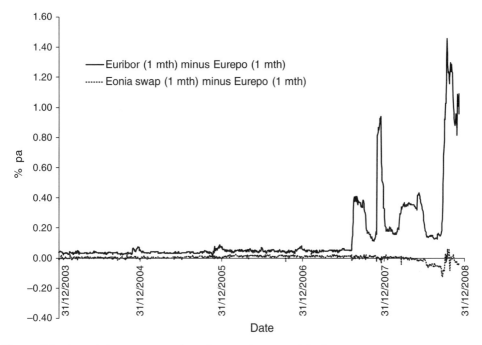

Figure 5.3 Spreads between 1 month Eonia swap, Eurepo and Euribor rates
Source: Bloomberg (end 2003 to 5 December 2008)

to reflect the differential credit risk between unsecured and secured interbank lending. After July 2007, this spread exhibited a strong term structure, see Figure 5.4.

Conversely, over most of this period there has rarely been much spread between 1 month Eurepo and the 1 month Eonia swap rate (other than close to the end of the period, see Section 5.3.3). This is also true across the term structure (of the underlying floating rate) from 1 week to 1 year, see Figure 5.5, except for occasional apparent discrepancies on individual days (perhaps due to short squeezes or the like).[15]

A justification for the different characteristics of Euribor and Eonia swaps in this respect is given by Creedon *et al.* (2008). It is there called the 'refresh effect'. Consider the positions of two synthetic bond investors, one that rolls over semi-annual deposits in conjunction with a 6 month Euribor-based swap and one that rolls overnight deposits in conjunction with a Eonia-based swap. Both are exposed to the risk of default of the bank with whom they hold the

---

annum higher than Euronia for the first five months of 2008, probably principally reflecting the different bank panels applicable to the two rates.

[15] In times of crisis there appears to be a desire by central banks to keep overnight rates relatively close to central bank rates. For example, on 17 March 2008 around the time of the near collapse of Bear Stearns, a major US investment bank, the Bank of England held an 'exceptional fine-tuning Open Market Operation' offering GBP £5bn of extra reserves in a 3 day repo maturing when the regular weekly short-term Open Market Operation would next take place. In the same communication the Bank indicated that it would 'take actions to ensure that the overnight rate is close to the Bank Rate', see Bank of England (2008a).

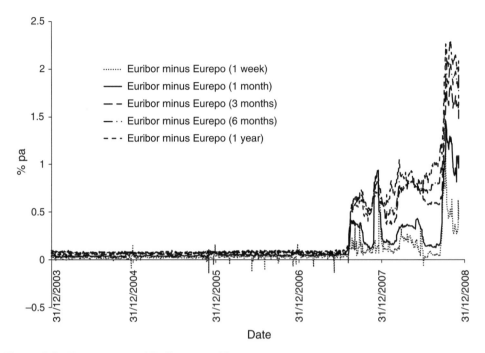

Figure 5.4 Term structure of Euribor versus Eurepo
Source: Bloomberg (end 2003 to 5 December 2008)

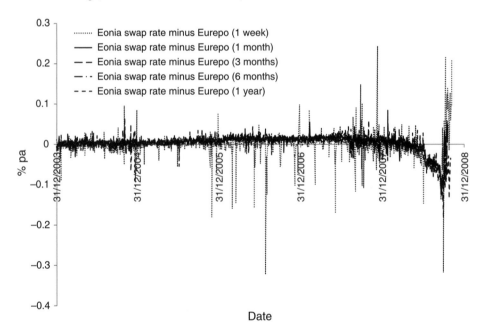

Figure 5.5 Term structure of Eonia swap versus Eurepo
Source: Bloomberg (end 2003 to 5 December 2008)

deposit. Banks (like other entities) ultimately default (if at all) on some particular day. However, bank failures in practice are rarely entirely overnight affairs. Usually, a bank's difficulties will feature in the news for at least several weeks prior to collapse. The Euribor-based investor is still exposed to the bank failure unless he is fortunate enough to have one of his rolling deposits mature during the window between bad news appearing and subsequent collapse. In contrast, the Eonia-based investor typically has time to switch elsewhere.[16]

The fundamental issue with use of swap rates as reference 'risk-free' rates can thus be encapsulated in the beguilingly simple question: *'Which swap rate?'*

The market could, if it so wished, have developed a truly 'risk-free' swap rate by arranging for the floating rate of interest on such swaps to be in line with a readily available short-term truly 'risk-free' interest rate. This idea is perhaps one of the reasons why the European Banking Federation has launched Eonia swap rates.

Unfortunately, longer-term swap rates typically quoted in practice do not necessarily incorporate floating rates that are as apparently free of credit risk as Eonia. For example, as at end February 2008, swap rates (out to 30 years) available from the *Financial Times* market data pages (source ICAP plc) involved the following conventions: 'bid and ask rates are as of close of London business. US $ is quoted annual money actual/360 basis against 3 month Libor. £ and Yen quoted on a semi-annual actual/365 basis against 6 month Libor, Euro/Swiss Franc quoted on annual bond 30/360 basis against 6 month Euribor/Libor with the exception of the 1 year rate which is quoted against 3 month Euribor/Libor.'

Whilst historically the difference between such swap types might have been perceived to be modest, it is less easy to make such a claim at the time of writing in 2008, see Figure 5.4. Some fixed income strategists, e.g. those from Barclays Capital according to Financial News (2008), have argued that investors wishing to gauge the relative value of different types of bond instruments should do so not only relative to Libor/Euribor but also relative to overnight index swap rates.

Indeed, such is the magnitude of the difference between these two possible definitions of swap rates that at the time of writing some commentators are even floating the not obviously very practical idea of rebasing existing swap agreements away from Libor or Euribor onto other 'cleaner' reference floating rate bases such as Sonia, Eonia or equivalents in other currencies.[17] More plausible is that market practice will result in a move away from Libor/Euribor towards Sonia/Eonia type swaps for transactions entered into in the future. It is interesting to note that in June 2008 Bloomberg started to make available Eonia swap rates for 20 and 30 year

---

[16] There is an echo here back to the discussion on derivative pricing in Chapter 4. There are two conceptually different kinds of bank failure, namely, those where build up to failure involves a 'visible' state variable, i.e. you would in principle know about the failure an instant before it happens, and those where it is 'hidden', i.e. the failure appears to you to have come completely out of the blue. Structural models of default are often driven by a Brownian motion applied to a firm's assets, with default triggered when assets fall below a certain barrier level. Such defaults in principle have a 'visible' driving state variable (i.e. are 'previsible') which can warn us in advance if default is just about to happen. Conversely, reduced form models of default typically incorporate no such underlying driving variables, and failure is thus less easy to see in advance. In the continuous time limit (probably closely approximated by overnight index deposits), the refresh effect should protect you against the former sort of default but not the latter. Therefore, in theory it ought to be possible to test which model type is more accurate by reference to how, say, Eonia compares with Eurepo.

[17] Sonia is the Sterling market equivalent of Eonia. Like Euronia it is published by the Wholesale Markets Brokers' Association. More generally, an overnight index swap (OIS) is an interest rate swap agreement where a fixed rate is swapped against a predetermined published index of a daily overnight reference rate, such as Sonia or Eonia, or equivalents in other major currencies such as US dollar OIS.

terms, making it no longer correct to assume that data on overnight index swap rates were only available for relatively short maturities.

Some of the commentary around this topic has also questioned whether 3 or 6 month Libor rates were necessarily being reliably 'fixed' (i.e. determined) in market conditions where few interbank deposits were being placed for such long durations given the mechanisms used in these fixings (which typically merely require the bank to indicate where they would strike such deposit rates if asked to do so), see e.g. Rule (2008) and Financial Times (2008c). Another concern aired was that these fixes were organised by the British Bankers' Association and relate to a specified panel of banks identified by the BBA, which might not therefore be representative of US banks operating in the US dollar interbank market.

Principle P26: Practitioners should not assume that swap rates contain no element of credit risk premium merely because the two parties to a swap may be protected from each other's default via collateralisation techniques. The main way in which swaps incorporate a credit risk element is indirectly, via the way in which the interest payable on their floating leg is defined. If practitioners wish to use swap rates to derive 'risk-free' rates then they should adjust observed swap rates by the market implied credit risk implicit within the underlying floating rates.

A practical complication for anyone wanting to follow Principle P26 is that any such adjustments may not compound uniformly over time. Suppose that the floating rate leg of a 5 year Sterling interest rate swap involved 6 month Sterling Libor.[18] Suppose also that 6 month Sterling Libor currently carried, say, a 30 basis point per annum spread to 6 month Sterling GC repo. Unfortunately, it is not then necessarily correct to assume that the implied forward spread between 6 month Sterling Libor and 6 month Sterling GC is 30 basis points throughout the term of a 5 year swap, and hence that the rate applicable on such a 5 year swap should be 30 basis points per annum higher than the corresponding 5 year Sterling GC repo rate, were such a rate to be observable in practice.

5.3.3   How risk-free is government debt?

A perhaps even bigger practical challenge with all of the above is hinted at by the divergence between Eonia and Eurepo that appeared in late 2008 (albeit comparatively modest compared with the divergence between either and Euribor rates), see Figure 5.3. The equivalent discrepancy between Sonia and Sterling GC repo was considered sufficiently anomalous to be explicitly referred to in Bank of England (2008d).

The Bank of England in Bank of England (2008d) observed that, over a long period, secured borrowing rates (secured on highly creditworthy assets such as GC repo) have typically traded close to rates on equivalent-maturity overnight index swap contracts, since both are considered to reflect minimal risk premia and hence to provide a close read on risk-free interest rates. It observed that any liquidity premia in OIS rates were likely to be small, since OIS are derivatives that involve no exchange of cash at inception of the trade. It therefore concluded

---

[18] The term 'Libor' is so widely used in a generic sense that one should also be slightly careful about currency, unless the context makes this obvious. Strictly speaking there is no 6 month 'Libor' rate as such, rather there are 6 month 'Sterling Libor', 'US dollar Libor', … rates (one for each currency) and these of course in general differ because interest rates in different currencies differ.

that the divergence was most likely to reflect liquidity premia due to conditions in the cash and/or collateral markets. Some of their market contacts suggested that strong demand from banks and securities dealers for secured borrowing might have boosted liquidity premia in secured borrowing rates. There also seemed at the time to have been increased activity in trades that exchanged government collateral for more risky trades, via tri-party repo. Some other of their market contacts suggested that the increased availability of government collateral (via, for example, in the UK, the Special Liquidity Scheme) might have meant that relatively more government collateral was available for use in repo, thereby increasing repo rates. The Bank of England noted that this latter logic might also explain the somewhat wider spreads between Sterling secured rates and gilt yields that were also observed in the latter part of 2008.

Perhaps a more obvious, if more troubling, reason for this divergence was increased market concern about the longer-term creditworthiness of the governments of major developed countries, as highlighted in Figure 5.1(a). Another apparent anomaly had appeared at about the same time as the divergence referred to above, at the long end of the Sterling yield curve. By November 2008, yields on long-dated Sterling-denominated UK government debt had started to trade higher than GBP Libor swap rates (and GBP OIS rates), see Figure 5.6. Figures 5.7 and 5.8 show that similar developments had occurred at the long end of the Euro and US Dollar yield curves, to the extent that long-dated OIS swap rates were observable there. A common market interpretation for this anomaly (in the UK) at the time was market pressures arising from liability driven investment strategies implemented by UK pension funds.

However, the differential between, say, the 30 year yield on UK government debt and the 30 year Sonia swap rate shows a strong correlation over time with the 10 year sovereign

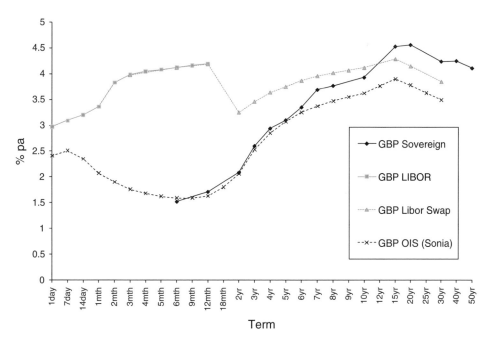

Figure 5.6   Different Sterling yield curves as at 24 November 2008
Source: Bloomberg

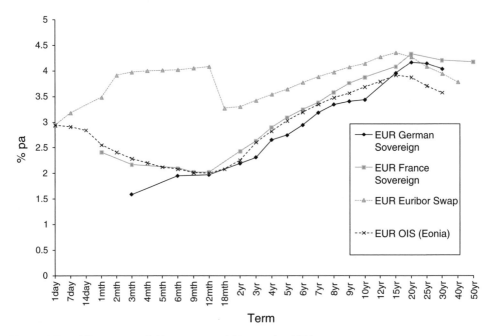

Figure 5.7 Different Euro yield curves as at 24 November 2008
Source: Bloomberg

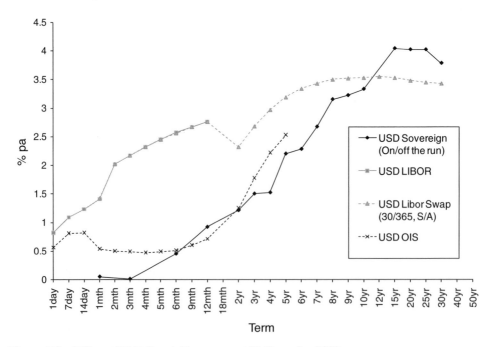

Figure 5.8 Different US Dollar yield curves as at 24 November 2008
Source: Bloomberg

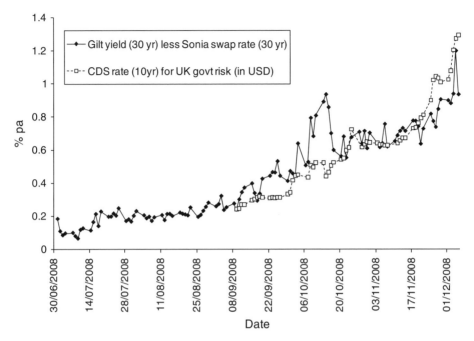

Figure 5.9 Comparison between UK government bond (gilt) spread over GBP OIS swap rate (Sonia) and CDS rate on UK sovereign risk (to 5 December 2008)
Source: Bloomberg

CDS spread on the UK government, see Figure 5.9. The corresponding spread on German government debt versus Eonia swap rates also shows a reasonable level of correlation with the market implied creditworthiness of the German government, see Figure 5.10.

How should we interpret 'risk-free' when government debt is not itself considered by the market to be risk-free? As Creedon *et al.* (2008) point out, there are a number of ways in which government bonds can be economically in default while legally honouring their terms, because governments write the law. For example, governments can introduce new types of taxes on coupon or capital, or impose conversion of one bond for another, less valuable, one, etc.

The differential present in late 2008 between long-dated government yields and OIS rates appears to imply that markets were then attributing a non-zero market implied probability to these governments rewriting the rules at some stage in the future, altering downwards previously ruling coupon rates (or principal amounts outstanding) on some or all of their then outstanding long-term debt in ways that did not create corresponding downward revisions in money held in bank accounts accruing overnight interest rates. These restructurings, if they were to occur, might perhaps be similar to those arising from the Brady Plan of the 1980s and 1990s (or other more recent equivalents). These involved conversion of defaulted bonds issued principally by Latin American countries into new (dollar-denominated) bonds with either lower coupon or lower principal amounts but typically incorporating greater guarantees of payment perhaps via additional collateral, etc.

Other possible contributory explanations to this apparent anomaly (and for why it seemed to persist) are given in Smith (2008).

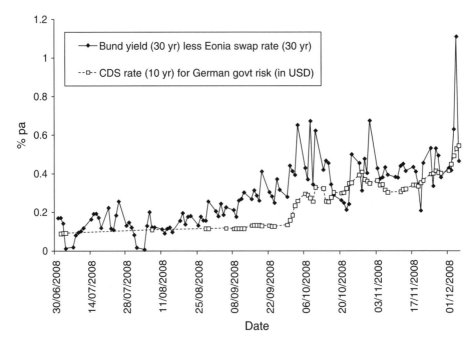

Figure 5.10 Comparison between German government bond (Bund) spread over Euro OIS swap rate (Eonia) and CDS rate on German sovereign risk (to 5 December 2008)
Source: Bloomberg

Firms that have entered into long-dated fixed liabilities and matched them by purchasing corresponding government bonds should therefore be asking themselves what would happen if these governments defaulted. If their own customer liabilities fell commensurately (e.g. because they related to the market values of assets in a unit-linked fund) then the firm would presumably be able to pass on the impact of any such market value declines to their customers. However, if the liabilities were fixed in monetary terms then the negative financial impact might fall to the firms themselves.

5.3.4 Impact of choice of reference rate

The choice of how to define the risk-free reference rate will probably remain contentious for some time. For some liquidity types and in some market conditions the impact on valuations can be large. In Figure 5.11 we show the spread between Euribor swap rates and Eonia swap rates. For long durations the spread appears to diminish, but this is partly because the rates are annualised. We therefore in Figure 5.12 quantify approximately the impact (at different times) of using Euribor swap rates rather than Eonia swap rates for payments of different durations. For simplicity, for any given duration we have ignored variations in the term structure of either Euribor or Eonia interest rates. The present value of a liability payable in T years time, discounting at Eonia swap rates, divided by the corresponding present value discounting at

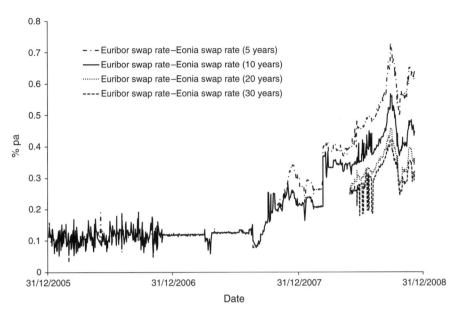

Figure 5.11 Spread between longer-term Euribor swap rates versus longer-term Eonia swap rates for different floating rate terms
Source: Bloomberg

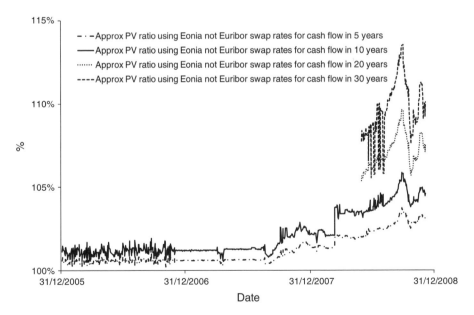

Figure 5.12 Approximate present value differential between discounting at Eonia swap rates and discounting at Euribor swap rates
Source: Bloomberg

Euribor swap rates, if i_{Eonia} is the Eonia swap rate (per annum) and $i_{Euribor}$ is the Euribor swap rate, is then approximately:[19]

$$V_{ratio} = (1 + i_{Eonia} - i_{Euribor})^{-T} \qquad (5.1)$$

In November 2008, the differential for cash flows of a 20 or 30 year swap using this computation was c. 5–15 %, i.e. non-trivial. As we have already noted above, at a similar time, long-dated government bond yields in the Euro-zone, UK and USA were trading above corresponding Libor/Euribor swaps, so the differential between discounting at government bond yields and OIS swap rates would have been larger (for long-dated liabilities) and larger still for discount rates derived from corporate bond yields.

> **Principle P27: Choice of methodology for determining risk-free rates can have a significant impact on the value placed on long-term liabilities.**

---

[19] See e.g. Kemp (2009) for an analysis of more accurate ways of extrapolating present values from swap yield curves.

6

Liquidity Theory

6.1 INTRODUCTION

The extent to which individuals or markets as a whole focus on particular types of risks at particular points in time is strongly linked to how much the particular risk is in the public eye. Turbulence and lack of liquidity in worldwide money markets during 2007 and 2008 sharply focused attention on liquidity risk, including the crucial role that adequate access to liquidity plays in the effective functioning of the banking sector and related markets.

Liquidity has a very direct interaction with market consistency. If all assets and liabilities that financial entities might hold were readily traded on deep, liquid and transparent markets then carrying out market consistent valuations would be conceptually quite straightforward. All that you would need to do is to source price data from these markets and then apply these prices to the assets and liabilities actually held by the entity in question. It is when markets are not deep, liquid and transparent that challenges arise.

We noted in Section 3.4 that even the phrase 'deep, liquid and transparent' can be open to interpretation, but the basic emphasis is that of a market where participants can relatively easily trade in the instrument in question and can do so in size without moving the price very much. In this chapter we explore *liquidity theory*, i.e. the underlying principles involved in understanding such concepts. We then apply these insights in later chapters to identify how to take account of liquidity (or lack of it, i.e. illiquidity) when seeking market consistency.

It is worth bearing in mind that liquidity theory is a less well-developed branch of financial economics than some other risk disciplines. This can be inferred from its relative lack of prominence, say, in Basel II, where it does get some mention but much less than market or credit risk and its mention is mainly in the context of stress testing. The Basel Committee sought to address this potential imbalance in subsequent documents setting out additional principles applicable to liquidity risk management, see e.g. BCBS (2008). National regulators are also focusing increasing attention on these risks, see e.g. FSA (2008b).

6.2 MARKET EXPERIENCE

Lack of adequate access to liquidity, it can be argued, was the proximate cause of the collapse or near collapse of Bear Stearns, a US investment bank, in early 2008 and several other banks later on in 2008, as well as a large US insurer, AIG. Following the US government engineered rescue of Bear Stearns by JP Morgan, rules were changed so that US investment banks could access government liquidity assistance to a similar extent to that available for US commercial banks. However, this did not stop Lehman Brothers collapsing later in the year and the other main US investment banks converting to commercial bank status.

Even larger, perhaps, were the rescues of Fannie Mae and Freddie Mac, two US government sponsored entities at the heart of the US housing mortgage market. It can be argued that their need for rescue arose not because their own paper had become illiquid. Rather, they had become overburdened with illiquid credit risk, a reminder that credit and liquidity risk are very closely intertwined.

In the UK, a particular focus of attention during 2007 and early 2008 was Northern Rock, a medium-sized bank with a prime residential mortgage book, which experienced a bank 'run' (the first material run on a bank in the UK for many years). Its business model, which was predicated on access to funding from wholesale money markets, came unstuck and it called on the Bank of England for emergency liquidity assistance. After attempting to find a private buyer, the UK government nationalised Northern Rock in early 2008. In late 2008, Bradford and Bingley, another UK bank that had previously been a building society, collapsed, triggering a call on the UK's Financial Services Compensation Scheme (FSCS). At around the same time, as interbank lending dried up across the world, several other European and US banks also collapsed, were rescued by their governments or relevant government-sponsored bodies or were taken over to prevent collapse.

In December 2007 the FSA published FSA (2007), a discussion paper that aimed to review some of the lessons that were already becoming clear early on in the 2007–09 credit crisis regarding managing and regulating banks' liquidity, and to set out some preliminary ideas for reform. Points noted in FSA (2007) included:

(a) A bank's role in financial intermediation, i.e. transforming the maturity of short-term deposits into longer-term loans, makes it inherently susceptible to the risk that creditors' demands for repayment may outstrip the bank's ability to liquidate its assets. Banks thus rely on ready access to the money and asset markets, where liquidity is reallocated from banks with surplus liquidity to those with liquidity needs. A number of other participants in financial markets face similar exposures even if they are not explicitly involved in this maturity transformation.

(b) In an orderly, transparent and well-functioning market, adequately capitalised entities ought always to be able to obtain additional liquidity, since they ought then to be able either to liquidate assets as needed or to borrow funds against such assets, to meet their debts as they fall due.

(c) However, this may be obstructed by market failures. These market failures may be specific to the entity seeking liquidity, e.g. asymmetric information leading to uncertainty about a participant's true net worth and hence an unwillingness by others to lend them funds. Or they may be more generalised, e.g. because of a more widespread uncertainty which leads to a wide range of market participants hoarding liquidity due to uncertainty about their own needs (including those who might normally be expected to be providers of liquidity). This may limit the market's willingness to reallocate liquidity at prices that seem commensurate with the risks involved, or even at all.

(d) A fundamental driver of prudential liquidity requirements is how the country's central bank generally supplies domestic currency, either to the market as a whole or to individual banks unable to satisfy liquidity needs in the market. Generalised activity by the relevant central bank in this sphere can, usually, be differentiated from a central bank's specific role as 'lender of last resort' (known in some jurisdictions as 'emergency liquidity assistance' or ELA), since usually the stigma attached to explicit access of such a backstop lending facility is considerable and may in itself trigger a 'run' or loss of access to other sources of liquidity.

(e) Usually, but not always, diversification of liquidity sources is desirable. However, banks active in more than one currency should be aware that market circumstances can arise in which it is difficult for a bank to use liquidity sourced in one currency to meet liquidity needs in another currency.

(f) Events in 2007 highlighted that even banks that appeared otherwise solvent could suffer liquidity problems. Creditors may be uncertain about a bank's solvency position, and so may be unwilling to lend to it, even though it may be fundamentally solvent. Even if creditors do not doubt that it is solvent they may doubt that it has sufficient access to liquidity and so may be worried that if they advance it short-term funds then they may not be repaid in a timely manner. This worry may be compounded if there is a general seizing up of money markets, and hence a tendency towards hoarding of liquidity by those who might otherwise have been expected to be willing to advance funds. A 'run' can thus be self-fulfilling. In trying to generate cash to repay creditors a bank may suffer losses (from 'fire-sales') that it would not otherwise have incurred. Moreover, once a 'run' has started, or even if one is merely feared, it may be individually rational for creditors to 'run'.

(g) Management of liquidity involves a trade-off. Typically, assets that are easier to liquidate, or more readily acceptable as collateral when borrowing funds from other market participants (and/or from a central bank), may be expected to generate lower rates of return than assets less effective for these purposes, because their presence on a bank's balance sheet mitigates liquidity risk.

(h) There are some features of liquidity risk that seem to differentiate it from other sorts of risk. First, liquidity risks can grow in severity very rapidly. Second, it can be very hard to predict, because it is dependent not only on a bank's own internal liquidity needs, but also on the extent to which there is more general appetite to advance liquidity. Generalised liquidity shortages are often associated with panics and herd behaviour, and hence it can be very hard to assess probability of occurrence from historical data.

Based on the FSA's observations, particularly those in (g) and (h) above, we may expect illiquid assets to carry a yield premium. The size of this yield premium could potentially vary significantly depending on the liquidity 'climate'. We might also expect a high proportion of this illiquidity premium to constitute recompense for carrying liquidity risk in 'extreme' scenarios. This means that the illiquidity premium is likely to have characteristics somewhat akin to a strongly out-of-the-money option. Its 'market consistent' level (if it can be observed) is therefore likely to be materially different to what the generality of investors might think represents the 'real world' likelihood of occurrence of the relevant liquidity risks. Investors willing to forego such yield premia presumably place a large negative utility on the sorts of outcomes in which these risks materialise and are prepared to pay handsomely for not being left with these risks on their own books.

Liquidity premia may therefore be difficult or impossible to differentiate from premia that investors presumably also demand for carrying exposure to uncertain systematic default experience. This highlights the point made in Section 5.2(7) that disentangling these contributions to the observed spread on an instrument may be very difficult if not impossible.

Principle P28: Liquidity risk tends to show up only in extreme scenarios. But in such scenarios it can grow in severity very rapidly and can then be strongly influenced by the overall liquidity market 'climate' as well as by a firm's own internal liquidity needs.

6.3   LESSONS TO DRAW FROM MARKET EXPERIENCE

6.3.1   Consideration of 'extreme' events

Lessons that FSA (2007) suggested could be drawn from the liquidity shortages experienced during the second half of 2007 included:

(a) The need for firms to carry out liquidity stress tests that encompassed both firm-specific and market-wide stresses. The FSA had already introduced the concept of liquidity stress testing into its regulatory framework, bearing in mind the difficulty of analysing in a statistical fashion some factors influencing liquidity.[1] Firm-wide stress tests might involve, say, the firm suffering a multi-notch credit ratings downgrade, or some other impairment to the firm's reputational ability to access a particular funding source. Implicit assumptions about there being a low correlation between firm-specific and market-wide stresses or between stresses in shorter and longer-term markets should be questioned, since they would not have correctly reflected experience during 2007.[2] The FSA also thought that market-wide stress tests should:
   - Include disruptions to both primary sources of liquidity and to secondary ones, e.g. secured funding markets such as the secured finance repo market; and
   - Encompass both one-off 'shocks' that relatively quickly revert to 'normal' as well as more 'chronic' market failures, e.g. extended partial or total closure of a particular market over multi-month periods.

(b) Diversification of funding source is an important mitigant of liquidity risk, but does not always prove effective, e.g. in late 2007 diversification across wholesale deposits, corporate paper, certificates of deposit, secured finance such as repo, covered bond and securitisation, etc. only proved to be of limited use. All of these markets can become impaired simultaneously if there is extensive enough liquidity hoarding.

(c) Off-balance sheet vehicles (such as conduits and Structured Investment Vehicles, see Section 7.6) do not necessarily remain stand-alone in times of market stress, given the reputational (and legal?) risks that a bank may face if these vehicles are not brought back onto the bank's own balance sheet in such circumstances.

(d) During more generalised market-wide stresses liquidity scarcity can be particularly concentrated on assets where banks are particularly prominent purchasers in normal times, given the propensity of banks to hoard liquidity in times of stress.

(e) Assets held in a bank's treasury for liquidity purposes that are complex and thus potentially difficult to value can become particularly difficult to value (or to sell) and hence less effective at providing liquidity in times of market stress, since their effectiveness for this purpose depends in part on how credible is the valuation placed on them. If present in large quantities, difficult to value assets may bring into question just how solvent the firm might be, causing a firm-specific liquidity problem. This highlights a strong link between liquidity and trading costs such as bid–offer spreads.

(f) Some market participants wishing to access liquidity sources with which they were not familiar found that this could be operationally challenging, due to lead times involved in

---

[1] Liquidity stress testing is also mandated by Basel II, see Chapter 8.

[2] Or, it turned out, the even larger liquidity stresses some banks faced in late 2008 when a significant number of leading banks across the globe needed to be rescued by their respective governments.

implementing the appropriate operational practicalities, e.g. sorting out audit/rating agency reviews, legal documentation, etc. The FSA's view appeared to be, as a generalisation, that a bank that is not used to raising liquidity from a particular asset type prior to a liquidity stress is unlikely to find it easy to do so during a stress (at least not in a timely manner) even if the relevant market is open.

(g) Perhaps less obviously, during the second half of 2007, firms that held liquidity lines with other private sector firms proved extremely reluctant to call upon them (and arguably the same applied to some of the liquidity lines being offered by central banks). According to FSA (2007), there appear to have been two linked reasons. First, there seemed to be a perception that if a bank was actually seen to draw on these lines then this might be seen as a sign of weakness, making it more difficult for the bank to draw on other lines, possibly more than negating the help to liquidity that the original draw might otherwise have offered. Second, there appeared in some cases to have been a strong commercial expectation that the line would not be drawn, perhaps again because of the reputational damage that doing so would create. Paradoxically therefore, liquidity 'promises' (by which we mean legally binding pre-commitments to a bank or to a bank's off-balance sheet vehicle(s) to provide liquidity if called upon to do so) may have been less effective during this period at managing liquidity risk than liquidity 'facilities' (by which we mean agreements that allow but do not compel a counterparty to lend to the bank in similar circumstances), because of the lesser stigma attached to exercising the latter type of facility. Some of this stigma seemed subsequently to fall away when central banks introduced generalised liquidity assistance schemes deliberately designed to be used by wide swathes of the industry.

6.3.2   Or maybe not such extreme events?

Some commentators have argued that the banking crisis of 2007–09 was depressingly familiar. For example, the Economist (2008), reporting on Rogoff and Reinhart (2008) as presented to an American Economic Association meeting, suggested that, although details may vary, banking crises typically seem to follow a similar script, which this one also followed. Their thesis is that each such crisis is preceded by rising home and equity prices; an acceleration in capital inflows driven by optimistic foreign investors; a rapid build-up of debt; and an inverted V-shaped path for the economy, with growth first picking up and then faltering.

Brunnermeier (2008) expresses a similar opinion, noting that 'while each crisis has its own specificities, it is surprising how "classical" the 2007–08 crisis is'. He notes that an increase in delinquencies in sub-prime mortgages triggered a full-blown liquidity crisis, primarily because of a mismatch in the maturity structure involving banks' off-balance sheet vehicles and hedge funds. The only element that he thought was really 'new' was the extent of securitisation, which made more opaque (and more difficult to value) the exposures that firms had to credit and counterparty risk, creating additional spill-over effects.[3]

---

[3] Brunnermeier (2008), like several other writers, has chronicled in detail developments in the 2007–09 credit crisis (up to a point in time prior to the collapse of Lehman Brothers, the US government rescue of Freddie Mac, Fannie Mae and AIG, the passing into law in the USA of the Troubled Asset Relief Program and the bank rescue arrangements instigated by several European countries in October 2008). For example, he describes the way in which investment banks' financing became more dependent on overnight financing in the years prior to the crisis (noting

6.3.3 Contagion

Turbulence in one market often unsettles other markets. The banking crisis of 2007–09 was again true to form in this regard. The knock-on turbulence can be at the overall market index level, if the contagion involves larger-scale economic uncertainties. Or, it can be more security specific, if the contagion takes more subtle forms.

For example, a sudden jump in uncertainty in money markets and credit markets in late July and early August 2007 probably led to loss of risk appetite and a reining in of leverage that banks were willing to extend to certain active quantitative hedge fund managers. A few large such funds then unwound some of their positions. This led to knock-on unwinds by quant funds more generally, because these funds had grown significantly in prior years and had more commonality in their types of active positions than many of them had appreciated. In the hedge fund world this type of syndrome is often called a 'crowded trade'. Crowded trades are, of course, not limited to quantitative fund managers; one could, for example, argue that the dot-com boom and bust during the late 1990s and early 2000s was ultimately a crowded trade (and subsequent unwind), just one that rather a large number of investors crowded into at the time.

As might be expected, the August 2007 travails of quant fund managers generated a fair amount of analysis, particularly amongst quant researchers themselves. Some of this research has included arguments linked to liquidity. For example, Emrich and Crow (2007) point out that active investment strategies all involve the attempted identification and exploitation of mispricing in the market. Such mispricings mean that investors are hoping to receive more than fair compensation in exchange for taking on certain risks. In almost all cases (private equity being a possible exception), the compensation is received when a position that was taken based on a perceived mispricing is unwound. They note that this means that active investment decisions can be viewed as *liquidity provision* strategies – positions are taken on in expectation of a P&L-positive unwind later, when the mispricing has been corrected.

A corollary is that the level of liquidity prevailing in a particular market is likely to be linked to the extent to which different market participants are willing to express (and change) their active views on instruments being traded within that market. Thus active portfolios such as hedge funds (and bank proprietary trading desks run on similar principles) can be significant providers of liquidity, and if they collectively rein in their risk appetite (e.g. because their own investors start pulling money from them) then this can have a leveraged impact on liquidity for everyone else.

---

that almost 25 % of their total assets were financed by overnight repos in 2007, an increase from about 12.5 % in 2000). He expresses forthright opinions about incentives that encouraged markets to develop in ways that would make them more exposed to liquidity risk, e.g. the incentives banks had to expand their use of SIVs (including CDOs and money market conduits) due to regulatory and ratings arbitrage, the 'ratings at the edge' and other behavioural characteristics of banks and ratings agencies that in tandem may have devalued the appropriateness of credit ratings awarded to paper issued by such SIVs, and the willingness of other market participants such as asset managers and end investors to 'look the other way' because it may have suited their own business goals to do so. His view is that these factors collectively resulted in credit becoming extremely cheap, causing credit spreads to shrink to historically low levels, leading to a private equity boom (boosting value stocks, hence boosting quant funds which often had a bias towards such investments), etc. As a result, his view is that no single player had an incentive to derail the system (as is typically the case in all such bubbles). He exemplifies this by the now oft repeated words ascribed by FT (2007) to Chuck Prince, Citigroup's former CEO, when referring to Keynes' analogy between bubbles and musical chairs, namely, 'When the music stops, in terms of liquidity, things will be complicated. But as long as the music is playing, you've got to get up and dance. We're still dancing.'

Hayes (2007) also believes that the pattern of quant equity returns during August 2007 (involving a dramatic sell-off in long positions and a simultaneous rally in short positions, followed quickly by a significant retracement of these moves) indicates a technical, liquidity-based explanation for the turmoil.

6.4 GENERAL PRINCIPLES

A problem that we face is that the term 'liquidity' has many different connotations. For example, the markets in which the quant funds referred to above were invested were not classically 'illiquid'. By this we mean that it was not difficult for the funds in question to buy or sell assets. Indeed, many of the positions could be easily traded, and in some instances volumes traded were higher than normal! The issue (for the funds in question) was that trades were happening (for funds on the wrong side of the 'crowded trade') at prices significantly less favourable than where they might have been only a short time before.

However, we do still seem to be able to draw out the following general principles:

(a) Liquidity risk mitigation has an intrinsic economic benefit, and hence cost. Banks are prepared to accept lower interest rates on some assets that they hold, because these assets facilitate their access to liquidity. They are also prepared to pay preferential interest rates to certain depositors if the terms on which these deposits are made reduce the likelihood of these depositors withdrawing their funds at an inopportune time. The liquidity characteristics of particular assets and liabilities can therefore be expected to influence their market values, particularly if trading in them is strongly driven by market participants sensitive to such issues.

(b) Whilst the particular maturity transformation activities focused on in earlier parts of this chapter are principally (but not exclusively) the province of banks, it is likely that other types of market participants have similar liquidity needs. Therefore, we should expect that the market prices placed on other instruments will also be influenced by their liquidity characteristics.

(c) The effectiveness of a holding as a means of accessing liquidity, if needed, depends in part on how credible others believe its valuation to be, which we might potentially proxy by some assumed bid–offer spread that it might exhibit. Hence, illiquidity premia can in some sense be thought of as options expressing the risk that the hypothetical (variable) bid–offer spread (including market impact) on the asset or liability in question might become very wide in times of stress. This links to Principle P9 in which we noted that preparing market consistent valuations may require not just a view to be formed about the price at which one might reasonably expect an asset or liability to trade were a market to exist for it, but also a view on the bid–ask characteristics that one might reasonably expect such a market to exhibit.

(d) If markets were perfect, then organisations known to be economically solvent would be able to access whatever liquidity they needed when they needed it. So, liquidity premiums are to some extent costs incurred by organisations because markets are (or are believed to be) imperfect and/or because there is uncertainty in the financial health of the entity seeking funding. Liquidity premiums can be expected to exhibit strong option-like characteristics, since they involve an option-like protection against the risk that markets might become materially less perfect at an inopportune time. They are therefore likely to vary significantly depending on the liquidity 'climate'.

The challenge is that whilst most commentators seem to agree that some types of highly liquid assets seem to command a 'liquidity' *price* premium and some less liquid assets ought to command a corresponding 'illiquidity' *spread* premium, there is much less consensus on:

(a) What precisely we mean by the term 'liquidity' and what the (illiquidity) premium actually consists of, i.e. what exactly it is recompensing the investor for;
(b) What impact, if any, such issues should have on market consistent valuations; and
(c) Even if it is thought that (il)liquidity premia should influence market consistent valuations how to work out the size of the relevant premia in the first place.

In the rest of this chapter we explore these challenges further.

6.5   EXACTLY WHAT IS LIQUIDITY?

6.5.1   Different points of view

Brunetti and Caldarera (2006) define liquidity as 'the ability to trade quickly any amount at the market price with no additional cost'.

This definition, simple though it seems, actually hides a divergence of viewpoints on what exactly liquidity is in the first place. Essentially, we can characterise liquidity in several different ways all staying within the spirit of the above definition:

> **Principle P29: Liquidity is a concept that is quite complicated to pin down (and therefore to measure). Emphasising some elements of the concept over others can materially influence how much (il)liquidity premium we might expect different instruments to exhibit.**

(1) *Liquidity can be viewed as largely a single 'universal' market factor that some instruments have more of and some have less of*

The most obvious way in which such a view can arise derives from Section 6.4(b), if we focus on liquidity as relating to the time that it might take to find a willing seller (if we wanted to buy) or a willing buyer (if we wanted to sell) with whom we can transact at a willing buyer/willing seller price (or from/to whom we can raise/lend cash using the security as collateral).

'Liquidity', understood in this manner, is then largely a single universal characteristic, being essentially derived from the future time line itself, which is universal for all market participants and instruments.[4]

A corollary of this interpretation of liquidity is that illiquidity in assets and illiquidity in liabilities ought in principle to net off against each other, since each is travelling in the same direction along the same time line. For example, if we have a bond with a fixed redemption date or a liability cash flow with a known payment date, we know (ignoring default risk) that

---

[4] Readers who have a physics background may spot that in making such a claim we have ignored insights arising from Einstein's theories of relativity, which indicate that in certain circumstances one observer's interpretation of time can differ from another's. Readers particularly interested in exploring this analogy further might note an echo within FSA (2007) to the effect that liquidity in one location does not always easily translate to liquidity in a different location.

however illiquid the instrument might be prior to maturity we will be able to find a willing buyer or seller no later than the maturity date. This is because the bond or liability payment will redeem at maturity, and thus will automatically be realised, if it is still on our books, at par. Hence, from this perspective, any current 'illiquidity premium' expressed by a given asset is a 'free lunch' as far as the firm holding these assets or liabilities is concerned, as long as assets and liabilities are sufficiently well 'matched'.[5]

(2) *Alternatively, liquidity can be viewed as more market or instrument specific, deriving from uncertainty in the instrument's own bid–offer spread*[6]

The basic premise here derives from Section 6.4(c) and views wider bid–offer spreads (or greater market impact,[7] which can be thought of as akin to an implicit bid–offer spread) as an indication of poorer liquidity (or perception of potential poorer liquidity). The greater the uncertainty in the likely evolution of the instrument's bid–offer spread and the greater the size of this spread, the larger the illiquidity premium we might expect would apply to the instrument in question, assuming that typical market participants are risk-averse.

Whilst there probably are systematic elements that apply across major market segments (witness developments in the 2007–09 credit crisis in which liquidity fell across most or all credit markets simultaneously), such a perspective would not view illiquidity in assets and liabilities as necessarily netting off against each other. Indeed, the two might even be expected to have opposite signs and thus compound. If you had to liquidate both assets and liabilities in the near term then you would need to 'sell' the assets and 'buy' the liabilities back (or settle them on someone else by paying them something), so exit-to-mid spreads would be suffered on both sides of the balance sheet.

(3) *Some mixture of (1) and (2)*

Most probably, real life lies somewhere between these two extremes. For example, if matching is good enough and the bonds are sure to mature before the liabilities fall due (if they do not default in the meantime) then at least one-half of the full bid–offer spread should be avoided, because the bonds will mature at par not at par less the mid-bid element of the spread.

---

[5] By (cash flow) matching, we mean arranging for the cash flows generated by assets and liabilities to coincide in relation to both timing and underlying economic exposure. The concept is widely referred to in actuarial literature, and is also, for example, referred to in Basel II.

[6] 'Bid–offer spread' is here shorthand for all transaction-specific effects that might influence market price dynamics, including 'market impact' and 'market depth'.

[7] The 'market impact' of a trade is an estimate of the impact that the trade itself has on the price of the relevant security, as other market participants react to the new information implicit in any particular trade. The larger the trade, the larger, usually, is the market impact as a percentage of trade size, although this percentage may be relatively insensitive to trade size changes within a wide range of sizes deemed within the range of 'normal' bargain size. The total cost of a trade can therefore be thought of as the sum of any taxes (such as stamp duty), any explicit bid–offer spreads, any commission payable to brokers and any market impact. Market impact is difficult to identify for any one trade in isolation (e.g. was the price changing anyway as the trade was executed?) but can be estimated statistically for a suitably large sample of trades by identifying the typical price movement occurring between the start and end of the trade execution. Market impact is often the largest single contributor to the total cost of a trade (particularly in markets that use an order matching process, since the explicit bid–offer spread may then be zero). Some trading strategies incur more market impact than others. For example, a momentum trading strategy typically buys as the market is temporarily rising and sells when it is temporarily falling, and thus may suffer higher market impact than other trading strategies.

This assumes that the entity is not somehow forced to liquidate (or to assume that it might have to liquidate) both sides prior to maturity (e.g. to meet some regulatory requirement), see Section 6.6.

(4) The term 'liquidity' may also be used as a shorthand for other well-recognised economic exposures

An example would be use of the term 'liquidity' to refer to short-term borrowing costs. If an entity needs rapid access to cash and it cannot raise the sums needed from asset sales or the equivalent then it will need to borrow the cash it needs from some other entity.

In such a context, 'liquidity' may be equated (at least for banks) with spreads on interbank interest rates (versus, say, corresponding risk-free rates on short-dated government debt). It can thus be said that we had a 'liquidity' crisis in 2007 and 2008 because Libor/Euribor rates were high versus Sonia/Eonia (and GC repo rates). However, others might describe this spread as reflecting the short-term market implied credit risk applicable to deposits with the relevant panel(s) of banks underlying Libor or Euribor. This highlights once again the extreme difficulty of untangling 'liquidity' risk from 'credit' risk, at least in the short-dated interbank market.

6.5.2   Funding versus market liquidity

Brunnermeier (2009) also characterises liquidity into two types, which loosely but not exactly correspond with (1) and (2) above. He calls them *funding liquidity* and *market liquidity*. This subdivision also appears in Malz (2003), although he calls the latter *asset liquidity*.

Brunnermeier views funding liquidity as relating to the ease with which expert investors and arbitrageurs can obtain funding. So, funding liquidity is high, and markets are said to be 'awash with liquidity', when it is easy to borrow money, either uncollateralized or with assets as collateral. He subdivides risks relating to this type of liquidity into three sub-categories, *margin funding risk*, *rollover risk* and *redemption risk*, all of which he views as ultimately arising from the maturity mismatch that can exist between a purchased asset and its funding.

In contrast, in his terminology, market liquidity is high when it is easy to raise money by selling the asset (instead of borrowing against it), i.e. when selling the asset does not depress the sale price too much. The literature seems to distinguish between three sub-forms of such liquidity, namely:

(a) *Bid–offer spread* (how much money will traders lose if they sell a unit holding and immediately afterwards buy it back?);
(b) *Market depth* (how many units can traders sell, or buy, at the current bid, or offer, price without moving the price further?); and
(c) *Market resilience* (if the price drops temporarily due to trading activity, how long will it take to bounce back?).

Brunnermeier (2008) highlights different ways in which the interaction of market and funding liquidity can cause liquidity to evaporate very rapidly. He focuses on *loss spirals* and *margin spirals*. Loss spirals arise because lenders typically require borrowers to put some of their own capital at stake before lending them money, to reduce moral hazard. As the value of the borrower's assets falls, their net worth also declines, reducing the amount that they can borrow, hence forcing them to sell more.

Moreover, whilst we might perhaps expect such distressed selling to provide attractive investment opportunities for others, such loss spirals are often also associated with increased margins and haircuts, i.e. margin spirals, meaning that lenders may also at the same time reduce the amount that they are prepared to lend per unit of underlying net worth (potentially across most or all market participants simultaneously), leading to further forced sales. He suggests that margin spirals may be rationalised by higher expected future volatility (particularly for structured products such as CDOs, whose value depends on the correlation structure of the underlying assets), increased information asymmetries and non-rational behaviour by lenders.

A subdivision between funding and market liquidity has also been introduced into Basel II, see BCBS (2008) or Davidson (2008). In this context, 'funding' liquidity is defined as 'the risk that a firm will not be able to meet efficiently both expected and unexpected current and future cashflow and collateral needs without affecting either daily operations or the financial conditions of the firm'. Meanwhile 'market' liquidity is defined as 'the risk that a firm cannot easily offset or eliminate a position at the market price because of inadequate market depth or market disruption'.

6.5.3   The impact of these different points of view

Researchers have attempted to quantify the impact of liquidity and therefore the likely magnitude we might expect to see for illiquidity premia. The majority of these analyses appear to have focused on equities, presumably because they trade on recognised exchanges. This makes it easier to obtain reasonably reliable estimates of statistics like volumes traded, frequency of transactions, price spreads, etc. that are often used as proxies for measuring liquidity. However, it does also potentially limit the relevance of these studies to the sorts of markets most immediately affected by the 2007–09 credit crisis, i.e. credit and money markets.

The likely magnitudes of liquidity premia that these studies appear to predict seems to depend heavily on which of the two meanings for liquidity given in Section 6.5.1 is the one the researcher is most focusing on in the analysis.

This is illustrated by Longstaff (2005). He develops a stylised model of a continuous-time economy with more than one (i.e. two) assets and more than one (i.e. two) heterogeneous agents. The agents have identical (logarithmic) utility functions but differ in their subjective time discount factors, so agents can be classified as 'patient' or 'impatient' according to the sizes of these discount factors. Assets are also in essence split into two types. Liquid ones can always be traded. In contrast illiquid ones can be traded at outset but thereafter only after some fixed horizon or trading 'blackout' period. Such a model is therefore subscribing to the 'liquidity is a universal factor linked to the time line' type of viewpoint.

Longstaff develops a quasi-analytical solution to the way in which such an economy should price the two assets. It includes elements relating to the expected 'intrinsic' returns and volatility/uncertainty dynamics for each asset and assumes that both agents act rationally. Using this solution he comes up with some indicative magnitudes of effects that introduction of illiquidity of this sort might be expected to create.

He concludes that effects relating to illiquidity are potentially large and very economically significant, i.e. have first order impact on the clearing prices applicable to each asset. He argues that these effects extend not just to the prices of the two assets but also to how much each agent would optimally hold in each (and hence on the expected observed returns and price volatilities of the two assets). He presents examples in which a liquid asset can be worth up to 25 % more than an illiquid one with otherwise identical cash flow dynamics. Longstaff worries that these magnitudes are implausibly large, although he quotes a number of other papers that appear to suggest that illiquidity effects can be this large in practice.

Conversely, Acharya and Pedersen (2005) develop a model in which liquidity is characterised by the existence of variability in the bid–offer spread through time. Whilst they also conclude that liquidity effects can potentially be large enough to be economically significant, the magnitudes of the effects that they predict appear to be substantially smaller than the ones that Longstaff appears to be coming up with, for plausible sizes of bid–offer spreads and instrument terms.

Others like Brunetti and Caldarera (2006) seek to apply econometric analysis (regression techniques) to different equity sectors, postulating the existence of liquidity discount factors applying to different instruments. Das *et al.* (2003) provide a further review of the literature in relation to liquidity and bond markets.

Decomposing liquidity between a funding and a market component as per Brunnermeier (2008) highlights the practical importance that leverage levels can have on liquidity evolution. However, assets will only provide effective collateral for funding purposes if they have a clearly realisable value were their market funding characteristics to be tested. The investor does not at the time actually need to suffer a bid–offer spread. However, the wider the bid–offer spread lenders think might apply to the asset, the more expensive will be collateralised funding secured against such an asset (or the greater the haircuts demanded). So, to some extent we end up with a similar conceptual picture, even if we slice up the definition of funding slightly differently.

6.5.4   Modelling liquidity premia on different instruments

What all of these commentators seem to agree upon, although they do not articulate this agreement as such, is that liquidity premia are heavily linked to how uncertain might be the evolution of the future price dynamics of the instrument in question. This becomes of particular importance when we try to infer what liquidity premium we ought to include in market consistent values of insurance liabilities or other types of liabilities that rarely if ever trade in practice.

In the UK, market practice in this respect has been significantly influenced by Webber and Churm, see Bank of England (2008b) and Section 5.2(7). This study, like Brunetti and Caldarera (2006), seeks to decompose observed spreads (but here relating to corporate bonds) into different elements, some of which may be associated with liquidity. Despite this study not explicitly identifying any specific figure for the liquidity premium applicable to corporate bonds (the study merely estimates the size of a 'residual' component, part of which is assumed to relate to liquidity), market practitioners have used its results to justify a material liquidity premium add-on to apply to the discount rate used to value illiquid insurance liabilities, such as annuity liabilities. Given the long-term nature of these liabilities, such an add-on materially reduces the value placed on these liabilities, see Section 5.3.4.

In essence, practitioners appear to have adopted a model in which spread (versus government bonds) is built up as follows. In this formula, c_s is the (corporate bond) spread we are attempting to explain, c_d is the 'pure' credit default risk to which the bond is exposed (including, presumably, an adjustment to cater for the possibility of a recovery in the event of default), c_u is a 'credit uncertainty' risk element (i.e. the spread investors presumably want as compensation for being exposed to uncertainty in how big c_d actually is), and l_a is the additional spread investors require to compensate for the instrument's illiquidity, i.e. uncertainty in how much the investor might receive in practice when selling the instrument versus the theoretically correct price that would apply were the bond's price merely to be driven by the 'credit' and 'credit uncertainty' components:

$$c_s = c_d + c_u + l_a \tag{6.1}$$

Whilst such a model has a simple and hence appealing form (and produces answers that market practitioners find convenient), it arguably contains an important methodological flaw. It assumes that contributions to spread are *additive*.

More plausible, given the analysis set out above, is a model which is mainly *multiplicative*, i.e. has the following form. Here c_d and c_u are the same as above, c_y is a convenience yield adjustment described below and l_m is the multiplier that we apply to $(c_d + c_u)$ to derive the liquidity risk element. In such a model, the greater the 'credit' risk that an instrument expresses, the greater is assumed to be its potential exposure to liquidity risk. However, we might also ascribe possibly different values to l_m at different times and for different types of instrument (in part depending on prevailing leverage levels of market participants most active in the market for the instrument in question). Arguably, we can also claim support from Bank of England (2008b) and Wilson (2008) for such a model, given that the 'residual' term in Figure 5.2 (which is the term that market practitioners typically associate with 'liquidity') appears to be roughly one-half of the total corporate bond credit spread at both start and end of the period under analysis.

$$c_s = c_y + (c_d + c_u) \times (1 + l_m) \tag{6.2}$$

An additive term in the form of a convenience yield adjustment, c_y, is included in the model to cater for convenience yield effects of the sort described in Section 5.2, to the extent that it is not already included in the base yield against which the spread is being determined.[8] These are additive rather than multiplicative, because it is the same issuer (i.e. the government, for GC repo) that provides the different bonds in question.

Principle P30: It is virtually impossible to measure the price or value that the market places on liquidity in isolation, because most or all market observables that might incorporate that value depend on other risks that also cannot themselves be observed in isolation. Whilst it is tempting to seek to measure proxies and to extrapolate from their behaviour in 'normal' market conditions, the validity of such extrapolations may be limited because liquidity risk manifests itself most in 'stressed' market conditions.

6.6 LIQUIDITY OF POOLED FUNDS

Investors in pooled funds such as mutual funds, UCITS and unit-linked life insurance contracts typically receive payouts that are largely or wholly determined by the assets held in relation to these liabilities. We should therefore expect any liquidity premium in the assets to carry

---

[8] In other words, if the spread is relative to the GC repo rate (or some deemed proxy, e.g. OIS, see Chapter 5), then c_y would presumably be zero. However, it is more common for spreads to be quoted relative to the yield on a reference government bond or government bond index, in which case there would typically be a positive convenience yield, which in normal conditions is likely to be relatively small.

through to the liabilities, unless there are situations where the vehicle provider might provide a liquidity backstop.

Units in such funds can usually be surrendered on demand, creating a need for payment from the fund to the investor typically within at most a few days. Exceptions may apply where the underlying assets are relatively illiquid (e.g. property, i.e. real estate). It is common (although not universal) for providers of such funds to reserve the right to delay payment for some time (potentially several months or even longer), whilst sufficient assets are liquidated in an orderly fashion to meet redemption requirements. These exceptions are typically justified to investors on the grounds that such restrictions should reduce the likelihood of the fund being a forced seller, and therefore potentially only realising assets at firesale prices, to the detriment of all unit holders.

Ordinarily, the liquidity characteristics of the underlying assets flow through to the end investors, so one can still identify market consistent valuations for such liabilities for solvency and other purposes directly from the valuation of the underlying assets.

However, in some cases such an assumption may prove inaccurate. For example, the fund provider may feel for reputational reasons that it cannot turn off the liquidity tap (e.g. because no competitor has ended up in a similar position). It may then find that it has to take onto its own balance sheet[9] the illiquid exposures. In such circumstances the liabilities in question do not have the same liquidity characteristics as the assets. There is a mismatch, which might either appear within some deemed market consistent valuation placed on the provider's liabilities or within additional capital requirements it might wish or need to set up to protect itself against the possibility of such a mismatch.

Switching to an orderly liquidation of assets when redemptions exceed immediately available or accessible cash resources and then spreading the impact across the unit-holder base can also come unstuck if the fund makes more aggressive use of leverage, as might be the case for some hedge funds. There are many different types of hedge funds. However, most of them:

(a) Are particularly focused on delivery of alpha (i.e. outperformance);
(b) Respond rapidly to market events. Hedge funds typically seem to behave as if they operate to a faster internal 'clock' than more traditional portfolios. Investors typically accept a shorter track record before investing, but are correspondingly less forgiving of a short-term performance downturn;
(c) Take sizeable positions, often employing leverage and shorting; and
(d) Use sophisticated and potentially relatively illiquid instruments. Hedge funds are constantly innovating in order to keep one step ahead of the competition, but this means that their portfolios are perhaps more likely to behave in unexpected and idiosyncratic fashions.

Leverage affects this mix in a variety of ways:

(a) It can magnify upside (which is normally the main rationale for its use by hedge funds) and downside;
(b) It can introduce risks not present in other more traditional sorts of portfolio. These include *lender liquidity risk* (i.e. the entity lending to the portfolio to implement the leverage

---

[9] Assets in unit-linked life insurance funds are normally already 'on balance sheet', but ring-fenced in accounting terms so that policyholders invested in such funds receive benefits linked to the behaviour of the assets within the fund. In this instance we mean by 'taking onto its own balance sheet' the insurer using its own shareholder capital to buy the assets off the relevant unit-linked fund.

may become unable or unwilling to continue to support the leverage, or may be willing to do so only at a significantly increased cost), *forced unwind risk* (i.e. the funding arrangements may only be available alongside terms that require automatic unwinding of positions in certain adverse circumstances, potentially locking in poor returns) and *variable borrow cost risk* (i.e. the market rates for the type of borrowing in question may rise unexpectedly);[10] and

(c) It seems to be linked to an increased risk of fat tails, i.e. extreme outcomes seem to become more common, see Chapter 8, which may materially magnify the impact of some of these additional risks.

Forced unwind risk can be particularly problematic, since it is a normal part of most prime brokerage arrangements and of derivative master agreements that such funds use to implement investment views. Hedge funds may therefore find that it is not their investor base who turn off the liquidity tap but other parties with whom they themselves have contracts. If such third parties turn on a fund, this may trigger the equivalent of a 'run' by the fund's own investors.

Hedge funds do attempt to limit this risk by, for example, use of 'side pockets' (that only specified investors may be invested in) to hold particularly illiquid assets, or 'gates' or other investor redemption deferral mechanisms. However, actually triggering redemption deferral clauses in a hedge fund's governing documentation may have a catastrophic impact on the fund's viability not dissimilar in practice to the impact that a 'run' on a bank might create.

Principle P31: Pooled funds may give the appearance of providing customers with additional liquidity, even for intrinsically less liquid assets. However, this appearance can prove ephemeral in stressed circumstances. If a firm offering such funds cannot pass on this illiquidity to its customers in such circumstances then it may need to include in its own balance sheet a (negative) market consistent value relating to this liquidity mismatch.

6.7 LOSING CONTROL

There is another important reason why we should be wary of the logic that implies that we can place a lower value on illiquid liabilities if we can deem them to be well matched by appropriate illiquid assets. Such logic depends on the arguably unwarranted assumption that the firm will not be an involuntary seller in the meantime.

Consider the situation where a firm has only a small exposure to illiquid assets and liabilities of the sort for which this type of argument is being advanced, and that this liquidity risk is 'independent' of other types of risk to which the firm is exposed.[11] By 'small' we mean that the evolution of these assets and liabilities by themselves has a negligible impact on the way in which the firm as a whole develops.

---

[10] Another risk that some (equity) hedge funds found to their cost when Lehman Brothers defaulted related to the common practice of rehypothecating the hedge fund's assets into the name of prime broker. This made it very difficult to work out what they were actually then exposed to, hindering effective portfolio management.

[11] Strictly speaking the argument that follows relates to the marginal impact of such assets and liabilities, which will also depend on their correlation with other risk exposures within the portfolio, and we assume 'independence' to allow us to ignore this second order effect.

We can subdivide the future evolution of the firm into two camps. Either the firm defaults or it doesn't. In neither case, given the small size of the illiquid assets/liabilities in question, do the behaviour of these assets and liabilities make any (material) difference to whether or not the firm defaults.

The logic set out in Section 2.8 indicates that solvency capital requirements ought to be aiming to establish an amount of capital needed to achieve a given (market implied) level of protection for customer liabilities. Derivative pricing theory as set out in Chapter 4 indicates that this can be found (in a market consistent manner) by averaging customer losses weighted in line with the risk-neutral likelihood of those losses occurring. In the example above we see that the *only* future paths that have a non-zero contribution to this figure are the ones where the company ends up defaulting and we have also just concluded that the realisation or not of such paths will be essentially independent of how we value these marginal illiquid assets and liabilities.

To put it another way, because we are seeking a quantum of capital sufficient to provide adequate protection *against* firm defaults, we are only interested in outcomes that are extreme enough to result in default.

We should thus take credit for any supposed illiquidity premium when valuing liabilities *only* if we expect the firm and/or its administrators to be able to access it in the event of default (or in the run-up to such a default).

Here the experience of bankruptcies such as Lehman Brothers is extremely sobering. Lehman Brothers was a large investment bank that defaulted in September 2008 after a frenzied weekend when the US government tried to broker a rescue, the market having finally lost confidence only a few days earlier that it would be able to withstand the stresses then pummelling the financial markets. In the few days prior to its collapse, its equity market capitalisation was of the order of a few billion US dollars (a figure far less than its value a few months earlier). Several weeks later when an auction of its senior debt was sorted out to expedite its orderly wind-down, senior debt holders found that their paper was worth only c. 9 cents in the dollar, with insurers of Lehman debt out of pocket to the tune of c. $365bn, according to *The Times* (2008).

In percentage terms, such losses are not particularly unusual. A typical assumption for recovery value on a company's senior debt in the event of default is c. 40 %, meaning that in many instances there will be no value left to equity holders once the business has been wound up. A firm default typically wipes out any future franchise value for the firm, and may considerably disrupt value implicit in its existing business commitments. Once a firm is put into administration, its administrators may have legal responsibility to seek the best value for all of its creditors, but they typically have little if any interest in looking after the interests of shareholders and other solvency capital providers if such actions risk depleting protections afforded to those higher up the capital structure.

So, for solvency capital computation purposes we should generally take credit for the value of a marginal asset (and liability) within the portfolio only to the extent that we think that we can access this value in the firestorm of asset (and liability) unwinds that often characterise a default. This is true of the entire asset (and liability) portfolio. However, an illiquid asset and liability pairing may suffer the most in this maelstrom, particularly if we have been incautious and written up its value to the firm on the assumption that we could ignore the possibility of such a catastrophe.

To put it another way, consider two otherwise identical companies A and B, each of which has a 1 in 200 likelihood of defaulting in the coming year and each of which has the same specified quantum of illiquid customer liabilities. They differ in only one respect. Company A invests assets matching these illiquid liabilities in liquid government debt instruments, whilst company B invests the same amount in illiquid bonds with otherwise similar cash flow characteristics. Which of the two companies should customers prefer? The answer, of course, is company A! As far as customers are concerned, the only relevant scenarios in which they would suffer with either company is if the company runs into difficulties. But in these circumstances, customers of company A are likely to be better off than customers of company B, because the administrators of company A are likely to get a higher sum than those of company B when they try to liquidate the assets matching the customer liabilities.[12]

Market behaviour during the 2007–09 credit crisis provides some support for this type of logic. Bank of England (2008c) notes that when probability of default is low then the value of assets on banks' balance sheets seems to be determined (by market participants) by reference to their 'economic value', i.e. a value built up from underlying expected cash flows on those assets on the assumption that they are held to maturity. But as default probabilities rise, so do the chances of the assets needing to be liquidated prior to maturity at market prices. The Bank of England sought to estimate the aggregate sizes of these values and concluded that as expected probability of default rose during September 2008, it became rational for market participants to alter the way in which they assess the underlying value of banks' assets, placing greater weight on mark-to-market values. This influenced the size (and nature) of the rescue package the UK government came up with in October 2008 to support banks with a significant presence in the UK.

The point is that market participants are chillingly rational when it comes to behaviour towards others in distress. It may be rather rash for a firm within its own solvency computations to assume that it will somehow live a charmed life relative to how the market has treated others in similar situations.

Principle P32: In stressed scenarios, market participants can be chillingly rational towards others in distress. Assumptions by a firm that it can access illiquidity premia on specific assets because it will be a long-term (e.g. a hold-to-maturity) investor in these assets may prove unfounded if the firm gets into distress and cannot then continue to be a long-term holder of the asset. As far as customers are concerned, capital is present to provide protection as and when such stressed scenarios *do* occur. Capital adequacy tests should treat with caution the assumption that a firm will always remain a long-term holder of such assets merely because this is its current stance.

---

[12] This example highlights several other points. Current regulatory frameworks typically seem to cope poorly with liquidity risk, see Chapter 8. Typically, current regulatory capital computations in the main implicitly or explicitly involve tests designed to ensure that a company has no more than some specified probability of insolvency, e.g. the 1 in 200 year likelihood used here. They thus involve a VaR style risk measure, see Chapter 7. But as we note in Section 7.3.3, VaR style risk measures take no account of differentials in the tail of the distribution *beyond* the relevant VaR cut-off. In this example, the difference between the more liquid and the less liquid investment strategy *only* shows up in the tail (as far as the customer is concerned), i.e. *only* in those circumstances extreme enough for the company (or its administrators) to have become a forced seller of the relevant assets!

7
Risk Measurement Theory

7.1 INTRODUCTION

'Risk management' can mean many different things to different people. For example, the job of a risk manager within an oil refinery might be to minimise the likelihood of industrial accident (or to arrange insurance cover to protect the company and others against the adverse consequences of such an accident). Alternatively, it might involve attempting to ensure that personnel management activities are unlikely to lead to the company being (successfully) sued for unfair dismissal. Practically any business discipline can benefit from and therefore apply its own definitional flavour to risk management. Risk management such as this has been around for a long time, even if some modern aspects of it, such as 'Enterprise Risk Management', presume a depth of quantitative analysis and a level of holistic approach that might rarely have been feasible before the advent of modern computers.

Financial risk management can be viewed as akin to these more general sorts of risk management activities but focusing on a business's *financial* activities, either a specific subset or when taken as a whole. It is a field that has seen big changes in recent years, driven in part by similar pressures to those that have been favouring greater focus on market consistency in asset and liability valuations.

Going hand in hand with the management of risk is the need to measure it. Ideally, the metrics used should be relatively straightforward to understand, capable of being tracked through time and able to be compared across different portfolios/organisations.

My aim with this chapter, like the chapter on derivative pricing theory, is to provide a general introduction to risk measurement theory. Again, my hope is to do so without getting too involved in mathematical technicalities, although once again it is difficult to do justice to the subject without some reference to mathematical ideas. Readers with a more technical mathematical bent can again peruse a more in-depth mathematical treatment of this subject in Kemp (2009).

7.2 INSTRUMENT-SPECIFIC RISK MEASURES

At one level, the 'risk' expressed by a single instrument can be thought of as the way in which the value of the instrument might move in response to changes in factors that affect its price.

For example, suppose an individual owns a house. When viewed as a financial asset, houses can be thought of as having exposures, and hence expressing risks, to the general housing market. If the housing market in general rises then all other things being equal so will the value of any particular house. Of course, it is incorrect to assume that all parts of the housing market move in tandem. Any individual house will also express somewhat more idiosyncratic risks, such as exposure to the behaviour of other houses in its immediate vicinity (or of its particular type). It will also express even more idiosyncratic risks not even typically shared with the generality of houses in its own immediate vicinity, such as the risk that its particular bath might flood.

Typically, such risk exposures are quantified by reference to the sensitivity of the value of the asset or liability to small changes in the value of the underlying factor characterising the risk. Ascribing an asset or liability some 'sensitivity' to a particular type of risk exposure implicitly requires certain regularity conditions, such as if one (small) quantum of movement in some (economic) factor creates a certain amount of movement in the value of the asset or liability then two such quanta of movement, all other things being equal, create twice the price movement. These regularity conditions are very similar to the axioms of additivity and scalability referred to in Chapter 2.

Risk exposure sensitivities can also be viewed as first partial differentials of the value of the asset or liability with respect to a movement in some underlying factor. They are conceptually equivalent to the option 'greeks' involved in derivative pricing theory that we explored in Chapter 4.

Perhaps use of instrument specific risk exposures is most advanced in bond-land. For example, measures such as DV01 (i.e. the change in the value of the asset if there is a one basis point move in the underlying yield curve), duration and convexity are common ways of quantifying a particular bond's exposure to interest rate movements. The value of a bond can typically be built up in a relatively mathematical way from its component cash flows. At least, one can do this relatively straightforwardly if we ignore the possibility of non-receipt of these cash flows because of issuer default.

A good memory for terminology can help here. For example, concepts like DV01 that have non-intuitive names can be given different names by different people, e.g. the term PV01 ('present value at risk from a one basis point move in the underlying yield curve') is essentially synonymous with DV01. Terms that have a natural intrinsic meaning may also be modified, if the resulting statistic has some other useful property. For example, the term 'duration' has a 'natural' meaning referring to the length of a time period. A bond's duration is therefore typically understood to be a suitably weighted average time to payment of the coupons and redemption proceeds expected from the bond. But a bond's *modified* duration, which can be derived from a bond's basic duration (also known as its *Macaulay* duration) using Equation (7.3), is a concept also used in bond-land. Modified duration has the convenient property that a bond's sensitivity to small parallel shifts in the yield curve is proportional to its modified duration. This means that modified duration is another term nearly synonymous with DV01 or PV01:

$$dirty\ price,\ i.e.\ value,\ V = \sum_t \frac{C_t}{(1+i)^t} \qquad (7.1)$$

$$duration,\ Dur = \sum_t \frac{tC_t}{(1+i)^t} \qquad (7.2)$$

$$modified\ duration,\ Mdur = \frac{dV}{di} = \frac{d}{di}\left(\sum_t \frac{C_t}{(1+i)^t}\right) = \frac{1}{(1+i)}\sum_t \frac{tC_t}{(1+i)^t} = \frac{Dur}{1+i} \qquad (7.3)$$

What impact does market consistency have on how we might calculate a single instrument risk measure such as a bond's duration? Implicitly, a market consistent mindset asks us to focus on the *market's* view of the worth of the bond, i.e. it implicitly asks for the bond's duration to be calculated by reference to the market value of the bond. This is how it is typically calculated. One can perhaps envisage circumstances in which someone might say: 'the duration of a particular bond, were it to have a market value of P, would be d'. However, it is unlikely that a bond duration computation unless otherwise qualified in this manner would ever intentionally be calculated other than by reference to what is believed to be a reasonable estimate of the bond's market value.

One might therefore think that a sensitivity statistic such as a bond's duration is well defined and to the extent that two individuals are asked to calculate the same type of duration and are given the same market price to assume for the same bond they ought to come up with the same duration. However, there are at least three ways in which life may not be quite this simple:

(a) If the calculation of duration is to be reproducible without further assumptions then the payments that the bond will generate need to be known with certainty. This is analogous to the way in which only symmetric derivatives can be priced purely from no-arbitrage criteria whilst asymmetric ones require further assumptions wrapped up within the risk-neutral distribution. Quite a few bonds nowadays have callability or putability features.[1] Analysts seeking to quantify the yields or spreads available on these assets may calculate statistics such yield to worst[2] or option adjusted spread,[3] together with corresponding duration measures.

(b) The concept of duration (and hence DV01) was originally developed to cater for situations where there is some single unambiguous yield curve applicable to the currency in question. The growth in credit markets has rendered this implicit assumption invalid. Instead, nowadays, one conceptually differentiates between 'interest rate DV01' (IRDV01) and 'credit DV01' (CRDV01). The former would be the sensitivity that an instrument's value has to a parallel shift in the benchmark yield curve applicable to the generality of fixed interest instruments denominated in a given currency. The latter would be the sensitivity that an instrument's value has to parallel shifts in the (annualised) credit spread applicable to the instrument in question (measured relative to the generic currency-wide yield curve used in the calculation of the corresponding IRDV01). Some types of instrument can express a significant amount of IRDV01 but very little CRDV01, whilst the opposite can be the case for others.[4]

(c) Not all bonds involve fixed coupon and redemption payments. Nowadays, issuers, particularly governments, may also issue inflation-linked bonds in which future payments on the bond depend on movements in some stated inflation index in the meantime. Such bonds express different economic exposures to fixed rate bonds. So, one can calculate equivalent 'real' (as opposed to 'nominal') durations on such instruments, but the two are

---

[1] A bond is 'callable' if the issuer has the option to redeem the bond (typically at par) at some stage prior to its quoted maturity date. A bond is 'putable' if the investor in the bond has the right to have the bond redeemed at some set price prior to its quoted maturity date. Bonds may also have, say, more complex call features. For example, the issuer may have the right at maturity either to redeem at par or to convert the bond into a floating rate note paying some coupon above Libor that may itself have further call features. Tier 1 and Tier 2 debt instruments issued by banks and insurers often have such features, including the ability to defer redemption indefinitely, because issuance of such capital provides greater protection to such companies in stressed business scenarios (and as a consequence it is looked upon more favourably within regulatory solvency computations).

[2] The 'yield to worst' would be calculated by considering the different possible times when the option embedded within the bond might be exercised, and taking whichever was the least desirable (typically, as far as the issuer was concerned). Likewise, we have 'duration to worst', 'duration to best', 'yield to best', etc.

[3] The 'option adjusted spread' would be the spread provided by the bond (i.e. yield minus some predefined reference rate) taking into account the value of any optionality embedded within the bond, i.e. by finding the yield that results in the present value of the cash flows plus this optionality equalling the current market price.

[4] For example, bonds issued by highly creditworthy governments are typically viewed as expressing interest rate duration but little credit spread duration, whilst the opposite is typically true for credit default swaps.

not interchangeable. Likewise, a particular Euro denominated bond may have the same duration as a particular Dollar denominated bond. However, this does not mean that the value of the two will move in tandem if only Euro yields (and not equivalent Dollar yields) move, or if neither Euro nor Dollar yields move but there is a change in the Euro–Dollar exchange rate.

Sometimes terms can have different meanings in different parts of the financial markets. For example, convexity in bond-land typically refers to how the sensitivity of a bond's value to interest rate movements changes as the interest rate movement becomes larger. It quantifies a second order dependency not captured by duration alone. In contrast, in equity-land 'convexity' is typically a concept applied principally to options, see Section 4.3. However, at a deeper level, one might treat terminology in either market as indicative of a desire to capture a second order element in the pricing behaviour. One can perhaps even view it as indicative of a deeper synthesis between equities and bonds, in which a bond's spread is in some sense related to an equity's volatility, given the relationship that typically exists between these sorts instruments via the 'firm model', see Section 4.8.

It is equally possible to identify portfolio-wide sensitivities. These are typically calculated by taking the average of the risk sensitivities expressed by each individual holding within the portfolio, weighted by market value. A subtlety that is sometimes worth worrying about is that a risk sensitivity such as a duration includes second order dependency on yield (as yields rise, the durations of coupon-paying fixed rate bonds fall, because a higher proportion of their value then relates to earlier payments than previously). Hence, the duration of a portfolio when considered as a single unit is not exactly the same as the weighted average of the individual durations of the instruments it contains. The calculation of the instrument-specific durations will in general use (instrument-specific) yields that may differ from the (average) yield applicable to the portfolio as a whole (if you were to view it as a single instrument with a much larger number of cash flows than a typical bond). The discrepancy will in general be more noticeable if the yield curve is strongly upwardly or downwardly sloping and if the portfolio exhibits a barbell type structure,[5] see e.g. Kemp (2009).

7.3   PORTFOLIO RISK MEASURES

7.3.1   Introduction

Instrument-specific risk exposures of the sorts described above are typically agnostic about the likelihoods of movements of different sizes to the underlying risk factors. Instead, they seek to provide sensitivities that (to first order) can be scaled up whatever the size of such a movement. Once we seek to include views about the possible magnitudes of movements in factors influencing an instrument's value we move into the realm of *portfolio risk analysis*. We use this term because it does not normally make much sense to consider the impact of such movements on individual instruments in isolation. It is far more likely that an entity will have several different assets and liabilities each of which might be influenced by several risk exposures. The overall movement in the entity's asset and liability position will thus be driven by the way in which different factors might move in tandem, as well as by the size of the movement of each factor in isolation.

---

[5] A 'barbell' type structure is one that involves a portfolio skewed towards a mixture of long and short dated instruments, with few (by weight) medium dated instruments.

Tools that are commonly used to measure portfolio risk include *Value-at-Risk*, *expected shortfall*, *tracking error* and *stress testing*. Most of them implicitly or explicitly require the measurer (and hence ultimately the user) to frame assumptions about how values of different assets and liabilities might change in the future, including how they might (or might not) *co-move* in tandem. From a mathematical perspective this involves formulating some hypothetical underlying joint probability distribution describing their behaviour. Such a hypothetical distribution is even present if all we do is tabulate the past and use it to characterise the future, which is the so-called 'historical simulation' approach to risk modelling. The assumption that we are then making is that what has happened in the past (and moreover the particular 'past' we have analysed) is a relevant guide to what might happen in the future.

The interaction between the past and the future is at the heart of many issues to do with risk measurement and management. Consider, for example, active investment management.[6] At its most fundamental level, this management style is aiming to deliver good performance at an acceptable level of risk. But what in this context do we mean by risk?

We first note that it is possible to measure risk in two complementary, but different, time directions:

(a) The *past*. This attempts to answer questions such as 'what level of risk did the manager adopt and was the reward worth the manager taking these risks?' Risk measures that focus on actual past outcomes are called 'backward-looking' or *ex-post* risk measures, and

(b) The *future*. This attempts to answer questions such as 'what level of risk might the portfolio experience, looking forwards?' Risk measures that focus on potential future outcomes are called 'forward-looking' or *ex-ante* risk measures. Usually, we assume that the portfolio structure remains the same going forwards. However, if we were, say, attempting to analyse a dynamic strategy (e.g. seeking to estimate how effective it might be at hedging some dynamical risk exposure) then it would be more natural to model the possible outcomes assuming that the hedge strategy in question was actually being carried out (if this was a reasonable assumption to make!).

Principle P33: Risk can be measured both looking backwards in time and looking forwards in time. The two, whilst related, aim to answer somewhat different questions. We can only influence the future not the past, so most practical risk management focuses on forward-looking risk measurement.

A truism is to note that we can only influence the future and not the past.[7] Therefore, most practical risk measurement and management is (or at least claims to be) focused on ex-ante risk.

---

[6] Typically, one understands an 'active' investment manager to be one who is seeking to outperform a particular benchmark, whilst a 'passive' investment manager is one who is seeking to perform in line with a particular benchmark. However, sometimes the term 'passive' management is used to describe a style that involves very little activity rather than explicitly trying to perform in line with a particular benchmark.

[7] We here assume that no-one will ever discover a way of travelling backwards in time. Of course, a common human trait is to exhibit selective memory or to try to rewrite history to favour one's own position. Wise risk managers bear in mind that hindsight may judge organisations and people (including themselves) unkindly, particularly if extremely adverse outcomes happen to arise, irrespective of the likelihood of occurrence of these outcomes (or anyone's ability to predict these likelihoods)!

Different types of portfolio risk can typically be viewed as relating to different types of *benchmark*. For example, if a client expresses a desire to avoid capital loss, such as with the 'absolute return' objective often applied to hedge funds, the benchmark would be a suitable cash return. For a traditional long-only portfolio, the benchmark would more usually be an investible market index[8] or some suitable mix of such indices.[9] For liability-driven benchmarks, the benchmark might be some proxy investible index (or composite of such indices) or it might merely be some set of predefined cash flows (plus possibly other characteristics, e.g. credit quality criteria) which the investment manager aimed to outperform or match.

Measurement of risk involves some assessment of how far away from the benchmark the portfolio is, or has been. By implication, choosing the right sort of risk to focus on (and therefore the right benchmark to give to the manager) is a key task for any client. The benchmark forms the manager's neutral position. To outperform, the manager will need to deviate from the benchmark. But the further the manager deviates from it, the more the manager might underperform.

In essence, the same applies to any other financial entity interested in measuring and managing portfolio or 'financial' risk, with the main differences boiling down to the benchmarks against which risk is measured and the precise metrics used to quantify 'how far away' the portfolio is (or might be) from the benchmark.

7.3.2 Ex-post (i.e. historic, backward-looking, retrospective) risk measures

7.3.2.1 Drawdown

Perhaps the simplest type of ex-post risk measure involves a concept that in the hedge fund world is known as *drawdown*. This involves calculating the maximum, say, monthly underperformance (for a 'monthly' drawdown) during some set past period (e.g. the last five years). Closely allied is the concept of *cumulative drawdown* which would be the worst cumulative amount of underperformance during the same period under analysis (e.g. from month ends to month ends, particularly if units in the hedge fund can only be bought and sold monthly).

Drawdown style statistics, in line with many other types of risk measures, can be particularly sensitive to one or two extreme movements within the period being analysed. Two funds may have been adopting equally risky types of positions in the past. The first may have been particularly 'unlucky' in that its positions may have been particularly hard hit by the market circumstances that it encountered. The second may have been more 'fortunate', without necessarily running any less 'risk' in some fundamental sense of the word. Taleb (2004) eloquently explores some of the fallacies that can arise when we attempt to extrapolate past behaviour into the future without properly taking into account the impact of randomness (and of uncertainty in the level of this randomness).

7.3.2.2 Ex-post tracking errors

All practical historic risk measures suffer from these sorts of difficulties. They are only imprecise measures of the 'intrinsic' (but ultimately unobservable) risk that a portfolio has been running.

---

[8] Most main market indices are 'investible', in the sense that a passive investment manager could in principle replicate their behaviour by buying every single constituent of the index (in the correct proportions) and adjusting these weights/holdings whenever the constituents (or their weights) changed.

[9] If the benchmark involves a mix of indices then it is in principle necessary to specify the rebalancing frequency.

Statisticians faced with this problem tend to prefer risk measures that are not overly sensitive to a small number of extreme movements, and have other intuitively appealing mathematical characteristics, whilst still being appropriate for the task in question. For this reason, the most usual sort of historic risk measure adopted in the fund management industry is the *ex-post* (i.e. historic) *tracking error*. Tracking errors are based on the statistical concept of *standard deviations*. If the returns relative to the benchmark are (log) Normally distributed then in roughly two periods out of every three we would expect the (log) return to be within plus or minus one standard deviation of the average.[10] The historic tracking error is merely another way of describing this standard deviation, usually annualised, referring to the actual spread of returns experienced in the past.[11]

Principle P34: All historic risk measures are only imprecise measures of the 'intrinsic' but ultimately unobservable risk that a portfolio has been running. A portfolio that seems in the past to have run a low level of risk may actually have been exposed to latent risks that just happened not to show up during the period under analysis.

7.3.2.3   Downside risk measures

Standard deviations give equal weight to positive and negative outcomes, whereas in practice the negative ones are the ones that are the most disliked. There are various ways of constructing *downside risk statistics* that focus more on adverse events, e.g. the *downside semi-standard deviation*, which involves a calculation akin to the basic standard deviation but only taking into account negative returns (or more generally ones below some given threshold). More generally, we can give differential weight to any part of the distribution we like.

Whilst such adjustments are intuitively appealing, blind use of them can be inappropriate. Take, for example, a portfolio that has always to date exhibited a minimal level of downside risk (e.g. minimal drawdowns to date) but is exhibiting relatively volatile levels of outperformance. It would most probably be rash to assume that the portfolio is low risk merely because its volatile behaviour hasn't to date impacted on the downside. To do so would be at odds with the concept that risk involves deviating from the benchmark. As we have noted earlier, it can be difficult to distinguish between funds that were 'fortunate' that their high risk stances did not come home to roost and funds that actually adopted a low risk stance. Common parlance does not help here. Often people characterise the world as 'volatile' when what they mean is that 'things are going down'. A danger with this sort of thinking is that people may then ignore or place insufficient focus on 'volatility' when 'things are going up', to their subsequent cost.

---

[10] The reason that we focus here on log returns is that returns compound over time. If r_1 is the return in the first time period and r_2 the return in the second time period then the return over the combined time period is r_c where $1 + r_c = (1 + r_1)(1 + r_2)$. Hence log returns, i.e. $\log(1 + r)$ add through time. There is therefore greater economic rationale for believing that log returns are Normally distributed than there is for believing that unadjusted returns are Normally distributed. Moreover, the minimum possible return is -100%, i.e. the tail is finite when expressed in unadjusted terms, whilst no such finite lower limit exists for log returns. Despite this, tracking errors are typically in practice calculated by reference to unadjusted returns; only when the mean or spread of returns is large does this typically make much practical difference.

[11] Typically, tracking errors are measured in per cent per annum terms (or in basis points per annum), but can also be expressed in £, $, ... terms instead, by multiplying by the net asset value of the fund.

7.3.2.4   Skew, kurtosis and other moments of distributions

More extreme (adverse) outcomes are typically particularly disliked by recipients and returns that display too many of these sorts of outcomes, i.e. are too 'fat-tailed' versus the Normal distribution (particularly on the downside), may be viewed particularly negatively. For a probability distribution to be fat-tailed, it must deviate from Normality. This traditionally is associated with the distribution exhibiting non-zero *skew* (or 'skewness') and/or positive (excess) *kurtosis*. Hence, skew and kurtosis may also be calculated and displayed, even though we shall discover in Chapter 9 that these measures are not necessarily very effective ways of characterising fat-tailed behaviour in distribution extremities.

7.3.2.5   Risk/return comparisons: information ratios, Sharpe ratios, Sortino ratios

Since the fund manager is aiming to deliver good performance at an acceptable level of risk, historic risk and return statistics may be considered jointly. If there are other portfolios against which the particular portfolio in question can be compared then this might be done via scatterplots showing the risk–return characteristics of each portfolio in the peer group. The ideal is to have performed well relative to the benchmark whilst also seeming to have exhibited a relatively low level of risk when doing so. Of course, low apparent risk in such a plot may hide some 'intrinsic' risks that the portfolio had been running that fortuitously didn't happen to show up in the period under analysis, see Principle P34.

A statistic often quoted in this context is the *information ratio*. It is the ratio between the relative return and the historic tracking error, i.e. it is the slope of the line joining the origin to the point representing the fund in question in a scatterplot showing return (y-axis) versus risk (x-axis). If the fund manager concerned could have doubled the sizes of all the positions (relative to the benchmark) then both the risk and the return of the portfolio (relative to the benchmark) would be doubled, leaving this ratio unchanged. If the benchmark is cash (or an absolute return) then this statistic more normally goes under the name of the *Sharpe ratio*. If instead we are focusing on downside risk then the equivalent statistic is the *Sortino ratio*. A glossary of such terms is given in Kemp *et al.* (2000). Changes in a fund's own risk–return characteristics can also be plotted in such a chart through time.[12] Other ways of analysing returns through time include plots showing individual discrete returns for consecutive time periods (perhaps onto which might be superimposed trailing standard deviations or other envelopes to indicate how the spread of such returns might be changing through time) and cumulative return plots, see e.g. Kemp (2009).

7.3.2.6   Peer group benchmarks

Some funds explicitly have the peer group median (or some other percentile) as their 'benchmark'. Peer group benchmarks have both advantages and disadvantages. From the perspective of some firms, particularly ones selling funds to retail investors, a key goal is to have funds that perform well versus where end investors might otherwise park their money. Unfortunately, peer group benchmark returns do not exactly compound over time and are not therefore 'investible' (which complicates performance attribution versus them). They may also encourage 'herd' behaviour, i.e. a tendency for most of the funds in the peer group to veer off from what

---

[12] Such a plot through time is colloquially called a 'snail trail', see Kemp (2009).

might be intrinsically reasonable for the investor base in question, merely because others in the peer group are doing likewise.

7.3.3   Ex-ante (i.e. forward-looking, prospective) risk measures

7.3.3.1   Ex-ante tracking error

Forward-looking risk measures are estimates of how much the portfolio return might deviate from benchmark return in the future. An obvious forward-looking metric, bearing in mind Section 7.3.2.2, is to use forward-looking (i.e. 'ex-ante' or 'prospective') tracking errors. An ex-ante tracking error is an estimate of the standard deviation of future returns (relative to the benchmark) that the portfolio might experience if the portfolio's current active positions stay unchanged.

The further the fund is from its benchmark the more its performance might deviate from the benchmark performance, and the greater is the risk that the fund will be running. So we should expect there to be an analogy between measuring 'distance' in the physical world (i.e. typically Euclidean geometry) and 'risk' in the financial world. This analogy is particularly strong with forward-looking tracking errors.

7.3.3.2   The geometrical analogy for ex-ante tracking error

The geometrical analogy works as follows. Suppose that our positions relative to the benchmark can be described via a position vector **x** whose components, x_i, indicate the relative position in the ith security. Suppose that we describe the random variable that is the future (relative) contribution to return[13] arising from holding **x** (over a suitably defined time period) by the equivalent italicised capital letter, i.e. here X. Suppose now that we have two different sets of positions, **a** and **b** with corresponding future contributions to returns A and B. The combination of the two positions, $\mathbf{c} = \mathbf{a} + \mathbf{b}$, then creates a corresponding future contribution to return $C = A + B$. We note that C will have a standard deviation (i.e. forward-looking tracking error) of σ_C, which can be calculated as follows, where $\rho_{A,B}$ is the correlation between the random variables A and B.

$$\sigma_C^2 = \sigma_{A+B}^2 = var(A + B) = var(A) + 2\,cov(A,\,B) + var(B) = \sigma_A^2 + 2\sigma_A\sigma_B\rho_{A,B} + \sigma_B^2$$

$$(7.4)$$

If $\rho_{A,B} = 0$ then this formula is very similar to Pythagoras' celebrated theorem, which tells us that the length, P, of the hypotenuse of a right-angled triangle can be found from the lengths, Q and R, of the two sides next to the right angle using the formula $P^2 = Q^2 + R^2$. Indeed, one can derive it mathematically using similar principles. If $P_{A,B} \neq 0$ then the fomula is very similar to the more general formula $P^2 = Q^2 + 2QR \cos \theta + R^2$ applicable to a non-right-angled triangle, where θ is the angle between sides Q and R, if we equate $\cos \theta$ with $\rho_{A,B}$, see Figure 7.1.

The one difference is that in Euclidean geometry the 'magnitude', i.e. length, of a vector from the origin to a point **x** with Cartesian coordinates x_i is calculated using a 'norm' defined as $|x| \equiv \sqrt{\sum x_i^2} \equiv \sqrt{\mathbf{x}^T \mathbf{I} \mathbf{x}}$, where **I** is the identity matrix, whilst in tracking error analysis the equivalent 'magnitude', i.e. tracking error, of a set of relative positions **a** is calculated as

---

[13] By 'contribution to return' we mean return weighted by position size.

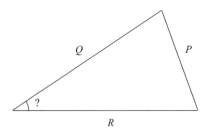

Figure 7.1 The geometrical analogy between tracking error $\sigma_C^2 = \sigma_A^2 + 2\sigma_A\sigma_B\rho_{A,B} + \sigma_B^2$ and distance $P^2 = Q^2 + 2QR\cos\theta + R^2$

$||a|| \equiv \sqrt{\mathbf{a}^T\mathbf{V}a}$, where $\mathbf{V}$ is the covariance matrix of the joint probability distribution from which the X_i are drawn.

We can therefore expect the same underlying geometrical concepts that apply to 'distance' in the physical world to apply, in the main, to 'risk' in the financial world (as long as 'risk' is equated with something approximating to forward looking tracking error). However, we may need to bear in mind that the introduction of a matrix component can in effect involve scaling the different axes in suitable ways. It can also involve shears to the coordinate framework, which in the risk management context reflect non-zero correlations between different securities.[14] For example, in such a framework, the process of considering the risk impact of a small number of risk exposures on a range of instruments is geometrically equivalent to projecting the multi-dimensional space describing the risks arising from all possible different factors onto a smaller-dimensional space describing the risks merely of the factors we wish to retain.

Other conclusions that we can draw from this analogy are:

(a) Forward looking tracking errors (and risk measures more generally) are dependent on assumptions both about the likely future volatility of individual stocks or markets relative to the benchmark (i.e. the degree of scaling required) and about the correlations between different stocks/markets (i.e. the extent of shearing referred to above).

(b) If we wish to rank portfolios by their riskiness then, as long as the sort of risk (ultimately deriving from the benchmark being used) is similar, the rankings will often be relatively insensitive to the precise risk methodology used, see Kemp *et al.* (2000).

7.3.3.3 Value-at-Risk

A more common forward-looking risk metric in many parts of the financial community is *Value-at-Risk* (VaR). VaR is enticingly simple as a concept, and therefore relatively easy to explain to lay-people. It requires specification of a confidence level, say 95 %, 99 % or 99.5 %, and a time period, say, 1 day, 5 days, 1 month or 1 year. If we talk about a fund having a 5 day 95 % confidence VaR of, say, X, then we mean that there is a only a 5 % chance of losing more than X over the next 5 days, if the same positions are held for this 5 day time frame.[15]

---

[14] In general, the operation of a matrix on a set of coordinates can be thought of as imposing a series of geometrical transformations on the coordinates, namely combinations of rotations (which do not alter distances), expansions or contractions along a given direction, and shears between directions.

[15] As with tracking error, VaR (and other similar risk measures) can be expressed in percentage terms or in monetary amounts.

If we talk about a 99.5 % 1 year VaR (as per some current regulatory solvency frameworks, see Chapter 8), then we are aiming to describe events only expected on average to occur once every 200 years.[16]

VaR originally referred merely to losses on some absolute numerical basis, but it is more helpful to use a generalised definition in which VaR can also refer to percentage losses versus a suitably chosen benchmark.[17]

There are several reasons why VaR is potentially more attractive as a risk measure to lay-people than (forward-looking) tracking errors, including:

(a) Tracking error requires a potentially greater understanding of statistical concepts like standard deviations.
(b) Tracking error can be applied both in a fully backward-looking and in a fully forward-looking manner, which can lead to confusion or misunderstanding. VaR can in principle be applied likewise, but in practice it would be applied in a forward-looking manner unless the context demanded otherwise. For example, even the term 'historic' VaR is most usually taken to mean taking current positions and working out what would have happened based on, say, the last 5 or 10 years' worth of past daily market movements. It is therefore still properly a forward-looking statistic, as it is an estimate of what might happen going forwards if the current positions are retained (to the extent that past market movements during the part of the past that has been analysed are a guide to how markets might move in the future). 'Historic' tracking error, in contrast, would usually be taken to refer to historic positions as well. A fund that is perfectly indexed should therefore have a nil VaR (versus the index), whether 'historic' or otherwise (using the above terminology), but could still have an appreciable 'historic' tracking error if it has only recently been converted into an index fund.
(c) If returns are Normally distributed then an annualised forward-looking tracking error is the same as a 15.9 % 1 year VaR. But which client is interested in a 15.9 % breakpoint?
(d) Flexibility in choice of confidence interval means that it may be easier to take practical account of the non-Normal distributions typically perceived to apply to returns in the 'real' world, see Chapter 9.

However, life is not actually this simple. Estimating VaR, like estimating forward-looking tracking error, involves subjective inputs that may not be immediately apparent to the recipient of the statistic. It is helpful to realise that VaR is frequently calculated using the same Normal distribution assumption as might be used to derive a forward-looking tracking error, by first calculating this tracking error and then applying a multiplier derived by reading off the appropriate confidence interval from a tabulation of the standard Normal distribution (or by using corresponding spreadsheet functions). Such a VaR computation is called 'variance–covariance VaR'.

In such circumstances, VaR becomes merely an alternative way of presenting tracking error, albeit in a format which may be more intuitively appealing and perhaps focusing on a

---

[16] Of course, a moot point with 99.5 % 1 year VaR figures is that there is insufficient data, at least in the context of modern finance, actually to observe such time periods directly, highlighting just how hypothetical such statistics actually are. We instead need to extrapolate from less extreme events and/or shorter time frames (or perhaps from relevant market implied data, see Chapter 10) to derive such measures.

[17] If we do for any reason need to differentiate between VaR relative to a benchmark and VaR in absolute monetary sense then the former can be referred to as 'relative VaR'.

different (and often shorter) time horizon. *If* returns are Normally distributed then the return distribution is completely characterised by two parameters, its mean and standard deviation, which means that mathematically the 'best' way of estimating any VaR statistic will typically involve reference to the sample standard deviation.[18]

7.3.3.4 Non-Normal returns

Sometimes the situation directly prescribes a non-Normal distribution. For example, the performance of a poorly diversified corporate bond fund is naturally likely to be significantly skewed because of the risk that one or more of the bonds held might default, causing a significant relative loss versus the benchmark. Similar skews can naturally be expected to arise with portfolios that contain significant exposure to options (or other financial instruments with option-like characteristics).

But in most other circumstances, it is more difficult to identify exactly how skewed or fattailed might be the underlying distribution of future returns. The distributional form underlying the VaR statistic might be directly taken from the historical data distribution (or from Monte Carlo or from bootstrap simulations that themselves ultimately derive from this distribution). However, this may be placing too much reliance on the particular sample of the past that was observed. Sampling errors may be particularly acute if we are focusing just on the extreme tail of the distribution. Better may be to adopt more robust methodologies that are less sensitive to the actual sample used, see Chapter 9.

Alternatively, we might dispense with any distributional assumptions and merely use scenario tests (or 'stress tests') to identify the impact that some particular set of events occurring simultaneously might have, see Section 7.8.

7.3.3.5 Other forward-looking risk measures

As Leippold (2004) points out, the x day y% confidence level VaR of a portfolio is actually the *minimum loss* that a portfolio can suffer in x days in the y% *worst* cases when the portfolio weights are not changed during these x days. His reasons for clarifying the definition of VaR in this manner are to highlight that VaR fails to take any account of the shape of the distribution *beyond* the VaR cut-off point and to highlight that it is not a *coherent* risk measure in terms of how risks might add together.[19]

For example, suppose we have two return distributions both with the same 95% VaR of £1m, but in one the average loss, in the event that the VaR cut-off point is breached, is £1.5m and in the other it is £15m. The latter would in most people's eyes be riskier than the former, even though both have the same 95% VaR statistic. Or consider an insurer only underwriting a single catastrophe insurance risk, without any reinsurance. If the probability of it occurring is 1 in 300 years then the insurer's yearly 99.5% VaR will be zero (or better, if it takes credit for the premium it receives). However, every once in a while it will suffer a massive loss way beyond its VaR. But if the same insurer underwrites 1/10th of 10 such risks, each independently with

---

[18] The reason that the sample standard deviation is 'best' in this context is because the sample variance, i.e. the square of the sample standard deviation, is then the minimum variance unbiased estimator of the underlying population variance.

[19] A coherent risk measure is one that satisfies the technical properties of monotonicity, sub-additivity, homogeneity and translational invariance, see e.g. Artzner *et al.* (1999).

the same 1 in 300 year chance of occurring, then its yearly 99.5 % VaR will be much higher, even though it has a more diversified book of business. Or take a bond. Such an instrument might have an expected default rate if held to maturity of, say, 1 %, which would imply that its 95 % VaR over this period is 0, but it is not thereby riskless.

Possible risk metrics that are more useful in these circumstances are *expected shortfall*, sometimes called *tail Value-at-Risk* (TVaR) which is the *average* loss that a portfolio can suffer in x days in the y % worst cases (rather than the *minimum* loss as is used in the basic VaR computation), or other similar metrics that take better account of the shape of the tail.

7.4   TIME SERIES-BASED RISK MODELS

7.4.1   Risk 'models' versus risk 'systems'

To calculate a forward-looking portfolio risk statistic you need a *risk model*, i.e. a mathematical framework for estimating the future spread of returns a portfolio might generate were its positions versus the benchmark to remain unaltered in the future.[20] Most current commercially available systems derive these estimates principally using time series analysis applied to past data.

We can conceptually differentiate between a risk 'model' and a risk 'system'. The latter is a practical software tool (within which is embedded one or more risk models) that can be used to derive the sorts of statistics described above or carry out other related tasks, e.g. risk–return optimisation, see Chapter 12. The underlying risk model defines what answers you will get out of a risk system, even if ease of use, cost and run times are also key elements firms consider when deciding which systems to buy. There are now quite a few specialist third party providers of risk systems. Quantitative research departments within investment banks may also provide such services to their broking clients. Some asset managers have their own internally developed systems (which they sometimes then try to commercialise for third party use). Pension fund investment consultants provide similar services to their pension fund clients (usually in conjunction with a commercial risk system provider). Risk modelling capabilities are increasingly being added to asset-liability software supplied by insurance consultants and actuaries.

7.4.2   Mathematical characterisation of different types of risk model

We can characterise the main sorts of commercially available risk models in several different ways, including:

(a) *The way in which factors assumed to drive the behaviour of multiple securities are developed.* The main sub-classifications here are between fundamental, econometric and statistical models.
(b) *The shape of the underlying joint probability distribution(s) that the risk model assumes will govern the behaviour of different securities.* There are typically differences here between equities and bonds (and between securities/portfolios that do or do not contain optionality).

---

[20] Or if the positions were to change in the pre-specified dynamical manner under consideration, see Section 7.3.1.

(c) *The mathematical algorithm used to calculate the risk metric.* The main distinction here is use of *analytical* versus *simulation* techniques. The latter is typified by Monte Carlo simulations, although more sophisticated approaches are possible, see Section 4.11.

But actually there are fewer underlying distinctions than appear at first sight. For example, categorisation by mathematical algorithm does not really define different underlying risk 'models' per se. As we saw in Chapter 4, if we had unlimited computing power and unlimited Monte Carlo sample sizes, simulation techniques would in the limit give the same answer as any corresponding exact analytical result. At issue is that in most cases it isn't actually possible to identify an exact analytical answer without making some approximations that we may not feel are appropriate for the task in hand.

7.4.3   Intrinsic ways of estimating risk models from past data

The blurring that exists in practice between different types of risk model is perhaps most relevant to how we might develop factors that characterise succinctly future market movements.
There are three apparently different ways of estimating risk models from time series data:

(a) A *fundamental* risk model ascribes certain fundamental factors (such as price to book) to individual securities. These factor exposures are exogenously derived, e.g. by reference to a company's annual report and accounts. The factor exposures for a portfolio as a whole (and for a benchmark, and hence for a portfolio's active positions versus a benchmark) are the weighted averages of the individual position exposures. Different factors are assumed to behave in the future in a manner described by some joint probability distribution. The overall portfolio risk (versus its benchmark) can then be derived from its active factor exposures, this joint probability distribution and any additional variability in future returns deemed to arise from security-specific idiosyncratic behaviours.
(b) An *econometric* risk model is similar to a fundamental model except that the factor exposures are individual security-specific sensitivities to certain pre-chosen exogenous economic variables, e.g. interest rate, currency or oil price movements. The sensitivities are typically found by regressing the returns from the security in question against movements in the relevant economic variables, typically using multivariate regression techniques.
(c) A *statistical* risk model eliminates the need to define any exogenous factors, whether fundamental or econometric. Instead, we identify a set of otherwise arbitrary time series that in aggregate explain well the past return histories of a high proportion of the relevant security universe, ascribing to elements of this set the status of 'factors'. Simultaneously, we also derive the exposures that each security has to these factors. This can be done using *principal components analysis* or other similar techniques, see Kemp (2009).

However, these three apparently rather different types of risk model are rather less different in practice than might appear at first sight.
It would be nice to believe that factors included within a fundamental or econometric model are chosen purely from inherent a priori criteria. In reality, however, the factors will normally be chosen in part because they seem to have exhibited some explanatory power in the past. They are therefore almost certain to have some broad correspondence to what you would have chosen had you merely analysed past returns in some detail as per method (c). How can we ever expect to decouple entirely what we consider to be a 'reasonable' way of describing

market dynamics from past experience regarding how markets have actually operated? There is ultimately only one past that we have to work with!

The blurring is particularly noticeable with bond risk models. A key driver of the behaviour of a bond is its duration. Is this a 'fundamental' factor, since we can calculate it exogenously by reference merely to the timing of the cash flows underlying the bond? Or is it an 'econometric' factor, because a bond's modified duration is also its sensitivity to small parallel shifts in the yield curve? Or is it a 'statistical' factor, because if we carry out a principal components analysis of well-rated bonds we typically find that the most important statistical explanatory driver for a bond's behaviour is closely allied to its duration?

All three types of risk model have the same underlying mathematical framework which we can derive from the geometrical representation of risk developed in Section 7.3.3, if we proxy risk by tracking error or an equivalent. We can model the ith security's return as coming from 'exposures' $f_{i,j}$ to the jth 'factor loading'. Here one unit of each factor generates a prospective return (in the relevant future period) of r_j which are random variables with a joint covariance matrix of $\mathbf{V}$, say. So a portfolio described by a vector of active weights $\mathbf{a}$, say, will have an overall ex-ante tracking error of σ where $\sigma^2 = \mathbf{a}^T (\mathbf{F}^T \mathbf{V} \mathbf{F}) \mathbf{a}$, where the matrix $\mathbf{F}$ is formed by the terms $f_{i,j}$.

It is worth noting here that there are two different ways in practice that risk models handle 'residual' risk within such a framework, i.e. the idiosyncratic risk that is relevant only to specific individual securities:

(a) The matrix $\mathbf{F}$ may be deemed to include all such idiosyncratic risks, i.e. our set of 'factors' includes idiosyncratic factors that predominantly affect only individual securities; or
(b) The matrix $\mathbf{F}$ may exclude these idiosyncratic risks. In such a formalisation, the idiosyncratic risk of the ith security might be, say, σ_i, and we might calculate the total risk of the portfolio as $\sigma^2 = \mathbf{a}^T (\mathbf{F}^T \hat{\mathbf{V}} \mathbf{F}) \mathbf{a} + \sum a_i^2 \sigma_i^2 = (\mathbf{F} \mathbf{a})^T \hat{\mathbf{V}} (\mathbf{F} \mathbf{a}) + \sum a_i^2 \sigma_i^2$, where $\hat{\mathbf{V}}$ is now a much smaller sized matrix characterising merely the covariance matrix between 'factor' returns (an $m \times m$ matrix, if there are just m different factors included in the model). There are typically far fewer parameters to estimate using this sort of methodology, so estimation of these parameters is likely to be more robust.

In practice, there may be good reasons for believing that certain securities may share what would otherwise be purely idiosyncratic exposures. For example, some companies have a dual holding company structure, or are listed on more than one exchange. The two listings do not necessarily trade at identical prices (there may be differences in how they are taxed, etc.) but are still likely to exhibit strongly linked behaviours. Likewise, corporate bonds issued by the same issuer are likely to share many common characteristics, even if their behaviour won't be identical (e.g. because the bonds may have different terms, priority status in the event of company wind-up or different liquidity characteristics). Computation of ex-ante tracking error can then be characterised as $\sigma^2 = (\mathbf{F} \mathbf{a})^T \hat{\mathbf{V}} (\mathbf{F} \mathbf{a}) + \mathbf{a}^T \mathbf{Y} \mathbf{a}$, where $\mathbf{Y}$ is a sparse $n \times n$ matrix, with few terms other than those along the leading diagonal.

7.4.4 Matrix analysis

The above analysis highlights the deep links that typically exist between risk modelling and matrix algebra. Carrying out a principal components analysis on a multivariate return distribution characterised by a covariance matrix $\mathbf{V}$ can be characterised as identifying a matrix $\mathbf{L}$ for which the matrix $\mathbf{M} = \mathbf{L}^T \mathbf{V} \mathbf{L}$ contains non-zero elements only along its leading diagonal, with the elements of the leading diagonal in $\mathbf{M}$ also typically sorted into, say, descending order. The sizes of these terms, and the structure of $\mathbf{L}$, are intimately related to the *eigenvalues* and *eigenvectors* of $\mathbf{V}$, which thus play an important role in risk measurement theory. The application of the matrix $\mathbf{L}$ in this manner to the original matrix $\mathbf{V}$ is said to involve the application of a *matrix transformation* to the original matrix.

For those not familiar with such aspects of matrix algebra, any symmetric $n \times n$ matrix $\mathbf{V}$ (of the sort that might describe the covariance characteristics of an n-dimensional probability distribution) has n (normalised) eigenvectors and associated eigenvalues (although the eigenvalues may not all be distinct). These are solutions to the matrix equation $\mathbf{V}\mathbf{x} = \lambda\mathbf{x}$. By 'normalised' we mean $\mathbf{x}^T\mathbf{x} = 1$. Any vector can be decomposed into a suitably weighted composite of these (normalised) eigenvectors.

Usually, when people talk about 'principal' components analysis they mean 'truncating' $\mathbf{M}$ so that all bar a few of the leading diagonal terms are set to zero. This is mathematically equivalent to applying a further matrix transform characterised by a matrix $\mathbf{P}$ which is unity for the first few leading diagonal terms and zero everywhere else and then backing out an adjusted covariance matrix $\bar{\mathbf{V}} = \mathbf{L}^{-1}\mathbf{P}\mathbf{L}\mathbf{V}\mathbf{L}\mathbf{P}\mathbf{L}^{-1}$ from the original covariance matrix $\mathbf{V}$ (or $\hat{\mathbf{V}}$).[21]

For example, if we carry out a principal components analysis on the entire (conventional) UK government fixed interest (i.e. gilt) market then typically we find that nearly all of the behaviour of nearly all of the gilts is well explained by a very small number of factors. By 'nearly all of the behaviour' we mean that only the first few of leading diagonal terms in $\mathbf{M}$ (i.e. only the largest few eigenvalues) are much different to zero. Bond interest rate risk models often focus on just the first three principal components, equating them with, say, 'shift' (i.e. parallel shifts in the yield curve), 'twist' (i.e. steepening or flattening of the curve) and 'butterfly' (i.e. curving up or down of the curve).

Multivariate regression can be expressed using similar matrix algebra, see e.g. Kemp (2005) or Kemp (2009). The process of creating (covariance-based) econometric risk models is thus mathematically equivalent to deriving a covariance matrix using (typically) the historic returns on each security, and then projecting this matrix onto a (typically) lower dimensional space (in a manner that equates to regressing these return series versus whatever are the base econometric times series being used in the analysis).

So, econometric risk models essentially differ in mathematical terms from statistical risk models only in the way that they rank and discard eigenvectors and corresponding eigenvalues. Of course, there are some differences. With statistical models the explanatory variables – the principal components – emerge endogenously from the covariance matrix whilst with econometric risk models they are selected on a priori grounds, i.e. exogenously. But the point is that the econometric time series most likely to be incorporated in an econometric risk model are ones that correspond (in aggregate) with a significant fraction of the leading eigenvectors, so the two modelling approaches should actually produce relatively similar results to the extent that they are being based on the same underlying data set.

What econometric risk models really bring to the party is a more intuitive description of the covariance matrix, i.e. primarily presentation rather than underlying mathematical content. Presentation should, however, not be dismissed as unimportant, not least because it makes

---

[21] As we noted in Section 7.3.3, we are in effect applying (matrix) transformations characterised by a matrix $\mathbf{A}$ that translates $\mathbf{X} \to \mathbf{A}^T\mathbf{X}\mathbf{A}$ and which geometrically involve rotation and/or stretching and/or shearing, except that here we are also including cases where we shear away an entire dimension, i.e. we project the geometrical representation of the matrix onto some lower dimensional space.

explanation of the results much easier to non-experts. Perhaps it can also be argued that if there is some underlying economic logic to the ranking of eigenvectors then their use for prospective risk analysis may become more reliable.

Such risk models typically not only include factor exposures but also security-specific idiosyncratic elements. In our geometrical representation the inclusion of these sorts of idiosyncratic elements involves reinserting additional dimensions into the covariance matrix by reinserting non-zero eigenvalues whose eigenvectors largely align with individual securities (i.e. correspond to active weights that are unity for a given security and zero for all others). One can in principle also do this within a statistical model framework. We discuss below some of the challenges that arise in practice in choosing a suitable structure for these 'residual' terms.

Similar mathematics also underlies fundamental risk models. In these models, we exogenously assign factor exposures to individual securities. We then back out the returns on individual factors from these factor exposures by a suitable matrix inversion and projection into a suitably dimensioned space (assuming that there are fewer factors than there are securities, as otherwise the problem becomes ill-defined). Once again, therefore, the essential difference (from a mathematical perspective) is in how we rank and discard eigenvalues and eigenvectors (and then, in effect, reinsert other eigenvectors defining the 'residual' terms). Once again, the factors deemed useful in this process are likely to be ones that have exhibited predictive power in the past, i.e. ones that in aggregate span the main eigenvectors that a principal components analysis might generate.

Principle P35: Practitioners have developed many different forward-looking risk models and ways of estimating them. However, on closer analysis there are fewer variants than may appear at first sight, because most models and ways of estimating them extrapolate, in some way, the past into the future and we only have one past on which to base this extrapolation.

7.4.5   The link back to pricing algorithms

Developers of bond risk models will have spotted that we have glossed over a rather important subtlety in the above discussion. The specifications of most bond risk models also include pricing algorithms.

In equity-land we normally assume that the return in time t from the ith equity under consideration is characterised by a simple linear formula such as $r_{i,t} = \alpha_i + \beta_{i,1} f_{1,t} + \beta_{i,2} f_{2,t} + \sigma_i \varepsilon_{i,t}$ where the betas are sensitivities that the particular equity has to the factors analysed above and the $\varepsilon_{i,t}$ are independent unit Normal random variables.

In bond-land, in contrast, the formulae become potentially more complicated, because of the more complex ways in which bond prices can depend on yields, etc. Even if we seek to 'linearise' the return formula in an equivalent manner as per Section 7.2, it is often simplest to calculate these linear sensitivities by building up a pricing model for the instruments in question.

A corollary is that the risk analysis involves, in part, a marking-to-model.

7.4.6   Choice of underlying distributional form

The other main way (mathematically speaking) in which risk models can be differentiated is in terms of choice of distributional form. Here there are potentially larger inherent differences.

7.4.6.1   (Log)-Normality

Risk models for equity securities often but not always assume that returns on individual securities are jointly (log) Normally distributed over suitable time intervals, with the same mean for all securities and with some suitable *covariance matrix* that defines the joint second moment of the distribution.

The use of a common mean involves taking an a priori stance that risk measurement ought not to assume any expected added value from investment 'skill' in an analysis that is attempting to assess the downside implications if this skill fails to materialise. This assumption would, however, be suspect if, say, known charge differentials between the portfolio and the benchmark justified a non-zero differential expected return between them (or if there were liquidity arguments that justified the same conclusion, see Chapter 5).[22] From a formal mathematical perspective such risk models are therefore completely characterised by their underlying covariance matrix.

7.4.6.2   The Central Limit Theorem

However, equities do not exhibit perfectly Normal return distributions. The methodology is therefore relying on the active positions within the portfolio being sufficiently diversified for the Central Limit Theorem to bite. This mathematical law states that the probability distribution of the sum of a large number of independent random variables tends to a Normal distribution as the number of underlying random variables tends to infinity, subject to certain regularity conditions such as each random variable having a (known) finite standard deviation. So, we need to treat with caution tracking error and VaR computations for highly concentrated portfolios (particularly extreme examples consisting of, say, just one security), as any deviations from Normality may then have less scope to be smoothed away by the Central Limit Theorem.

7.4.6.3   Time-varying volatility

A less obvious way in which the Central Limit Theorem can break down is if returns exhibit time-varying volatility, see Chapter 9. Various time series analysis tools can be used in an attempt to make risk models more responsive to such time-varying characteristics. For example, practitioners may use GARCH (i.e. *generalised autoregressive conditional heteroscedastic*) processes in which the current level of, say, index volatility (or perhaps even sector or security volatility) is derived from its recent past level and the covariance matrix is then adjusted accordingly. Correlations also appear to exhibit time-varying characteristics (i.e. do not appear to be stable over time). GARCH style modelling may also be used in an attempt to capture their dynamics.

7.4.6.4   Bond portfolios or other portfolios exposed to credit risk

For many types of bond portfolios, an assumption of (log)-Normality is more suspect. One can conceptually split the return behaviour of bonds into several parts:

---

[22] It is not entirely clear how such an assumption ties in economically with the existence of the market price for risk vector described in Section 4.3, which implies that different asset types can in principle still have different risk-neutral implied mean drifts in a multi-asset economy.

(a) A part driven by general levels of interest rates (*curve* risk). This is generally taken to refer to prevailing interest rates as derived from yields on relevant well-rated government bonds of different durations (also known as the *government* or, in the UK, the *gilt* yield curve), but the arguments in Chapter 5 about what constitutes the 'risk-free' rate are in principle relevant here too;

(b) A part driven by the currency of the bond (*currency* risk);

(c) A part driven by changes in general levels of spreads versus government bond yields for issues with a similar credit rating as the issue/issuer in question (*spread* risk, also called *credit spread* risk), or strictly speaking non-idiosyncratic spread risk, see (e) below;

(d) A part driven by spread changes not being uniform across industries/sectors (*industry/sector* risk); and

(e) A residual element arising from issuer-specific idiosyncratic features (*idiosyncratic* risk), mainly the possibility that a particular issuer might default (*default* risk), but also covering other issuer-idiosyncratic characteristics, e.g. idiosyncratic yield differentials between different issues from the same underlying issuer (perhaps driven by credit risk uncertainty or liquidity considerations, see Chapter 6).

In essence, exposures to (a) to (d) are similar, in a mathematical sense, to the sorts of equity style factor exposures described above, just translated into bond-speak. For certain types of bond portfolio, e.g. single-currency/country government debt, there may be so few factors (or one so dominating, e.g. duration) that the point noted in Section 7.4.6.2 becomes particularly relevant. We may then want to spend more time attempting to estimate more accurately the distributional form applicable to just that factor.

Portfolios containing significant amounts of credit will typically have less to worry about from this perspective. But instead they will typically be exposed to default risk. This sort of risk (for any given issuer) can be highly non-Normal because of the highly skewed returns that such bonds can deliver depending on whether or not they default.

7.4.6.5 Granularity-based risk models

The geometrical analogy we developed in Section 7.3.3 is arguably less effective for highly skewed returns. But it still provides hints as to how we might develop risk models that cater for such skewed behaviour. We might, for example, develop a *granularity-based approach* to risk modelling by noting that we can decompose the relative return (and the risk) that a credit portfolio exhibits (versus its benchmark) into parts that derive from:

(a) Its active 'factor' exposures, as per Section 7.4.6.4(a) to (d) (e.g. its relative duration, industry positions and exposures by rating bucket), as if the portfolio had *infinitely diversified active credit exposures* within each such dimension; and

(b) Its issuer-specific credit exposures (relative to the benchmark) as per Section 7.4.6.4(e) that arise because the portfolio (and benchmark) exhibits *credit granularity*, i.e. is not infinitely diversified as per (a).

We can, for example, use this approach to define suitable single name limits, dependent on credit rating, to include in portfolio guidelines. An example of how this might be done is set out in Kemp (2005), who suggests that such limits might then scale approximately 1:2:3 for BBB:A:AA rated corporate debt. Such an analysis relies on the possibly questionable assumption that *historic* default and recovery rates provide a reasonable guide as to the relative magnitudes of the *future* residual risk components for instruments with different credit ratings.

Granularity type arguments are also used by regulators when framing standardised regulatory solvency computation frameworks, see Chapter 8.

7.4.7 Monte Carlo methods

We need to be slightly wary of how simulation techniques such as Monte Carlo can sometimes be put on a pedestal by some members of the financial community. This is because such techniques can appear to be more sophisticated than they really are. We can be fooled into thinking that if a system uses millions of simulations then it is somehow 'better' than one that uses thousands of simulations or even no simulations at all. The point is that if the simulations are drawn from the 'wrong' distribution then even use of billions or trillions of runs will result in the Monte Carlo exercise converging on the 'wrong' answer. Rubbish in, rubbish out!

That being said, Monte Carlo simulations do have some nice computational features that make them perhaps more common than might otherwise be expected for top of the range risk systems, particularly when combined with a comprehensive library of instrument pricing algorithms. A common algorithmic framework can then be used to compute any desired risk statistic, namely:

(a) Tabulate random scenarios of how all economic factors (including idiosyncratic factors) influencing the price of any instrument held in the portfolio might behave;
(b) Re-price the portfolio under each simulated scenario;
(c) Tabulate and characterise its resulting distribution; and
(d) Read off whatever risk statistic you like from the distribution derived from the answers in (c).

7.4.8 Summary

Most commercially available risk systems can be categorised into one of the above forms. In essence, we can view time series risk modelling as an example of the more general problem of forecasting the characteristics of return series, see Kemp (2009), but applying the constraint that all assets (and liabilities) must have the same mean return.

A common complaint levied at risk systems is that they typically understate (or overstate, depending on the time period) the overall risk characteristics of a portfolio. This may partly reflect cognitive bias. People typically remember those times when the estimated tracking errors significantly misstate actually observed tracking errors more than they remember the times when they are closer (even though tracking errors are statistical tools and therefore necessarily subject to error). It also reflects the so-called heteroscedastic nature of most financial time series, i.e. that they seem to exhibit time-varying volatilities.

7.5   INHERENT DATA LIMITATIONS APPLICABLE TO TIME SERIES-BASED RISK MODELS

7.5.1   The sparsity of the data available

A major issue that afflicts all time series risk models, and indeed time series return forecasting more generally, is the *sparsity of the data available for the task*. We are used to thinking that there is a veritable cornucopia of data relating to financial markets available from brokers or via third party data vendors. How then can there be insufficient data for such purposes?

High dimensional vector spaces are incredibly large. If, for example, one could conceive of a 100-dimensional cube each side of which is 10 units long, then its volume would be 10^{100}. The distance between two randomly selected points within such a cube is roughly Normally distributed, with mean 41 and standard deviation 2.5, meaning that the likelihood of coming across two points that are substantially closer together (or further apart) than any other pair of randomly chosen points is very low. In our geometrical representation of risk, each instrument in principle creates a new dimension, and there are hugely more than 100 securities traded in the global marketplace (let alone all the liabilities that might also be considered, if, say, we treated each individual insurance policy as a separate 'instrument'). The vector space describing all such instruments is truly vast!

For time series risk modelling purposes, an arguably even more important constraint is the limited history available to us.

> **Principle P36: Forward-looking risk measures that are ultimately derived from extrapolation, in some shape or form, of the past into the future are subject to the inherent limitation that there is relatively little data contained within 'the past' compared to what we would ideally want to have available for risk modelling purposes.**

Take, for example, the S&P 500 index of 500 US equities. Suppose, for example, that we wish to develop a risk model for the S&P 500 index or the FTSE All-Share index using monthly returns over a 5 year period. Ignoring for the moment that not all of the 500 companies in the S&P index will have a complete 5 year history, the covariance matrix for the S&P 500 would appear to have $500 \times (500 + 1)/2 = 125,250$ separate terms. However, the observed covariance matrix only has at most 59 non-zero eigenvalues. This is because we can replicate every single return series using linear combinations of 60 different base series (the jth return series having a 1 in month j and a 0 in every other month), and one further degree of freedom drops away because for risk purposes we a priori assume a common underlying mean for all the security returns.

This means that the covariance matrix is in this instance embedded in at most a 59-dimension vector space however many securities we are analysing. Even fewer will exist if some of these 59 degrees of freedom are 'consumed' by incorporating time-varying behaviour within the model. The true underlying probability distribution describing the joint behaviour of different securities almost certainly contains many more factors. *But there is no possible way of identifying any of the remaining factors from the historic return data alone.*

Even this understates the magnitude of the estimation problem. If we actually analyse the observed eigenvalues, we discover that nearly all of them appear to be little different to what might arise purely by chance, see Figure 7.2. This plots the magnitude of the observed eigenvalues of the covariance matrix described above (giving equal weight to each month's return in the computation of the covariance matrix), ordered by size, against those that would typically occur by chance even if all the securities were independent (log) Normally distributed returns (each scaled to have the same volatility). Some of the observed eigenvalues of such random data will be randomly larger than others, so they too will show a declining pattern when ordered by size. Only perhaps 5 to 10 of the eigenvalues appear to be obviously different

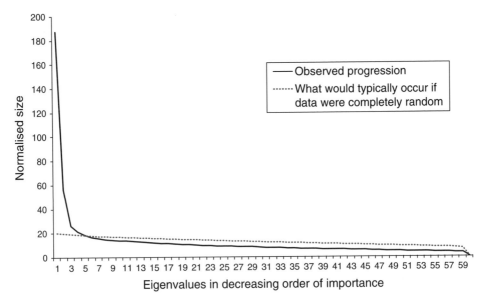

Figure 7.2 Contribution to predictive power (principal components analysis) for FTSE All-Share index – 60 months data to 30 August 2003
Source: Thomson Datastream

to what you might observe by chance. Using weekly data seems to increase the number of statistically significant eigenvalues, but not by very many, see Kemp (2009).[23]

7.5.2 Idiosyncratic risk

The inherent mathematical limitations described above make choice of idiosyncratic risk elements in time series risk models highly subjective. There simply isn't enough data to estimate these contributions reliably. We could in principle attempt to overcome this problem by increasing the time period over which we carried out the analysis. But long ago individual securities may have had quite different dynamics (if they existed at all). There comes a point where what you might gain in this respect will be lost because the information is more out

---

[23] Scherer (2007) describes how we might judge the extent to which a given (empirical) correlation matrix (i.e. standardised covariance matrix) is statistically different from a correlation matrix that exhibits zero correlation using so-called random matrix theory, see e.g. Kemp (2009) or Edelman and Rao (2005). Given certain regularity conditions, we can identify the distribution of eigenvalues for a random correlation matrix (or we can estimate the distribution by simulation techniques). He suggests a simple prescription for de-noising the correlation matrix, which is to:

(a) Calculate the empirical correlation matrix, together with its (ordered) eigenvalues
(b) Compare the largest observed eigenvalue with the range of eigenvalues that might randomly occur. As long as it is deemed large enough to be significant then remove the principal component associated with this eigenvalue from all underlying series used to estimate the empirical correlation matrix
(c) Repeat steps 1 and 2 for the new (filtered) data series until the largest eigenvalue is no longer significant, and set all remaining eigenvalues to zero.

However, it is important to add back a suitable amount of idiosyncratic risk after the truncation in step 3. Otherwise, we will on average understate the riskiness of portfolios.

of date. Moreover, the challenge of working out what to do for securities that do not have a complete history becomes greater. Often risk systems allow users to choose how to 'fill in' such missing data. Alternatively, they may merely model aggregates, such as industry, sector, rating or duration bucketed sub-indices (if these do have complete histories) and ignore or otherwise guess at the idiosyncratic risk characteristics of securities within these sub-indices.

It is important to bear this fundamental limitation in mind when using optimisers based on time series risk models, see Chapter 12, as it means that some of their answers are more subjective than might at first sight appear to be the case. It also highlights some of the challenges that arise if we want to develop a risk model that can simultaneously estimate risk well both for a broad global or regional portfolio and for a narrower market segment, e.g. just securities in some individual sector within a single country. The problem is that the eigenvalues (or to be more precise the corresponding eigenvectors) that work well at the big picture level are unlikely to be the same as the ones that work well at every single micro level at which the model might be used.

We also glossed over another subtle issue in this respect. We presented principal components analysis as if there was only one way of applying it to extract out the 'most important' eigenvectors and hence drivers to observed return series. But suppose that instead of using each of the return series unadjusted in any way, we scale one by a factor of 100 and only after doing so calculate the covariance matrix on which we then carry out our principal components analysis. It has the same number of non-zero eigenvalues (and hence eigenvectors) as before. However, much greater weight will now be given to the return series of the security that we scaled up in magnitude. The largest eigenvalue would then typically be much closer to this security's return series (adjusted to have the same mean as the other return series).

Time series risk modelling actually always includes a weighting schema. Implicitly, we have assumed earlier in this chapter that we should use a weighting schema that gives equal weight to each security being analysed. But when we attempt to create risk models that simultaneously cater for widely different types of portfolios we ideally want to use different weighting schemas for each discrete type of portfolio, to focus on the assets and liabilities that are most likely to appear in that portfolio. We will be rather lucky if we can get consistent risk models across all possible such weighting arrangements.

7.6   CREDIT RISK MODELLING

7.6.1   Introduction

Whilst conceptually credit risk modelling can be included in the above framework, astute readers will have noticed that much of the above analysis revolved around manipulation of covariance matrices and the like. It thus implicitly focuses on a world in which returns are tolerably close to being (log) Normally distributed. This is a dubious assumption to adopt for some types of instrument, most notably instruments sensitive to credit risk. Moreover, the Central Limit Theorem does not necessarily in these instances make the position much better even at a portfolio level.

Traditionally, therefore, the risks expressed by credit sensitive instruments have been analysed in a somewhat different fashion, focusing on likelihood of default and the sudden (large) jump that can occur in the value of an instrument when a credit event such as a default occurs.

In essence, this is the same division that we saw in Chapter 4 between volatility-based derivative pricing models and jump-based derivative pricing models. For assets and liabilities expected to progress 'smoothly' through time, volatility-based approaches are most commonly used, but these do not cater effectively for sudden discontinuities. In reality, few instruments actually fit wholly into one or other of these camps. We should expect the theoretically ideal approach to involve a synthesis between the two. The problem is that such mixed, i.e. more generalised, approaches can be expected to be quite complicated to frame and implement, given the analogy with pricing of hybrid derivatives, see Section 4.10.

It is therefore not surprising that in practice there has been a bifurcation in risk modelling, between instruments seen principally to express 'market' risk (which are implicitly assumed to progress in a quasi-Brownian manner through time) and instruments seen principally to express 'credit' risk (which are implicitly assumed to progress in jumps as and when the credit in question defaults).

Arguably, there have also been other more institutionalised reasons why in practice market risk and credit risk have been differentiated. For many decades, the Glass-Stegal Act in the USA largely prohibited the same company from undertaking both market making and corporate lending activities. Market makers were perceived to be principally exposed to market risk, whilst corporate lenders were perceived to be principally exposed to credit risk (albeit it has always been accepted that some 'high level' risks like interest rate risk might influence them both). The same division was retained in the notion of there being a division between a bank's 'trading' book and its 'banking' book.

Within the investment management world, 'market risk' and 'credit risk' are also often considered separately, because asset managers are often split into equity and bond teams, and 'credit' is then seen as part of bond-land.

Risk management tools are thus in the main sold to different constituencies and so often differentiate between these two types of risk, with risk models designed for credit portfolios incorporating credit spread widening factors and credit rating bucket factors that are not considered relevant for other sorts of portfolios. However, the division is not absolute. Asset managers, banks and the like often have centralised risk teams, who have an interest in harmonisation across disparate desks. Their preferences may also strongly influence risk tool selection. Some (but not necessarily all) of the underlying data management framework that a risk system needs can also be reused across different instrument types.

7.6.2   Credit ratings

One further apparent differentiator is the existence of credit ratings. Credit rating agencies such as S&P, Moody's and Fitch assign ratings ranging from AAA (least risk) to BBB to C to D, etc. to individual instruments. These are perceived to provide an external guide to investors as to how likely an instrument is to default. If bonds are downgraded then typically their spread versus, say, government debt widens.

The existence of external credit ratings allows one to think of a bond as potentially migrating between rating buckets over time. Based on actual histories of defaults, it then becomes possible to model what losses ought to arise (and when they might occur) on bonds of any given rating, see e.g. Schönbucher (2003). The theory is much like that used by actuaries to model state dependent behaviour in general insurance, and so is sometimes referred to as the 'actuarial' approach to credit ratings.

There is a key underlying assumption involved in any such analysis. It is that the credit ratings given to issuers or issues by a rating agency (or by a firm's internal ratings department if there is one) actually provide a meaningful differentiator between instruments with different likelihoods of default. If this is not true then any such approach will be no more effective than randomly assigning some score that we happen to refer to as a 'rating' to the different instruments.

An important subsidiary assumption in this respect is that a given rating when applied to one sort of instrument has a similar meaning to the same rating applied to a different sort of instrument. Some have argued that overreliance on this latter assumption was a significant contributor to some of the problems banks incurred in the 2007–09 credit crisis, when the price behaviour of asset-backed securities (particularly CDOs and asset-backed money market instruments) deviated markedly from those of more mainstream corporate bonds given the same credit rating. When faced with such criticisms, ratings agencies may fall back on a number of defences such as:

(a) Ratings are merely the rating agencies' own opinions (e.g. are covered by freedom of speech exemptions under the US constitution). They are thus 'no substitute for investors doing their own homework properly'.
(b) Ratings are 'ordinal' rather than 'cardinal', i.e. they are merely designed to indicate an ordering of likelihood of default (so AAA bonds should be less likely to default than AA bonds, etc.) rather than designed to provide a numeric figure corresponding to that likelihood (as is implicitly done by those who extrapolate from past history to estimate likely future default rates for a given rating bucket).
(c) Ratings only measure 'through the cycle' default rates, and price dynamics are driven by many other factors as well.
(d) And, following on from (c), actual 'through the cycle' default rates for different types of instrument given the same ratings haven't typically been too far out of line with each other, albeit this might be further caveated by comments such as 'the Credit Crunch has thrown up lessons that we are taking note of and will incorporate into our ratings assessment methodologies going forwards'.

The worry that undue emphasis has been placed by investors on credit ratings, particularly ones sourced from external ratings agencies, has resulted in greater scrutiny of these organisations. For example, some commentators have highlighted possible conflicts of interest that might exist in their business models that might have led them to give more favourable ratings to some instruments than was actually warranted.

Perhaps the biggest issue with ratings that some commentators have alighted on is that they have become institutionalised within regulatory solvency computations, see Chapter 8. This is in part because they have been seen as providing a relatively convenient way for investors to compare different bonds and other sorts of credit-sensitive instrument.

For example, Persaud (2007) paraphrased the then prevalent 'originate and sell' banking business model as 'originate, rate and relocate', because of the importance that end investors had ascribed to the credit rating given to an instrument by one of the main credit rating agencies. He argued that one fundamental flaw in this model is that credit risk is then transferred in part to traders of risk who did not intend to hold on to these risks over the longer term, and hence had relatively little incentive to understand in detail what it was that they were actually buying. He thought that banks and certain other market participants are naturally well placed to hedge and hold credit risk. He therefore suggested that one way out of what he saw as the 'quagmire' that credit markets got into during the summer of 2007 was for regulators to alter the system that incentivises banks and the like to transfer credit risk to others who do not share these natural advantages.

Partly in the light of these and other similar criticisms, the US Securities and Exchange Commission indicated in June 2008 that it was planning to reduce as much as possible the number of references in its rulebook to credit ratings from ratings agencies, see Financial Times (2008d).

Principle P37: A feature of modern credit markets is the assignment of credit ratings to different instruments by external credit ratings agencies. However, the existence of such ratings does not by itself ensure that these ratings are directly relevant to whatever activity the practitioner might want to use them for, or even that the ratings ascribed by such an agency to different types of instrument have the same degree of relevance for these activities.

7.6.3 Market consistency

As elsewhere, market consistency is a great leveller. A bank's trading book will in general have credit exposures to the issuers of any securities it holds. The bank is just as exposed to the risk of default via these securities as it is from any loans it has made within its banking book to the same entity (if the loan and the security rank pari passu in the event of default).

Some might disagree with this rather bold claim, particularly if the banking book typically has long-term exposures expected to be held to maturity.

However, in a market consistent framework, the value of any loan that the bank holds in its banking book should in theory (like the securities it holds in its trading book) be marked-to-market. The rise and fall in this market value (including its fall in the event of the issuer of the bond defaulting) is just as much an example of 'market risk' as any other sort of market price dynamic to which the bank might be exposed.

7.6.4 Collateralised debt obligations (CDOs)

The distinction between market risk and credit risk is also arguably rendered theoretically unsound by the development of collateralised debt obligations (CDOs) and analogues. Before explaining the rationale for this view, we describe below the main characteristics of CDOs and how risks expressed by them might be assessed.

7.6.4.1 Traditional CDOs

Traditionally, a CDO involved the establishment of a Special Purpose Vehicle (SPV) that held one set of debt instruments and funded these positions by itself issuing several different tranches of debt, see Figure 7.3.[24] This diagram is visually very similar to the schematic diagram of a financial services firm in Figure 2.1. The different tranches would have different priority levels and therefore command different credit ratings and credit spreads.

A bank could, for example, have a portfolio of debt or loans that it wanted to remove from its balance sheet. It could do so by creating an SPV and selling this portfolio to the SPV. The

---

[24] The CDO issuer might have aimed for the super senior to be given a AAA rating by an external credit rating agency, the senior tranche an AA rating, the mezzanine tranche an A rating, etc., given the importance typically placed by investors on an endorsement by an external credit ratings agency, see Section 7.6.4.3. However, this does not mean that such debt would necessarily retain these ratings through time, see Section 7.6.5.

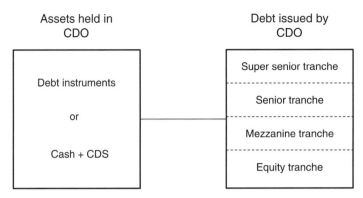

Figure 7.3 Schematic diagram of a traditional CDO

SPV needs to raise sufficient funds to be able to purchase the portfolio from the bank. So the SPV would have its own capital structure, issuing various tranches of debt (and at the bottom of the priority ladder an 'equity' tranche[25]). Different entities would subscribe to the different tranches of the SPV's debt, the spreads being demanded being dependent on where in the priority ladder the relevant paper lay. The 'technology' underlying CDOs is also known as *tranching*, as it involves a rearrangement of who suffers what if there are credit losses within a portfolio.

To understand better the impact of tranching, consider the following example. Suppose that the underlying portfolio contained 10 debt securities (equally weighted). If one of them defaulted with zero recovery value then the portfolio value would fall from say 100 to 90. This loss would be borne first by holders of the CDO's 'equity', i.e. the lowest priority tranche of the SPV's own balance sheet structure. If the equity tranche was not sufficiently large to absorb the loss then other tranches sequentially higher up the priority ladder would suffer a loss. Holders of super-senior debt, i.e. the tranche at the top of the priority ladder, would typically only suffer a loss in the hopefully highly unlikely situation of there being multiple defaults in the asset portfolio. Actually, what is relevant is not the default frequency per se, but the degree to which the observed default frequency exceeds the default rate implied by the credit spreads ruling on the bonds held within the CDO. All other things being equal, this spread (net of costs) accrues to the CDO in the absence of defaults.

Each tranche is defined by its attachment and detachment points. The *attachment point* is the level of loss which if not reached results in that tranche being repaid in full at maturity. The *detachment point* is the level of loss which if exceeded means that the tranche holders receive nothing at maturity. Figure 7.4 shows how, in broad terms, the maturity proceeds provided by

---

[25] The term 'equity' is used for the lowest tranche in the capital structure mimicking the name given to the corresponding element in the priority structure of a normal corporate. However, there is one difference that normally exists versus a standard corporate. This is that the CDO, being an SPV, is not really aiming to generate a 'profit' for its shareholders as such, and hence these equity tranches cannot normally be expected to grow because, say, the management successfully times a shift to a new sort of business. SPVs are not supposed to deviate from the specific purpose for which they are set up. It is perhaps better to think of CDOs and other SPVs as more akin to a unitised fund, but with the ownership of the fund apportioned between different tranche holders in a more complicated way than having each unit ranking pari passu with any other. In this respect, CDOs are in some ways akin to split-capital investment trusts, which also have different unit classes with different priorities and rights attaching, that in aggregate form the entire capital structure of the trust in question.

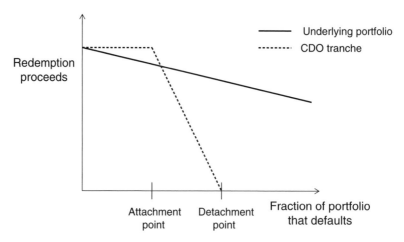

Figure 7.4   Redemption proceeds for a particular CDO tranche

a specific tranche might differ from those arising from the portfolio as a whole depending on the default experience of the CDO.

The underlying economic rationale for CDOs (and tranching more generally) is that different market participants may find different parts of the credit risk spectrum particularly relevant to their own needs. For example, different investors will have different risk profiles, perhaps because of regulatory considerations. By repackaging risks so that each tranche can be sold to the sort of investor to which it is most suited, the theory is that the sum of the parts can in some sense be 'worth'[26] more than the whole. This is also the ultimate economic rationale behind the development of other risk transference or risk sharing mechanisms such as derivatives and insurance markets.

Originally, the debt instruments held within CDOs were typically passively managed or subject to very limited substitution rights, i.e. defined rules for replacing, say, a bond that had defaulted with another non-defaulted bond, to avoid the CDO having defaulted paper on its books. More recently, it has become more common for CDOs to be actively managed. Good active management benefits the investors in the CDO (just as it benefits investors in any other sort of actively managed investment product). The primary beneficiaries are the equity tranche holders, because they are then more likely to be repaid in full. But good security selection can also result in the more highly rated tranches being upgraded and hence revalued upwards.

7.6.4.2   Single tranche CDOs

Traditional tranched CDO structures suffer from the significant disadvantage that the SPV needs to sell all of its tranches to raise the funds it needs to buy its debt portfolio. A particular problem here is the equity tranche. It would typically not be rated by a ratings agency. This in

---

[26] By 'worth' we here mean utility weighted, weighted by the investors actually holding the tranche.

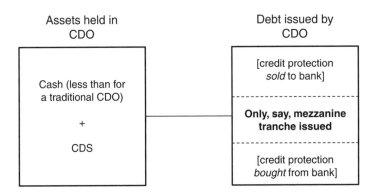

Figure 7.5   Schematic representation of a single tranche CDO

practice makes it difficult to sell to third parties.[27] It is also typically the piece of the capital structure that the creator of the CDO usually most wants to pass to someone else.

To circumvent this difficulty, investment banks developed the concept of the *single tranche CDO*. In this structure an investment bank synthetically acquires all bar a given tranche by selling to (and/or buying from) the SPV some credit protection that replicates what would have happened had there been the remaining tranches and these had been sold to third parties, see Figure 7.5. These transactions can be thought of as specific examples of *basket credit default swaps* (i.e. credit derivatives dependent on a whole basket of credit names), rather than the more standardised *single-name credit default swaps* (which depend merely on the behaviour of a single credit).

The investment bank will want to hedge the risks it incurs by entering into these *tranche CDSs*. A good way for it to hedge at least some of these risks is for it to buy single-name CDS protection on each of the individual credit risk exposures contained within the underlying portfolio. Typically, these sorts of hedges would reside in some notional hedge portfolio that the investment bank owns. Single tranche CDOs are nowadays typically actively managed, so the investment bank will ideally want to be able efficiently to modify its hedge portfolio whenever the investment manager makes a change to the underlying portfolio.

A single tranche CDO is therefore typically structured so that its credit exposures are implemented using credit default swaps rather than physical bonds, and so is often called a *synthetic CDO* (but see below for an alternative meaning that might be ascribed to this term). This makes it easier for the investment bank to alter its hedges whenever the investment manager wants to alter the underlying exposures. The fund manager adds an extra element on behalf of the investment bank to any transaction it wants to undertake, which implements a corresponding change to the investment bank's hedge portfolio. Such a CDO is typically not required to carry out its trades through the relevant investment bank, but it does need to alter the part of the hedge portfolio that it controls according to some suitable pre-agreed mathematical algorithm whenever it changes its own underlying portfolio.

---

[27] This is because, as explained in Section 7.6.2, investors have typically placed a lot of emphasis (some would say too much emphasis) on the ratings awarded by third party ratings agencies in their investment decisions regarding such instruments.

There is a further subtlety, at least with more modern single tranche CDOs. Suppose a manager wishes to alter the underlying reference portfolio in some way. Then all other things being equal, this will alter the value of the tranche CDSs. Originally, there were restrictions on what the manager could do to stop the manager changing the value too much to the detriment of the issuing bank (i.e. in this case the other side of the tranche CDS transactions). Nowadays what happens instead is that the attachment and detachment points are altered whenever a trade occurs, in a manner that leaves the replacement tranche CDSs worth the same as the value of the tranche CDSs immediately prior to the trade. Or rather it does so if the tranche CDS transactions implicit in this process are priced fairly.

The use of CDSs to 'manufacture' single tranche CDOs highlights a close linkage between these two relatively recent financial innovations. Indeed, it is possible to avoid having a SPV entirely, i.e. to have a *totally synthetic CDO*. This would involve the owner retaining the debt portfolio on its balance sheet, rather than transferring it into an SPV, and for the owner then to purchase a suitable basket CDS that provides the same risk transference as an SPV structure would have done. Again the debt portfolio could be actively managed, and again it may then be beneficial to devise mechanisms that allow the provider of the basket CDS to hedge the basket CDS efficiently. This would again imply a preference (if practical) for exposures to be traded in a hedge friendly way such as via single-name CDSs.

7.6.4.3   Risk analysis of CDOs

As we have noted above, investors typically rely heavily on the rating assigned to each tranche by a third-party ratings agency when assessing its attractiveness. The ratings agencies use Monte Carlo simulation and other techniques to identify how likely they think a given tranche is to suffer a default (and its likely recovery rate). Usually, attachment and detachment points are set so that the tranche in question achieves a certain rating, which the manager will typically wish to protect quite vigorously. Paper actually issued may not use the minimum possible subordination level, to provide some protection against a downgrade in somewhat adverse circumstances.

The detailed methodologies used by different credit rating agencies to rate CDO paper vary. For example, in 2008, one agency apparently concentrated just on the subordination level (i.e. where the attachment point is placed), whilst another one apparently took into account the expected loss if the attachment point were reached (which depends on where the detachment point is placed).

A perhaps more important point is that the rating that a given agency assigns to a traditional bond may not necessarily mean the same as an apparently identical rating that it awards to a CDO tranche. Or rather, it may do as far as the formal meaning assigned to a rating by the rating agency is concerned, but not as far as the actual purpose to which the investor then puts this rating, see Section 7.6.2.

7.6.4.4   Why CDOs render theoretically invalid any distinction between market risk and credit risk

The main reason that the tranching 'technology' used to create CDOs renders any distinction between 'credit' and 'market' risk rather spurious is that CDOs are not the only type of collateralised structures in existence. SPVs exist in which other sorts of credit assets substitute for the debt held within a traditional CDO, e.g. loans (in which case the SPV is called a collateralised loan obligation vehicle) or even other CDOs (in which case the SPV is called a CDO-squared vehicle). There are also structures where the substitute assets are not what anyone would typically associate with 'credit', e.g. they can involve equities or hedge funds. How do the resulting structures then differ economically from equity investment trusts and other similar closed end vehicles such as Real Estate Investment Trusts (*REITs*) and where then is the boundary between 'market' and 'credit' risk?

Principle P38: Collateralised debt obligations and other similar structures render theoretically invalid the distinction between market and credit risk because they make it possible to convert one into the other. Their existence therefore also highlights the need for risk measurement and management to be holistic, considering all types of risk simultaneously.

7.6.5 An accident waiting to happen?

An important element in understanding CDO tranches is to appreciate their typically *leveraged* nature. There are several angles to this. One can tell that there must be some possibility of leverage by noting that if, say, a tranche is £100m in size and has an attachment point at, say, 6% and a detachment point at, say, 10%, then this £100m must in some sense have some underlying 'reference portfolio' of £2.5bn, i.e. £100/(0.10 − 0.06)m. However, it is difficult using just this sort of basic analysis to work out the actual characteristics of any tranche, given the subordination protection that a tranche typically benefits from.

If spreads widen, i.e. market implied default rates rise, then the market implied likelihood of total or substantial loss from holding at least some CDO tranches is likely to increase by significantly more than the spread increase on the CDO's underlying holdings. Thus, all other things being equal, CDO paper may experience a magnified mark-to-market spread movement. The magnification ratio, called the tranche delta, is sensitive to a number of parameters, but JP Morgan estimated that the weighted average delta across all CDOs issued in 2004 was roughly as per Table 7.1. We note that with a traditional CDO structure the combination of all of the individual tranches has the same redemption characteristics as the overall underlying portfolio. This explains why there are some tranches which have delta of less than one. However, Table 7.1 shows that these are not the ones most typically purchased by investors in single tranche CDOs.

Of course, all other things are not always equal. In particular, CDO paper is itself subject to supply and demand considerations. The observed volatility in the price of such paper may not

Table 7.1 Approximate average delta of different CDO tranches during 2004

Tranche Type	Subordination	% of Issuance	Average Tranche Delta
Junior	0 to 3%	12	14.3
Mezzanine	3 to 7%	33	9.6
Senior	7 to 10%	24	4.3
Super	>10%	31	0.4
Total/Average		**100**	**6.0**

Source: JP Morgan, Kemp (2005)

therefore exhibit the same degree of magnification (or dampening in the case of super senior) as implied above, at least if volumes traded are limited. Or so the theory went.

The problem with such theory was that, if unpacked, such dampening would only in practice be sustained if the issuing banks themselves were somehow (perhaps unconsciously) dampening the underlying volatility. This type of price dynamic is more typically associated with instruments like real estate where volatility is dampened because liquidity characteristics can be relatively poor.

With the benefit of hindsight, it can be seen that these structures contained implicit latent liquidity risk exposures. These would be hidden if risk appetite for such instruments was strong, but could come home to roost if risk appetite fell away, as occurred in the 2007–09 credit crisis. When exacerbated by the great difficulty market participants then had in identifying realistic mark-to-market prices for such structures, transaction volumes (other than perhaps forced sales) dried up almost completely.

7.6.6   Conduits and structured investment vehicles (SIVs)

Whilst CDOs were acquiring an almost pariah-like status as the risks described above came home to roost, banks were also suffering from application of tranching in other parts of their business. Most notable were losses they were also suffering on their so-called mortgage conduits, which were SPVs also known as *structured investment vehicles* (SIVs) designed to finance mortgage debt from money raised in the wholesale money markets.

These off-balance sheet vehicles had typically been set up because they had been capital efficient from a regulatory perspective. They too often had structures in which different providers of capital shared returns differentially depending on how the underlying assets in which they were invested (i.e. typically mortgages) performed. As the underlying mortgage markets soured, some of the note holders in these structured vehicles found that their notes involved highly leveraged exposures to these mortgages. As a consequence, appetite for such instruments from money market funds and other wholesale providers of finance fell away. This meant that some of the conduits were unable to refinance short-term elements of their capital structure and in some cases ended up collapsing. But often the conduits had back-stop funding lines from their originating bank (or there was intense moral pressure put on the banks to avoid having their conduits collapse), which returned the risk back to the bank in question.

Thus we had another example of a repackaging of relatively illiquid assets into what were apparently more liquid structures, which worked fine as long as risk appetite was supportive, but ran aground when risk appetite turned negative. The negative effects of leverage hit home magnified by the coming home to roost of the previously implicit liquidity risk expressed by these structures.

7.7   RISK ATTRIBUTION

7.7.1   Intrinsic rationale

Whatever risk metric is used, there will be a natural desire to understand the sources of risk, just as there is a natural desire to understand the sources of past performance. This process is known as *risk attribution*. As with performance attribution, there is no unique way to decompose risk into its various parts, see Kemp (2009).

7.7.2   Traditional (covariance-based) risk attribution

Traditionally, risk attribution (if the risk model is characterised by a covariance matrix) proceeds as follows. We assume that there are n different instruments in the universe in question. We assume that the portfolio and benchmark weights can be represented by vectors $\mathbf{p} = (p_1, \dots, p_n)^T$ and $\mathbf{b} = (b_1, \dots, b_n)^T$ respectively. The active positions are then $\mathbf{a} = \mathbf{p} - \mathbf{b}$. If the risk model is characterised in the parsimonious manner described in Section 7.4.3 then $\sigma^2(\mathbf{a}) = \sigma^2(\mathbf{p} - \mathbf{b}) = (\mathbf{F}(\mathbf{p} - \mathbf{b}))^T \hat{\mathbf{V}}(\mathbf{F}(\mathbf{p} - \mathbf{b})) + (\mathbf{p} - \mathbf{b})^T \mathbf{Y}(\mathbf{p} - \mathbf{b})$. The matrix that describes the covariance structure between factors, i.e. $\hat{\mathbf{V}}$, corresponds to a *projection* of an n-dimensional space onto a smaller m-dimensional space.

Factors might be further grouped into one of, say, z different factor types, using what we might call a *factor classification*, $\mathbf{T}$, i.e. a $z \times m$ projection matrix that has the property that each underlying factor is apportioned across one or more 'super' factor types. By apportioned we mean that if $T_{k,j}$ corresponds to the exposure that the jth factor has to the kth factor type then the sum of these exposures for any given factor is unity, i.e. $\sum_k T_{k,j} = 1$ for all j.

Usually, such a factor classification (at least in equity-land) would involve unit disjoint elements, i.e. each factor would be associated with a single 'super' factor type. For example, equity sector classification structures are usually hierarchical, so each industry subgroup is part of a (single) overall market sector. More generally, factors might be apportioned across more than one factor type. The aggregate (relative) exposure to the different factor types is then, in matrix algebra terms, equal to $\mathbf{TFa}$.

To decompose (or 'attribute') the tracking error into its main contributors it is usual to decompose the tracking error, $\sigma(\mathbf{a})$, in the manner described in Kemp (2005) or Heywood *et al.* (2003), i.e. in line with partial differentials (scaled if necessary by a uniform factor so that the total adds up to the total tracking error). For example, if the aim is to identify the risk contribution coming from each individual security then we might calculate the *marginal contribution to tracking error*, m_i, and the *contribution to tracking error*, c_i, from the ith instrument as follows:

$$m_i \equiv \frac{\partial \sqrt{\sigma^2(\mathbf{a})}}{\partial a_i} = \frac{\partial \sqrt{\mathbf{a}^T \mathbf{F}^T \hat{\mathbf{V}} \mathbf{F} \mathbf{a} + \mathbf{a}^T \mathbf{Y} \mathbf{a}}}{\partial a_i} = \frac{1}{\sigma(\mathbf{a})} (\mathbf{F}^T \hat{\mathbf{V}} \mathbf{F} \mathbf{a})_i \tag{7.5}$$

$$c_i = a_i m_i \tag{7.6}$$

This has $\sum_i c_i = \sigma(\mathbf{a})$, so the sum of the individual contributions assigned to each instrument is the total tracking error of the portfolio. Sometimes writers focus on decomposing the variance instead of the standard deviation. However, the answers are the same up to a scaling factor.[28]

An individual security's marginal contribution to risk is closely allied to its *implied alpha*, α_i, i.e. the expected outperformance (or underperformance) you need to expect from the instrument if the portfolio is to be 'efficient' in the sense of optimally trading off risk against return. For the portfolio to be efficient we need to have all of the following n equations (one for

---

[28] This is to be expected since, for any two functions, $f(x)$ and $g(x)$, with first differentials f' and g', we have $\partial f(g(\mathbf{x}))/\partial x_i = f'(g(\mathbf{x}))\partial g(\mathbf{x})/\partial x_i$, i.e. the vector of partial differentials is the same, up to a scaling factor, for all functions of same underlying risk measure. Variance and standard deviation in this context relate to the 'same' underlying risk measure, since variance is the square of standard deviation.

each i) satisfied simultaneously, for some portfolio risk aversion parameter, λ:

$$\frac{\partial}{\partial a_i}(\alpha_i \alpha_i - \lambda(\mathbf{a}^T \mathbf{F}^T \mathbf{VFa})) = 0 \tag{7.7}$$

This implies that $\alpha_i = C + \lambda \sigma(\mathbf{a}) m_i$. Here C is an arbitrary constant that might be chosen so that the weighted average implied alpha of the benchmark is zero. The implied alpha of a given portfolio or instrument is then more directly related to the expected excess alpha that such a portfolio might deliver versus the benchmark.

We can group the c_i in whatever manner we like, as long as each relative position is assigned to a unique grouping or if it is split across several groupings then in aggregate a unit contribution arises from it. We can also attribute risk between the part that comes from the contribution to the overall 'beta' of the portfolio from each individual security and the residual (non-beta) component. The residual component derived in this manner may then be more stable than that stock's overall contribution to risk if there are small cash increments or decrements to the portfolio, see Kemp (2009).

7.7.3 Risk attribution applied to other types of risk measure

For other risk measures such as VaR, risk attribution can be developed in an analogous manner as follows. Suppose that the risk measure is defined as a function of the active positions, say, $f(\mathbf{a})$. Given suitable regularity conditions on f, we can expand this as a Taylor series for marginal changes to $\mathbf{a}$, i.e. small $d\mathbf{a}$:

$$f(\mathbf{a} + d\mathbf{a}) = f(\mathbf{a}) + \sum_i \frac{\partial f}{\partial a_i} da_i \tag{7.8}$$

We can always calculate marginal contributions to the risk measure using this sort of decomposition. But the sum of these marginal contributions won't necessarily add up to the total risk measure. Instead, the total might need to be reapportioned in proportion to the individual marginal elements to force additivity in the presentation.

An example of how such ideas can be applied to decomposition of TVaR in a credit risk context is given in Tasche (2007).

Historic risk measures can be decomposed in a similar manner, see e.g. Kemp (2005).

7.7.4 'Stand-alone' risk statistics

Any linear decomposition of risk as above depends heavily on the assumptions made concerning how instruments might co-move in tandem. If positions are assumed to be likely to move in opposite directions then their contributions will often have opposite signs in the risk decomposition, whereas if they are assumed to be likely to move in the same direction then they are more likely to have the same sign in the risk decomposition.

Managers might therefore gain a false sense of comfort or understanding of portfolio dynamics if they only study these linear decompositions, if the co-movement behaviour turns out not to be as expected. In a linear decomposition, an instrument might show up as contributing little to the overall risk of the portfolio even though the position might be quite risky in isolation.

One way of tackling this issue is to show the risk of each position in isolation (or maybe of each sector in isolation, etc.), as well as to show the overall risk decomposition. This might be called 'stand-alone' tracking error.

Any part of the risk model characterisation could be wrong, so why pick on elements relating to co-movement in particular? We perhaps see here risk managers noting that correlations seem to be unstable (and seem to exhibit the annoying habit of being most unstable, indeed most adversely wrong, at the most inopportune times). We may also be seeing risk managers noting that the impact of correlations is difficult to grasp or visualise effectively. As one might expect, risk managers, being human, are thus seeking to protect themselves from being caught short by deficiencies in their models and are seeking to remind their audience about the existence of model risk.

7.8 STRESS TESTING

7.8.1 Introduction

A more fundamentally different way of catering for *model risk* (i.e. the risk that our model of how the future might behave is wrong and not just that a particular sample drawn from it might prove undesirable) is to place less emphasis on traditional statistical measures of risk like VaR and (ex-ante) tracking error and to supplement these tools with *stress testing*.

Considerable emphasis has recently been given by risk practitioners, regulators and internal and external auditors to the use of stress tests to complement VaR-like measures of risk. This is particularly true in areas like liquidity risk that are perceived to be less well suited to VaR-like risk measures. More generally, portfolios (or risks) that are perceived to be less well diversified or non-linear or skewed may be viewed as less suited to VaR style risk measures, so stress testing may be considered potentially more important in, say, bond-land and currency-land than equity-land.

The basic idea behind stress testing is to identify a range of scenarios which in aggregate describe what might 'go wrong'. The term 'stress testing' is used nearly synonymously by risk managers with the term 'scenario analysis', but arguably scenario analyses might also include focus on what might 'go right'. We again see a natural bias on the part of risk managers to worry about what might 'go wrong' (since this is what they are typically paid to do).

The Basel Committee on Banking Supervision thinks that greater emphasis on stress testing is important, e.g. it wants to make sure that 'stress testing is incorporated systematically into the regular process for generating market risk information' according to Rowe (2005). However, as Rowe (2005) also points out, not everyone shares quite such a rosy view of stress testing. For example, he quotes the following comment from Barry Schachter regarding the Basel Committee's stance: 'it appears to have been accepted as a self-evident matter of fact' that 'the results from portfolio stress testing generate additional knowledge about potential portfolio losses not obtainable from value-at-risk . . . it is not easy to find any concrete discussion of how stress testing generates additional knowledge, what that knowledge is, how great is that increment over VAR-obtainable knowledge and whether stress testing can provide sufficient additional knowledge to fill the gap between VAR-obtainable knowledge and "enough" knowledge'.

7.8.2 Different interpretations

This apparent difference of opinion seems to stem from the existence of four possible interpretations of what we mean by stress testing:

Principle P39: Important tools in the armoury of practitioners wishing to mitigate against 'model' risk are to think outside the box and to carry out a range of stress tests that consider potentially different scenarios. However, stress testing should not be seen as a perfect panacea when doing so, since the stresses tested will often be constrained by what is considered 'plausible' in relation to past experience.

---

(1) *Stress testing may be equated with analysis of the impact on the portfolio (or firm as a whole) contingent on movements in specific market drivers, the sizes of these movements being considered to be appropriately within the tail of the plausible distribution of outcomes*

Typically a range of such scenarios would be considered in turn, e.g. oil price up 30 %, equity market down 40 %, leading counterparty defaults, . . ., and there might also be some consideration of what are considered to be plausible combinations of such events.

It may be that this is the interpretation that Barry Schachter was focusing on. For such stress tests to be 'reasonable' and hence, in a sense, for them to be 'market consistent' they will naturally need to take some account of what is considered a sensible range of outcomes. This will ultimately be influenced in people's minds by what has already happened. In a sense, therefore, they can be thought of as VaR-like in nature, using a range of different underlying VaR models, one for each stress test considered.

For example, a common way in practice to frame such scenarios is to identify every observed movement in the driver in question that has actually happened over some extended period of time in the past, to identify what impact each of these movements might have on the portfolio/firm as currently positioned if the movement was repeated now, and to use as the stress test the worst such outcome (or the second such worst outcome, . . .).

This is called a (historic) 'worst-loss' stress test. However, we could also characterise such a stress test (albeit to do so would be rather a mouthful) as an 'x-quantile historic simulation VaR using a VaR model derived by considering the impact of just one single factor driver'. Here x would be set by reference to the number of observations in the past dataset, to correspond to the worst observed outcome. Indeed, one advantage of using this terminology would be to remind us that the larger the number of past periods included in the worst loss computation the more onerous a worst loss stress test is likely to be, because the more likely it becomes that it will include a really adverse outcome. Even if users in practice show a range of worst loss scenarios relating to different drivers, each one is still in isolation VaR-like in derivation.

(2) *Stress testing may be equated with specific industry-wide stress scenarios mandated by a regulator and directly applicable in the computation of regulatory capital*

Examples here would include many of the so-called 'standardised' approaches set out in Basel II (and likely to be defined under Solvency II) as well as the so-called 'resilience' reserving computations mandated by the FSA for UK insurance companies, see Chapter 8.

For these stress tests to be intellectually credible their derivation will typically need to exhibit a suitable level of logical consistency. Although driven in part by the prior beliefs of whoever has formulated them, this means that their derivation will almost inevitably also take due account of what has actually happened in the past, see e.g. Frankland *et al.* (2008). This is particularly true if the relevant 'standardised' framework involves several different stress test elements and there is a need for the stress tests to be seen to exhibit consistency relative to each other.

The natural way to achieve this consistency is again to build up each one of them in a VaR-like manner. Most probably this would be done repeatedly, in each case limiting attention to one or at most a few drivers at a time. Deriving different stress tests from different underlying models will to some extent mitigate model risk. Moreover, a given regulatory stress test often typically involves a combination of sub-stress tests (a particularly simple example would be if the stress test involves consideration of both an up and a down move and focuses only on the one that is more onerous). Nesting stress tests in the overall capital computation may also further protect against model risk.

One problem with such a nested stress test regulatory framework, however logical is the derivation of each stress test in isolation, is that the ways in which the stress tests are combined is ultimately rather ad hoc. This can result in an overly prudent framework and/or one that does not foster suitable incentives for enhanced risk management.

Regulatory frameworks are increasingly encouraging firms to adopt more sophisticated ways of measuring risk, which one can think of as more fully VaR-like in nature, placing greater emphasis on more accurately assessing how different contributors to risk might interact.

An opposite problem is then that in isolation there may be insufficient incentive for firms to take account of the possibility that they will be hit (singly or in tandem) by events that have no direct prior market analogue but which if they did occur might hammer or even imperil the continuing viability of a firm. These are the 'unknown unknowns' or 'black swans' of, say, Taleb (2007). This leads us to a third interpretation of the term 'stress testing', and probably one that is gaining ground relative to the first two.

(3) *Stress testing may be equated with a greater focus on the sorts of configurations of market events that might lead to large losses, involving something of a mental adjustment away from purely probability theory and towards hypothetical scenario construction*

Such a form of stress testing involves some group of individuals within a firm ideally starting with a clean slate and then brainstorming up potential scenarios that might adversely impact the firm. They would then endeavour to quantify what impact these scenarios might actually have on the firm (bearing in mind how effective previously considered risk mitigants already in place might actually prove to be in such circumstances). The hope is that such a process may highlight potential weaknesses in existing risk mitigants, and thus suggest refinements that might help improve the firm's risk management practices. Regulators encouraging this sort of activity often want to see that the 'use test' is satisfied, i.e. that the firm's senior management actually knows what its appetite for risk is and takes due regard of results coming out of such analyses.

The challenge, as we have highlighted above, is that typically stress testing ultimately still has, as its starting point, assumptions about how underlying markets might behave. If the target audience for the stress tests (e.g. senior management) consider these assumptions to be unrealistic or too onerous (or not onerous enough) to involve implausible correlations between events or to lack credibility in some other way, then they may place little credence on the chosen stress tests and their effective informational content may thereby be lost.

CRMPG-III (2008) makes an interesting suggestion here, which is to promote the use of so-called 'reverse stress testing'. This terminology seems to derive from the ideas of 'reverse optimisation' (see Section 12.5) or 'reverse engineering' (i.e. the process of analysing what a piece of hardware or software does and working out from it how it does it).

The starting point in a reverse stress test would be an assumption that over some suitable period of time the firm suffers a large loss. For a large integrated financial institution of the sort that CRMPG-III focuses on this might be a very large multi-billion dollar loss. The analysis would then work backward to identify how such a loss might occur given actual exposures at the time the reverse stress test is conducted. For very large losses these would most probably need to include contagion or other systemic (i.e. industry-wide) factors or compounding operational issues that might not typically be included in a conventional stress test built up the other way round. Done properly, CRMPG-III argue, this 'would be a very challenging exercise, requiring the engagement of senior personnel from both the income-producing and the control functions in a context in which the results of such exercises would be shared with senior management'. CRMPG-III is particularly focused on issues such as systemic liquidity risk and counterparty risk and hence it is perhaps particularly apposite that it should focus on stress testing methodologies that might be expected to cater for industry-wide business disrupting stresses of the sort that happen very infrequently but are of very serious magnitude for large numbers of industry participants simultaneously.

The idea of reverse stress testing has been picked up by regulators. For example, in FSA (2008c), the FSA indicate that they are planning to require most types of UK financial firms to carry out reverse stress testing involving consideration of scenarios most likely to cause the firm's business model to fail (however unlikely such scenarios might be deemed to be). They note that a firm's business model might fail before it actually runs out of regulatory capital. The FSA thought that senior management at firms less affected by the 2007–09 credit crisis had more successfully established comprehensive firm-wide risk assessment processes in which thoughtful stress and scenario testing played a material part, allowing better informed and more timely decision making.

Another name for this sort of reverse stress testing might be 'stress testing to destruction' although some of the connotations of such terminology may not be ones that regulators are comfortable promoting.

(4) *Finally, stress testing may actually be a coded reference to a sentiment such as 'you messed up in the past, make sure you do better in the future'*

A big challenge for risk managers is that stress tests are typically perceived by their recipients to provide the plausible boundary of what might happen in practice (excluding 'really extreme' events such as an asteroid striking the earth or a major nuclear war which are much too doomsday to be typically considered worth bringing up in such contexts!). They can therefore always with hindsight be shown to have been inadequate, if something even more extreme does come along in the meantime. So, whenever something more extreme comes along we can expect there to be calls for additional stress testing methodologies to be applied that would have included such an outcome within the range of results considered by the set of stress tests under consideration.

We can see such a phenomenon at work in developments surrounding the 2007–09 credit crisis, see Chapter 5, or perhaps in, say, the recommendations of CRMPG-III (2008) in relation to large integrated financial intermediaries carrying out stress tests regarding their maximum liquidity outflow, bearing in mind how their normal sources of liquidity, both secured and unsecured, could be disrupted for the firm, the markets or both. The considerable pain that firms suffered as a result of a drying up of liquidity was typically well outside the spectrum of risks that their liquidity stress tests (that Basel II encouraged them to do) might have implied, so the message here is to use stress tests that are more 'market consistent', i.e. more plausibly consistent with potential adverse actual market dynamics (particularly ones that are in the sufficiently recent past that they are high up in people's minds).

7.8.3   Further comments

There does seem to be a trend towards an interpretation of stress testing that sees it as a complement to, rather than a restatement of, VaR-like techniques. This is particularly true in areas where, for whatever reason, VaR-like techniques are less well entrenched, which can be because:

(a) The risks are more 'jumpy' or more 'skewed' in nature;
(b) The regulatory framework has yet to develop standardised approaches to risk management in the area in question and regulators want to put more of the onus back on management to consider appropriately the risks of extreme events; and/or
(c) There is a desire to encourage a mentality that 'thinks outside the box' to help highlight appropriate risk mitigants that might reduce the downside impact of existing exposures and to foster a business culture able to react more effectively to whatever actual stresses the future holds.

Whatever the interpretation adopted, any stress testing requires the re-evaluation of an entire portfolio or firm balance sheet assuming some set of market events (the stress 'scenario') occurs. It thus in principle requires employment of the full panoply of valuation tools described earlier in this book. CRMPG-III (2008) makes a similar point, noting the importance of suitable valuation disciplines in mitigating systemic risks and highlighting the impact that challenges in the valuation of complex instruments might have in this respect.[29] For example, CRMPG-III (2008) highlights the increased possibility of valuation disputes relating to collateral flows that might further exacerbate systemic issues. This in turn may need a fair investment in time, money and effort, e.g. to ensure that positions, exposures and valuations are available in a timely manner and in suitably consolidated/aggregated form.

Another thing that can be said about the more 'complementary' style of stress testing that seems to be coming to the fore is that it typically requires a fair amount of subjective input, indeed potentially significantly more than is the case with VaR (particularly if the firm buys in a VaR system from a third party). It may therefore be potentially more time consuming (and more IT intensive) to do, if you want to do it well.

---

[29] As an aside, CRMPG-III (2008) makes an interesting point in this regard that an instrument that some might intrinsically view as 'high risk' and/or 'complex' in nature may not necessarily be regarded as such by the market as a whole because of its liquidity and price transparency, and vice versa. For example, large capitalisation equities are generally considered neither high risk nor complex because they are actively traded on the stock market. However, if such stocks were priced in a vacuum based on, say, a dividend discount model, then the analyst trying to build up such a model might well conclude that they were rather complex entities. Likewise, futures markets relating to high risk complex financial instruments might not be considered to circumvent the inherent complexity in their underlyings merely because of the transparency that the futures market might bring to the price of the futures themselves. Complexity is clearly in this instance in the eye of the beholder!

One final comment is that stress testing, even the sort of reverse stress testing or 'testing to destruction' described in Section 7.8.2(3), focuses on loss up to the level of the stress rather than beyond it. Stress testing is thus closer to VaR than TVaR in terms of underlying mindset. As conventionally implemented it may not give adequate focus to the financial implications of events in the downside tail, see Section 10.2. More appropriate than 'testing to destruction' may be some sort of 'testing beyond destruction', to capture better the differential impact that tail risks can have on customers versus shareholders.

8

Capital Adequacy

8.1 INTRODUCTION

An accepted feature of modern developed capitalist economies is the regulation of businesses and organisations operating within the financial sphere. Sometimes this involves self-regulation by the industry concerned but it is much more common for it to be carried out by governments or by government established bodies, e.g. the relevant central bank or some other financial regulatory authority. The work of individual practitioners within these fields, if they belong to professional bodies such as the accountancy or actuarial professions, may also be subject to professional standards or codes of conduct. There may be 'reserved' activities that can only be carried out by appropriately qualified professionals (or firms of them). Examples include auditing and approval of life insurance company insurance reserves which in nearly all developed economies are required to be carried out by accountants and actuaries respectively.[1]

Why is regulation in this sense so pervasive within the financial services industry?

It is said that 'bad money drives out good'.[2] Governments of virtually all hues subscribe to the thesis that public confidence in the sound functioning of the financial system is an essential prerequisite for economic stability and prosperity. The perceived need to maintain *financial stability* is so strong that many regulatory bodies specifically have such a mandate written into their charters or governing framework.[3]

In this chapter we explore key characteristics of financial regulatory regimes, with particular focus on their capital adequacy elements. As in Chapter 2 we introduce the topic by considering some of the key characteristics of money itself and how these characteristics can be expected to influence the structures of regulatory regimes relating to monetary matters. We also summarise or comment on a number of existing or soon to be introduced international capital adequacy frameworks, including Basel II (for banks) and Solvency II (for insurers).

The aim here is not to provide a comprehensive analysis of such frameworks. To do so would make the book much too long and liable to be out of date as soon as it was published. Instead, the aim is to pick out key aspects of existing regulatory frameworks and to benchmark them against how we might expect regulatory regimes to operate were they to embed fully market consistent principles in their construction. The focus in this chapter is on the regulated

---

[1] Such codes of conduct can also be imposed more widely on most or all individuals working within the financial services industry, e.g. a substantial proportion of all individuals working within the UK financial services industry are required to sign a contract with the FSA to achieve the status of an 'approved person'. By doing so, they assent (personally) to adhering to certain personal codes of conduct established by the FSA.

[2] This saying perhaps originated around the time of the Napoleonic wars when the British government introduced paper money in addition to the gold-based money that was also in circulation. The gold previously used for carrying out transactions was rapidly hoarded with people switching to using the paper money.

[3] For example, the UK's Financial Services Authority has four statutory objectives, of which the first according to their website, www.fsa.gov.uk, is 'market confidence: maintaining confidence in the financial system'. This argument was at the forefront of many of the banking rescues that occurred around the world in late 2008. According to Roach (2008), the US Federal Reserve does not have a similar mandate to maintain financial stability, but ought to.

entity itself. We leave to Chapter 11 the topic of what impact such regimes might have on the wider economic fabric of society, including the topic of pro-cyclicality.

8.2   FINANCIAL STABILITY

The perceived need to maintain public confidence in money and in the sound functioning of the financial system is particularly true of money in its role as a medium of exchange. Only if there is public confidence in the soundness of money, particularly the government's own legal tender, is the economic catastrophe of having to return to a barter economy avoided. In this sense we all at heart subscribe to the economic merits of specialism and division of labour. We know that we cannot ourselves possibly fulfil efficiently everyone else's role in the economy as well as our own.

Somewhat more circumspect are society's views on the soundness of money in its other role, as a store of value. Here governments (generally) accept the futility of standing in the way of the inevitable. There is an acceptance that stock markets, housing markets, etc. rise and fall as investor sentiment changes. A government prop-up of an unsustainable market level is ultimately seen as a recipe for disaster for the public purse.

This circumspection also shows up in the relatively common historical phenomenon of monetary inflation. This has the incidental impact of inflating away the real value of any fixed coupon debt that governments might previously have issued. Economists debate at length the interaction of different inflationary drivers, what levers governments and central banks have over these drivers and how any such levers should be used in practice. For our purposes it suffices to note that monetary inflation increases the 'convenience yield' on legal tender, described in Chapter 5. Only when it becomes large (or is perceived to be at risk of becoming large) does it seem to lead to a really serious breakdown in confidence in money as a medium of exchange.[4] More moderate inflation does not seem to have the same undesirable (immediate) impact on the financial system, although it may still have undesirable consequences for the wider economy and a redistributionary effect on wealth between different members of society.

The different views that seem to apply to the different functions of money also seem to influence how regulatory systems have developed for different parts of the financial services industry. The commercial entities most closely associated with the role of money as a medium of exchange are banks and equivalents.[5] A major goal of regulation of such entities (at least within this sphere of their business activities) is to ensure that bank failures are rare, and that if they do occur they should not wipe out too many small depositors or be likely to lead to wider systemic concerns about the soundness of the monetary system. Most money is nowadays held in bank accounts. If failures do occur then the regulator or central bank may intervene and arrange for the bank in question to be nationalised or to be taken over by a bank perceived to be more soundly capitalised.[6] Regulatory frameworks also typically try

---

[4] The experience of the Weimar Republic (and the subsequent rise of the Nazi party) in Germany is a haunting example of the catastrophe that can arise if hyperinflation takes root.

[5] Many countries also have bank-like entities that may be regulated more or less like commercial banks depending on historical precedent, e.g. credit unions, building societies, local savings banks, state funded banks, government sponsored entities, etc.

[6] For it to be economically rational for other banks to be willing to support the regulator or central bank with such rescues there must either be some belief in a residual value attaching to the bank being rescued, or the regulatory authority must be able to 'strong arm' the banks in question to see the wider economic merit (to them) of participating

to take account of lessons learned from previous crises, e.g. the dangers of moral hazard and adverse selection highlighted by the US savings and loans crisis of the 1980s and 1990s.[7] The dangers of regulatory arbitrage are also well understood (if not necessarily easy to eliminate), i.e. the risk that entities or activities will focus on the weakest links in the entire regulatory superstructure, if there are financial incentives to do so. This has led banking regulatory frameworks in different countries (and to the extent that they are applied differently within a country) to converge over time towards internationally agreed capital adequacy frameworks, most notably the ones encapsulated in the Basel Accords, see Section 8.3.

Financial services firms majoring on activities more related to 'money as a store of value' are also typically regulated, but here the focus seems more about trust and honouring promises. Honouring promises is an essential part of money being a medium of exchange.[8] But for, say, life insurers, key are the actual promises being made and ensuring that they are adequately covered by the insurer's financial resources. Different types of insurance policies can have quite different economic characteristics (e.g. unit-linked versus annuities). They thus express different forms of promise and as a result may need different levels of capital to be set aside for them to secure such promises.

General (i.e. property/casualty) insurance business is typically shorter term, but still involves a monetary 'promise' by the insurer, which customers expect to be honoured. So these sorts of firms are also typically regulated. A particular challenge is that it is rarely easy for customers to assess possible outcomes in advance of entering into an insurance contract (in contrast to the scope a customer has to view what he might get if he were, say, to want to buy a car or a fridge). So there may be requirements built into such regulatory frameworks designed to include what the customer might reasonably have expected any such promise to involve, even though the promise itself may be more difficult to pin down with precision.

Historically, therefore, it is not surprising that insurance companies have been regulated in different ways to banks. However, the existence of yield curves reminds us that time is a continuous dimension. Whilst we may all view the long-term as diverging from the short- term, pinning down the dividing line between the two is notoriously difficult, if not impossible. There are many ways in which insurance companies and banks encroach on each other's space.[9] A

---

in such a rescue. The latter ultimately requires the banking industry as a whole to have sound economic prospects, highlighting the ultimate importance of future new business profitability in the intrinsic capital adequacy of players within the financial services industry (even if it is not something typically incorporated explicitly within solvency computations).

[7] The US savings and loans crisis of the 1980s and 1990s led to large numbers of failures of savings and loans associations (S&Ls) there. These are financial institutions somewhat akin to the building societies found in the UK and some Commonwealth countries specialising in accepting savings deposits and making mortgage loans. Some estimates put total losses at around US$160bn, most of which was ultimately paid for by the US government, i.e. the US taxpayer. Perceived causes of the crisis included widening of their investment powers and giving them greater scope to behave like banks via the Depository Institutions Deregulation and Monetary Control Act 1980 without at the same time imposing adequate regulatory capital requirements on them. The changes introduced new risks and speculative opportunities which many managers pursued with gusto, even though they may have lacked the ability or experience to evaluate or administer them.

[8] E.g. the wording 'I promise to pay the bearer on demand the sum of . . .' on many bank notes.

[9] Examples include guarantee type contracts that either type of firm may offer, or longer-term derivative instruments such as swaps that may be longer even than most long-term insurance contracts. Also, the rescue by the US Federal Reserve Bank in late 2008 of AIG, a large US insurer, indicated that banking authorities there believed AIG's failure would present systemic risks to the US banking system, given the extent to which it had become involved in activities more traditionally associated with the banking industry.

consequence has been a tendency for the regulatory frameworks within which each operates to converge, to the extent that the risks involved are similar. This can be seen in the evolution of the EU-wide Solvency II insurance company regulatory framework due to be implemented shortly, see Section 8.4.

Principle P40: An accepted feature of modern economies is the regulation of firms operating within the financial services industry. The formulation of the different regulatory frameworks applicable to different parts of this industry should bear in mind the different types of roles different players undertake within this industry and how they interact with the fundamental attributes of money, namely how money is a medium of exchange and how it is also a store of value. For practical reasons, harmonisation across different types of firms may also be desirable, to avoid regulatory arbitrage, given that many firms are involved in many different parts of the industry simultaneously.

Pension fund capital adequacy presents an interesting case study in the evolution and articulation of such 'promises', see Section 8.5. There is less harmonisation across countries, particularly in relation to defined benefit (DB) pension schemes, which involve scheme members being 'promised' pension benefits that may depend on future salary movements and the like. Much of the debate about how these entities ought to be regulated and capitalised is driven by views about what their members have actually been promised.

Asset managers, wealth managers and the like typically try to make as few asset-related promises as possible, realising that 'assets go down as well as up' and 'past performance may not be a guide to the future'. However, they still typically 'promise' to behave in an appropriate manner in the context of financial markets, e.g. to avoid market abuse, to act in the best interests of their clients, etc. and are thus still typically subject to financial regulation.[10]

Often, asset managers will be agents of other sorts of institutions mentioned above. However, they may often also manage assets directly for members of the public, usually within specially established legal vehicles designed to facilitate efficient pooling of investors' interests. Some of these vehicles are themselves tightly regulated, e.g. EU-based UCITS style pooled vehicles, or their US mutual fund equivalents. Others may be subject to less regulation, e.g. hedge funds established in offshore jurisdictions. Sales of less regulated pooled vehicles are often not allowed to general members of the public, again highlighting the point that the 'promise' here is really to behave in an appropriately customer-focused manner. However, more sophisticated and wealthier investors may be able to access less regulated vehicles, as long as the asset manager takes reasonable care to ensure that the investor really is sophisticated enough to understand the potential additional risks involved.

The regulations applied to the vehicles themselves do not typically include explicit capital adequacy type requirements but are more focused on the 'promise' that the fund in question will be run in a suitable manner. There may be requirements on risk management disciplines and processes used, see e.g. CESR (2008), and on transparency, valuation disciplines and expense levels, etc.

---

[10] Although asset managers are subject to capital adequacy requirements, it can be argued that for them a more important element of financial regulation is the application of conduct of business rules (including rules about treating customers fairly).

The world is never static and regulatory frameworks change, becoming more or less onerous through time. That being said, compliance requirements and regulatory sophistication have been on a fairly steady upward trend for my entire working life. It is difficult to see behavioural factors that might seriously reverse such a trend any time soon unless society as we know it changes radically too. Modern sophisticated economies involve complex monetary interactions between different economic participants. Given the importance of financial stability to the sound workings of such economies, it seems a small cost to impose reasonably sophisticated regulatory frameworks on parties that might endanger this stability, as long as the frameworks actually promote such stability and are not disproportionate in terms of effort to apply.[11]

Regulatory capital requirements for both banks and insurers increasingly recognise that an adequate capital base is not necessarily the only or even in some cases the most important way of protecting against insolvency. Both Basel II and Solvency II adopt in broad terms a three pillar approach to supervision, involving:

(a) a Pillar 1 element focusing on explicit quantitative requirements (i.e. how much capital a bank or an insurer should hold);
(b) a Pillar 2 element focusing on internal governance, risk management and supervisory review; and
(c) a Pillar 3 element focusing on market discipline and transparency.

8.3   BANKING

8.3.1   The Basel Accords

The Basel Accord of 1988, commonly known as 'Basel I', was the first attempt by the Basel Committee on Banking Supervision (BCBS) to unite bank regulatory and economic capital, see BCBS (1988). It went through a number of refinements over time, e.g. BCBS (1996) and BCBS (1998). Basel I addressed only market risk and credit risk, the former in some detail and the latter only cursorily. For credit risk, it became apparent that Basel I was too conservative in some respects and too lax in others. Basel I also ignored operational risk.

Some of these shortcomings have been addressed in Basel II, implemented in 2007, see BCBS (2006). Basel II contains a significantly enhanced treatment of credit risk, as well as methodologies to assist in the estimation of operational risk. Market risk has been left largely unchanged in Basel II.

However, it is highly unlikely that Basel II will remain unchanged. Like many other aspects of the financial system, it has come in for high-level criticism as a result of the 2007–09 credit crisis. In an interview with the *Financial Times* in October 2008, the new chairman of the UK's Financial Services Authority said that regulators should be prepared to engage in a fundamental debate about how to set banks' minimum capital requirements following state bank bailouts in Europe and the USA, see Financial Times (2008e).

Examples of high level weaknesses that Basel II might exhibit are described in Yetis (2008) and Wood (2008). They each highlight several ways in which banks can 'game' Basel II (and probably have already done so) by tranching credit risk in different ways, thereby reducing

---

[11] One of the principles of good regulation that the UK's Financial Services Authority is required to adhere to is 'proportionality', i.e. that the restrictions imposed on the industry must be proportionate to the benefits that are expected to result from those restrictions. Judgements here include costs to firms and consumers.

their required capital base. They have been strongly incentivised to use such techniques given the extreme capital stresses that banks have faced as a result of the 2007–09 credit crisis.

We can draw out some high-level observations about Basel II from the structure of the consolidated Basel II framework as set out in BCBS (2006), including:

(a) The majority of BCBS (2006) relates to the first pillar, i.e. to minimum capital requirements, although a reasonable amount of attention is also placed on the sound internal governance and on supervisory review. Within the first pillar, the majority of the focus is on credit risk (perhaps reflecting the substantial exposures to credit risk that many banks have), and there is also a fair amount of attention paid to market risk, given its importance to some (often larger) commercial and investment banking groups. Operational risk is specifically mentioned, but the section is relatively modest in size compared with corresponding sections for market and credit risk, probably reflecting the lack of consensus on how to measure such risks most effectively. Liquidity risk is not much focused on in Pillar 1, although it is referred to within Pillar 2 in relation to stress testing and more recently in BCBS (2008). There is a requirement to take account of potential illiquidity of lower-quality assets when assessing the effectiveness of haircuts within collateral management.

(b) Tools and techniques familiar to those advising longer-term investing institutions also appear in Basel II, e.g. taking into account maturity mismatches. This highlights the extent to which the maturity profiles of banks can nowadays stretch out in time.

(c) The basic premise underlying credit risk measurement appears to be that estimates incorporated in the computation should be grounded where possible in historical experience and empirical evidence, rather than subjective or judgemental considerations, see e.g. paragraph 449 of BCBS (2006).[12] This is also reflected in the backtesting disclosures included in Pillar 3, which aim to provide externally some assessment of whether the risk measurement estimates used by the firm corresponded in a statistical sense with (subsequent) observed outcomes.

8.3.2 Market risk

Under Basel II, banks are required to segregate their business into two parts, a trading book and a banking book. The former includes positions held with trading intent. These are positions held intentionally for short-term resale and/or with the intent of benefiting from actual or expected short-term price movements or to lock in arbitrage profits (including, for example, proprietary positions, matched principal broking and market making). Banks are required to have clearly defined policies and procedures that identify which exposures should be included and which should be excluded from the trading book.

Market risk is then defined as the risk of losses in on- and off-balance sheet positions arising from movements in market prices, which in BCBS (2006) are taken to be risks relating to interest rate related instruments and equities in the trading book and foreign exchange

---

[12] It is possible to construe reference to 'empirical' evidence in, for example, paragraph 449 of BCBS (2006) as leaving open the door to the sort of fully market consistent-based risk modelling we describe in Chapter 10. In paragraph 450, banks are also required to demonstrate that economic or market conditions that underlie the data being used for such estimation purposes are relevant to current and foreseeable conditions. However, elsewhere BCBS (2006) mandates set confidence levels on outcomes (rather than on costs of hedging such outcomes) and, for example, indicates that loss given default estimates must be grounded in historical recovery rates.

and commodities risk throughout the bank. However, as we saw in Section 7.6, differentiation between market and credit risk is at times rather artificial at best, so banks carrying out their own internal capital adequacy assessments may not themselves adopt such a compartmentalised approach to their own exposures.

Various market consistent elements are included within Basel II, e.g. the need to focus on marking-to-market as much as possible. Basel II mandates using the more prudent side of bid–offer unless the institution is a significant market maker in a particular position type and it can close out at mid-market.

As with other elements of Basel II there is generally flexibility to choose between a 'standardised' risk measurement method and a 'more sophisticated' version, the latter here being called the 'internal models approach'. The use of the latter is conditional on explicit approval of the bank's supervisory authority.

The simplified approach can be thought of as mandating a (relatively) straightforward methodology for adding up exposures. For example, for options, the delta and gamma are calculated and a specified shift is assumed to occur to the underlying. Some allowance is also included for volatility (i.e. vega) risk, by inclusion of a standardised up or down shift in volatility levels. Some but only limited offset is allowed to reflect correlation between different exposures.

The internal models approach can be much more sophisticated. It will generally aim to assess more accurately the risks being covered, presumably with the expectation that the extra sophistication will lead to lower capital requirements and/or more efficient allocation of capital and hence business management. The results are presented in the form of a value-at-risk computation along the lines described in Chapter 7, involving a 99th percentile (one-tailed) confidence interval and a 10 day holding period. The historical observation (i.e. data sample) period is constrained to a minimum of 1 year (or where, say, exponential weighting is used, a minimum average time lag of 6 months). No specific type of model is prescribed as long as it is considered to capture all the material risks run by the bank, including non-linear price characteristics. Specific risk components, see Section 7.5, can be included as long as they satisfy certain requirements, e.g. they explain historical price variations, capture concentrations, capture name-related basis and event risk, are robust and are validated through backtesting.

Irrespective of the precise methodology involved, the relevant supervisory authority is only supposed to approve an internal model approach if it thinks that:

(a) the bank's risk management system is conceptually sound and implemented with integrity;
(b) the bank has adequate numbers of staff skilled in the use of sophisticated models, not only in the trading area but also in risk control, audit and, if necessary, back office areas;
(c) the bank's models have a proven track record of reasonable accuracy in measuring risk (highlighting the potential backward-looking bias noted above); and
(d) the bank also regularly conducts stress tests, which in this context are seen as trying to identify extraordinary configurations of market events or influences that are not well described by VaR-style models.

The models (and the backtesting of them) also need to be validated by external auditors and/or the regulator itself. Validation is supposed not only to refer to the concepts involved but also to their implementation. There is little point in adopting sophisticated risk measurement and management tools if they are applied to the wrong dataset.

8.3.3   Credit risk

It is in the area of credit risk where Basel II is perhaps most different to Basel I. The popularity of Value-at-Risk as the metric of choice for measuring market risk is perhaps particularly due to its endorsement in Basel I, but its simplicity, adaptability and applicability to a wide range of products have also played an important role. Credit risk, one might argue, is more complex, being more characterised by large jumps (on default) and hence greater skews and fat tails. It may involve more complicated mathematics (e.g. copulas) and it involves an understanding of, and differentiation between, asset and default correlations, as well as a more refined understanding of the capital structure of an issuer's balance sheet. It also perhaps requires somewhat more parameters (e.g. loss given default, probability of default, exposure at default) than market risk.

Banks may choose between two approaches to calculate capital requirements for credit risk, namely, the standardised approach (which is a slightly modified version of Basel I) or the Internal Ratings Based (IRB) approach. Within IRB, banks are permitted to use their own internal ratings as inputs to the capital calculation. Regulatory minimum capital for a loan portfolio is calculated in a bottom-up manner, by estimating and then summing capital requirements at the individual loan level.

The underlying theory used for the IRB is the Asymptotic Single Risk Factor (ASRF) model. Although the BCBS neither cites nor documents this model, it is widely believed that the precursor to Basel II in this respect was Gordy (2003). This was itself derived from an adaptation of the single asset model of Merton (1974), later extended to an entire portfolio by Vasicek (1977), as well as Pykhtin and Dev (2002).

In this model, portfolio credit risk is separated into two categories, systematic and idiosyncratic risk. Systematic risk can be considered as representing the effect of unexpected changes in macroeconomic and financial market-wide conditions on borrower performance. Idiosyncratic risk represents the effects of risk connected with individual companies. One of the key assumptions of the ASRF approach is that the credit portfolio comprises a large number of relatively small exposures, so portfolio idiosyncratic risk becomes diversified away. All systematic risk, such as industry or regional risk, is modelled with only one single common systematic risk factor that drives all dependence across credit losses in the portfolio. This can be thought of as akin to the LHP pricing model approximation used in CDO pricing, see Section 4.8. The result is that the total capital charge can then be built up in a linear fashion, i.e. as the sum of the contributions from each individual name.

The IRB approach is itself further divided into a Foundation IRB and an Advanced IRB approach. In the Foundation IRB, banks may only determine and use their own internal ratings (and associated probabilities of default). In the Advanced IRB, banks may measure and use other inputs (over and above their own internal ratings) in the (specified) regulatory capital calculations.

In either case, the bank is expected to forecast the average level of losses that they can reasonably (on average) expect to experience over a 1-year horizon, known as expected losses (EL). Losses above this expected level – known as unexpected losses (UL) – may occur, but both their timing and severity are unknown.

Banks are expected to cover their EL continuously via provisioning, write-offs and the incorporation of expected losses within instrument pricing. In effect, capital, under Basel II, only needs to be held against UL. The IRB approach estimates the annual loss that can be expected to be exceeded with a small, pre-selected, probability $1 - \alpha$, which can be thought of as akin to an assumed probability of bank 'insolvency'.[13] Basel II's regulatory capital charge for the IRB approach – per unit quantum of credit – is then, see BCBS (2006):

$$RCC = LGD \times \left(N \left(\sqrt{\frac{1}{1-\rho}} N^{-1}(PD) + \sqrt{\frac{\rho}{1-\rho}} N^{-1}(\alpha) \right) - PD \right) \times M^* \qquad (8.1)$$

where LGD is the assumed loss given default, PD is the assumed probability of default, $N(x)$ is the cumulative distribution function for a unit Normal random variable, $N^{-1}(x)$ is the inverse of $N(x)$, i.e. the value z such that $N(z) = x$, ρ is the assumed 'asset correlation' that indicates the dependence of the asset value of a borrower on the general state of the economy in the ASRF model, α is the confidence level (set by Basel II at 99.9 %, i.e. an institution is expected to suffer losses that exceed its economic capital only once in a thousand years on average), and M^* is a maturity adjustment reflecting the empirical observation that longer-term loans appear to be riskier than shorter-term ones (e.g. are more likely to experience ratings downgrades) and that these effects appear to be more pronounced for obligors with low probabilities of default.

The ASRF model has the property of asymptotic capital additivity, i.e. the total capital for a large portfolio of loans is the weighted sum of the marginal capital for individual loans. It is thus said to be *portfolio invariant*, a feature that depends strongly on the assumption of a single systematic risk factor and on the portfolio being asymptotically fine-grained.

In practice, under IRB the LGD and the asset correlation are not estimated by banks but instead are calculated according to equations provided by the BCBS, based again on empirical observations.

8.3.4 Operational risk

Operational risk is defined within Basel II as the risk of loss resulting from inadequate or failed internal processes, people and systems or from external events. Within this type of risk Basel II includes legal risk but not strategic risk or reputational risk.

As with other types of risk considered within Basel II, firms have a choice of different possible risk measurement approaches of varying degrees of sophistication, namely, the Basic Indicator Approach, the Standardised Approach and the Advanced Measurement Approaches (AMA). With the Basic Indicator Approach, the capital requirement is a specified multiple (15 %) of the average over the previous 3 years of annual gross income. The Standardised Approach is similar but more granular, apportioning the business into eight business lines (corporate finance, trading and sales, retail banking, commercial banking, payment and settlement, agency services, asset management and retail brokerage).

With AMA, the regulatory capital is set in line with the results of the bank's own operational risk measurement system. As with equivalent advanced measurement frameworks allowable for other types of risk there are a number of qualitative and quantitative requirements that such a system must satisfy before it can be approved by the regulator, including:

(a) Active involvement by the firm's board and senior management;
(b) Conceptual soundness, implementation with integrity and adequate resources allocated to it (and to relevant control and audit functions);

---

[13] The term insolvency is here used in a broad sense, including, for example, the bank being unable to meet obligations under its senior loans.

(c) Validation by external auditors and/or supervisory authorities;

(d) Adequate granularity;

(e) Adequate tracking of relevant historical data, here internal loss data (minimum 5 year period, or 3 year when first implemented); and

(f) Internal data to be supplemented by external data, particularly relevant here to exposure to possible severe but infrequent losses that may be difficult to estimate reliably from a bank's own internal data.

The confidence level used is supposed to be comparable with that applicable to the internal ratings-based approach for credit risk (i.e. 99.9th percentile, 1 year VaR). As with credit risk, there is an assumed subdivision between expected loss (EL) and unexpected loss (UL), with the former supposed to be met as it arises.

There is some ability to take into account risk mitigation, e.g. insurance, in specified circumstances.

As with credit risk we see a bias towards computations that focus on probability of outcome rather than cost of hedging against that outcome.

8.4   INSURANCE

8.4.1 Solvency II

The Solvency II Project aims to harmonise solvency requirements for insurance businesses across all EU Member States, see European Commission (2007a) and European Commission (2007b). Solvency II is due to come into force on 31 October 2012 and includes the following:

(a) A 'total balance sheet' type regime where all the risks and their interactions are considered;

(b) Harmonised economic risk-based solvency requirements applicable across all EU Member States and applicable to all but the smallest insurance undertakings;

(c) An emphasis that capital is not the only (or necessarily the best) way to mitigate against failures. Hence, new rules will for the first time compel insurers specifically to focus on and devote significant resources to the identification, measurement and proactive management of risk. These include the introduction of the *Own Risk and Solvency Assessment* (ORSA). There will also be a new *Supervisory Review Process* (SRP)[14] that aims to enable supervisors to identify more effectively and more quickly insurers that might be heading for difficulties;

(d) Increased public disclosure of information, to improve the market disciplines applicable to insurers; and

(e) More efficient and strengthened supervision of multinational insurance groups, via allocation to a group supervisor in the home country of the group of specific responsibilities to be exercised in close cooperation with the relevant national supervisors.

The Pillar 2 requirements being introduced by Solvency II are likely to impact the governance structures of insurers. It will mean that they will have to establish certain specific 'functions' (i.e. specific areas of responsibility and expertise) to deal with risk management, risk modelling (for internal model users), compliance, internal audit and actuarial issues. Other requirements include ones relating to internal control, the need to carry out a self assessment

---

[14] The FSA has a similar requirement under its ICAAP requirements called its *Supervisory Review and Evaluation Process* (SREP).

of the company's risk and solvency position (the ORSA mentioned above) and the need for board members and senior management to be 'fit and proper'.

The proposed directive is not planning to review state run insurance guarantee schemes. It also only covers prudential valuation rules rather than accounting practices. However, the Commission has indicated that it is aiming to reduce as far as possible the initial implementation and ongoing administrative costs arising from the introduction of Solvency II. One way of doing this is where possible to limit the number of separate types of valuation that insurers might need to carry out for different purposes.

The proposed directive also does not apply to pension funds covered by Directive 2003/41/EEC (the directive on the activities and supervision of institutions for occupational retirement provision, i.e. IORP), but the Commission is planning to review this directive to examine whether and how suitable solvency requirements can or should be developed for such funds.

CEIOPS has carried out or coordinated several impact analyses regarding the proposed directive, including Quantitative Impact Study number 3 (QIS3) and Quantitative Impact Study number 4 (QIS4), see Section 3.4. Similar Quantitative Impact Studies were undertaken for Basel II.

8.4.2 Underlying approach

As at present, insurers will need to establish technical provisions to cover expected future claims from policyholders. The aim is for these to be the amount that another insurer would be expected to pay in order to take over and meet the insurer's obligations to policyholders, i.e. it is based on market consistent principles. In addition, insurers will need to have available resources sufficient to cover both a Minimum Capital Requirement (MCR) and a (typically higher) Solvency Capital Requirement (SCR). In certain circumstances, the regulator can require capital in addition to the SCR, if it does not think that the SCR reflects the specific risk profile of an undertaking.

The SCR aims to follow VaR-based principles calibrated to a 99.5 % confidence level over a 1-year time horizon. It thus adopts the current industry paradigm relating to risk management as described in Chapter 9. The SCR aims to cover all risks that an insurer faces and may be calculated using either a new European Standard Formula or an internal model validated by the supervisory authorities, in much the same way as Basel II applies to banks. At the time of writing, the European Standard Formula is expected to be finalised only after the results of QIS3 and QIS4 have been carefully analysed. If an insurer's available resources fall below the SCR then the supervisors are required to take action with the aim of restoring the insurer's finances back to the level of the SCR as soon as possible, with further deterioration leading to increased supervisory intervention. Only if the resources fall below the MCR is it envisaged that supervisors would apply the 'ultimate supervisory sanction' of forcibly liquidating the insurer.

8.4.3 Best estimate calculations

According to the proposed directive, best estimate calculations involve probability weighted averages of future cash flows, taking into account the time value of money. Future cash flows need to be split into guaranteed and discretionary benefits because, according to proposed

Article 107, the loss absorbing capacity of technical provisions is limited by the need to meet each policyholder's guaranteed benefits.

QIS4 used the following definition of guaranteed and discretionary benefits:

(a) 'Guaranteed' benefits include any benefits to which the policyholders are already individually and unconditionally entitled (as at the valuation date). For unit-linked policies these include unit entitlements, which will be of uncertain monetary value (since they depend on future movements in the value of the assets underlying the unit pool), but are still 'guaranteed', in the sense that the insurer cannot unilaterally cancel unit holdings.[15]

(b) 'Discretionary' benefits include all payments to policyholders and beneficiaries in addition to the guaranteed benefits. Their amounts may be influenced by legal or contractual factors, market practice and/or management actions.

To value guaranteed benefits, firms need to calculate a deterministic value of all future expected cash flows on a policy-by-policy (or model point[16]) basis, using realistic assumptions that are neither deliberately over- or understated. QIS4 mandates discounting at its deemed risk-free rate, see Chapter 5. Firms also need to assume normal policyholder behaviour (consistent with the financial or other demographic assumptions in that scenario) and management actions consistent with the normal operation of the insurer in that scenario.

Assumptions regarding management actions are much more important for some sorts of insurance contracts than for others. In particular, many jurisdictions have the concept of 'participating' or 'with-profits' contracts, in which policyholders have some right to share in the profits of the business. Exactly how profits are then allocated between policyholders (or between them in aggregate and the firm's shareholders) may not be specified precisely, but may be subject to some management discretion.

In the UK (and in some other Anglo-Saxon jurisdictions), with-profits contracts can be of two types, namely, 'conventional' with-profits and 'unitised' with-profits. Policyholders with a *conventional* with-profits endowment policy are typically entitled to a sum assured payable on death or maturity plus reversionary bonuses plus a terminal bonus. At any point in time typically only the sum assured and reversionary bonuses already declared to date are 'guaranteed'.[17] Traditionally, firms declared further reversionary bonuses year by year as profits accrued and also a terminal bonus at maturity of the policy (perhaps linked to the 'asset share' that premiums paid by the policyholder had accumulated to through time based on actual fund performance), with the amounts of profits released in the form of yearly reversionary bonuses being designed to provide a smoothed trajectory through time for policyholders. Exactly how the smoothing and profit sharing algorithms might be applied typically involves some discretion by management, thereby affecting potential future benefits payable to policyholders.

---

[15] In actuarial terminology, the total actuarial reserve or liability attaching to a unit-linked policy will be the sum of the 'unit reserve', i.e. the value of the units assigned to the policyholder, and the 'non-unit' reserve (called, e.g. 'Sterling' reserve in the UK) which is the remainder, e.g. any reserve required to cater for the impact of possible expense overruns, guarantees on unit values, etc.

[16] Insurance companies may have many hundreds of thousands or even millions of policyholders. To simplify their reserving computations, they may 'model' their business using a smaller number of 'model points', which are a series of hypothetical policies which in aggregate are expected to model closely the insurer's overall policyholder book.

[17] However, management practice may be such that in law, or via regulatory requirements, policyholders may have become entitled to some assumed minimum level of 'terminal bonus', despite it having originally been a discretionary payment at maturity, in which case this element of assumed future terminal bonus would also have become 'guaranteed'.

Unitised with-profits contracts are still participating in nature, but may be structured to look more like unit-linked contracts. The participating nature of the contracts typically arises via their surrender value mechanism. Surrender values are typically based on some roll-up of premiums received assuming a set rate of interest, but crucially also then involve multiplication by a so-called *market value adjustment* (MVA), which typically bring the surrender value back towards the actual market value of the assets underlying these contracts. The use of an MVA mechanism thus allows insurers to invest in riskier asset categories and still adopt the sorts of value smoothing behaviours that are the hallmark of with-profits contracts. However, there may be limits on management discretion actually available to the company, e.g. the policies might include MVA-free dates from time to time, thus introducing guaranteed surrender values and hence guaranteed benefits.

Management discretion can also arise with non-participating policies, e.g. there may be discretion to raise future charges (possibly qualified, with qualifications imposed either by explicit policy wording or by the regulatory requirement to treat customers fairly).

Valuation of discretionary benefits is also supposed to use realistic assumptions that are neither deliberately over- or understated. Included within these values are the values of options or other guarantees linked to the discretionary benefit, calculated using Monte Carlo or alternative methods.

The total best estimate is then the discounted value of both the guaranteed and the discretionary benefits. Various stress scenarios are included in the computation of the SCR which can alter the size of either or both of the guaranteed and the discretionary elements of the total best estimate, limiting the extent to which it is possible to take benefit for risk-mitigating effects of future discretionary benefits on some policy reserves.

8.4.4 Surrender rates

Certain EU regulators have spotted that the above approach may result in firms having insufficient resources to be able to meet a potential 'run' on the firm, in which nearly all policyholders that can, seek to surrender their policies at the earliest available opportunity. This reflects the link between 'best estimate' and *realistic* assumptions in the above framework, because it may not be 'realistic' for a firm to expect a very high level of surrenders in the 'normal' run of events. One of the SCR tests under QIS4 involved a 30 % level of mass surrenders, which many firms argued should be more than sufficient based on statistical projections. However, such a level might still not take account of plausible changes in policyholder behaviour in very adverse circumstances.

This debate replays some of the issues we have already discussed in Chapter 2 relating to the typical need for solvency computations to strip out the impact of discretion. In this instance, customers have discretion to surrender, but QIS4 would be valuing the business assuming that in no circumstances more than 30 % of customers do so. It seems unsound to incorporate adjustments for discretion on the part of the insurers themselves but not then fully on the part of policyholders. A 30 % upper limit on surrenders may prove a dubious assumption if for some reason it becomes rational for nearly all policyholders to surrender (e.g. because the solvency of the business looks to be imperilled and non-surrendering policyholders might expect to suffer if default does occur).

Moreover, with the benefit of hindsight, regulators would look to have been living in cloud-cuckoo land if such a run did then occur (if they had mandated assuming that only 30 % of the policyholder base able to 'run' then did so). Presumably, a course of action that 30 % of the policyholder base considers sensible may well seem sensible to most of the remaining policyholders, to the extent that they are able to follow it. Ideally, the starting point should be rational exercise of any and all possible ways policyholders might try to mitigate personal loss on hypothetical default of the company, even if it involves a higher capital base. Companies could, of course, try to mitigate such risks by designing policies that contain less onerous 'promises' in the event of the company running into difficulties.

8.4.5   UK regulatory capital computations for insurers

The UK's Financial Services Authority (FSA) regulates a large part of the UK's financial services industry having taken over responsibility from several predecessor organisations (e.g. the Bank of England for banks, IMRO for asset managers, the DTI for insurers) when the UK adopted a unitary regulatory framework.

The regulatory capital computation that became applicable to UK life insurers as at 1 January 2005 introduced three regulatory computations. Two derive from Pillar 1 style computations mandated by FSA rules (although it is possible to obtain waivers from certain of these requirements in certain circumstances from the FSA). They are called the *regulatory peak* and the *realistic peak* computations.

The third computation derives from Pillar 2 requirements. It involves each insurer preparing its own *Individual Capital Assessment* (ICA), potentially supplemented, if the FSA thinks that it is too optimistic, by the FSA issuing further Individual Capital Guidance, i.e. ICG. 'ICAS' is often used as shorthand for the combination of the Individual Capital Assessment and Individual Capital Guidance but more accurately stands for *Individual Capital Adequacy Standards*. The corresponding 'own' assessment the FSA mandates for banks and asset managers is called the Internal Capital Adequacy Assessment Process (ICAAP).[18]

As with Basel II there appear to be a number of issues with how credit risk is catered for in the relevant insurer computations. At the time of writing, the regulatory peak computation involved, in broad terms, a computation along the following lines:

(a) Calculate the spread of each bond held by the insurer over the corresponding government bond yield curve;
(b) Calculate, using the rating assigned to the bond in question, the spread corresponding to a prudent estimate of its expected default loss, based on historic default experience;
(c) Deem the spread differential between (a) and (b) to be an 'illiquidity premium' ascribable to the bond; and
(d) Capitalise this illiquidity premium (if the liabilities are also illiquid and therefore are deemed to be 'matched' by the illiquidity in the assets) and take credit for it as a reduction to the insurer's required capital base by increasing the yield at which the liabilities are discounted.

The insurance company 'regulatory' peak computation thus has the characteristic that moving away from gilts into less creditworthy debt can reduce rather than increase capital requirements. It also typically seems to be carried out on a security-by-security basis and may thus fail to take full account of the diversifying effects of holding portfolios of bonds rather than isolated ones. One has to be a little careful with this logic as there is plenty of

---

[18] Asset managers and the like also have corresponding 'regulatory', i.e. Pillar 1, requirements, but for asset managers they are typically simpler to calculate (e.g. involving set percentages of expenses).

flexibility in practice afforded in exactly how the illiquidity premium is calculated. Even if it is exactly as described above, its actual computation often assumes that each position is actually a diversified basket of bonds of that particular rating category.

The *realistic peak* computation was only introduced a few years ago and is a little closer to what we might describe as 'underlying reality' (as one might hope given the use of the term 'realistic' in its name). Strictly speaking, the realistic peak Risk Capital Margin (RCM) only applies to larger with-profits companies (or smaller ones that have opted to adopt it) and then only for their with-profits business. Broadly speaking, at the time of writing, the RCM element for credit risk (as a proportion of the market value of the bond) was calculated as follows (for each bond and then summed), where *Dur* is the duration of the bond, *s* is the (yield) spread over corresponding government debt and F_C is a factor dependent on credit rating:

$$RCM = \begin{cases} F_C \times Dur \times \sqrt{s}, & \text{if rated } B(\text{minus}) \text{ or better} \\ \max(F_C \times Dur \times \sqrt{s}, 5\%), & \text{if rated below } B(\text{minus}) \text{ or unrated} \end{cases} \qquad (8.2)$$

Credit Rating	F_C
AAA	3.00
AA	5.25
A	6.75
BBB	9.25
BB	15.00
B or below	24.00

There are several ways in which such a computation struggles to cater for credit risk in a fully *market consistent* manner:

(a) It relies on credit ratings. These are 'real world' views of credit ratings agencies about how likely an issuer might be to default. However competent the credit rating agencies might be at forming such opinions, their subjective views are not necessarily going to reflect market implied levels. There is also the significant issue of whether the rating applied to one type of instrument (e.g. a CDO) means the same as the same rating applied to a different type of instrument (e.g. a mainstream corporate bond).
(b) Even relative to differential *historic* default experience on differently rated paper and paper of different durations, this computation appears to favour better rated shorter duration paper at the expense of worse rated longer duration paper.
(c) The computation of the RCM does not obviously tie in closely with the idealised theoretical model we set out in Section 2.8. For example, it involves a calculation that is also carried out on a security-by-security basis and therefore presumably may not fully reflect portfolio diversification effects.

The ICA is potentially able to come closer to 'underlying reality' but only if carried out appropriately. The ICA is designed to reflect what the insurer believes is the 'true' amount of risk capital that it needs as a business, based on some standardised 'ruin probability'. Current FSA guidance favours use of a 99.5 % 1 year confidence limit, which the FSA considers broadly to equate to a BBB rating. Similar guidance applies for ICAAP. We see again a bias towards computations that focus on probability of outcomes rather than the cost of hedging against these outcomes, and so such computations are not 'fully' market consistent in the context of Chapters 9 and 10.

8.4.6 Categorising risks

We described in Chapter 1 a six-way split of risks that different sorts of financial firms might face and we noted that there could be some blurring between the different categories. In Chapter 6 we noted some of the difficulties that can arise when trying to identify an exact demarcation between market risk and credit risk.

Another example of a potential blurring is *expense risk*. Actuarial guidance (and Solvency II) seems to assume that, within an insurance company, expense risk is a form of insurance risk. However, banks and other non-insurance financial services entities are also exposed to expense risk (although not necessarily over quite such long timescales). We would not typically view them as carrying insurance risk merely because there is uncertainty in their future expenses.

Another area of potential blurring is *asset-liability risk*. Within an insurance company this too has perhaps traditionally been viewed as an example of insurance risk, the primary control of which has often fallen to the actuarial function. But again there is just the same sort of need to focus on asset-liability risk in other sorts of financial services entities like banks, since they too have both assets and liabilities. Banks nowadays typically have an *asset-liability committee* (ALCO), or an equivalent with a similar function but a different name, that monitors and manages this sort of risk.

8.5 PENSION FUNDS

Different viewpoints about what 'promises' have been made (and to whom) are perhaps most prevalent within the pension fund industry.

Pure defined contribution (DC) arrangements are relatively non-contentious in this regard. In such arrangements, members receive pension benefits equal in value to the fair market value of whatever their contributions (and those made on their behalf by their employers) accumulate to. The underlying vehicles in which these contributions are invested are typically pooled vehicles such as UCITS or unit-linked life insurance funds and they are regulated accordingly, perhaps with some further requirements imposed on the legal entity actually forming the pension scheme (if different).[19]

The issues arise principally with defined benefit (DB) arrangements. The UK is perhaps a good historical example of these issues. In their heyday, final salary schemes (the form of defined benefit arrangement most prevalent in the UK), covered a substantial proportion of the workforce. Their size meant that they had a major influence on market structure and on the recycling of capital across businesses. Employers were encouraged to use such structures to fund retirement provision because of tax breaks. They were also supported by labour unions, who sought to include pension provision in collective bargaining discussions, to try to ensure that their members were adequately looked after financially in retirement as well as in employment. With the rise of inflation, DB pension funds in the UK shifted into assets perceived to provide better long-term inflation protection, e.g. equities. Surpluses accruing from such investment strategies were often used to award discretionary benefit improvements

---

[19] It can be difficult to see exactly what extra protections and benefits are created by including such an extra layer in the legal structure. In the UK this might take the form of an additional trust structure. These extra layers might be subject to regulatory scrutiny, and hence might incur additional costs. The tendency in, say, the UK has therefore been towards arrangements that involve a direct contract between the DC scheme member and the relevant vehicle provider. In the UK and EU the provider is often established as an insurance company. In the US it is more common for DC arrangements to adopt a 401(k) structure investing in mutual funds.

including discretionary pension increases that aimed to protect the real purchasing power of former employees' pensions. Employers also found that they could use such surpluses to support redundancy arrangements when restructuring businesses.

Over time, however, these discretionary improvements became more formalised and guaranteed in nature, culminating in a government decision to make pension scheme deficiencies on wind-up a debt on the sponsoring employer. Aspirations had become promises!

As we noted earlier, opinions differ between those who view pension schemes as financial institutions not dissimilar to insurance companies and those who view pensions as a cross between a strict financial product and a 'best endeavours' initiative to deliver certain social policy objectives. The EU may refine the Institutions for Occupational Retirement Provision (IORP) Directive and impose Solvency II style capital adequacy requirements on pension funds, albeit suitably modified. However, this issue is something of a political hot potato. Many private sector pension schemes in some States would struggle to raise from their sponsors the required capital needed to satisfy Solvency II style capital adequacy tests, including some States where occupational pension schemes play a major role in old age retirement provision. Conversely, in other States, occupational pension provision is less prevalent because old age retirement provision is mainly provided by State pension arrangements, which fall outside the remit of the current IORP Directive.

Perhaps the best way to characterise this state of affairs is as a journey. The European Parliament is believed to favour the principle of 'same risk, same capital'. At a very high level this principle is very difficult to fault[20] but ultimately it implies imposition of more tightly articulated regulatory capital requirements. In practice a rather important extra dimension is added by the involvement of a sponsor alongside the pension fund and its members but even so, aspirations have been shifting towards promises.

Employers have spotted this trend and are trying to unravel their DB arrangements, or at least to limit accrual of future risk exposures. This explains the large numbers of DB pension schemes (in the UK) that have closed to new members, closed to new benefit accrual for existing members or even transferred their liabilities to a third party, such as a life insurance company. Pension schemes have become more aware of the credit exposure that they have to their sponsor (i.e. the *employer* or *sponsor covenant*). In the UK, DB pension schemes and the Pensions Regulator have become more focused on ways in which employers might diminish the value of this covenant, e.g. by seeking greater protection in the event of corporate activity. However, the Pensions Regulator has been reluctant to intervene in how individual schemes set capital adequacy requirements (via scheme-specific funding plans) because there is, as yet, no consensus on exactly how strongly funded a pension scheme 'ought' to be.

Different interest groups stand to gain or lose as this journey progresses. Specialist buy-out organisations can probably expect to gain if higher capital requirements are imposed, because the schemes would then probably be more likely to wind up sooner. Conversely, sponsors would need to find more capital sooner.[21]

---

[20] It is particularly difficult to fault for sponsors that are themselves insurers and who could then buy out their own pension benefit exposures within their own insurance funds.

[21] To some extent this journey is about when capital is needed. Capital adequacy requirements ought only ultimately to have a second order impact on the long-term cost of honouring any specific given promise. But this is again linked to the shift from aspiration to promise. Only when something has become a promise do you have to honour it! As schemes become more mature (which becomes inevitable once they close to new benefit accrual), the pension entitlements to which their members are entitled become more like those that an insurance company might provide. Other issues that get raised in the debate include the greater investment flexibility that might be available if there is

Pension fund capital adequacy requirements are also influenced by other regulatory trends, such as the increasing adoption of unitary regulation, see Section 2.3. For example, in Holland the PVK regulates pension funds, banks and insurance companies. It wrote to pension funds in September 2002 requiring them to get to a 105 % solvency level in one year and on 1 January 2006 introduced a new regulatory framework for pension funds, requiring the use of 'fair values' for liabilities.

Pension fund valuations are carried out for many different purposes, not all of which are related to solvency, see e.g. IAA (2008b). For example, actuaries commonly carry out forecasts for pension funds of likely future smoothed contribution rate requirements to maintain a healthy ongoing surplus of assets versus liabilities. We have already noted in Chapter 2 that we can always reexpress these sorts of computations in the form of a fully market consistent solvency style valuation plus a balance, but this does not necessarily provide the simplest of presentation formats. As noted in IAA (2008b), there is less intrinsic need for these sorts of computations to be framed in an explicitly market consistent manner because they are not necessarily aiming to be market consistent in the first place.

Indeed, some commentators believe that undue focus on market consistency when presenting the results of pension fund contribution rate calculations may unduly encourage adoption of matched investment strategies and that these strategies might not be in the best interests of scheme beneficiaries and other stakeholders. IAA (2008b) recommends that where possible advocacy of risk investing should be separated from discount rate choice.

8.6   DIFFERENT TYPES OF CAPITAL

Regulators often go to great lengths to stress that they do not necessarily subscribe to the view that extra capital is the only, or even always the best, way to protect customers against risk. However, it is generally accepted that financial services providers do need to be adequately capitalised. Capital may not be the best way of protecting against every type of risk, but lack of capital certainly is a hindrance!

By 'capital' (i.e. *own funds*) we mean funding (or contingent funding) via issuance of shares, debt or other instruments that rank *below* customer liabilities in the event of the firm becoming insolvent. Thus 'capital' can include equity (i.e. share) capital, preference share capital (i.e. preferred stock), many forms of debt and other financial support arrangements.[22]

Given the wide range of instrument types that a firm might issue, Basel II and Solvency II go into some detail regarding what is or is not acceptable capital for solvency purposes.

For example, under Solvency II, a distinction is made between 'basic' own funds and 'ancillary' own funds, see e.g. FSA (2008a). Basic own funds are defined as the excess of assets over liabilities (net assets) and subordinated liabilities, as per Figure 8.1. Ancillary own funds are defined as any other capital resources that could be called upon to absorb losses, i.e. contingent capital items, including e.g. letters of credit or other guarantees.

In both Basel II and Solvency II, own funds are classified into *tiers* depending on the characteristics of the capital in question. The aim is to ensure that the firm has the right sort of capital to meet its regulatory capital requirements.

---

less pressure on capital and the greater returns that might be available from such flexibility, balanced by the greater risks of failing to honour the 'promise' by following such strategies.

[22] For pension funds, these 'support arrangements' might include future contributions from their sponsoring employer (if they have one).

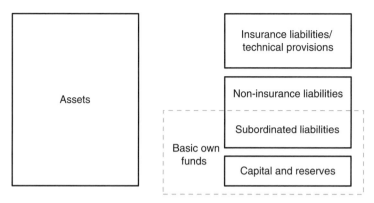

Figure 8.1 Characterisation of 'own' funds in Solvency II

Capital has two main purposes. The first is to enable firms to continue operating as a going concern (e.g. to protect against unexpected loss without triggering insolvency). This is called *full loss absorbency on a going concern basis*. The second is to protect creditors (particularly, for financial firms, customers) in the event of insolvency. This is achieved via *subordination*. The difference is fundamental to the differentiation of capital into two main tiers, namely:

(a) Tier I capital, which is meant to exhibit full loss absorbency characteristics on both a going concern basis and in a winding-up scenario; and
(b) Tier II capital, which provides loss absorbency in a winding-up scenario.

Other characteristics that such capital is required to exhibit (for Solvency II) are:

(a) The instrument must be of sufficient duration in relation to the customer liabilities;
(b) The instrument must be free from requirements or incentives to redeem the nominal amount;
(c) The instrument is free of mandatory fixed charges; and
(d) The capital is free of encumbrances.

Under Solvency II, dated capital instruments (i.e. ones that have a finite life) can be included in Tier I capital as long as the instrument is of sufficient duration in relation to the firm's insurance liabilities. Tier II capital does not need to absorb losses in a going concern situation but must absorb losses in a gone concern scenario and satisfy the other requirements set out above.

The current draft Solvency II directive introduces a further type of capital, i.e. Tier III. This type of capital is not referred to in Basel II or in, say, current UK insurance regulatory frameworks. It involves capital that is deeply subordinated (i.e. subordinated to all policyholders and senior creditors) but does not meet all the characteristics required for Tier II capital. Tier III capital is not eligible to meet the MCR but can be used, within limits, to meet the SCR.

Calibrating Risk Statistics to Perceived 'Real World' Distributions

9.1 INTRODUCTION

Forward-looking risk statistics ultimately depend on the positions contained within a portfolio and on the risk model that is applied to these positions to calculate risk statistics. Calibrating risk statistics to the market is thus intimately bound up in how we 'apply what the market has to say' to the task of constructing a risk model.

There are two intrinsically different ways of interpreting 'market consistency' in this context. These arguably mirror the 'real world' versus 'market consistent' debate that we have come across several times already within this book.

Traditionally, the goal of a well-calibrated risk model has been to characterise as accurately as possible the ways in which markets might be expected to behave in the future. By 'characterise' we here mean defining a probability distribution that in theory matches the true underlying likelihood of a given outcome occurring. Such a goal is traditionally implemented by postulating that the past provides some guide to the future. In this paradigm we characterise the probability distributions inherent in how the relevant markets (and/or instruments) have behaved in the past (or would have behaved had they existed) and, to the extent that it is possible, we use this characterisation to predict how markets might behave in the future. Risk measurement and management is generally principally interested in avoiding too many adverse outcomes (or even a relatively small number that are too extreme). So, typically, the process would be biased, if at all, towards greater consideration of the negative impact of downside outcomes. It would also typically avoid (except perhaps in external marketing presentations!) positive assumptions about any ability to add value by active repositioning of the portfolio through time.

The reliability of the risk model would then be tested either *in-sample* (by reviewing the past and identifying how well it would have predicted past outcomes given the portfolio prevailing at the time) or *out-of-sample* (by running the risk model regularly going forwards in time). The aim is to see whether as time progressed the distributions of outcomes that the model forecasted were consistent in a statistical sense with the emerging observed outcomes, see Section 9.3.

However, there are two potential flaws with such a paradigm:

(a) There may be contemporaneous pieces of market data that may be better estimates of future market behaviour than any that are derived from observations further into the past. Thus, the future volatility of a security or of a market might perhaps be better predicted by relevant market implied volatilities than by historic volatilities, however recent the past time period used to derive the historic volatilities.[1]

---

[1] For example, Christensen and Prabhala (1998) conclude that implied volatility outperforms past volatility as a means of forecasting future volatility (for the S&P 500 index) and even subsumes the information content of past

(b) Trying to identify the probability distribution that best describes likelihoods of future outcomes may not be the right thing to be aiming for in the first place. The most obvious reason for proposing this currently non-consensus view is that when deriving market consistent *valuations* we explicitly rejected in Chapter 2 the notion that these could be reliably identified from likelihoods of occurrence expected to apply in the 'real world'. Instead, we discovered that to put monetary values on pay-offs in a manner that correctly catered for the time value of money we needed to focus on risk-neutral probability distributions (or the equivalent 'deflator' approach in which we use state dependent discount rates for cash flows occurring at the same time). Generally speaking, for risk management purposes we are not interested in outcomes in an abstract sense only. Rather, we are more normally interested in their *monetary consequences* (e.g. that a firm may have insufficient financial resources to be able to cope with a particular financial loss and thus become insolvent). If 'monetary value' is most objectively identified by reference to risk-neutral probability distributions and if we view risk management (particularly solvency assessment) as in some sense integrally bound up with consideration of the monetary consequences of a particular business or investment strategy, then there would also seem to be a strong case for focusing in risk management on 'risk-neutral' distributions rather than 'real world' distributions.

We can think of (a) as merely a possible methodological flaw. We can ultimately test whether use of such additional contemporaneous data makes our risk model 'better' (in the sense of predicting more accurately the likelihood of future outcomes) by using suitable (out-of-sample) backtesting as described further in Section 9.3.

In contrast, (b) is much more fundamental. If we follow this idea then it is no longer possible even in principle to assess how good a risk model is merely by using (out-of-sample) backtesting. We no longer 'expect' the distribution of future outcomes we are seeking to identify to match in distributional form what might actually occur. Instead, the risk-neutral distribution will in general reflect the cost of hedging away the relevant risk, which in general will include a risk-aversion factor (driven by the utilities of different market participants). If on average market participants are risk averse towards a given outcome then its likelihood as described by the relevant risk-neutral probability will typically be higher than the actual likelihood of occurrence we might intrinsically think would apply to it.

So, superficially, these two refinements might both appear to be heading in the same direction, i.e. encouraging greater use of market implieds than might historically have been the norm within the risk management industry. However, in reality, the two perspectives are fundamentally different. With the former we would only use market implieds if we thought that they provided *better* estimates (or an improved explanation) of what might happen in the future. With the latter, we would favour use of market implieds even if we did *not* believe that

---

volatility in some of their specifications. However, they also note that others had previously concluded the reverse, i.e. that implied volatility was a biased and inefficient estimator of future volatility, with past volatility containing predictive information about future volatility beyond that contained in implied volatility. Christensen and Prabhala (1998) note the apparent presence of a regime shift around the time of the October 1987 stock market crash which may explain the apparently biased nature of implied volatility noted by earlier researchers. They also note the importance of sampling methodologies in such analyses, arguing that use of overlapping data periods (as had been used by some of the previous researchers coming up with results contradicting their own) would tend to overstate the actual explanatory power of past volatility.

they provided better estimates of what might happen in the future, but because we thought that they provided a better reflection of the *market price* for the risk in question.

At the heart of this issue is the question of what is the best way to encapsulate in a single *monetary* amount the impact of uncertainty in future outcomes. Applying the same logic as we expounded in Chapter 2 we may conclude that for many (although not all) purposes these monetary quantifications should respect the axioms of additivity and scalability and should focus on market implied rather than real world probability distributions. The conceptual framework we introduced in Section 2.8 indicates that capital adequacy is one such purpose where use of market implied probability distributions has merit.

Section 4.3.1.2 might be thought to provide a way of resolving this dichotomy. It shows that we can respect these axioms and achieve market consistency whilst still retaining use of real world probability distributions by use of 'deflators', i.e. state dependent discount rates. However, this approach doesn't really resolve the issue. The relevant state dependent discount rates are equal to the non-state dependent discount rate(s) we would otherwise use in the risk-neutral formulation multiplied by the ratio of the risk-neutral to the real world probability densities. So this alternative approach merely moves the dichotomy between real world and risk-neutral probability distributions into the computation of the deflator. If we are going down this route then we should ideally establish a second set of validation procedures to check that our choice of deflators is appropriate.

Given that the philosophy underlying (b) is one that is not universally shared across the industry (and that Section 2.2.5 implies that it is not always appropriate to seek full market consistency), I have split the discussion of how we might calibrate risk models 'to the market' into two chapters. In this chapter we focus on what market consistency means within the context of traditional time series-based risk modelling (potentially supplemented using point (a) as above). Only in the next chapter do we focus on the further implications of abandoning the aim of best characterising the 'real world' likelihood of future occurrence and instead aiming for best characterising the market consistent price for the risk in question.

Throughout this chapter it is therefore assumed that construction and calibration of the risk model is aiming to provide as accurate as possible a characterisation of the future 'real world' likelihood of occurrence of some specified event.

**Principle P41: The risk management paradigm currently adopted by most prac-
titioners in the financial community involves assessing risks by reference to their
perceived 'real world' likelihood of occurrence. It does not therefore necessarily provide effective estimates of the market costs of hedging against such risks, which are
instead driven by their risk-neutral probabilities of occurrence. It is arguably therefore an inappropriate basis to use when formulating economic (or regulatory) capital
requirements.**

9.2   REFERRING TO MARKET VALUES

Fundamentally, a risk model aiming to characterise future likelihood of occurrence of specified events is only likely to be 'market consistent' if it focuses on the evolution of market prices and other market observables. The assets and liabilities it is attempting to model therefore need to be marked-to-market or marked-to-model, with the model reasonably believed to describe how the assets and liabilities would have been valued if a ready market in them had existed. Thus many of the principles we explored in Chapters 2–6 apply here too. So too do the many issues that arise in practice with market consistent valuations.

A particular issue applicable to marking-to-model is that many of the methodologies used can result in modelled prices exhibiting artificially smooth trajectories and thus understated future volatility. For example, valuation methodologies used by surveyors in real estate markets typically appear to introduce smoothing, see e.g. Booth and Marcato (2004). Surveyor valuations typically seem to overestimate prices at which transactions can actually be completed when the market is depressed, and to understate them when the market is buoyant. As a result, surveyor valuations also seem to exhibit autocorrelation and an artificially low volatility relative to what one might have expected to apply on intrinsic economic grounds.

This smoothing of price trajectories is often seen with less liquid assets and liabilities or with pooled vehicles that contain such instruments[2] as it can arise merely because of unconscious behavioural biases that creep into the pricing process. For example, there is a natural tendency to benchmark what is considered a sensible price quotation by reference to the last transaction in the instrument. It can be a particular issue for a hedge fund of funds manager seeking to analyse candidate hedge funds, as some hedge fund strategies involve extensive use of less liquid instruments. Incidentally, the fact that Booth and Marcato (2004) find evidence for such behaviour with surveyors' valuations indicates that the issue does not necessarily go away merely by ensuring that the valuation process is carried out independently of the fund manager, since such independence is the norm in the real estate market.

Price smoothing should show up as autocorrelation in the return series. It can therefore be unwound by *de-correlating* the return series, r_t, e.g. by assuming that there is some underlying 'true' return series $\tilde{r}_t$, and that the observed series derives from it via, say, the formula $r_t = (1 - \rho)\tilde{r}_t + \rho\tilde{r}_{t-1}$, estimating ρ (from the autocorrelation characteristics of r_t) and then backing out $\tilde{r}_t$.

One can then, for example, regress the assumed true underlying return series against the different reference factors to identify the instrument's 'underlying' exposure to each factor (or do the equivalent also incorporating a pricing model, as might be needed for bond risk analysis, see Section 7.4.5).[3]

---

[2] An important corollary of this is that such structures can contain implicit liquidity risk, borne either by the end investor in the structure or by the issuer of the structure (or both) depending on who bears the pain when investors try to exit from the structure at times when this dampening of apparent volatility means that the structure is valued at a premium to its underlying constituents. See, for example, Section 7.6.

[3] Regression analysis can also be used to characterise fund behaviour in instances where the underlying constituents of the fund are unavailable to the analyst. For example, hedge fund analysts may carry out such regressions to try to understand better the style characteristics of hedge funds in which they might invest (and, after investment, to check for apparent style drift). There are, of course, lots of potential reference factors that could be used (e.g. large cap, small cap, value and growth indices, etc.). The selection of which ones to use (and how many of them to use) could be found by stepwise regression or by some sort of criterion that balanced model fit versus model complexity, e.g. the Akaike Information Criterion, Schwarz's Bayesian Information Criterion or the Empirical Information Criterion, see Billah et al. (2003). A perfect regression fit would be achieved if there are at least as many independent factors as there are return observations to fit, in much the same way as there is a limit to the number of non-zero eigenvalues for an observed covariance matrix based on a finite number of observation periods. Such techniques also form the basis of hedge fund replication strategies, which seek to mimic the behaviour of hedge fund indices by investing in a (possibly dynamic) mixture of cheaper substitutes.

Another issue relating to marking-to-model is that risk modelling often implicitly includes assumptions about the dynamics of price evolution for the instrument in question. For example, an option's short-term future price evolution might be assumed to be accurately characterised by how a delta-weighted hedge portfolio equivalent would behave, as long as the price of the underlying does not move by very much. However, even if the price of the underlying moves little (if at all), the hedge portfolio can still deviate in value from the original instrument. For example, its implied volatility might change.

The risk model may therefore end up merely being a very good characterisation of how the mark-to-model price of an instrument might move, but this can still be well out of line with its actual mark-to-market movements as and when it does trade.

More generally, as we highlighted in Chapter 4, identifying market consistent *hedging parameters* is materially more difficult than identifying market consistent *prices*. This is because there are far fewer reliable market observables that might guide us to market consistent views on how effective a hedge might be. Thus intrinsically we may expect to find it harder to achieve such 'market consistency' with risk models than with valuations, except perhaps for risk models that only refer to very liquid instruments.

9.3 BACKTESTING

9.3.1 Introduction

The intrinsic rationale behind VaR style risk measures (and stress tests derived in a similar manner), at least as far as this chapter is concerned, is that they provide a guide, albeit imperfect, regarding the potential range of future outcomes. This means that they are amenable to verification by comparing predictions with actual future outcomes.

There are two ways of thinking about backtesting:[4]

(a) It can be thought of as a quick and 'cheap' way to carry out such a comparison without actually having to wait for the future to arrive. It involves identifying how well a risk model would have worked *in the past* had it been applied to the positions then present.
(b) Perhaps more importantly in the context of this chapter, it can be thought of as a core step in the calibration of a risk model to (past) market behaviour. To calibrate a risk model to observed market behaviour, we parameterise the risk model in a suitable fashion and we choose which parameters to adopt by finding the model variant that best fits the data.

Backtesting also has a prominent (if sometimes just implicit) role in regulatory frameworks. Regulatory frameworks have increasingly incentivised firms to use their own risk models when determining their own regulatory capital requirements. Such models typically need to be approved by regulators before they can be used in such a manner. Given the complexity of the types of firms most likely to go down this route, it is not surprising that regulators are less than sanguine about their own ability to mitigate the possibility that firms might adopt overly optimistic assumptions in risk modelling. Hence, these regulatory frameworks also often include elements that penalise firms in capital terms if their risk models too often seem to underestimate actual magnitudes of outcomes. This makes it natural for firms to want to

---

[4] Backtesting is also relevant when testing a quantitative idea generation process (and to some extent a non-quantitative one too).

understand how well their risk models might have worked in the past (and for regulators to want to be provided with such information before approving a firm's model).

For firms opting to use industry-wide regulator-specified capital computations, backtesting might appear somewhat less important. However, this is because it has been (or ought to have been) carried out by the regulator itself when specifying the computation in question.

More generally, as risk measurement and management have acquired greater importance in business management it is natural for greater scrutiny to be placed on the validity of risk measures. Backtesting provides one way of 'quality assuring' such statistics.[5]

9.3.2   In-sample versus out-of-sample backtesting

Short-cutting the future by referring merely to the past introduces *look-back bias*. Exactly how this works out in practice depends on how the backtesting is carried out.

One way of carrying out a risk model backtest would be to take a single model of how the future might evolve and then to apply the *same* model to every prior period. The key issue with this so-called *in-sample* approach is that the model will typically have been formulated by reference to past history including the past that we are then testing the model against. Thus, unless we have been particularly inept at fitting the past when constructing the risk model in the first place, we should find that it is a reasonable fit in an in-sample, i.e. ex-post, comparison. We cannot then conclude much from its apparent goodness of fit. Or to be more precise, we oughtn't, as this subtlety does not stop practitioners from applying such methods in practice.

Backtesters attempt to mitigate this problem by using so-called *out-of-sample* testing. What this involves is a specification of how to construct a model using data only available up to a particular point in time. We then apply the model construction algorithm *only* to observations that occurred *after* the end of the sample period used in the estimation of the model, i.e. out of the sample in question. The model might be estimated once-off using a particular earlier period of time and then the same model might be applied each time period thereafter. Alternatively, the model might be re-estimated at the start of each time period using data that would have then been available, so that the time period just about to occur is still (just) after the in-sample period.

Whilst out-of-sample modelling does reduce look-back bias it does not eliminate it. Risk models ultimately involve lots of different assumptions about how the future might evolve, not least the format of the risk model itself. In the background there are lots of competing risk models that we might have considered suitable for the problem. Not too surprisingly, the only ones that actually see the light of day, and therefore get formally assessed in an out-of-sample context, are ones that are likely to be tolerably good at fitting the past even in an out-of-sample context. Risk modellers are clever enough to winnow out ones that will obviously fail such a test before the test is actually carried out. This point is perhaps more relevant to backtesting of return generating algorithms, given the human tendency to rationalise explanations for success or failure, perhaps even if there is no such explanation, see e.g. Taleb (2004).

---

[5] Following from Section 7.3.3.2(b), if the principal business application of risk measurement is to *rank* different portfolios, rather than to assess their intrinsic riskiness *in isolation* at a given point in time, then 'backtesting' should focus on how well the ranking derived from the risk measure corresponds with the ranking observed in practice. We do not explore this type of backtesting further in this book.

> **Principle P42: How well a risk model might have performed had it been applied in the past can be assessed using backtesting. However, practitioners using such techniques should bear in mind that it is tricky in any such backtesting to avoid *look-back* bias, even when the model is tested out-of-sample, i.e. even when any parameter estimates used at a particular point in time within the model are derived from data that would have been historic at that time. This is because look-back bias will creep in via the structure of the risk model itself and not just via the input parameters used in its evaluation at any particular point in time.**

9.3.3 Testing backtest quality statistically

Any statistic such as a VaR estimate that is ultimately derived in part from analysis of a finite data sample is itself just an uncertain estimate of whatever is its 'true' underlying (but ultimately unobservable) value.[6] It therefore comes with some error. Moreover, outcomes that arise in the future will also ultimately be probabilistic in nature.

Thus, suppose we experienced a significantly adverse outcome in the next period, well outside the typical spread of ranges we might have otherwise predicted. Does this mean that our model is wrong? Not necessarily. It might just mean that we have been unlucky.

Statisticians face this sort of issue with any type of modelling. The way that it is typically tackled is to postulate a hypothesis and then to identify the likelihood that the hypothesis is wrong (with the model being rejected if the hypothesis is too likely to be wrong). But even then, we might have alighted on the right model but might reject it because of a fluke series of outcomes.

Statistical backtesting of risk models typically thus proceeds in one of two ways:

(a) We tabulate past estimates from our risk model (with suitable out-of-sample adjustments as appropriate) of the specific statistic that we are most interested in 'estimating correctly' versus past outcomes. For example, the statistic in question might be a given quantile level, i.e. a suitable VaR estimate. We then apply suitable statistical tests applicable to that particular statistic, see e.g. Campbell (2006), Hurlin and Tokpavi (2006), Pena *et al.* (2006), Zumbach (2006) and Kemp (2009) to test if past actuals suitably fit past predictions. For example, we might use a one sided likelihood ratio test which provides a confidence interval on the number of rejects that we would expect to see, rejecting the model if too many actuals exceed corresponding predictions.
(b) Alternatively, we may seek to test whether the entire distributional form that our model would have predicted when applied to past data seems to fit the observed range of actual past outcomes, using appropriate statistical tests, see e.g. Campbell (2006), Dowd (2006) and Kemp (2009).

Statistical techniques might also typically be supplemented by corresponding graphical comparison of the data. This might, for example, indicate visually that the model was a poor

---

[6] We do not here do justice to some of the philosophical issues that arise if the future really is 'truly' unknown, or for that matter that arise if one adopts a 'Bayesian' view of statistics.

fit only during a limited 'exceptional' period in the past which might permit some suitable explanation or refinement of the model to cater for this historic period.

Commonly, we want the model not only to fit the data in aggregate but also to fit it 'period by period'. By this we mean that we want exceptionally adverse outcomes to occur apparently randomly through time rather than being strongly clumped together into narrow time windows. The latter might imperil the solvency of a firm more than the former, since there would be less time during such a window to generate new profits or raise new capital needed to maintain a solvent status or credible business model.[7]

Campbell (2006) explains that the problem of determining whether a 'hit' sequence (i.e. for, say, VaR, an indicator of the form $I_t(\alpha)$ which is 1 if the actual outcome for time period t is worse than the α-quantile VaR, and 0 otherwise) is acceptable involves two key properties, namely:

(a) *Unconditional coverage*, i.e. actual probability of occurrence when averaged through time should match expected probability of occurrence; and
(b) *Independence*, i.e. that any two elements of the hit sequence should be independent of each other.

The former can be tested for by using, for example, Kupiec's (1995) test statistic as described in Campbell (2006), which involves a proportion of failures *POF*, defined as follows, where there are T observations:

$$POF = 2\log\left(\left(\frac{1-\hat{\alpha}}{1-\alpha}\right)^{T-I(\alpha)}\left(\frac{\hat{\alpha}}{\alpha}\right)^{I(\alpha)}\right) \tag{9.1}$$

where $\hat{\alpha} = \frac{1}{T}I(\alpha) =$ observed number of failures, and

$$I(\alpha) = \sum_{t=1}^{T} I_t(\alpha) \tag{9.2}$$

Alternatively, it can be tested for by using a z-statistic also described in Campbell (2006):

$$z = \frac{\sqrt{T}(\hat{\alpha} - \alpha)}{\sqrt{\alpha(1-\alpha)}} \tag{9.3}$$

Campbell (2006) also describes several ways of testing for independence, including Christofferson's (1998) Markov test (which examines whether the likelihood of a VaR violation at time t depends on whether or not a VaR violation occurred at time $t - h$ by building up a contingency table). This idea could presumably be extended to correlations between times further apart. He also describes a more recent test suggested by Christofferson and Pelletier (2004) which uses the insight that if VaR violations are independent of each other then the

---

[7] The practical importance of future profitability, and having sufficient time for it to make a material contribution, should not be underestimated in relation to the solvency of financial organisations. Any business that is largely in run-off and does not have access to future profit streams is much less resilient to future shocks than one that has opportunities to mitigate past or present losses with future profits. But even a generally profitable business with a good business franchise can be brought down if a one-off stress, e.g. a fraud, creates a large enough loss. Its business franchise isn't necessarily then transferable at anything like its pre-stressed value, if the stress has undesirable reputational consequences.

amount of time between them should also be independent, which Christofferson and Pelletier apparently argue may be a more powerful test than the Markov test. Campbell (2006) also describes ways of testing for unconditional coverage and independence simultaneously.

9.3.4   Intra-period position movements

Future outcomes are influenced not just by current positions but also by how these positions change thereafter. This obvious truism can be particularly important if portfolios change rapidly through time. For example, suppose a trader always closes all of his or her positions out by the end of each day. Then the risk present in his or her positions at the end of each day will be zero. But this does not mean that the portfolio is not running risks, merely that they are not present overnight. In the context of backtesting, it may be necessary to capture intra-period movements in positions as well historic period closing positions, which may complicate considerably the data requirements of the exercise.

9.3.5   Calibration of credit default models

In Section 4.13 we commented on calibration in the context of derivative pricing. The term 'calibration' can be used more generally to describe how to arrange for *any* model's predicted probabilities to closely match *any* sort of desired outcomes.

In particular, models do not need to be calibrated to *valuation* data. However, it should then be borne in mind that the predictive efficacy of the model for characterising how market valuations might move may be lessened. For example, credit models could instead be calibrated to observed default rates (which are not *market implied* data items). This is the sort of calibration involved in, say, Stein (2007) which focuses on validating default prediction models applicable to credit markets. Spreads do not necessarily behave in the same way as actual or even 'real world' predicted default rates; there are other contributors too, see e.g. Chapter 5. Stein (2007) also explores topics such as in-sample and out-of-sample testing (which he calls the 'walk-forward approach') and how to identify how powerful a statistical test might be. He focuses on modelling corporate defaults whilst Rösch and Scheule (2007) focus more on stress-testing of retail loan portfolios. Dwyer (2007) focuses on how to derive and validate Bayesian models where the model structure is updated as additional default data becomes available through time. In an actuarial context, model updating of this sort might be described as applying Kalman filters.

9.4   FITTING OBSERVED DISTRIBUTIONAL FORMS

The basic mathematical challenge throughout this chapter is how to estimate a risk statistic. Often the focus is on an order statistic such as VaR. Calculating the corresponding (observed) order statistic is not typically the most accurate way of estimating an order statistic such as a VaR if, a priori, we actually know something about the form of the distribution from which the observed returns are drawn.

For example, suppose we wish to estimate the 50% confidence interval VaR, i.e. the median, and we also know a priori that the distribution is Normally distributed. We know that for a Normal distribution, the mean and the median are the same, so estimating either will immediately give us an estimate for the other. Statistical theory indicates that the minimum variance unbiased estimator of the mean of a Normally distributed sample is the average of the sample. For a large sample, the sample median has approximately a 37 % higher forecast error than the mean. So in these circumstances, it is better to estimate the 50 % confidence interval VaR from observed parametric estimators (in this case the observed mean), rather than from observed order (i.e. non-parametric) statistics. The same is true for other confidence level VaRs (for a sample drawn from a Normal distribution), except that more generally you need to use the observed mean and observed standard deviation. Indeed, if we know that the distribution is Normally distributed then the more into the tails we go the better (relatively speaking) becomes the parametric estimation route. Such logic provides theoretical support for the use of ex-ante tracking errors for risk management purposes within the investment management arena, since these metrics are designed to be estimates of the standard deviation of future relative returns.

We may not know a priori what the actual form of the distribution should be, and in particular we may not be confident that it is likely to be well approximated by a Normal distribution. For example, we may have analysed tail behaviour and concluded that it is highly unlikely to be well characterised by a Normal distribution. But even in these circumstances, it is still potentially inappropriate merely to use a particular percentile (aka 'quantile') from the observed distribution, because the fewer the data points that we consider the greater is the sampling error that might then be introduced. There is a potential trade-off between incorporating in the estimate merely observations in the immediate vicinity of the relevant quantile to be estimated (which reduces errors potentially arising from making inappropriate assumptions about distributional form) versus incorporating in the estimate a greater number of observations (to reduce sampling error).

The challenge is that there are a very large number (indeed an infinite number) of possible distributional forms we might choose from.

Some commentators focus on the generalized beta distribution of the second kind, as described in Bookstaber and McDonald (1987) or Kemp (2009). This distribution contains as special cases a large number of well-known distributions, such as the log-Normal, log-t and log-Cauchy distributions. Such distributions are characterised by four parameters, and thus can fit any arbitrary mean, variance, skewness and kurtosis. The mean of the distribution is in some sense redundant in this sort of analysis, since in general we typically set it equal to the risk-free rate in a risk-neutral world. Interestingly, Bookstaber and McDonald conclude in their paper that the longer the time period, the less justification there is for adopting a model different to a log-Normal one.

Other commentators have explored Levy stable distributions (otherwise known as stable Paretian distributions), see e.g. Kemp (2009). These play the same sort of role as the Normal distribution does in the Central Limit Theory when we accumulate random returns with infinite variances. Indeed, the Normal distribution is a special case of the more generalised Levy stable distribution. They too have four parameters which relate to the position of the 'middle' of the distribution, its dispersion, its skewness and how fat tailed it is. However, they have the practical disadvantage that they have infinite variances (apart from the special case of the Normal distribution) and are not particularly easy to manipulate mathematically. Longuin (1993), when analysing the distribution of U.S. equity returns, concluded that their distribution was not sufficiently fat-tailed to be adequately modelled by Levy stable distributions, even if it was fatter tailed than implied by the Normal distribution.

Another approach to distribution fitting, related to the relative entropy or analytical weighted Monte Carlo approach described in Section 4.12, involves using entropy densities, see e.g. Rockinger and Jondeau (2000). This aims to provide, for a given set of moments, a probability density function that involves the smallest amount of prior information. They focus on the case where the first four moments of the distribution are given, and show how such a technique can then be used to estimate a GARCH type model in which skewness and kurtosis (as well as volatility) are time-varying.

However, the above techniques are rather high powered mathematically. Is it possible to identify simpler approaches that facilitate visualisation of the problem at hand, and thus possibly reduce the risk that we inadvertently equate sophistication with accuracy and hence introduce model risk?

We consider first in Section 9.5 the situation where we have a single return series we wish to calibrate. Then, in Section 9.6 we consider the more complex situation where we want to fit the co-movement characteristics of more than one series. In each case the aim, in essence, is to model the 'fat-tailed' characteristics of the distributional form, i.e. how it differs from the Normal distribution so well loved by economists.

9.5 FAT-TAILED BEHAVIOUR IN INDIVIDUAL RETURN SERIES

9.5.1 Identifying the true underlying return series

Our first task is to ensure that we have the true underlying return series. If we are analysing a unitised fund then the quoted unit return may not derive directly from the mid-market values of the underlying assets. There may be a bid–offer or swing mechanism (or a fair valuation adjustment) applied by the fund manager that is not relevant to the underlying reference series. We would ideally want to analyse separately such adjustments, as well as the impact of other extraneous factors like fund expenses. The observed return series may also be distorted by smoothing, perhaps due to liquidity issues, see Section 9.2

9.5.2 Fat tails

By 'fat tails' we mean the well-known phenomenon that extreme outcomes seem to occur more frequently than would be expected were returns to be coming from a (log) Normal distribution. Practical risk management (and investment management more generally) is typically very interested in modelling and catering for these more extreme outcomes since although hopefully rare they can materially disrupt or (on the upside) materially benefit portfolio progress.

The probability density function of a (log) return series that is (log) Normally distributed has the well-known bell shape illustrated in Figure 9.1. Also illustrated in this figure is a probability density function with the same mean and standard deviation that is (two-sided) fat-tailed and thus has more outliers (at both ends of the distribution).

Two mathematically equivalent ways of describing the same probability distributions are their cumulative distribution functions (i.e. the likelihood of the outcome not exceeding a certain value), as per Figure 9.2, and their 'quantile–quantile' plots, as per Figure 9.3. The latter shows the return outcome (i.e. 'quantile') associated with a given (cumulative) probability level, plotted against the corresponding return outcome applicable to a (log) Normal distribution with equivalent mean and standard deviation. In it, a (log) Normally distributed return series would be characterised by the straight line, whilst (two-sided) fat-tailed behaviour shows up as a curve that is below this straight line at the bottom left-hand end of the curve and above it at the top right-hand end of the curve.

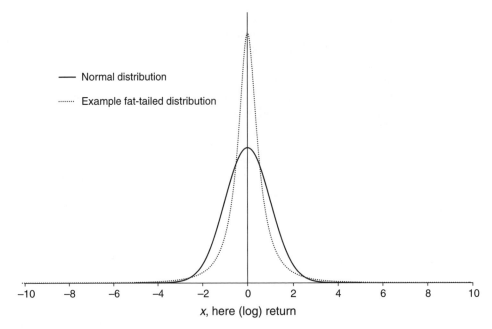

Figure 9.1   Illustrative probability density function plot

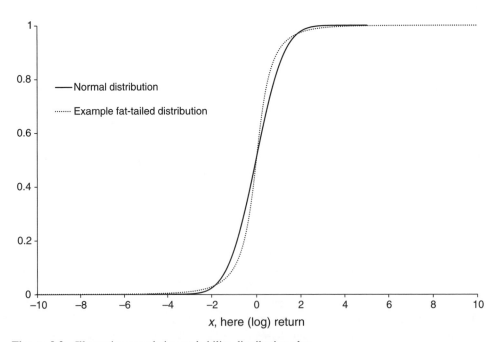

Figure 9.2   Illustrative cumulative probability distribution plot

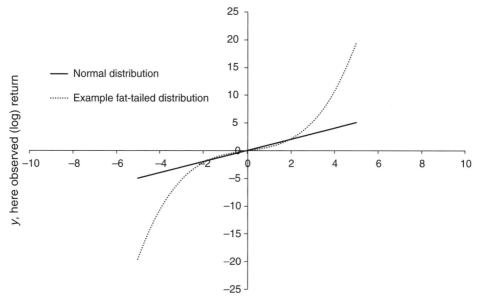

Figure 9.3   Illustrative quantile–quantile plot

Of the three graphical representations of these distributional forms described above, the one in Figure 9.3 is the easiest one in which to see visually the extent of any fat-tailed behaviour in the extremities. It is therefore the visualisation approach that we concentrate on in this section. The VaR for a given confidence level (e.g. 95 %, 99.5 %, ...) for a fat-tailed distribution can be read off such a quantile–quantile chart by using as the x-coordinate the relevant VaR level that would have applied to a (log) Normally distributed variable.

As we have already noted, fat tails are intrinsic features that we should expect to be exhibited by certain types of instrument, including many types of bonds. In other markets, there may be a less intrinsic reason to postulate strong asymmetric return characteristics, but they often still appear to exhibit fat tails, in either one or both directions. For example, the main equity market indices are often considered to exhibit such characteristics, witness October 1987. But even in more recent ('normal'?) times mostly prior to the 2007–09 credit crisis, there is evidence of fat-tail behaviour. In Figures 9.4–9.6 we plot the tail characteristics of the monthly, weekly and daily (logged) returns on the FTSE All-Share index (in GBP), the S&P 500 index (in USD), the FTSE-W Europe (ex UK) index (in EUR) and the Topix index (in JPY) for the period from end June 1994 to end December 2007. On the horizontal axis is shown the corresponding (sorted) size of movement expected were the (logged) returns to be Normally distributed (with mean and standard deviation in line with their observed values). The returns for each index have been scaled in line with their observed means and standard deviations, so that the comparator line is the same for each index.

The extent to which returns are fat-tailed seems to depend on the time-scale over which each return is measured (although some of the visual differences in tail behaviour in these three figures are because the more frequent the data are, the further into the tail the observation set

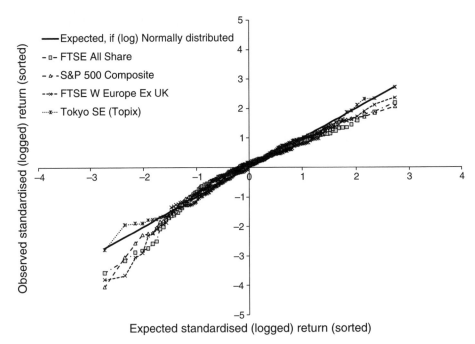

Figure 9.4 Fat tails in monthly returns on various major equity market indices from end Jun 1994 to end Dec 2007
Source: Thomson Datastream

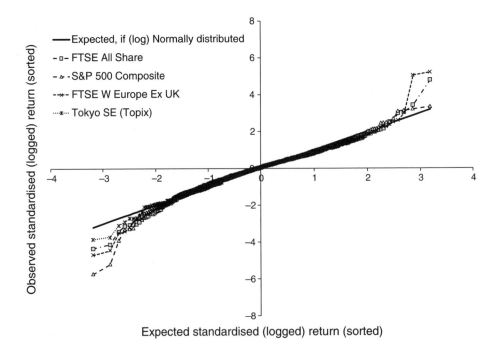

Figure 9.5 Fat tails in weekly returns on various major equity market indices from end Jun 1994 to end Dec 2007
Source: Thomson Datastream

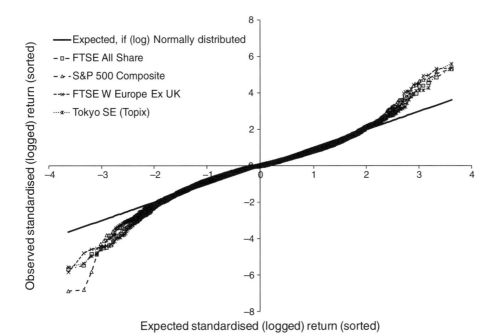

Figure 9.6   Fat tails in daily returns on various major equity market indices from end Jun 1994 to end Dec 2007
Source: Thomson Datastream

goes). For daily data, all four indices analysed appear to exhibit fat tails on both upside and downside, but there is less evidence of upside fat tails in monthly data.

It should be borne in mind that fat tails are not necessarily bad news – on the upside they may result in particularly *favourable* outcomes.

Principle P43: Most financial markets seem to exhibit fat-tailed returns for data sampled over sufficiently short time periods, i.e. extreme outcomes seem to occur more frequently than would be expected were returns to be coming from a (log) Normal distribution. This is true both for asset types that might intrinsically be expected to exhibit fat-tailed behaviour (e.g. some types of bond, given the large market value declines that can be expected to occur if the issuer of the bond defaults) and for asset types, like equities, where there is less intrinsic reason to postulate strong asymmetric return characteristics.

Practical portfolio construction may result in portfolio return series exhibiting somewhat more fat-tailed behaviour than is exhibited by the corresponding underlying asset class, see e.g. Kemp (2008a). This is particularly so if strong conviction is being expressed (as might be typical for a hedge fund) because such portfolios are likely to be quite concentrated in terms of idea expression. It is important for managers of such portfolios to understand and articulate these dynamics, both internally (to ensure that the best possible risk/reward profile

Table 9.1   Skew and (excess) kurtosis for several mainstream equity (log) return series end June 1994 to end December 2007

		Skew			(Excess) kurtosis		
	Currency	Monthly	Weekly	Daily	Monthly	Weekly	Daily
FTSE All Share	GBP	−1.0	−0.4	−0.3	1.6	2.0	3.2
S&P 500	USD	−0.8	−0.5	−0.1	1.3	3.0	3.8
FT World Eur Ex UK	EUR	−1.0	−0.2	−0.3	2.2	3.1	3.6
Topix	JPY	0.0	−0.1	−0.1	−0.2	0.5	2.5

Source: Threadneedle, Thomson Datastream

is delivered to clients) and externally (to help clients better understand the likely behaviour of the portfolios managed on their behalf).

> **Principle P44: Not all fat tails are bad. The extent to which a portfolio exhibits fat-tailed behaviour appears to be partly linked to the extent of conviction being expressed within the portfolio. If the manager can arrange for the fat tails to be concentrated on the upside rather than the downside then they will add to performance rather than subtract from it.**

9.5.3   Skew, kurtosis and the (fourth-moment) Cornish-Fisher approach

Any Normal distribution is completely characterised by its mean and standard deviation, which in effect correspond to its first two moments. A common way of measuring deviations from Normality is thus to calculate the higher order moments of the observed distribution, particularly the third and fourth moment. These correspond to the skewness and (excess) kurtosis[8] of a distribution (both of which are conveniently pre-canned functions within Microsoft Excel). Although it is possible for a distribution to be non-Normal and still to exhibit zero skew and kurtosis, such distributional forms are not often observed in practice. The skew and (excess) kurtosis of a Normal distribution are both 0. Those for the data referred to in Section 9.5.2 are summarised in Table 9.1.

Whilst we could use the observed skewness and kurtosis to fit distributions of the sorts mentioned in Section 9.4, a more common methodology within risk management circles appears to be to make use of the Cornish-Fisher asymptotic expansion, see e.g. Abramowitz and Stegun (1970) or Kemp (2009). The Cornish-Fisher asymptotic expansion takes into account non-Normality, and thus by implication moments higher than the second moment, by using a formula in which terms in higher order moments explicitly appear. Most commonly, the focus is on the fourth-moment version of this expansion, since it merely uses moments up to and including kurtosis. In effect, the fourth-moment Cornish-Fisher approach aims to provide a reliable estimate of the distribution's entire quantile–quantile plot merely from the first four moments of the distribution, i.e. its mean, standard deviation, skew and kurtosis, and

---

[8] A distribution's kurtosis is sometimes referred to in older texts as its 'excess' kurtosis (with its 'base' kurtosis then being 3 plus its excess kurtosis).

involves estimating the shape of a quantile–quantile plot by the following cubic, where γ_1 is the skew and γ_2 is the kurtosis of the distribution:

$$y(x) = m + \sigma \left(x + \frac{\gamma_1(x^2 - 1)}{6} + \frac{3\gamma_2(x^3 - 3x) - 2\gamma_1^2(2x^3 - 5x)}{72} \right) \tag{9.4}$$

For standardised returns as per Figures 9.4–9.5 (with $m = 0$, $\sigma = 1$), this simplifies to:

$$y(x) = x + \frac{\gamma_1(x^2 - 1)}{6} + \frac{3\gamma_2(x^3 - 3x) - 2\gamma_1^2(2x^3 - 5x)}{72} \tag{9.5}$$

9.5.4 Weaknesses of the Cornish-Fisher approach

Unfortunately, the fourth-moment Cornish-Fisher approach does not appear to give a visually satisfying fit (for the sorts of quantile–quantile plots introduced above) for the mainstream equity index return distributions considered above, particularly for more frequent data. Figure 9.7 repeats Figure 9.6 for just the FTSE All-Share index but now includes the relevant (fourth-moment) Cornish-Fisher estimate of the quantile–quantile plot (and an alternative method of estimating the quantile–quantile plot that fits the distributional form better, see Section 9.5.5).

For this daily return series the Cornish-Fisher approach seems to overestimate (by up to about a factor of 2) the extent to which the tail of the distribution appears to deviate from Normality. It is potentially even less effective at describing real life portfolio return distributions for high conviction portfolios, see Kemp (2008d).

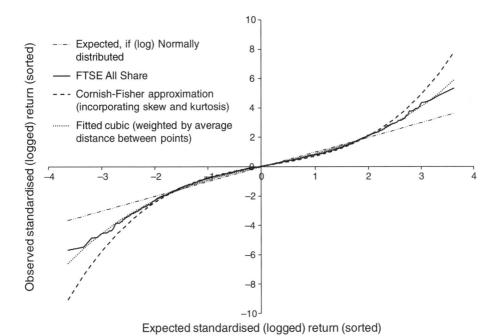

Figure 9.7 Fitting the distributional form for daily returns on FTSE All-Share index from end Jun 1994 to end Dec 2007
Source: Thomson Datastream

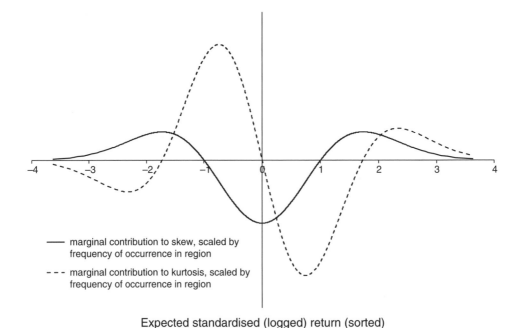

Expected standardised (logged) return (sorted)

Figure 9.8 Marginal contribution to skew and kurtosis if returns Normally distributed

One feature of Figure 9.7 is that the Cornish-Fisher approach expansion fits the distributional form much better in the more central parts of the distribution (i.e. in the area within, say, $m \pm 2\sigma$) than it does more extreme outcomes. This is because there are far more observations in the central part of the distribution than there are in the extremities. Because skew and kurtosis are parametric, they give equal weight to every observation and so might give more weight to the central part of the distribution than they do to the extremities.

We can quantify this effect by calculating the marginal contribution to the observed skew and kurtosis for any particular data point in the sample, scaled by its expected frequency of occurrence, were the observations to be coming from a Normal distribution, see Kemp (2008d). The results are shown in Figure 9.8. The horizontal axis is in units of standard deviation in this chart. Observations around the $\pm\sigma$ mark contribute very little to the skew, and observations around the $\pm 1.8\sigma$ mark contribute very little to the kurtosis of the distribution. The greater weight given to more central regions of the distribution is also apparent. No wonder the Cornish-Fisher approximation seems to fit the centre better than the extremities!

The failure to give an appropriate weight to the part of the distribution in which we are most interested does not appear to be the only potentially undesirable characteristic of the Cornish-Fisher approach. If we apply the Cornish-Fisher approach to a distribution that has materially non-zero (excess) kurtosis then it may not only be a relatively poor fit in the extremities but also a relatively poor fit in the middle of the distribution. Suppose that the distributional form was exactly in line with the one derived from the Cornish-Fisher approach, i.e. had a cubic quantile–quantile shape matching the equation in Section 9.5.3 for some particular values of γ_1 and γ_2. Suppose we now apply the Cornish-Fisher approach a second time to this distributional form. We might hope or expect that this would give the same distributional form

Table 9.2 Impact of applying the fourth-moment Cornish-Fisher adjustment to a distributional form already derived from such an adjustment

Characteristics of original distributional form		Characteristics after further application of the Cornish-Fisher adjustment	
Skew	Kurtosis	Skew	Kurtosis
0	0	0	0
0	0.5	0	0.5
0	1	0	1.3
0	2	0	3.6
0	3	0	6.9
1	1	0.9	0.8
1	2	1.1	2.4

as before, i.e. that the distributional form would be invariant under repeated application of the Cornish-Fisher approach. However, this is not the case as can be seen from Table 9.2. This issue is explored further in Kemp (2008d) and Kemp (2009).

Several other potential weaknesses of the Cornish-Fisher approach are noted in Jaschke (2002) in a paper that compares different ways of estimating quantiles alongside the Cornish-Fisher approach. Jaschke (2002) concludes that the Cornish-Fisher approach is a competitive technique if the portfolio distribution is relatively close to Normality, but that it is important to be aware of its many qualitative short-comings and its bad worst-case behaviour. The analysis in this paper suggests that return series of the sort often seen in asset management contexts may not be sufficiently close to Normality for the Cornish-Fisher approach to be a reliable tool for modelling fat-tailed behaviour.

Jaschke (2002) does suggest possible ways of generalising the Cornish-Fisher approach to circumvent some of the weaknesses highlighted above. For example, he suggests not starting with the Normal distribution but with a fatter-tailed base distributional form. Almost certainly, the resulting computations would no longer then depend in a simple way on the distribution's skew and kurtosis, obviating the practical computational advantages of the basic Cornish-Fisher approach.

A corollary is that over-reliance on use of just skew and kurtosis to characterise fat-tailed behaviour may also be inappropriate. It can be argued that the intrinsic justification for using these measures for this purpose is because one can then extrapolate from them to characterise the nature of the distributional form. If this really was the case then the fourth-moment Cornish-Fisher adjustment should be the relevant way of implementing this extrapolation process.

9.5.5 Improving on the Cornish-Fisher approach

Instead of, in some sense, using a curve that is derived giving equal weight to each data point, an alternative approach to estimating the distributional form would be to fit the curve directly, giving greater weight to observations in the part of the ranked sample in which we are most interested.

A simple example would be to use weights that corresponded to the distance between neighbouring expected (logged) returns (i.e. giving less weight to the observations bunched in the centre of the distribution). If we fit a cubic using a least squares methodology with this weighting approach then the fit in the tails becomes visually much more appealing than with the Cornish-Fisher approach, see Figure 9.7, but at the expense of a not quite such good fit towards the middle of the distribution. We could also use weights that placed particular focus on sub-elements of the observed distributional form, e.g. only ones between $m - 3\sigma$ and $m - 1\sigma$, if that part of the distribution was of particular interest to us.

This methodology can be thought of as another example of the distribution fitting approaches described in Section 9.4 but with the following special characteristics:

(a) The quantile–quantile plot is assumed to be expressible as a polynomial;[9] and
(b) We explicitly allow (indeed we even encourage!) the user to give different weights to different parts of the distributional form, depending on the use to which we intend to put the results.

> **Principle P45: Skewness and kurtosis are tools commonly used to assess the extent of fat-tailed behaviour. However, they are not particularly good tools for doing so when the focus is on behaviour in the distribution extremities, since they do not necessarily give appropriate weight to behaviour there. Modelling distribution extremities using the so-called fourth-moment Cornish-Fisher approach (an approach common in some parts of the financial services industry that explicitly refers to these statistics and arguably provides the intrinsic statistical rationale for their use in modelling fat tails) is therefore also potentially flawed. A more robust approach may be to curve fit the quantile–quantile form more directly.**

9.5.6   Time-varying volatility

As well as seeking effective tools for characterising fat tails, it is natural for us to be interested in why fat tails might arise in the first place. As mentioned earlier, some fat-tailed behaviour is intrinsic to particular instruments, but this is less obviously applicable to equity markets.

We can decompose the 'fat-tailed-ness' of observed equity market return distributions into two main components:

(a) A component arising because of the existence of time-varying volatility. Suppose we have two Normal distributions with the same mean, one with a relatively modest standard deviation and one with a much higher standard deviation. Consider the distribution of a random variable that 50 % of the time was randomly selected from the first distribution and 50 % of the time randomly selected from the second, i.e. a involves a *mixture* of two Normal distributions. Its probability density function will be denser in the tails (and in a central peak) than the corresponding (unmixed) Normal distribution with the same overall mean and standard deviation, see e.g. Kemp (2008d) and Kemp (2009). It will thus have

---

[9] Such distributional forms have the important added practical benefit that computation of statistics such as TVaR is then much simplified, see Kemp (2009).

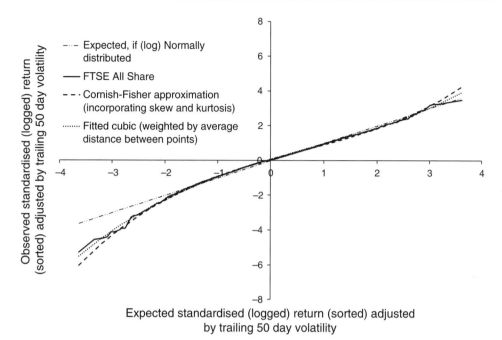

Figure 9.9 Daily returns on FTSE All-Share index end Jun 1994 to end Dec 2007, scaled by 50 business day trailing volatility
Source: Thomson Datastream

a non-zero kurtosis. Time-varying volatility will create a similar effect, and can thus also lead to fat-tails.

(b) A component which is not linked to time-varying volatility, but in some sense involves extreme outcomes 'coming out of the blue' (i.e. without prior 'warning' from changes in recent past shorter-term volatility).

A simple way of differentiating between these two components is to repeat the above analysis, but focusing on returns scaled by, say, past volatility of daily returns over, say, the preceding 50 trading days, see Figure 9.8. Assuming that the choice of a 50 trading day window is effective at capturing shorter-term movements in (time-varying) volatility, this picture should in the main show the contribution merely from the second of these components. The upside fat tail in Figure 9.7 largely disappears in Figure 9.8, suggesting that upside fat tails (at least for this index over this time period) may be largely explainable by the presence of time-varying volatility. The downside fat tail is somewhat less marked than before, but still quite noticeable.

Giamouridis and Ntoula (2007) analyse different ways of estimating downside risk measures (with particular reference to hedge fund strategies). Their conclusions seem to corroborate the analysis set out above. They note:

(a) The importance of time-varying volatility, by making reference to GARCH style models that might be used to adjust for time-varying volatility;

(b) The use of mean–variance models coupled with appropriate distributional assumptions seems to improve the ability to predict VaR, particularly VaR at a 1 % confidence level. The weighted quantile–quantile curve fit approach described above can be thought of as a way of defining a range of distributions (the higher the order of the polynomial the greater the flexibility of choice), together with a range of ways of best fitting these distributions to the observations in a manner that focuses on part of the distributional form of most interest to the user; and

(c) The estimation of expected shortfall is more influenced by the distributional form than the estimation of VaR. This reflects the greater sensitivity that expected shortfall may have to the extreme tail of the distribution, see Kemp (2009).

Hull and White (1998) also find that incorporation of time-varying volatility materially improves the goodness of fit in historical simulation Value-at-Risk estimation.

Principle P46: For major western (equity) markets, a significant proportion of deviation from (log) Normality in daily (index) return series appears to come from time-varying volatility, particularly in the upside tail. This part of any fat-tailed behaviour may be able to be managed by reference to rises in recent past shorter-term volatility or forward-looking measures such as implied volatility.

9.5.7 Crowded trades

Whilst the preceding section suggests that time-varying volatility is an important contributor to fat tails, it also suggests that it is not the only contributor, particularly on the downside. Another probable contributor is what are anecdotally called 'crowded trades'.

For example, we noted in Section 6.3.3 that several quantitative fund managers suffered performance reversals in August 2007. Rather too many of their supposedly independent investment views all declined at the same time, and the returns that they posted were in some cases well into the extreme downside tail.

Any style of active fund management is potentially exposed to 'crowded trades', since any style can be linked to rapid growth of assets under management, commonality of investment ideas, etc. Hedge funds are potentially particularly exposed to 'crowded' trades, whether they focus on less liquid strategies or whether they stick to more straightforward styles, e.g. equity long–short. Hedge funds can (potentially unwittingly) end up adopting similar positions to those of their close competitors. They can thus be caught out merely because there is a change in risk appetite affecting their competitors, and the consequential position unwinds then affect their own positions.

Crowded trade risk increases as the part of the industry that might be 'crowding' grows in size (as the quantitatively run part of the hedge fund industry had done prior to August 2007), but is latent until some set of circumstances triggers greater volatility in risk appetite. Hedge funds, like other high conviction fund management styles, typically seem to exhibit more fat-tailed behaviour than more traditional fund types. They may also be more at risk from such fat tails, since another typical feature of hedge funds, namely leverage, adds risks such as liquidity risk, forced unwind risk and variable borrow cost risk that may be particularly problematic in fat-tail scenarios.

At one level we might merely seek to understand whether and how the views that we might be adopting coincide with views that lots of other people are also adopting. If they are and there is a stress, will our portfolio be able to ride out the storm, or will it be one of the portfolios that has to unwind at the 'wrong' time? Crowded trades whilst often apparently relatively parochial can sometimes encompass entire markets. Examples of the latter arguably include both the dot-com boom and bust during the late 1990s and the early 2000s and the events before and during the 2007–09 credit crisis.

9.5.8 Bounded rationality

At a deeper level we might also explore why it is that investors have a propensity to get into crowded trades in the first place, to make sure that our own investment processes are cognisant of such risks (and if possible positioned to benefit from the behaviour of others).

It is unlikely that there will ever be general consensus on such matters, since if at any point there became such a consensus, the tendency to crowd would presumably move somewhere else. However, it is probable that behavioural finance and market structure may be relevant here. For example, there is some suggestion that a market involving heterogeneous investors or agents (perhaps with different agents principally focusing on different market segments or only able to buy and sell from a limited number of other agents) may naturally exhibit fat-tailed behaviour even when each agent is exhibiting 'bounded rationality' (i.e. fully rational behaviour within the confines of the bounds within which the agent is placed).

This idea is explored further in Palin *et al.* (2008) and Palin (2002) who develop (non-linear) models of the economy and financial markets that naturally give rise to fat-tailed return distributions even though their underlying drivers are more classically Normal (or log-Normal) in form.

9.6 FAT-TAILED BEHAVIOUR IN MULTIPLE RETURN SERIES

9.6.1 Introduction

We noted earlier how some quantitative fund managers posted particularly poor performance in August 2007. Movements in any one quantitative style, whilst sizeable, were not obviously particularly extreme. What was particularly problematic was the extent to which multiple factors that were supposed to behave independently all moved simultaneously in an adverse direction. In short, it was the *joint* fat-tailed behaviour of equity market elements that proved particularly problematic for them at that time.

In this section we focus on how to refine the techniques described in Section 9.5 to cater for fat-tailed behaviour in the *joint* behaviour of multiple return series. Most of the conclusions we drew there apply here too.

By 'fat-tailed' we again mean extreme outcomes occurring more frequently than would be expected were the returns to be coming from a (log) Normal distribution. However, instead of focusing on *univariate* Normal distributions we now focus on *multivariate* Normal distributions. Univariate Normal distributions are characterised by their mean and standard deviation. Multivariate Normal distributions are more complicated than a series of univariate distributions, because multivariate Normal distributions are characterised not only by the means and standard deviations of each series in isolation but also by the correlations between the different series.

9.6.2   Visualising fat tails in multiple return series

Effective visualisation of deviations from (now multivariate) Normality in co-movements of multiple series is more challenging than effective visualisation of fat tails in the univariate case. Even when considering just two return series in tandem, there are an infinite number of 'standard' bivariate Normal probability density functions, since their definition includes an extra parameter, ρ, corresponding to the correlation between the two series. This can take any value between -1 and $+1$ (if $\rho = 0$ then the two series are independent). With three or more series, we run out of dimensions for plotting joint behaviour (and there is even more flexibility in the correlation matrix structure that a 'standard' trivariate or higher dimensional Normal distribution might take).

The (joint) probability density functions corresponding to three 'standard' bivariate Normal probability distributions are shown in Figures 9.10 ($\rho = 0$), 9.11 ($\rho = -0.4$) and 9.12 ($\rho = +0.7$). These each have a hump in the middle that falls away at the edges (i.e. at the 'tails' of these bivariate distributions). In each case, cross-sections through the middle of the probability density function plot have the appearance of the traditional bell-shaped form of the univariate Normal distribution.

The difference between the three can be seen by considering different cross-sectional slices of the plot through an axis passing through the middle of the plot. The cross-sections are in general wider or narrower in different directions. If ρ is positive, as in Figure 9.12, then such cross-sections are widest towards the corners corresponding to the two series moving in the same direction (hence outcomes in which the two series move in the same direction are

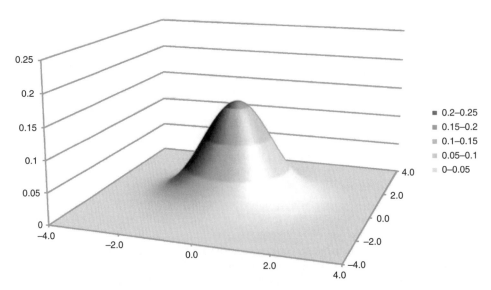

Figure 9.10   Standard bivariate Normal probability density function with $\rho = 0$

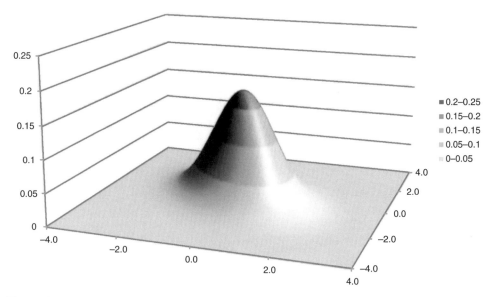

Figure 9.11   Standard bivariate Normal probability density function with $\rho = -0.4$

more likely than those where they move in opposite directions), whilst if ρ is negative, as in Figure 9.11, the opposite is the case.

As with univariate distributions, we can also display cumulative distribution plots, i.e. the likelihood of the (joint) outcome not exceeding a particular (joint) value. Those corresponding to the standard bivariate Normal distributions shown in Figures 9.10 and 9.11 are shown in

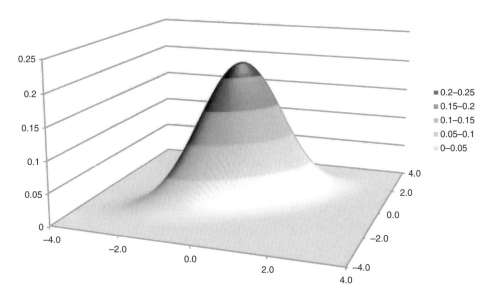

Figure 9.12   Standard bivariate Normal probability density function with $\rho = +0.7$

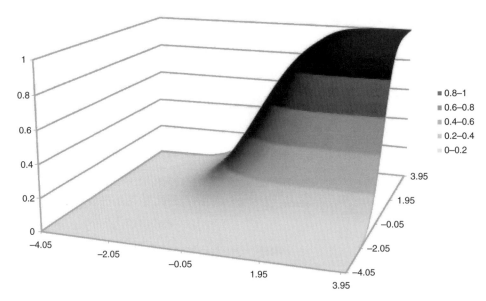

Figure 9.13   Cumulative distribution function for standard bivariate Normal with $\rho = 0$

Figures 9.13 and 9.14, respectively. It is not easy visually to spot much difference between these two figures.

9.6.3   Copulas, Sklar's theorem and quantiles

Perhaps the most usual way (in the financial community) of characterising more effectively the shape of the (multivariate) return distribution is to decompose the problem into

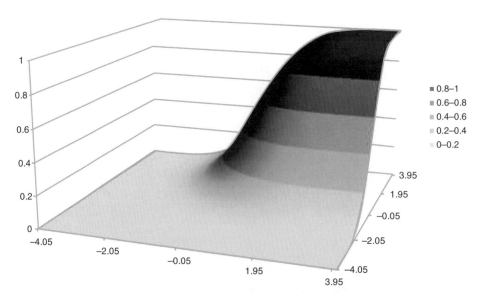

Figure 9.14   Cumulative distribution function for standard bivariate Normal with $\rho = -0.4$

two parts:

(a) A part relating to how fat-tailed each return series is in isolation, via the shape of their so-called marginal probability distributions (i.e. the distributional form relevant to each series in isolation ignoring any information about how other series might move); and

(b) A part relating to how the different return series might co-move together, having first standardised all of their original marginal distributions. The name given to the function describing these co-movement characteristics is the *copula* of the distribution.

The tools we introduced in Section 9.5 can be applied to tackle (a), so the 'new' element in this section is how to focus on the remainder, i.e. (b). By analysing both sources in tandem it may also be possible to identify what proportion of 'fat-tailed-ness' comes from each part, which may make effective portfolio construction easier, see Chapter 12.

The definition of a copula is a function $C : [0,1]^N \to [0,1]$ where:

(a) There are (uniform) random variables $U_1, \ldots, U_N$ taking values in [0,1] such that C is their cumulative (multivariate) distribution function; and

(b) C has uniform marginal distributions, i.e. for all $i \leq N$ and $u_i \in [0,1]$ we have $C(1, \ldots 1, u_i, 1, \ldots, 1) = u_i$

The basic rationale for copulas is that any joint distribution F of a set of random variables $X_1, \ldots, X_N$, i.e. $F(\mathbf{x}) = Prob(X_1 \leq x_1, \ldots, X_N \leq x_N)$, can be separated into two parts. The first is the combination of the marginal distribution functions for each random variable in isolation, also called the *marginals*, i.e. $F_i(\cdot)$ where $F_i(x) = Prob(X_i \leq x)$ and the second is the copula that describes the dependence structure between the random variables. Mathematically, this decomposition relies on Sklar's theorem, which states that if $X_1, \ldots, X_N$ are random variables with marginal distribution functions if $F_1, \ldots, F_N$ and joint distribution function F then there exists an N-dimensional copula C such that for all $x \in \mathcal{R}^N$:

$$F(\mathbf{x}) = C(F_1(x_1), \ldots, F_N(x_N)) = C(\mathbf{F}(\mathbf{x})) \tag{9.6}$$

i.e. C is the joint distribution function of the unit random variables $(F_1(x_1), \ldots, F_N(x_N))$. If $F_1, \ldots, F_N$ are continuous then C is unique.

A particularly simple copula is the product (or independence) copula $\Pi^N(\mathbf{x}) = \Pi_{i=1}^N x_i$. It is the copula of independent random variables. Indeed, because the copula completely specifies the dependency structure of a set of random variables, the random variables $X_1, \ldots, X_N$ are independent if and only if their N-dimensional copula is the product copula. The copula most commonly used in practice is probably the *Gaussian* copula (for a given correlation matrix). It is the copula applicable to a multivariate Normal distribution with that correlation matrix. In the special case where all the variables are independent, then the covariance matrix has non-zero terms only along the leading diagonal and the (Gaussian) copula for a Normal distribution with such a correlation matrix is equal to the product copula. All Normal distributions with the same correlation matrix give rise to the same copula, since the standard deviations that also drive the covariance matrix are part of the characterisation of the marginals, rather than of the dependency structure characterised by the copula.

Unfortunately, whilst any multivariate distribution can be decomposed into these two parts, this does not necessarily mean that copulas are much better for visualising joint fat-tailed behaviour than the cumulative distribution functions from which they are derived. Copulas corresponding to the two standardised Normal distributions shown in Figures 9.13 and 9.14 are shown in Figures 9.15 and 9.16, respectively. They are again relatively tricky to

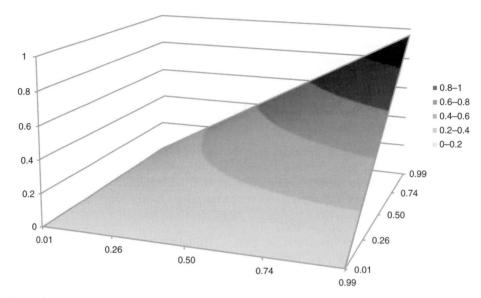

Figure 9.15   Gaussian copula with $\rho = 0$, also known as the *product* or *independence* copula

distinguish. Their differences are small in relation to unity, which drives the overall visual scale of the chart.

Rather easier to distinguish are *differences* between two copulas. The difference between the copulas in Figures 9.15 and 9.16 is shown in Figure 9.17. It is peaked upwards at the corners corresponding to situations where the two series move in opposite directions (which

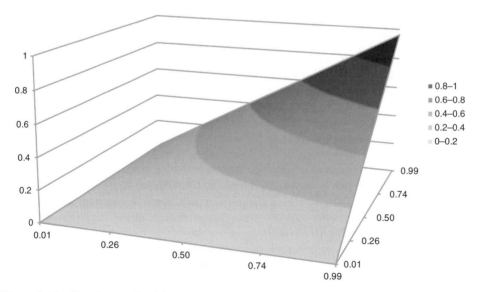

Figure 9.16   Gaussian copula with $\rho = -0.4$

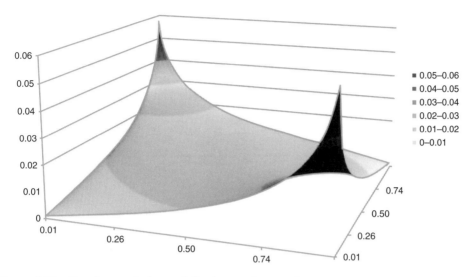

Figure 9.17   Gaussian copula ($\rho = -0.4$) minus product copula

become more likely when ρ is negative) and peaked down at the other two corners (which become less likely when ρ is negative).

9.6.4   Fractile–fractile (i.e. quantile–quantile box) plots

A closely related concept is a *fractile–fractile* or *quantile–quantile box* plot. *Fractiles* are the generalisation of percentiles, quartiles and the like. For example, suppose we were analysing the co-movement characteristics of two different return series. We might take each series in isolation and slice up the observed returns into, say, 20 buckets, with the top 5 % put into the first bucket, the next 5 % in the second, etc. We might then plot the number of times the observed return for the first series was in bucket x whilst the observed return for the second series was in bucket y. Another term used for this sort of analysis is *box counting*, see also Arbarbanel (1993) and Kemp (2009). Such a chart is essentially the same (up to a constant) as one that indicates how the density function equivalent to the copula for a particular distribution differs from the one for the product copula.

An example of how such plots operate is shown in Figure 9.18 and Figure 9.19. Figure 9.18 is a scatter plot of weekly (log) sector relative returns on the MSCI ACWI Utilities sector versus (log) sector relative returns on the MSCI ACWI Transport for the period 9 March 2001 to 4 July 2008, sourced from MSCI and Thomson Datastream.[10] Figure 9.19 is based on the same data but shows merely the ranks of these sector relatives within a listing of all of that sector's sector relative returns, i.e. it strips out the effect of the sector's marginal distribution. Figure 9.20 groups these ranks into deciles, and shows the number of returns falling into each decile–decile pairing.

---

[10] Weekly return data on these indices are available from end 2000 but we start 10 weeks into this period to allow us to include later on in this chapter adjustments relating to shorter-term time-varying volatility of returns, which we estimate using the preceding 10 weeks' worth of returns.

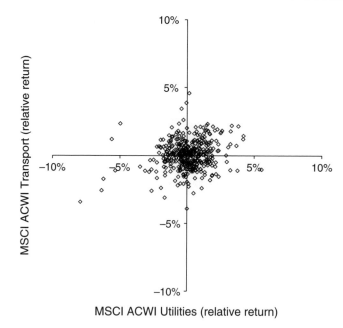

Figure 9.18   Scatter plot of weekly sector relative returns for MSCI ACWI Utilities vs Transport
Source: Thomson Datastream

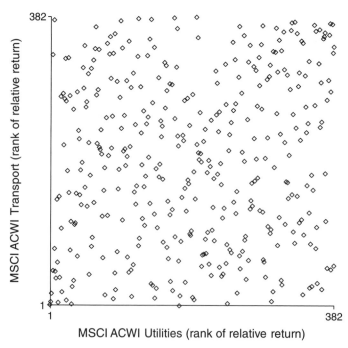

Figure 9.19   Scatter plot of weekly sector relative returns for MSCI ACWI Utilities vs Transport
Source: Thomson Datastream

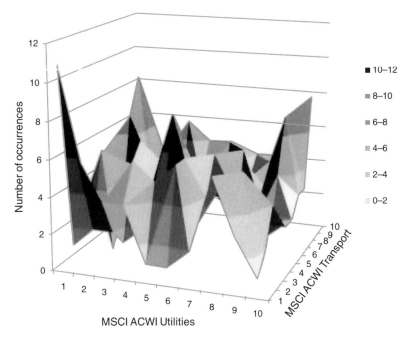

Figure 9.20   Decile–decile plot between MSCI ACWI Utilities and Transport sectors
Source: Thomson Datastream

All other things being equal, if we double the number of fractiles used, we can expect the number of observations falling into a given pairing to fall by a factor of 4. So if, for example, we have 20 quantile boxes (i.e. using increments of 5 %) then we would need 400 observations to expect to have more than one observation on average within each quantile pairing. This considerably limits the usefulness of quantile–quantile box analysis on a single sector pairing. However, we can instead look at numbers across all sector pairings simultaneously. Expected numbers in each fractile–fractile pair increase about four-fold as the number of sectors we can pair up is doubled.

In Figure 9.21 we show such an analysis, considering all pairs of the c. 20 MSCI industry sectors that have a continuous history over this period.

A noticeable feature of this analysis is the existence of four peaks in each of the four corners of the (sector pair averaged) fractile–fractile plot. From this we might conclude that extreme sector relative returns have a tendency to clump together. This is the phenomenon, articulated by risk managers, that all correlations seem to go to 'unity' in adverse times. By this is actually meant that they seem to have the annoying habit (unless the risk management is top-notch) of going to +1 or −1 depending on which is the worse outcome.

However, there is a possible error of logic involved in drawing this conclusion. As we have already noted, mixtures of Normal distributions are typically not themselves Normally distributed. We might expect the same to apply to mixtures of bivariate normal distributions. Even if (log) sector relative return distributions were accurately modelled by a multivariate Normal distribution, we should expect the corresponding bivariate Normal distributions for each specific sector pairing to differ, because they can be expected in general to have different pair-wise correlations. This mixing might create the same effect – i.e. the four peaks might

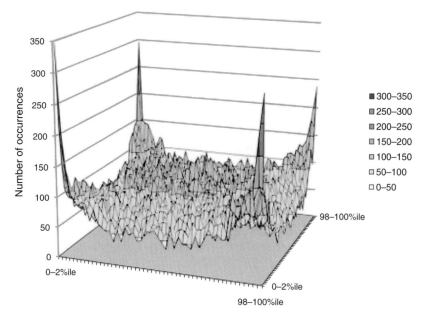

Figure 9.21 Fractile–fractile plot of sector relative return rankings, averaged across all sector pairings
Source: Thomson Datastream

merely be a feature of there being some sectors with relatively high positive and negative correlations.

9.6.5 Time-varying volatility

Another implication we have already drawn from consideration of mixtures of Normal distributions is that time-varying volatility can lead to fat tails. Indeed, it appears to be a significant contributor to fat-tailed behaviour of major developed equity market indices, particularly upside fat tails. The same effect also seems to explain a material fraction of the clumping into the corners seen in Figure 9.21.

There are two different types of ways of adjusting for time-varying volatility in multiple return series. We can adjust each series in isolation by its own recent past volatility, in the same way as was done in Section 9.5. Alternatively, we can adjust every series simultaneously by reference to changes in the recent past cross-sectional dispersion of sector returns.

In Figures 9.22 and 9.23 we show how the fractile–fractile plot in Figure 9.21 would alter if we incorporate such adjustments. Figure 9.22 adjusts for recent past changes in each individual series' own volatilities whilst Figure 9.23 adjusts for changes in recent past cross-sectional dispersion.[11]

---

[11] When adjusting each series in isolation by its own recent past volatility we have used the standard deviation of the last 10 weeks' worth of relative returns. When adjusting every series simultaneously by reference to changes in the recent past cross-sectional dispersion of sector returns we have used the average of the last 10 weeks' cross-sectional dispersion (calculated using the cross-sectional standard deviation of normalised sector relative returns, where 'normalised' here means scaling by the overall standard deviation of that sector's sector relatives over the entire period under analysis, to avoid giving undue weight to the behaviour of a small number of sectors).

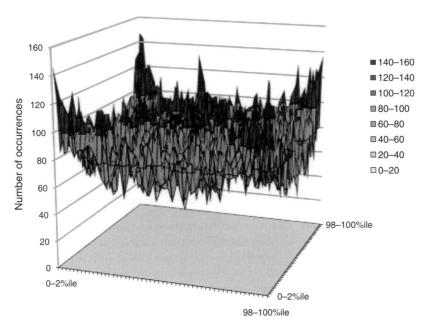

Figure 9.22 Fractile–fractile plot of sector relative return ranks, averaged across all sector pairings, if we adjust each series by its own recent past volatility
Source: Thomson Datastream

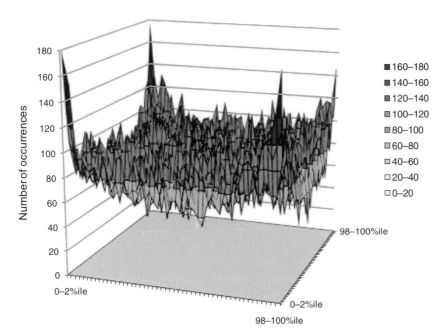

Figure 9.23 Fractile–fractile plot of sector relative return ranks, averaged across all sector pairings, if we adjust each series by recent average cross-sectional dispersion of returns
Source: Thomson Datastream

The clumping into the four corners of the fractile–fractile plot is materially reduced by such adjustments. As with single return series in isolation, a material fraction (but not all) joint fat-tailed behaviour (at least for mainstream equity sectors) does appear to be explained by time-varying volatility.

Principle P47: A substantial proportion of 'fat-tailed' behaviour (i.e. deviation from Normality) exhibited by *joint* return series appears to come from time-varying volatility. This part of any fat-tailed behaviour may be able to be managed by reference to rises in recent past shorter-term volatilities and correlations or by reference to forward-looking measures such as implied volatility and implied correlation or implied covariance.

Principle P48: Conversely, time-varying volatility does not seem to explain all fat-tailed behaviour exhibited by joint (equity) return series. Extreme events can still come 'out of the blue', highlighting the continuing merit of practitioners using risk management tools like stress testing that seek to reflect the existence of such 'unknown unknowns' or 'black swan' events.

9.6.6   Differentiating between return series

Plots focusing merely on average behaviour do not indicate spreads around the average, i.e. whether just a few sectors or sector pairings are much more prone to fat-tailed behaviour than others. They also do not provide much guide as to how important is fat-tailed behaviour in the marginals (i.e. analysable by considering each individual return in isolation) versus fat-tailed behaviour in the copula (i.e. the remainder).

In Figure 9.24 we show quantile–quantile plots (of the sort used in Section 9.5) for different sector relative return series in isolation, i.e. for the different marginal distributions. To avoid over-cluttering the plot we show merely the cross-sectional spread of these plots, which we characterise by the 10th to 90th percentile range (and the average) if we order across sectors the apparent size of deviation from Normality. As before, the plots have been normalised to a zero mean and unit standard deviation to make them more comparable. In practice, a fund manager may combine two sector positions via any linear combination. For simplicity we concentrate on just two cases, which we call:

(a) 'X + Y', i.e. the two sector positions are of the same (normalised) magnitude and have the same sign; and
(b) 'X − Y', i.e. the two sector positions are of the same (normalised) magnitude but are of opposite signs.

It appears that:

(a) Individual sector fat-tailed-ness seems to be on average of a similar order of magnitude to overall market index fat-tailed-ness. However, some sectors are noticeably more fat-tailed than others; and
(b) Combinations of two sectors as per 'X + Y' and 'X − Y' also appear to be noticeably fat-tailed, indeed not much less fat-tailed on average than single series analysed in isolation (and potentially exhibiting a similar range).

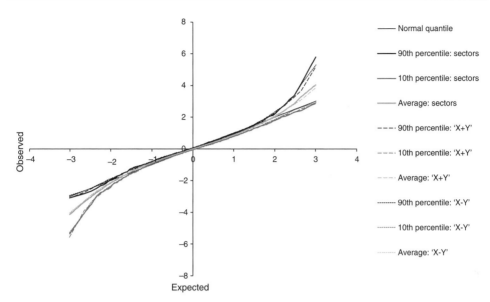

Figure 9.24   Standardised quantile–quantile plots of sector relatives and for all X + Y and X − Y combinations
Source: Thomson Datastream

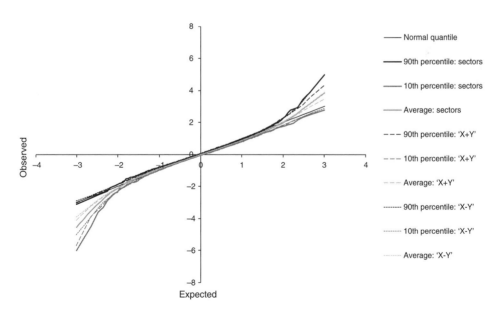

Figure 9.25   As Figure 9.24 but adjusting each series in isolation by its own recent past time-varying volatility
Source: Thomson Datastream

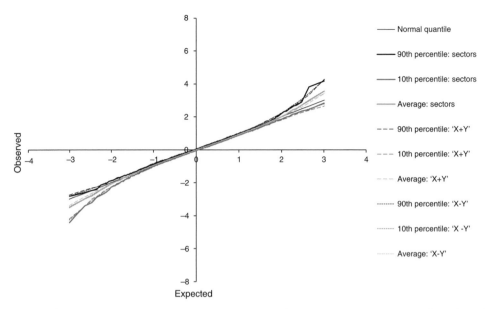

Figure 9.26   As Figure 9.24 but adjusting every series by the recent past cross-sectional dispersion of sector returns
Source: Thomson Datastream

Point (b) is potentially surprising. The Central Limit Theorem would suggest that the more distinct positions you have in a portfolio the closer to Normality is likely to be its behaviour. Thus we might have expected the 'X + Y' and 'X − Y' plots to have exhibited materially smaller fat tails on average (and hence a materially smaller spread of fat tails too) than single series because the combinations involve two positions whilst the individual return series in isolation involve just one. A material fraction of fat-tailed behaviour exhibited by portfolios involving two sector positions is not explainable in this manner and so must actually be coming from fat-tailed behaviour only capturable within the copula.

Just as in Figure 9.12, we can also analyse how much of the fat-tailed behaviour exhibited by 'X + Y' and 'X − Y' combinations of sector positions comes from time-varying volatility, and again there are two possible ways of interpreting time-varying volatility. Figures 9.25 and 9.26 are repeats of Figure 9.24, but incorporating adjustments designed to strip out time-varying volatility either in each return series in isolation (Figure 9.25) or in the cross-sectional dispersion of sector returns (Figure 9.26). As before, time-varying volatility of returns seems to explain a material fraction of fat-tailed behaviour in joint return series, with cross-sectional dispersion of return here seeming to be a more effective way of adjusting for time-varying volatility.

10

Calibrating Risk Statistics to 'Market Implied' Distributions

10.1 INTRODUCTION

We explained in Chapter 9 that the risk management paradigm currently used by the financial services industry involves, in effect, attempting to identify the 'real world' likelihoods of differently sized movements in market consistent valuations. It is therefore only, we might argue, *partly* market consistent.

In this chapter we explore how we might seek to identify *fully* market consistent risk measures rather than having market consistency apply merely to instrument valuations. We also explore some of the implications of adopting such a philosophy.

The key observation underlying the whole of this chapter is that whenever the main purpose of VaR and other similar risk measures is to place a 'price' on risk then we ought (if we are seeking market consistency) to be primarily interested in the *fair market price for the relevant risk*. As we saw in Chapter 2, this *fair*, i.e. market consistent, price will depend on *risk-neutral* probabilities and *not* on real world probabilities. Thus calibration needs as far as possible to replicate observed market prices of options that would hedge the entity against the risk in question. In general, such options will include a 'strike' price, i.e. the hedge will protect the entity against performance worse than some specified level, since in general implied volatilities and implied correlations vary by strike.

In particular, we saw in Section 2.8 that one of the disciplines to which this logic applies is capital adequacy, since it is attempting a fair quantification of the monetary implications to policyholders arising from the risk of default of the firm.

That being said, there are times when it may be inappropriate to seek full market consistency in our quantification of risk. Typically, these involve situations where we would be advising just one party within a transaction, e.g. when we are expressing a view as to whether the price we might pay for a particular risk looks attractive or not, see Section 2.2.5. The material in this chapter has potentially less relevance for these sorts of situations.

10.2 MARKET IMPLIED RISK MODELLING

10.2.1 Refining the granularity-based approach to risk modelling

We noted in Chapter 7 that time series-based risk models are subject to inherent data limitations. There just aren't enough data to estimate all of their elements accurately.

The granularity-based approach we proposed in Section 7.4 in relation to bond risk modelling appears to offer a way of estimating more accurately the residual instrument-specific contributions to risk that are otherwise impossible to estimate from time series data alone. It did so by referring to an exogenous characteristic of the instrument in question, i.e. its credit rating, which can be argued to have some link to the credit's idiosyncratic risk. However, to do so we needed to incorporate some possibly tenuous and over-simplistic assumptions. For example, we glossed over subtleties regarding ratings migrations. We also needed to rely on some exogenous mapping of rating to likelihood of default, perhaps derived from analysis of a rating agency's historic data (despite rating agencies elsewhere indicating that this might be unsound).

How accurate are the assignments of ratings to credits by rating agencies? And how relevant are default histories to the task of assessing how likely a bond is to default in the future? If we dislike *historic default rates* then we can instead use *market implied default rates*. Credit rating agencies can take some time to reflect in their ratings what is happening to a particular credit, so individual bonds can trade as if they have a different rating to the one assigned to them by the ratings agencies. Market implied default rates are easily derived from market data (as long as there is a market in the issuer's debt). As Schönbucher (2003) notes, they are essentially the same as the bond's *credit spread*, i.e. its yield spread versus an equivalent risk-free bond of similar currency and duration. These market implied default rates are 'risk-neutral' and market consistent.[1]

Default rates are a rather bond-orientated concept. Is there any corresponding market implied data that is relevant for equities? Yes. The financial theory of *firm valuation* demonstrates that bond default rates and equity volatility in some sense form two sides of the same coin, see e.g. Schönbucher (2003). This was recognised even within pioneering papers on derivative pricing such as the seminal Black and Scholes (1973) paper (which is actually titled 'The pricing of options and corporate liabilities') and Merton (1974). So, to create a market implied granularity-based risk model encompassing equities we should derive an individual equity's idiosyncratic risk from its implied volatility (assuming that there are options trading on it), or failing that from its credit spread (if available) and some analysis based on firm value theory.

Such an approach is conceptually a huge step forward compared with a pure time series-based risk model. It enables us in principle to populate all of the idiosyncratic risk components that were otherwise out of reach using purely time series data.

Why stop at idiosyncratic risk? In principle we ought also to be able to identify market implied idiosyncratic cross-correlations and industry/sector volatilities. If we have all of these too then we have an entire *market implied covariance matrix*. More generally, for non-(log)-Normal probability distributions, we can also in principle build up an entire market implied multivariate distributional form.

In practice, derivatives relevant to inferring the market implied distributional form do not trade very often, and even when they do they may not be very liquid. If we can't typically in practice observe the desired level of detail then do we not end up back using historic observed correlations, etc.?

---

[1] Credit portfolios may also include exposure to preference shares or debt instruments with similar economic characteristics, because they commonly form a part of the capital issuance of banks and other financial service providers. The spreads on these sorts of instruments do not necessarily reflect just credit risk. In normal circumstances, investors in such instruments might expect to receive a dividend or coupon fixed in monetary terms (or involving a fixed spread versus a reference floating rate level), plus, in due course, a redemption payment. However, if the firm runs into trouble then it may fail to pay (or it may defer) expected coupons, or it may fail to redeem the preference share as expected, without the firm being considered to have defaulted. The spreads on these instruments may therefore include an element of recompense akin to the equity risk premium applicable to a firm's common stock, as well as recompense for default risk.

There are three flaws with such reasoning:

(a) Financial markets have shown tremendous innovation over the last few decades. In certain markets it is now possible to identify from market observables some of this data. For example, in equity-land, we can infer an approximate average level of implied correlation from the relationship between index implied volatilities and single stock implied volatilities (some hedge funds attempt to arbitrage between the two). In bond-land, prices of different CDO tranches are sensitive to average implied correlation between defaults on different bonds. Who knows how much more will become possible over time?[2]

(b) Some of the more complicated structures used to back some retail structured products are sensitive to market implied average correlations between baskets of securities (*correlation*, in the parlance of the derivatives markets), and it is possible to buy instruments that express views on equity implied correlation or hedge such exposures, see e.g. Pengelly (2008). One might expect[3] sellers of such products to have satisfied themselves that there was *sufficient* access to pricing data to permit an appropriate level of price discovery and hedging for their own risk management purposes. Even if market observables are sparse they may not be *so sparse* that they are not, in some sense, 'fit for purpose' for at least some tasks that depend on knowledge of the market implied distributional form.

(c) In Section 4.13 we explored how we can blend together our own 'prior' views about market correlations (e.g. derived from analysis of historic data) with market observables that might help us infer something about market implied views. Indeed, one reason we focused there on elaborating how to combine them was because it would be relevant when we reached this chapter. Inability to source a *complete* market implied covariance matrix doesn't mean that we can't take into account more sketchy market implied information to the extent that such information is available.

The key point is that the philosophical basis of this form of risk modelling (which we might call 'fully market implied' or 'derivative pricing-based' risk modelling) is quite different to that of time series-based risk modelling. With time series-based risk modelling, we extrapolate the past to identify how the future might behave. With derivative pricing-based risk modelling we infer where possible how risky the future might be (or to be more precise, the monetary implications of this riskiness) from current market observables. Only if we can't find current market observables do we fill out the missing data via general reasoning (presumably usually by reference to historic data).

10.2.2   Time horizons

Fully market implied risk modelling caters for time horizons differently than historic time series-based risk modelling.

In general, forward-looking risk measures can be either *horizon dependent* or *horizon independent*. VaR is naturally a horizon dependent measure, e.g. we might be interested in a 5 day (rather than a 1 day, 15 day, 1 month, ...) 95 % confidence level VaR, in which case its *return horizon* is this 5 day period.

---

[2] The 'mileage' option referred to in Section 4.5 is an example of a conceptually interesting option type that for a long time was relatively hypothetical but which more recently appears to have become more practical to trade.

[3] For 'expect' perhaps read 'hope' given the losses that some organisations have suffered on more complex derivatives in recent years!

Tracking errors are less often apparently horizon dependent. They are usually annualised but this is actually a quotation convention. The underlying logic behind the convention is to assume that the return distribution through time has *stationary* second moments. This means that the standard deviation of the (log) return between t_1 and t_2 is dependent only on the length of the time period. In continuous time (subject to suitable regularity conditions) it would be proportional to $\sqrt{t_2 - t_1}$. The standard quotation convention therefore involves annualising tracking errors derived from, say, monthly returns by adjusting by the square root of time, i.e. in this instance by the square root of 12. Risk systems that quote a single annualised ex-ante tracking error typically implicitly assume that the tracking error applicable to any other return horizon can be derived by the same square root of time convention but in reverse. Some risk systems do quote horizon dependent ex-ante tracking errors, e.g. 4 % pa for yearly returns but 5 % pa for monthly returns.

Conventional risk modelling wisdom holds that we ought in principle to be interested in a *time horizon*. The argument goes that we are interested in risks that we might experience between now and when the portfolio might change, since if the portfolio is completely realigned then its risks become completely different. Such wisdom thus holds that the most appropriate time horizon to focus on for risk measurement and management purposes ought in principle to depend on your investment analysis and/or decision-making time horizon. A short time horizon (e.g. days or even hours or minutes) might be appropriate for a hedge fund, a somewhat longer one (e.g. weeks or months) for a more traditional long only asset manager, and a longer one still (quarters or years) for a longer-term investing institution such as a pension fund when considering asset-liability management.

Conventional wisdom also notes that observed return distributions typically do not have stationary second moments and so the time horizon you choose actually makes a difference to the answer. Observed return distributions typically exhibit at least some of what is typically called by financial practitioners *autocorrelation*, even though they actually mean *intertemporal dependency* (since the dependency does not always relate to the second moment and hence to correlation). There is, for example, some evidence of intertemporal dependency for major market indices (and more for some individual securities). The extent of their fat-tailed behaviour seems to depend on the frequency of the analysis, see Chapter 9.

However, there is a potentially puzzling angle to this conventional wisdom. If autocorrelation really were such a big deal, then why haven't people spotted its near universal existence and why hasn't it been arbitraged away more effectively over time? Most probably its existence or non-existence is less important in terms of market implieds than this conventional wisdom might otherwise suggest.[4]

One reason why in Chapter 4 we explored mileage options in some depth was because they highlight very effectively that the risk-neutral probabilities depend mainly on the behaviour of cumulative quadratic variations and *not* on how much autocorrelation these quadratic variations appear to exhibit in the 'real world'. Providers of options (of any type, not just mileage options) cannot generally in their pricing of such options take 'real world' autocorrelation effects into account, because the circumstances in which these autocorrelation effects might fail to materialise are typically the ones that have the highest dis-utilities as far as market participants in aggregate are concerned.

---

[4] It can also be shown that autocorrelation isn't actually inconsistent with efficient markets, if we posit a time-varying 'price of risk'.

That being said, option implied volatilities observed in practice not only exhibit a skew structure (i.e. different volatilities for different strikes) but also a term structure, see Figure 4.7. Option investors are not only taking views on *volatility* (and *volatility skew*) but also potentially on *volatility term structure*. There are intertemporal dependency effects present even within market implieds.

10.2.3 Additivity, scalability and coherence

In Section 7.3 we assumed that if we had two different sets of positions, **a** and **b**, that generated corresponding contributions to future returns A and B then the sum of these two positions, i.e. $\mathbf{c} = \mathbf{a} + \mathbf{b}$, would generate a corresponding contribution to future return of $C = A + B$.

Another reason why focusing on the 'price' of risk leads us to adopt fully market implied risk measurement is that this rather reasonable assertion requires us to assume that the valuations (and hence returns) are additive. Elsewhere in the same section is embedded an assumption that values are scalable. As we saw in Chapter 2, use of 'real world' probability distributions does not in general result in valuations that adhere to these axioms (unless discount rates are adjusted to compensate).

Indeed, it can be argued that the whole of the risk measurement framework set out in Chapter 7 actually *requires us* to adopt these axioms and hence a derivative pricing-based approach to risk modelling. Whenever risk statistics are being calculated primarily for capital adequacy or capital allocation purposes, not only might it be desirable to include some of the derivative pricing refinements described earlier in this chapter, it is actually theoretically required!

Principle P3 is important here. Some commentators describe an approach to risk modelling in which we attempt to calculate the 'real world' likelihood of different sized movements in market consistency valuations as relating to the economic capital that the business needs. But suppose that such a computation of economic capital comes up with a figure lower than the cost of hedging the risk in the open market. Then such a computation will encourage entities not to hedge risks. Use of the term 'economic capital' suggests a degree of objectivity that is not then actually present in practice (given the subjectivity involved in identifying 'real world' probabilities). It may also lead to false confidence and adoption of inappropriate levels of risk by the firms concerned (relative to the strategies they might have adopted had they sought to place a more market consistent 'price' on the risks in question).

Furthermore, if we adopt a regulatory framework in which additivity and scalability are not satisfied then it is likely that the regulatory framework will include scope for 'regulatory arbitrage'. For example, Kemp (2005) comments on the potential inconsistencies that can arise if structured credit instruments, such as CDOs, are valued by the market in one way, but the risks implicit within them are assessed for regulatory or risk modelling purposes using different methodologies.

The concepts underlying fully market consistent risk measurement also shed further light on the incoherence of VaR referred to in Section 7.3.3. The equivalent option to a traditional VaR is a digital option that pays out 1 if the loss is greater than the VaR and 0 otherwise. But life is not often this black and white. More appropriate may be risk measures that correspond to options with somewhat smoother pay-offs, such as TVaR.

Or rather, choice between VaR and TVaR depends in part on one's perspective, see Kemp (2009). The conceptual framework we introduced in Section 2.8 means that capital adequacy computations will in general depend not just on *probability of default* but also on *loss given default*. Generally speaking, shareholders in a limited liability firm will have lost all that they are going to lose once the firm has defaulted, so they do in effect have a flat pay-off in the region beyond default. VaR may thus be quite satisfactory from their perspective. In contrast, customer pay-offs in the event of default are much more sensitive to how bad the default turns out to be. They should be much more interested in metrics such as TVaR that include this tail sensitivity. At least they should be up to the detachment point (if any) at which their losses are capped by government or industry-wide protection arrangements. These wider stakeholders thus have a TVaR-like exposure further into the tail.

The design of regulatory frameworks is a topic that we principally cover in Chapter 11. It suffices to say at this juncture that capital adequacy ought principally to revolve around adequate protection of customers and these wider stakeholders against the risk of default of the firm. Thus, capital adequacy ought ideally to focus on TVaR-like rather than VaR-like measures of risk. The differential behaviour in the tail is borne by customers (or, further into the tail, by government-sponsored protection arrangements) rather than by shareholders.

10.3   FULLY MARKET CONSISTENT RISK MEASUREMENT IN PRACTICE

10.3.1   Comparison with current risk management practices

VaR, calculated using forecasted 'real world' probability distributions, is now very widely embedded within risk management practice, and is thus unlikely to be dislodged. As we saw in Chapters 8 and 9, it also comes embedded within a wide body of practice designed to give it greater intellectual rigour. This includes testing VaR estimates by comparing observed versus expected outcomes.

A framework that retains these advantages whilst also putting risk management on a firmer theoretical foundation involves the following:

(a) Continued calculation of 'real world' VaR, i.e. $VaR(p)$, say (for a confidence level p and a given timescale);
(b) Calculation of corresponding 'real world' expected shortfall, i.e. $TVaR(p)$, given the lack of coherence of VaR noted earlier (and its overly shareholder focus, if the purpose of the risk measurement relates to capital adequacy);
(c) Calculation of the corresponding 'risk-neutral' (i.e. fully 'market consistent') expected shortfall, $MCTVaR(p)$. This in effect includes an adjustment that takes into account the average (relative) disutility that market participants place on scenarios contributing to the VaR/TVaR; and
(d) A further step (for regulated entities) which we explain in Section 10.3.2 below.

If $A(x) - L(x)$ is the (present, i.e. discounted) value of the future assets minus liabilities at the end of the given timescale depending on random contingencies x that might happen in the meantime, $P^*(x)$ is the 'real world' probability distribution of these random contingencies, $P(x)$ is the 'risk-neutral' distribution of these random contingencies and $I(x)$ is the indicator function (i.e. $I(x) = 1$ if $x \geq 0$ and $I(x) = 0$ otherwise) then:

$$VaR(p) = k \quad \text{where} \quad \int I(A(x) - L(x) - k)P^*(x)dx = p \tag{10.1}$$

$$TVaR(p) = \int (A(x) - L(x) - VaR(p))(1 - I(A(x) - L(x) - k))P^*(x)dx \tag{10.2}$$

$$MCTVaR(p) = \int (A(x) - L(x) - VaR(p))(1 - I(A(x) - L(x) - k))P(x)dx \tag{10.3}$$

The formulae simplify to the following, using the notation of expectations introduced in Section 4.3, where $E^*(X_T)$ is the expected value now (i.e. at time t) of some contingency X_T at time T (where $T \geq t$) using 'real world' probabilities (and some suitable risk-free discount rate) and $E(X_T)$ is the corresponding expected value but using 'risk-neutral' probabilities.

$$VaR(p) = k \quad \text{where } E^*(I(A_T - L_T - k)) = p \qquad (10.4)$$

$$TVaR(p) = E^*((A_T - L_T - k)(1 - I(A_T - L_T - k))) \qquad (10.5)$$

$$MCTVaR(p) = E((A_T - L_T - k)(1 - I(A_T - L_T - k))) \qquad (10.6)$$

The $MCTVaR(p)$ is the market consistent price of buying an option to protect the portfolio or firm against losses beyond a certain amount over a given timescale. Building up its derivation in this manner provides transparency in the calculation steps (or at least in the impact that such steps have on the answers). The key innovation versus current practice is to include the step from (b) to (c).

To implement this innovation would in practice require the user to identify a risk-neutral analogue to the real world distribution otherwise implicit in the calculation of the VaR or TVaR. Most probably this would involve some sort of 'best fit' or credibility weighted inclusion of market implieds into the distributional form as per Sections 4.12 and 4.13. Indeed, those two sections provide the prototypical example of how this can be done in the situation where the underlying distributional form is assumed to be multivariate Normal.

Principle P49: Fully 'market consistent' risk measurement focuses on market implied, i.e. 'risk-neutral' probabilities of occurrence. It also favours use of coherent risk measures that satisfy additivity and scalability criteria, these being key axioms underlying market consistency more generally.

10.3.2   The CDO analogy

The framework described above still leaves slightly hanging in the air the issue of what timescale to incorporate within the computation. It also contains an inconsistency in that we have defined the VaR confidence level by reference to a 'real world' probability distribution, even though we claim to be wanting to focus on the 'risk-neutral' distribution.

For regulatory solvency purposes a desirable further refinement would therefore be to add a fourth step. This harks back to the idea that there is relatively little difference between the balance sheet structures of banks, insurance companies or pension funds and a suitably defined CDO structure.

For example, the 99.5 % 1 year ICA requirement introduced for UK life insurers by the FSA can in such a representation be thought of as identifying an attachment point deemed appropriate by the regulator for the policyholder tranche (and therefore a required minimum equity base), albeit with current practice mandating that this is calculated using some assumed 'real world' distribution of potential outcomes rather than the corresponding 'risk-neutral' distribution.

A *fully market consistent approach* to setting capital requirements would, in effect, seek to answer the following question:

> What capital does the company need (and in what form) to ensure that, if the company were to settle its assets and liabilities into a CDO-like structure, the tranche relating to customer liabilities would command a market spread (over the appropriate risk-free rate) of less than some desired solvency cut-off level s % pa?

The natural fourth step is thus to quantify the s % pa applicable to the firm in question. Possibly there might be several different values of s for different customers or stakeholders if they have different priorities in the event of wind-up.[5] s might also exhibit a term structure for customers with different maturities.

Principle P50: Fully 'market consistent' regulatory capital frameworks should focus on how much capital is required to arrange for the market implied risks expressed within customer liabilities to be lower than some pre-specified (but possibly time-varying) level.

The computation of s is conceptually straightforward once we have calibrated our distribution of future outcomes to any observable market implieds. 'All' it requires is to:

(a) Tabulate all possible future paths and their (market consistent, i.e. risk-neutral) probabilities of occurrence;
(b) Determine for each potential future path the present value of what the customer receives through time (including paths where there are insufficient assets to provide fully for the liabilities), discounting at the risk-free yield curve; and
(c) Calculate the weighted average of these present values using the risk-neutral probabilities of occurrence.

In practice, the task would probably not be so simple, because:

(a) Generally speaking, risk managers, actuaries and others involved in regulatory capital computations have not in the past typically explored what impact their own firm's default might have on payouts to customers;
(b) The VaR $\rightarrow$ TVaR $\rightarrow$ MCTVaR methodology set out in Section 10.3.1 might typically be implemented merely for a single given time period. To calculate s (and its possible term structure) we need the term structure of the market implied distributional form and probably its path dependence characteristics, since payouts in the event of default might be strongly path dependent; and
(c) Multi-period analysis will probably add considerable computational complexity (and hence increase run times).

Fortunately, the usual way in which high-dimensional multi-period derivative pricing problems are tackled is via Monte Carlo simulation or variants designed to improve run times. Modern stochastic modelling tools that have been developed by actuaries for insurance company

---

[5] A corollary is that if s is fixed then an increase in market risk aversion would require the company to find more capital even if the risk exposures haven't themselves changed. This potential for pro-cyclicality is intrinsic to market consistency. Thus, if we wish to avoid undue pro-cyclicality in market consistent regulatory frameworks we will need to include mechanisms that in effect alter s through time, see Chapter 11.

valuation and business planning purposes already typically include such simulation engines within their market consistent scenario generators. Thus it should be possible to reprogram these engines so that they focus on spread versus risk-free, rather than merely on liability valuation, as long as it is clear what payment occurs to which policyholders in circumstances where there are insufficient assets to meet all liabilities.[6]

The computations would need to take into account management and customer discretions, and profit sharing between the firm and the customer (which may itself include discretionary elements). As IAA (2008b) notes, the assets and liabilities settled should include future cash flow commitments from customers (e.g. future premiums from policyholders) only to the extent that these are contractual, and it should include on- or off-balance sheet assets or liabilities corresponding to options that either the firm has granted to the customer (e.g. guarantees relating to annuity conversion terms or surrender terms in the life insurance context or deposit withdrawal terms in a banking context) or vice versa. However, these factors exist already in many life insurance contexts. Methodologies already exist for catering for such liability elements, see e.g. CEIOPS (2008).

One possible management action, if there is continuing value in the franchise, is to raise new capital. This reminds us that regulated firms do not exist in splendid isolation. In the next section we consider the wider systemic issues that arise when we explore the interaction between regulated industries and the rest of the economy. Our CDO analogy is better suited to the scenario implicitly being tested in solvency computations where such a management action is excluded. Another way in which firms often differ from the idealised picture described above is that SPVs like CDOs are typically administered by someone else and therefore are not (generally) subject to operational risk (which instead would typically fall to this third party). Regulated firms typically internalise much or all of their operational activities. We therefore also need to include operational risk considerations in regulatory capital frameworks, see e.g. Section 8.3.4.

---

[6] Such simulation engines can even include nested computations in which we simulate outcomes using valuations in the future that are derived from simulations drawn from possibly other distributions, see e.g. Ledlie *et al.* (2008). The impression given by these authors is that typically these simulation techniques involve market consistent probability distributions used to derive simulated future valuations, coupled with simulations using real world probability distributions of economic outcomes to derive 'economic' costs or values to the firm of having such policies on its book (despite our earlier observation that for costs or values to be 'economic' they should be derived where possible from 'market implied' likelihoods of outcomes rather than 'real world' ones). Our proposed fully market consistent formulation may be *easier* to implement than some of these approaches, because it does away with the need in interim steps to simulate regulatory capital computations based on 'real world' likelihoods of occurrence.

11

Avoiding Undue Pro-cyclicality
in Regulatory Frameworks

11.1 INTRODUCTION

As I write this chapter in late 2008, doom pervades financial markets. In the last few months we have seen bankruptcies or government rescues of many previous stalwarts of the financial community, including Lehman Brothers, AIG, HBOS and Fortis. Governments around the globe have come up with rescue packages involving many hundreds of billions (collectively even trillions!) of dollars, to shore up their financial systems. Several countries have sought loans from the IMF. Stock markets have tumbled as a significant economic recession looms. The supposed decoupling of emerging markets from developed markets that some thought would stop the whole world descending into recession seems to have been wishful thinking. Easy credit has given way to retrenchment.

The natural tendency in such circumstances is to find someone or something to blame. No doubt future post-mortems will eventually unpick the possible causes, be it human greed, lax business management, misaligned incentives, consumers living beyond their means, etc.

One area that some have blamed is particularly relevant to this book. Some have argued that the growth in the practice of marking-to-market has itself contributed to the problem. The thesis put forward by such commentators is that marking-to-market exacerbates swings in the values placed on assets and liabilities. When times are tough, this supposedly leads to greater depletion of bank capital than would otherwise be the case, magnifying the negative impact of liquidity and funding spirals.

In short, the claim is that marking-to-market is supposedly too pro-cyclical, in the sense that it unduly exacerbates economic cycles. Banks, of course, ought to know their own exposures irrespective of how they are incorporated in published accounts or regulatory capital computations, so the argument is slightly more subtle than this. It is not that such commentators consider marking-to-market wrong per se, rather the issue is its use in published accounting data or in regulatory frameworks where the claim is that it provides third parties (including regulators) with 'wrong' answers, creating systemic instabilities, which could be reduced by using some better measure of the 'true' economic worth of the relevant assets (and liabilities). It behoves a book like this to consider carefully such a claim and its surrounding logic, to ensure that the way in which we adopt market consistency (if at all) is in the best interests of everyone.

11.2 THE 2007–09 CREDIT CRISIS

A book like this is inevitably influenced by the context in which it has been written. This context includes the 2007–09 credit crisis. A detailed analysis of the unfolding of this crisis through to late October 2008 is given in Bank of England (2008c). It describes the extended global credit boom that preceded the crisis, which involved a benign economic environment involving stable real GDP growth, a rise in borrowing, development of global financial imbalances and a 'search for yield' in financial markets. The corresponding prolonged spell of balance sheet expansion by many banks[1] across the globe was in part facilitated by increased dependence on wholesale and overseas funding. A housing boom saw loan to income ratios rising in the UK, USA and elsewhere.

The boom was brought to a halt by rising defaults on US sub-prime mortgages. Losses spilled over into other global financial markets with unexpected virulence. Securitisation markets used to distribute these assets broke down as the extent of the deterioration in credit standards was revealed. Valuation uncertainty rose sharply, particularly for more complex instruments, as end investors lost confidence in meanings ascribed to ratings given to these instruments by credit rating agencies. This led to their prices seeming to fall below levels that seemed plausible (if it could be assumed that the instruments would be held to maturity) based on credit fundamentals alone, as liquidity and uncertainty premiums increased significantly, see Figure 5.2.

Over the summer of 2008 it became clear that problems in the banking system were deep seated including:

(a) Inflated balance sheets that had grown far more rapidly than growth in the real economy;
(b) Expansion into certain sectors whose underlying value, credit quality and liquidity were uncertain;
(c) Funding that was in some cases overly short dated and overly reliant on the sustained availability of wholesale funding;
(d) Capital levels that, given these funding characteristics, had become in some cases low relative to underlying balance sheet risks; and
(e) Underappreciated, but potentially significant, interconnections between different firms in the global financial system.

Even as late as April 2008, commentators such as the Bank of England still typically thought that the most likely evolution, conditional on banks raising sufficient new capital, would involve a gradual recovery in market sentiment and confidence in financial institutions. This was not to prove to be the case.

Deteriorating global macroeconomic prospects and weakening housing markets internationally (disproportionately affecting first-time buyers and buy-to-let mortgagors) coupled with further falls in asset prices and sustained market illiquidity (particularly in some of the funding mechanisms that some banks had grown to rely upon), caused rising and more broadly based losses. Too little capital, it seemed, had been raised to avoid the coming whirlwind.

Over the late summer of 2008, institutional pressure became more and more evident as market implied bank default spreads rose alarmingly. The Bank of England (2008c) viewed the unfolding of the crisis during this critical period as having three key phases:

(1) *Problems at Fannie Mae and Freddie Mac led to concerns regarding major US securities houses*

As the US housing market continued to weaken, concern regarding these US government sponsored agencies increased markedly, as analysts concluded that the agencies were poorly capitalised given mark-to-market losses they were probably suffering. On 7 September 2008,

---

[1] For example, major UK banks' assets rose from c. £2,000bn end 2001 to over £6,000bn end 2008 H1, with median leverage rising from low 20s to low 30s over a similar period.

they were placed into conservatorship[2] and given access to capital and funding from the US Treasury in order to avoid unacceptably large dislocations within the financial sector and the economy as a whole.

The severe problems at Fannie Mae and Freddie Mac sharpened the focus the market was placing on other leading US financial institutions. Banks' equity prices fell and their credit spreads increased dramatically. Particular focus was turned on Lehman Brothers, with some investors believing that it was undercapitalised given its exposures to commercial real estate and the challenges to its business model going forwards with the previously prevailing 'originate and sell' banking model under pressure. On 15 September 2008, the holding company and European subsidiary went into administration. It had not been deemed to be 'too big to fail' by the US government. This was perhaps because almost at the same time the possible collapse of AIG, a large US insurer, was troubling the market because of losses related to its substantial structured credit exposures. On 15 September, its credit rating was downgraded, forcing it to post substantial amounts of additional collateral to its counterparties, and it was unable to liquidate sufficient assets quickly enough to meet these margin calls. On 16 September 2008, the US government announced a support package, agreeing to lend AIG $85bn in return for a 79.9 % stake in the company.

In a hectic few days, the remaining major US securities houses took steps to avoid suffering the same fate as Lehman Brothers. Merrill Lynch was acquired by Bank of America, and on 21 September 2008, Goldman Sachs and Morgan Stanley announced plans to become bank holding companies. This allowed them direct access to the US Federal Reserve's discount lending window and opened up the prospect of them building a base of retail deposits mitigating their potential overexposure to the wholesale funding markets.

(2) *International breakdown of interbank funding markets*

Interbank (e.g. 3 month) lending rates had become noticeably higher in August 2007 (when expressed as spreads versus more risk-free rates), see e.g. Figure 5.4. However, there was a further step increase in late September 2008 following the failure of Lehman Brothers. In Chapter 4 we refer to bankruptcies as often being 'previsible', i.e. there is prior warning of impending failure available in news feeds, etc. However, the speed at which the financial crisis was unfolding highlighted that one day an entity might be perceived to be sound and the following day it might have collapsed. Weekends were particularly worrisome. The concern was that some other important entity would have collapsed or been bailed out by its government by the time markets reopened on Monday.

This systemic uncertainty led to a flight to quality. Lending maturities in the interbank markets were shortened, with many banks and other institutions only able to borrow overnight. Money withdrawn from the market was reinvested in assets perceived to be a safe haven, such as gold and government debt. US Treasury bill yields fell towards, and briefly below, zero, i.e. to levels last seen during the Second World War.

Many investors also withdrew money from US dollar money market mutual funds (MMMFs), some of which had lost money on holdings of Lehman Brothers' commercial paper. Around 5 % of assets under management were withdrawn in the second half of September alone, and other amounts were switched to more conservatively run funds investing mainly or exclusively in government debt. This led to further sales of commercial paper, contributing

---

[2] Conservatorship is a legal process in which control of an entity is transferred to someone else – the conservator – by court order, or in the case of regulated businesses, via statutory or regulatory authority.

to a US$74bn (or 4.2 %) fall in the total amount of dollar-denominated commercial paper outstanding in the week following Lehman Brothers' failure.[3]

The failure of Lehman Brothers also led to wider disruption of international financial markets, as it took creditors some time to determine their total exposure (and/or what they could do to alter this exposure). The Bank of England (2008c) thought that ultimately this merely led to a redistribution of liquidity (and in the end settlements were relatively modest), but conceded that it temporarily intensified funding pressures and increased market uncertainty.

Central banks took unprecedented action to ease the intense funding pressures facing some banks, flooding the financial system with liquidity. The US Treasury also offered a guarantee to help stem withdrawals from MMMFs, the aim being to help stem the reduction in MMMF demand for commercial paper. Dislocation had also occurred in the foreign exchange swaps market because of the difficulties that some institutions outside the US faced when attempting to exchange funds raised in other currencies for US dollars. On 18 September a number of central banks in Europe introduced a US dollar swap facility with support from the US Federal Reserve. Some countries blocked short-selling of shares in financial institutions, and some countries took measures to stabilise banks' retail (and in some cases wholesale) deposit bases by increasing the value of retail deposits insured by the state or other centralised deposit insurance schemes (or by announcing guarantees on wholesale funding). On 3 October 2008 the US Congress approved a Troubled Asset Relief Program (TARP) (having turned down a similar proposal a few days before), which sought to address counterparty credit risk concerns by removing distressed assets from banks' balance sheets, making available c. US$700bn to the US Treasury for this purpose.

(3) *Broader institutional distress*

However, even these extensive measures failed to quell investor and public panic. Instead there was a spillover of distress into the international financial system. In response, governments facilitated bank mergers or nationalised firms to stabilise the financial system. On 8 October the UK announced a comprehensive package involving:

(a) Government-supported recapitalisation of the main UK banks and building societies, via purchase of preference shares or, if requested, ordinary equity. This was expected to involve a capital injection of c. £50bn;
(b) For all firms participating in (a), the UK government announced that it was prepared to guarantee senior unsecured debt obligations issued by the firm for terms of up to 3 years. Take-up was expected to be around £250bn in aggregate; and
(c) The UK government extended its Special Liquidity Scheme that allowed relevant firms to borrow from the government in return for posting a range of assets as collateral. It agreed to make available at least £200bn to banks via this scheme.

The comprehensive nature of this package, addressing capital, interbank lending and funding requirements, appeared to bring greater calm to markets and was copied in many respects by a large number of other governments, although at the time of writing in late 2008 interbank

---

[3] Money market mutual funds and equivalents elsewhere in the world had been substantial buyers of some of the more complex financial instruments when conditions were benign. It can be argued that their loss of appetite for this type of paper in preceding months had been a significant contributor to the valuation uncertainties and lack of liquidity that these markets had been suffering for some time prior to the failure of Lehman Brothers.

lending rates were still elevated. It appeared likely that governments would in many cases end up being majority owners of some of their most important financial institutions.

11.3   UNDERWRITING OF FAILURES

The massive size of the government bail-outs that the 2007–09 credit crisis triggered indicates the very real systemic and public interest concerns that arise when considering design of regulatory frameworks. As we have mentioned above, some commentators have argued that marking-to-market is part of the problem rather than part of the solution. If this claim were true, then we would need to think very carefully about the merits of marking-to-market, and by implication market consistency more generally, given the probable costs to the public purse that may arise from the underwriting of what now appears to have been prior banking folly.

There are, however, problems with the logic these commentators propound. These problems are also highlighted in Bank of England (2008c). As we have already noted in Chapter 5, the analysis in Bank of England (2008c) indicated that market participants seem to place *increased* weight on perceived mark-to-market valuations the more likely it becomes that the firm in question may get into difficulties. Failing to publish mark-to-market valuations does not stop other market participants being chillingly rational in their assessments in this regard. Rather, it whets their appetite for plausible data that they themselves can use to guess at the 'underlying' (mark-to-market) financial position of the firm in question. This point is also made by Escaffre *et al.* (2008). Lack of publicly available information in this respect does not solve the problem. Instead, it simply adds to a lack of transparency, which in troubled times can increase the sort of fear and mistrust that engenders the need for such bail-outs.

One of the interesting features of the troubled passage of TARP through the US Congress was that originally the US Treasury argued that the funds made available by TARP were likely to be used to buy troubled assets from the banks in distress at prices *above* their mark-to-market levels but *below* their underlying deemed 'economic' value based on the assumption that they were held to maturity. In short, the US Treasury, or so it was presented, might even be able to profit from 'saving' the banking system, by leveraging its relative lack of need for liquidity. Perhaps unsurprisingly, with the benefit of hindsight, this logic did not find favour with politicians (or with their constituents). The ultimate reason, most probably, is that once the proposed bail-out was presented in this manner it became more transparently a transfer from government to the banks. Why should banks benefit from this largesse when the same support was not (yet) on the table for others?[4]

From our perspective, this experience highlights that, at a time of maximum market stress, the US public distrusted valuations that were intrinsically not mark-to-market. They, in essence, objected to value transferring at other than market prices when it was going to be to their disadvantage, as we might reasonably expect them to do from Principle P2.

In this respect, the UK's rescue package has a more reasonable air to it. The value transfer, if any, that it mandates is more aligned to a corresponding transfer of ownership of the banks

---

[4] It can be argued that the rise in sovereign CDS spreads applicable to the external debt of major western economies at around the same time, see Figure 5.1, reflected a worry that such governments might overreach their ability to cope with such risk, i.e. it brought into question whether it would always be practical for such governments to take advantage of such liquidity arguments. Some smaller countries needed to seek loans from the IMF in part because of the additional financial burdens they took on when supporting their own financial systems.

into public hands, so more value should be recaptured from the public's perspective, at least if and when banks' profitability improves.

We thus see that, when push comes to shove, the public is no more interested in executing transactions away from market prices than anyone else, if it can possibly be avoided, even when it comes to saving the financial system!

> **Principle P51: In times of systemic stress, market consistency still has strong relevance, because the public still expects fair and equitable value to accrue from public expenditure, including public expenditure aimed at promoting financial stability.**

11.4 POSSIBLE PRO-CYCLICALITY IN REGULATORY FRAMEWORKS

Nevertheless, it is still essential that we analyse in more detail whether different sorts of regulatory frameworks have an inherent bias towards pro-cyclicality. Actions taken to try to solve the 2007–09 credit crisis highlight the extent to which governments in practice underwrite the financial health of the banking industry, in order to protect retail depositors. The unusual feature of this crisis is not that some public money has been forthcoming to bail out the banks, but rather the severity of the crisis and hence the amounts involved. The trade-off for providing this underpin is that governments impose regulatory requirements on firms, including requirements that they be 'adequately' capitalised, so that the cost to the public purse of providing such underpins is contained.

If these capital requirements are too high then few if any companies are likely to pursue the type of business in question. This is undesirable if we adopt the reasonable postulate that regulated industries within the financial services industry play useful roles in society.[5] Conversely, if capital requirements are set too low then customers will lose confidence in the providers. The effectiveness of the role that financial services firms play in society is in part conditional on them being unlikely to default.

This much is very widely accepted. Less consensus exists on whether and how we might want to vary the strength of capital adequacy requirements through time for wider economic reasons, and, if so, in what ways. At least since the Great Depression of the 1930s it has been recognised that declines in bank lending can lead to economic contraction, which can trigger a vicious downward spiral in economic activity.

Not surprisingly, therefore, central banks seek to understand the extent to which existing and planned regulatory frameworks might exhibit pro-cyclical characteristics. Economies that are unduly exposed to business cycles seem to perform worse than ones that are not. Governments have a legitimate interest in ensuring that the underpins they provide are structured appropriately and involve the minimum potential value transfer to bank shareholders and other stakeholders for the maximum potential economic benefit accruing from a sound financial system.

Relatively early on in the 2007–09 credit crisis Benford and Nier (2007) studied in some depth the possible pro-cyclical nature of introduction of the Basel II capital requirements.

---

[5] For example, we might argue that insurance facilitates pooling of risk and banking provides mechanisms facilitating purchase and sale of goods and services. Both facilitate savings.

They noted that the majority of banks' capital requirements under Basel II were likely to come from its credit risk requirements.

Under Basel I, capital requirements for credit risk exposures were set purely on the basis of the type of portfolio (with a fixed risk weight applied to each type of exposure, i.e. 0 % for sovereign exposures, 20 % for exposures to banks and qualifying non-bank financial institutions, 50 % for retail mortgages and 100 % for corporate as well as unsecured retail exposures such as credit cards). In contrast, Basel II introduced a more risk-sensitive capital regime, dependent on ratings ascribed to different exposures, prepared either by external credit rating agencies or internally by the bank itself, see Chapter 8.

The supervisory review process required if a bank is to adopt an Internal Ratings Based approach under Basel II requires that the relevant loss given default estimates and similar input assumptions are used for business and not just for regulatory purposes. Benford and Nier noted that this feature of Basel II creates a possible tension between the stable parameter estimates that the IRB formulae expect and the types of inputs most useful for business management. They characterise possible choices as either *point in time* (PIT) estimates or *through the cycle* (TTC) estimates. A single set of ratings cannot be both simultaneously. They refer to a survey by Treacy and Carey (1998) which found that almost all banks had chosen to assign ratings based on current economic conditions.

For banks adopting the Standardised Approach, the ratings come from external ratings agencies, and ratings agencies purport to provide TTC style ratings. But here again Benford and Nier indicate that empirical studies of the behaviour of such ratings find strong evidence that agency ratings are cyclical, quoting e.g. Amato and Furfine (2003).

The key point is that PIT type ratings involve (credit exposure related) capital requirements increasing in an economic downturn, and hence are inherently pro-cyclical, or to be more precise are *more* pro-cyclical than TTC style ratings. For example, Benford and Nier calculate that use of PIT style ratings might have resulted in a minimum to maximum spread for mortgage capital requirements of c. 300 % over the period 1983–2006 compared with only a c. 200 % spread for TTC style ratings. They also consider a 'smoothed' PIT style approach, involving merely a moving average of historical default rates over the preceding 5 years (perhaps on the basis that the 'typical' economic cycle is often supposed to last around 5 years), which whilst lower than an unadjusted PIT approach still had a spread of c. 170 %.[6] In really extreme circumstances, presumably even larger swings are possible, and this may be one reason why governments and investors became so worried about the impact that the 2007–09 credit crisis might have on the wider economy.

Benford and Nier concluded that use in Basel II of ratings to set capital requirements, while improving on the risk sensitivity of requirements (and hence presumably encouraging better risk management), introduced the risk that capital requirements might vary excessively with economic conditions. In response, the Bank of England and the FSA set up a system to monitor aggregate Basel II capital requirements and to identify whether shifts in these requirements might be resulting in capitalisation of the banking system not growing as rapidly as it should during periods of strong economic growth, or becoming such that the ability of the banking system to provide financial services might be undermined during weak economic periods.

The bank rescues of late 2008 led to a more comprehensive questioning of the merits of the Basel II computations, even from regulators themselves. For example, in October 2008,

---

[6] Benford and Nier note that a smoothing algorithm such as this would also result in peaks in capital requirements lagging peaks in mortgage defaults by several periods.

Lord Turner, the incoming chairman of the UK's Financial Services Authority, indicated that a fundamental review of the nature of regulatory frameworks was needed, including discussion about marking-to-market, the need for a new system for setting capital and liquidity requirements for banks, etc., see e.g. Financial Times (2008e). The Bank of England (2008c) also discussed possible counter-cyclical measures, possibly including additional leverage ratio limits (i.e. in effect reintroducing some of the methodologies present in the old Basel I Accord[7]) and/or dynamic provisioning.

Dynamic provisioning is a rules-based scheme, a form of which is used in Spain, in which banks are required to build up general reserves in good times according to a formula calibrated on loan growth and the rate of provisioning and losses experienced over the past.[8] The effect of such a scheme, if properly calibrated, would be that the cumulative stock of general provisions would rise when actual loan losses were low but loan growth was strong, and these general provisions could be drawn on in periods where actual losses were high. Banks following such requirements should therefore have less need to raise new capital in downturns, when the market appetite for new equity might be limited.

Another idea, that of capital insurance, is explored in Kashyap et al. (2008). They note the following:

(a) Agency issues play an important role in shaping banks' capital structures. Banks perceive equity to be an undesirable form of financing and try to use as little of it as possible. A key challenge for regulators is how to get banks to make more use of equity capital.[9]

(b) However, if banks' balance sheets are instead primarily financed by short-term market borrowings then this increases the systemic issues that can arise if past decisions go sour across the industry as a whole. During the 2007–09 credit crisis, as housing markets deteriorated, the perceived risk of mortgage-backed securities increased and it became difficult to roll over short-term loans. Banks then needed to sell assets that they could no longer finance, leading to possible fire sales and depressed asset valuations, depleting bank capital, and leading to a downward spiral. This in turn spilled over to bank borrowers as banks cut back on loans and hoarded liquidity, slowing the whole economy.

(c) If bank capital requirements are left unaltered in both good times and bad (or if they actually increase in bad times) then banks face an unyielding trade-off – either liquidate assets (i.e. reduce lending) or raise fresh capital. The latter tends to be sluggish. Raising capital is relatively costly at the best of times; it is particularly costly during times of greater uncertainty. Also, the benefits if they are systemic in nature may accrue principally to other banks and to the broader economy, rather than being internalised to the bank

---

[7] Some authorities, notably in the USA, already use a leverage ratio as an additional tool in their overall assessment of resilience of their financial institutions. However, it is not without its issues, e.g. if the required ratio binds then it might provide an inappropriate incentive on banks to invest in more risky assets. In addition, actually defining leverage is not as easy as it might sound. If, for example, (some) off-balance sheet items are excluded then this might increase the incentives on banks to circumvent such restrictions via such transactions.

[8] A challenge that dynamic provisioning of this sort faces is that current accounting rules largely prohibit banks from building up reserves against future losses that might possibly occur but for which there is currently no or insufficient evidence that they will occur.

[9] Kashyap et al. (2008) argue that equity capital is expensive to service and they also note that equityholders in banks may worry that bad decisions by management will dissipate the value of their shareholdings, and equity capital raising may in any case result in transfer of value to debtholders because it reduces the value (per unit of equity capital) of the shareholder put option referred to in Chapter 2. Thus the tendency for banks to finance themselves largely with short-term debt may reflect a privately optimal response to governance problems.

actually doing the capital raising. Hence, the tendency is to do the former, i.e. reduce lending, to the detriment of the economy as a whole. This is the wrong answer as far as governments, central banks and regulators are concerned in relation to their mandate to foster financial stability.

Kashyap *et al.* (2008) propose two possible ways of tackling this issue:

1. Relax capital requirements in times of stress. This reduces systemic issues, but probably requires heightened equity capital in normal circumstances (which, one hopes, correspond to most of the time!), consequentially increasing costs of funds and ultimately resulting in increased costs to customers. This is the dynamic provisioning referred to above.
2. Incorporate incentives that encourage companies to put in place contingent funding arrangements, i.e. insurance type arrangements (provided by, for example, sovereign wealth funds) that result in additional equity capital being injected when systemic stresses arise. This might involve allowing banks to choose between holding higher capital or buying capital insurance that would provide a capital infusion in the event of a systemic stress.

The idea of (2) is that banks could buy (or be required by the regulator to buy) catastrophe insurance from a deep-pocketed 'insurer' such as a pension or sovereign wealth fund, which would place a sum aside in a 'lock box', invested in safe assets such as Treasury bills, in return for a receipt of premium and interest on the investment. In a payout, the safe assets would be transferred to the bank, recapitalising it.

A problem with this proposal is that it has the potential to create new vulnerabilities, such as overreliance on such deep-pocketed 'insurers'. It would possibly also be subject to moral hazard. It can in any case be argued that use of different capital tiers within current regulatory frameworks already provides such a framework. Such a scheme might in any case not cope well with very substantial systemic stresses, since otherwise apparently deep-pocketed organisations may also be drawing on funds at the same time, potentially exhausting the resources of such 'insurers' (or causing them to rein in other exposures in a manner similar to how the banks themselves would act in the absence of new capital).

Such catastrophe insurance arrangements do exist in other spheres, e.g. covering natural catastrophes such as earthquake or hurricane risk, so the idea may be worth exploring further. However, a really large financial 'catastrophe' might easily exhaust the available coverage. Coverage against the very largest natural disasters is in practice only partly provided by the private sector. Such risks are too much even for the entire global insurance industry to handle and above a certain level coverage typically falls back to governments to handle.

11.5   RE-EXPRESSING CAPITAL ADEQUACY IN A MARKET CONSISTENT FRAMEWORK

We argued in Chapter 2 that the setting of regulatory capital requirements in a fully market consistent regulatory capital framework can be boiled down to the task of choosing a suitable value (or values) for s, the market implied spread on customer liabilities versus the risk-free rate.

In the market consistent regulatory formulation we describe above, the first of Kashyap *et al.*'s (2008) proposals, i.e. dynamic provisioning, corresponds to having s somehow varying according to market conditions.

Whilst it is difficult to fault the economic logic involved, this re-presentation of the approach also highlights some of the potential political challenges involved. Stressed market conditions may correspond with situations where customers also feel more risk-averse, and hence where they may be least keen to have their own assets (i.e. the firms' customer liabilities) exposed to heightened levels of market implied default risk. But that is the nature of such pro-cyclical overrides. If things get worse still then shoring up the problem in the meantime may ultimately be good money thrown after bad.

Of course, if governments do nothing then the result may be a Keynesian liquidity black hole and economic depression. A fully market consistent framework would at least make such anti-cyclicality adjustments somewhat more transparent, and therefore hopefully more proportionate and more fairly applied to different market participants.[10] We see here again the power of market consistency. Even when we feel for systemic reasons we need to temper its answers at an aggregate level, it still helps to spread the costs and benefits of doing so more equitably between different firms and other economic participants.

An intermediate step often exists in the unfolding of such issues. Centralised deposit insurance arrangements are often funded by other (better capitalised) firms, at least up to the point at which additional support from the taxpayer becomes inevitable. So other industry participants ought to want regulatory capital frameworks applied to their compatriots to be as fairly representative as possible of the true costs of protecting against the risk of insolvency, in order for the costs of such desposit insurance schemes to be borne as fairly as possible across the industry.

What about the second of Kashyap *et al.*'s (2008) proposals, i.e. catastrophe insurance? In our formulation, it is equivalent to including within the derivation of s some mechanism which incentivises firms to adopt capital structures that facilitate wider stability of the financial system. Ultimately, governments (i.e. taxpayers) end up bailing out regulated sectors when particularly extreme scenarios occur. It therefore does not seem unreasonable for them to have the right (via the way in which regulatory capital frameworks are framed) to favour capital structures that reduce the burden they would otherwise face as and when such scenarios do arise.

Is there a single right choice for s or even for how it might evolve through time as economic circumstances change? Most probably not. Ultimately, it is a matter for the customers themselves and, because it is implemented through capital adequacy regimes, the regulators charged with looking after their interests and the wider interests of society as a whole. Governments ultimately underwrite any particular level of s, and when setting its level (and how the level might change as economic conditions change) need to weigh up the conflicting costs and benefits of having a vibrant and competitive financial system versus having a financial system that might be more prone to instability and hence to potential extra expenditure from the public purse in adverse scenarios.

11.6 DISCOUNT RATES

In theory, we can use a variant of this argument to rationalise discounting long-term insurance liabilities at Libor/Euribor swap rates, see Chapter 5. However, the logic is problematic.

To first order, the impact of increasing s by a set amount is equivalent to the result of applying existing regulatory capital computation methodologies but increasing the discount

---

[10] Another point that is worth bearing in mind is that certain participants in the financial services industry may not themselves be subject to capital adequacy requirements set by the regulator. For example, the extent of leverage that hedge funds might be prepared to employ may be driven by VaRs calculated by their prime brokers. An approach that focuses only on visible manifestations of 'regulatory' capital may not therefore capture all pro-cyclical factors at work.

rate used in the valuation of the liabilities.[11] Thus we could in principle justify changing s in line with changes in the spread between Libor and 'truly' risk-free rates if we thought that such changes to s were appropriate on cyclicality grounds.

The problem with this line of argument is that it is difficult to see why there should be congruence between the implied default risk regulators think ought to be expressed on long-term insurance company policies with those observable in practice on 3 month or 6 month deposits with panel banks underlying the Libor fixing. The two are of quite different terms and relate to different parts of the financial services industry.

11.7   PRO-CYCLICALITY IN SOLVENCY II

Practically any regulatory framework can introduce pro-cyclical aspects. Solvency II is no exception. For example, the CRO Forum (2008b) note that equities are volatile investments and so insurers holding them should also hold risk capital as a buffer against adverse developments, as will be the case under Solvency II. However, they worry about the potentially pro-cyclical nature of Solvency II as currently framed in relation to equity markets, particularly the possible risk of forced sales in market downturns (as arguably occurred for some life insurers in 2002–03). They propose that the SCR (which in the context of Pillar 1 of Solvency II is determined by reference to a 99.5 % quantile over a 1 year time horizon) be supplemented by a separate reduced capital requirement SCR* (or 'Shadow-SCR') which would gradually revert back to the SCR over a time period linked to the duration of the liabilities covered by the assets in question (or immediately if the market in question recovered, i.e. ceased to be 'distressed'). In their proposal, the Shadow-SCR would be reduced by an amount related to the market value falls, subject to a certain floor. The treatment would only apply in situations where management intended (and had documented) that they would hold these assets over the duration of the liabilities covered by the assets. The CRO Forum viewed such an approach as 'intuitive' for distressed equity markets but also applicable to any other risky asset class, as well as to insurance risks. It accepted that such a proposal would need further refinement before it could be included in solvency frameworks such as Solvency II.

The UK life insurance solvency computation applicable towards the end of 2008 highlights some of the challenges that can arise if one attempts to adopt formulaic approaches for mitigating forced sales that are tied to specific asset markets. They included a requirement that sufficient capital be held to protect against a 'resilience test' which included an allowance for declines in equity market valuations. Some years previously this test had involved a fixed assumed 25 % market value decline. Adjustments were introduced towards the bottom of the 2002 equity bear market. This allowed smaller assumed declines to be used, depending on the relationship between equity income yields and government bond yields, as long as the assumed fall was no smaller than 10 %. By late 2008 the decline that could be used had been consistently at this floor of 10 % for some time, despite during October and November 2008 there being times when equity markets moved (down and up) by of the order of 10 % in a single day. One might question just how resilient to adverse market movements a company

---

[11] For this logic to be accurate, we also need to assume that the risks expressed by such spreads are 100 % correlated with the aggregate of the other risks that such a firm might face. To first order this might be reasonable for a fellow bank, but this assumption is also more questionable for a firm in another part of the financial services industry. The same point also arises if we want to justify discounting at government bond yields when there is no longer undoubted confidence in the government's creditworthiness.

writing long-term business like life insurance really would be if it were only capable of coping with one day's worth of adverse market movements.

It is interesting to compare and contrast such ideas, particularly when applied to equity market risk (as might be most relevant to life insurers), with corresponding suggestions for how to avoid pro-cyclicality in bank regulatory frameworks, see Section 11.4, which typically focus more on credit risk. Particular challenges that arise with applying such ideas to equities include:

(a) How would you define 'distressed'? In bond-land, 'distressed' usually results in assets becoming illiquid as well as falling in value, but equity markets (at least the main equity indices) have usually remained reasonably liquid even in times of stress. It is therefore less easy to dress up such proposals in terms of liquidity issues alone.
(b) Why should time to return to 'normality' in the equity market be dependent on the term of a firm's liabilities? With bonds held to match cash flows there might be some justification for a hold-to-maturity approach, since (if we ignore credit risk) we will be in a position where the bond's proceeds are known at maturity, i.e. its valuation should by then have returned to 'normality'. But there is no similar surety that equity markets will revert to 'normality' within any similar timescale. The longer the time to liability cash flow, the greater might be the deviation between adjusted value and market value. Hence, the greater might be the possible loss to the firm's customers if the supposed 'distress' does not unwind in a timely fashion.
(c) How would you avoid firms cherry-picking which assets to include in such computations?
(d) From the firm's perspective, the equity market risks incurred with many types of customer liabilities that have historically involved high equity coverage can to some extent be mitigated by dynamic hedging of the amount of equity exposure underlying these liabilities. To 'force' firms to hold on to these assets for the term of the liabilities may inadvertently restrict them from taking appropriate risk mitigating actions to the longer-term detriment of themselves and their customers.

These types of challenges are generic to any sort of regulatory framework in which valuations fail to be market consistent. They almost always seem to introduce scope for firms to 'game' the regulatory framework, by adopting strategies that focus on exploiting anomalies in the framework rather than have intrinsic merit per se. Better, at least in theory, would be to retain market consistency to whatever extent is practical, and more directly to alter the value of s as per Section 11.5 in whatever ways are considered most appropriate. More realistically, we might expect regulators to test how actual proposals that might be easier to implement in practice compare with this theoretical ideal.

For example, in such an idealised framework, s ought not to depend on stated intent but only on what the firm will actually do.[12] In real life, what you say you *intend* to do is a less

---

[12] This at first sight might appear to be inconsistent with, say, typical actuarial approaches for valuing with-profits business, see Section 13.4.8, which do take into account stated planned management actions. The point here is that there are actually two sorts of 'stated' planned management actions. There are those that are sufficiently 'contractual' that customers can rely on them and potentially seek redress if they are not then acted upon, and there are those (like a statement here that currently we expect to hold a particular asset to maturity) that are more along the lines of 'we will do this unless we come up with a better idea along the way'. The first sort, i.e. a quasi-contractual commitment, does of course need to be incorporated in liability valuations. At issue is whether the second sort has any relevance in a solvency computation, if the firm in effect reserves the right to change its mind further down the road.

than perfect guide to what you will *actually* do, especially if, when the chips are down, you do not have enough money to be able to honour your intentions. Moreover, whether equity markets are 'normal' or not is presumably a matter independent of any particular firm. Equity market indices cannot therefore take different times to return to 'normality' for different firms merely because the firms have different maturity profiles.

Expressing the problem in this manner also highlights that governments and regulators might not have the same degree of interest in equity market pro-cyclicality as they have in other types of pro-cyclicality more directly relevant to economic conditions and stability of the financial system. If governments are less interested in this type of cyclicality then the focus presumably moves away from consideration of the wider consequences of 'distress' in any particular asset type (even one that is closely associated with the firm type in question) towards consideration of the specific consequences of 'distress' with the particular segment of the financial services industry in question.

11.8   INCENTIVE ARRANGEMENTS

The topic of employee remuneration and incentive arrangements has risen substantially up the public agenda in recent months as countries tip into recession or even perhaps depression and belt-tightening is the order of the day. There has been increasing public anger at senior bank employees apparently being rewarded handsomely for failure, particularly where the bank in question has been bailed out by the government (since the rewards may then ultimately have been coming from the public purse).

It is not the aim of this book to explore this topic in any detail. However, we would note that the difference in perspective between shareholders and others (which led us in Section 10.2 to favour TVaR over VaR in capital adequacy calculations) is arguably mirrored in a similar difference in perspective between employee and shareholder at the level of individual employee remuneration. Consideration of tail risk is key in either debate. For example, business line profit measures used to determine the remuneration of relevant employees should ideally include adjustments reflecting the potential cost that might be incurred providing liquidity support to the business line if liquidity in the relevant markets were to dry up. Whilst such events might be rare, they might seriously compromise the business line if they did occur, as demonstrated by the 2007–09 credit crisis. If the tail risk is large enough then the losses can blow through the limited liability cap applicable to shareholders, and onto customers or other external stakeholders, so they too have an interest in effective design of employee remuneration arrangements.

At a systemic level, governments and regulators may also have a wider interest in aggregate incentives operating within the financial services industry and whether they are truly delivering what society might want. For example, Turner (2009) has argued that one of the causes of the 2007–09 credit crisis seems to have been excessive focus within the banking industry on structuring and trading activity linked to complex versions of structured credit. As a result, in his view, 'in the years running up to 2007, too much of the developed world's intellectual talent was devoted to ever more complex financial innovations, whose maximum possible benefit in terms of allocative efficiency was at best marginal, and which in their complexity and opacity created large financial stability risks'. Whilst firms might not like this level of intrusion in how they operate, it is difficult to argue that governments do not have a legitimate interest in such matters, since they typically are the ones who pick up the tab for tail risks large enough to create systemic problems.

11.9   SYSTEMIC IMPACTS OF PENSION FUND VALUATIONS

We saw in Chapter 7 that increasing attention is being placed on the solvency of pension funds. Given the large size of assets held by pension schemes and their societal importance in terms of intergenerational transfer of wealth and provision of financial security in old age, it is easy to appreciate the possible systemic impact that pension scheme solvency regulation could have on economies and societies as a whole.

Countries often set up industry-wide pension guarantee funds, which seek to compensate for at least part of the shortfalls that might arise in private pension funds. Examples include the Pension Benefit Guaranty Corporation (PBGC) in the USA and the Pension Protection Fund (PPF) in the UK. Like other industry-wide protection schemes, they typically involve some pre-funding and some post-funding, with part or all of the costs met by the industry itself.

Importantly, such protection schemes typically have an implicit government guarantee in the event that too much of the industry defaults to make it practical to make good the losses from levies on what remains. Governments (and hence taxpayers) thus have a legitimate interest in the solvency regulation being on a sound footing. This is another application of Principle P7, but at a society-wide level. If we want fair apportionment of the consequences of such contingencies between firms, between beneficiaries and between both and the rest of society then ultimately we need to refer to market consistent principles, even if the way in which these principles are then implemented in practice needs to bear in mind the wider systemic issues. To do otherwise runs the risk of some such entities or stakeholders ultimately free-loading off others (or off the state). This does not seem an equitable way of running society.

11.10   SOVEREIGN DEFAULT RISK

Throughout the rest of this chapter we have assumed that the creditworthiness of the state is unquestioned, and thus governments could always in extremis bail out their own financial services entities. However, we saw in Chapter 5 that this is not necessarily the case, even for well-developed economies.

If the long-term creditworthiness of the state itself becomes questionable then Principle P7 would suggest that ideally the implications of this are equitably apportioned between different members of society (and between different states themselves). We enter here into tricky ethical territory, to decide what is then 'equitable'.

The impact of a sovereign default (or quasi-default) would cascade via many different avenues through to individual citizens of the state in question, and potentially to citizens of other countries. Firms (and individuals) may seek to mitigate their own exposures to such outcomes. They may also be prepared deliberately to invest in debt issued by such governments if they think that the market is overstating the risk of such a default.

Individual states may wish to downplay the possibility that they might themselves default. They may, for example, continue to promote regulatory frameworks that encourage locally regulated firms to invest in their own debt. However, if sovereign default does come to pass then it may turn out to have been better to have spread the costs more widely (including across other economies). Sovereign defaults are usually very painful for the citizens of the state in question. There is a tricky line to walk here. Policy responses that smooth and thus stabilise the financial system may look good for a while. However, if they ultimately lead to the even larger systemic distress of the government itself defaulting then their adoption may not actually prove sensible for the country in question.

Firms (and their customers) would thus be wise to remember that even apparently well-run economies and countries can go awry and in extreme circumstances can default. Such defaults can have highly unpredictable consequences. How a country might default (and who will then be most affected by the default and in what ways) is not easy to predict in advance.

12

Portfolio Construction

12.1 INTRODUCTION

Portfolio construction should, in my opinion, be seen as the third strand in a single overarching branch of financial theory and practice, the other two strands being valuation methodology and risk management processes. There is ultimately little point in merely valuing and measuring positions or risks. The focus should be on managing them to best advantage.

Market consistency is in some sense both key and peripheral to this activity. Market consistency should underpin both the valuation and risk analysis framework within which portfolio construction takes place, to the extent that market consistency is a worthy focus in the first place. However, Principle P6 reminds us that assuming that the 'market' is the sole arbiter of knowledge is unlikely to win many friends in practice. Nor is it realistically reconcilable with the concept of active management, if by this we mean taking views about when the market is right and when it is wrong, and then acting accordingly. The key is to understand and take due notice of the market but not to let it be the sole input into the decision-making process.

Furthermore, whilst it is relatively easy to point out how greater application of market consistency is crucial to the evolution of valuation principles and practices, and most probably will be for risk measurement principles and practices too, market consistency is probably likely to have a less dominant impact on portfolio construction. It is only part of a wider mix of ideas synthesised together in the portfolio construction process.

In this chapter we first explore the basic principles of portfolio construction. We then highlight ways in which market consistency influences the application of these principles. Some of these influences require somewhat subtle analysis to appreciate well. However, since real money is passing hands as a result, it is particularly worthwhile for anyone aspiring to be involved in the financial management of a firm or portfolio to explore these implications.

Discussion of how we might better take account of 'what the market has to say' within investment idea *generation*, as opposed to *implementation* in practical portfolio construction, is beyond the scope of this book. It is suggested that readers interested in this topic refer to Kemp (2009). For those with a strong quantitative bias, Fabozzi *et al.* (2008) may also be a suitable reference text.

12.2 RISK–RETURN OPTIMISATION

12.2.1 Introduction

Managing risk involves more than just measuring it. The traditional quantitative workhorse used to help decide how much risk to take (and of what type) is *risk–return optimisation*, also referred to as *efficient frontier analysis*. With suitable time series data the basic principles are beguilingly straightforward even if the mathematics can get quite detailed in places.

12.2.2   The basic mathematics of risk–return optimisation

Mathematically, any optimiser requires some definition of *return* (also referred to as *reward*) and some definition of *risk*. The optimisation exercise then mathematically involves maximising, for a given risk aversion parameter, λ, some risk–reward trade-off (or *utility*) function subject to some *constraints* on the portfolio weights, and then repeating the exercise for different values of λ. The trade-off might be expressed as: $U(\mathbf{x}) = Return(\mathbf{x}) - \lambda \cdot Risk(\mathbf{x})$, where $\mathbf{x}$ is the portfolio asset mix, or using some equivalent mathematical formulation that leads to the same portfolios being deemed optimal.

This process creates a series of portfolios, one for each different λ, each of which optimally trades off risk against reward for some particular level of risk (or equivalently for some particular level of return). Such portfolios are therefore known as 'efficient portfolios'. Collectively, the line that they form when plotted in a risk–reward chart is known as the 'efficient frontier' since it is not possible (given the assumptions adopted) to achieve a higher return (for a given level of risk) or lower risk (for a given level of return) than a point on the efficient frontier, see Figure 12.1.

Implicitly or explicitly superimposed on this basic framework will be assumptions regarding the costs of effecting transactions moving us from where we are now to where we would like to be. Often the assumption made is that these costs are small enough to be ignored, but more sophisticated optimisation engines do not necessarily adopt this simplification.

Risk–return optimisation may also be 'dynamic' or multi-period, in which case we would work out the optimal strategy to adopt now and how it might change in the future as new information comes along.

12.2.3   Mean–variance optimisation

In a world in which returns are well characterized by multivariate (log) Normal distributions, risk–return optimisation defaults to so-called mean–variance optimisation,[1] otherwise known as Markowitz portfolio optimisation, because Harry Markowitz was the individual credited with first developing the relevant formulation, see Markowitz (1952).

Typically, we might assume that the 'return' component of the utility function depends on a vector, $\mathbf{r}$, of (assumed future) returns on the different asset categories and that the return to use in the optimisation exercise is then the weighted average (or mean) of these, weighted in line with the asset mix being analysed. We might also assume that the 'risk' component of the utility function is suitably proxied by an estimate of forward-looking tracking error (versus some suitable minimum risk position, say, $\mathbf{b}$) based on a covariance matrix as described in Chapter 7.[2] Most commonly a quadratic utility function is used, such as:

$$U(\mathbf{x}) = \mathbf{r}.\,\mathbf{x} - \lambda(\mathbf{x} - \mathbf{b})^T \mathbf{V}(\mathbf{x} - \mathbf{b}) \tag{12.1}$$

---

[1] The return distribution is then completely characterised by its mean vector and its covariance matrix. The investor's utility, to the extent that it depends on market derived factors, must therefore also merely depend on these parameters. Risk–return optimisation also defaults to mean-variance optimisation if the investor has a so-called quadratic utility function, i.e. again depends merely on these parameters, even if the distribution is not multivariate (log) Normal. However, quadratic utility functions are generally considered to be implausible representations of how an investor might actually view risk and return. Thus if return distributions are believed to deviate materially from Normality, some refinement of mean-variance optimisation is typically considered necessary, see Section 12.7.

[2] The common alternative involving measuring risk in absolute volatility terms typically produces similar answers to the above approach if a 100 % cash minimum risk portfolio is assumed.

(a) Illustrative efficient portfolio analysis (including risks and returns of individual asset categories)

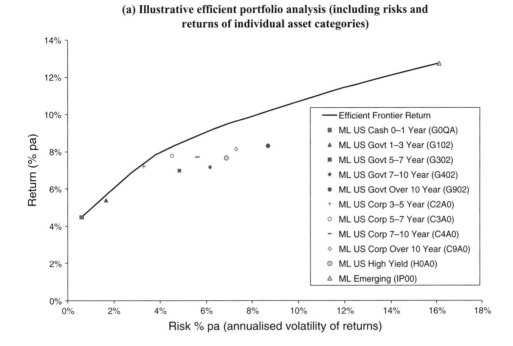

(b) Composition of corresponding efficient portfolios

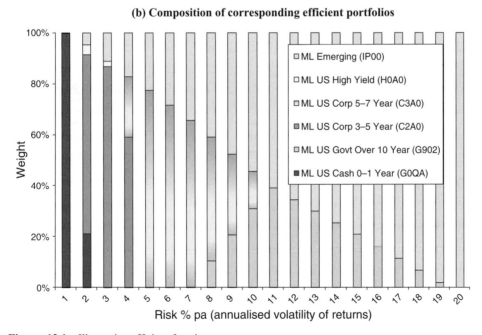

Figure 12.1 Illustrative efficient frontier
Source: Merrill Lynch, Bloomberg. Analysis uses merely illustrative forward-looking expected return assumptions applicable some years ago and is not therefore a guide to what might be a suitable asset allocation in current market conditions.

The same optimal portfolios arise with any other risk measure that monotonically increases in tandem with the risk measure used above. So, for example, we get the same efficient portfolios whether we use the ex-ante tracking error, the ex-ante variance (i.e. the square of the ex-ante tracking error) or any VaR statistic that has been determined using a Normal distribution approximation from the same underlying covariance matrix. The same is also true if we replace the original return measure by any other that monotonically increases in line with the original return measure.

Constraints applied in practice are often linear, i.e. of the form $\mathbf{Ax} \leq \mathbf{P}$. Equality constraints (such as requiring that the weights in a long-only portfolio add to unity) and limits (such as the weights in a long-only portfolio should all not be less than zero) can be included as special cases of this more general form as follows:

$$\sum x_i \leq 1 \text{ and } -\sum x_i \leq -1 \text{ (equality constraint)}$$
$$\text{and } -x_i \leq 0 \text{ for each } i \text{ (long-only constraints)} \tag{12.2}$$

If $\mathbf{V}$ is a positive definite symmetric matrix (which it should be if it is derived directly from historic data) and if there is no allowance made for transaction costs (or of deals needing to be in multiples of given lot sizes) then the exact solution to this optimisation problem can be found using a variant of the Simplex algorithm or other standard algorithms for solving *constrained quadratic optimisation* problems, see e.g. Kemp (2009) or references quoted by Press *et al.* (1992).

Application of mean–variance optimisation is very widespread in both academic finance circles and in actual business practice. Examples of its use in the public domain by the author include Kemp (2005), Kemp (2008a), Kemp (2008b), Kemp (2008c) and Kemp (2009).

12.2.4   Constraint-less mean–variance optimisation

If there are no constraints (other than that portfolio weights add to unity), and by implication short-selling is permitted, then all efficient portfolios end up merely involving a linear combination of two portfolios, a 'low-risk' portfolio and a 'risky' portfolio.[3] These are the minimum risk portfolio, **b**, as above (if it is investible) and some single 'risky' set of 'active' stances that represent the best (diversified) set of investment opportunities available at that time. All investors adopting the same assumptions about the future (multivariate) return distribution should then hold the same active stances versus their own minimum risk portfolios, see Section 12.4.3.

12.2.5   Alpha–beta separation

It is perhaps more common to reformulate this decomposition using language such as *alpha–beta separation*. Strictly speaking, alpha–beta separation involves physically splitting the portfolio into two parts, one explicitly aiming to deliver beta, i.e. desired market exposures (achieved via, say, the use of low-cost index funds or low-cost index derivatives) and the other aiming to deliver alpha (i.e. enhanced returns over and above those available purely from market indices, sourced by employing skilled managers in some particular investment

---

[3] More generally, although efficient frontiers generally look curved when plotted, they are actually (for mean–variance optimisation) multiple joined straight line segments if the axes are chosen appropriately, with the joins occurring whenever a new constraint starts or ceases to bite. This feature is used by some commercial optimisation packages to speed up computation of the entire efficient frontier.

area). Conceptually, any portfolio can be hypothetically decomposed in an equivalent way. Re-expressed in this fashion the optimal portfolio in the constraint-less mean–variance optimisation case involves:

(a) The minimum risk portfolio, i.e. the *liability matched beta*;
(b) The parts of the active stances that are market-index-like in nature, i.e. the *active beta*; and
(c) The remainder, i.e. the *alpha*.

The presence of (b) reflects the observation that investors typically expect there to be some intrinsic long-term reward for investing in risky assets per se (e.g. investors might consider there to be an equity 'risk premium' available over the long term by investing in equity market indices), whilst (c) reflects the hope that there are opportunities that can be exploited by skilled fund managers operating within a given asset class.[4]

12.2.6 Multi-period mean–variance optimisation

The decomposition in Section 12.2.5 is often implicitly relied upon for portfolio construction in a multi-period, i.e. dynamic, environment. For example, suppose that we have some desired goal that we would be uncomfortable failing to meet (e.g. some desired level of coverage of liabilities), but ideally we would like to do better than this. The portfolio construction problem can then be re-expressed mathematically in the form of a derivative pricing problem, in which our desired goal is characterised by some form of derivative pay-off involving as its underlyings the 'low risk' and the 'risky' portfolios noted in Section 12.2.4.

As the two portfolios are independently characterised, we find that the optimal portfolio, even in a dynamic environment, still involves combinations of two portfolios throughout time, although the minimum risk part may change through time (as may the mix between the two parts), if the liabilities (and client risk appetite) change.[5]

Classical index-orientated CPPI as per Section 4.2 can be viewed in this framework as a methodology for seeking to meet some specified liability goal (typically, delivery of an investment floor), whilst assuming that the optimal risky portfolio merely expresses an 'active beta' stance. More modern fund-linked variants assume that additional alpha is available from employing a fund manager within the risky portfolio.

12.3   OTHER PORTFOLIO CONSTRUCTION STYLES

Whilst traders, fund managers and the like do not necessarily articulate their portfolio construction disciplines as follows, any manager's approach to portfolio construction, if it is to have intrinsic rationale, can be viewed as involving the following:

(a) The manager will have positive and negative views on a range of different stocks. These views will differ in terms of strength of conviction that the manager would ideally wish to place on the relevant idea. All other things being equal, the greater the conviction behind the idea, the bigger should be the risk-adjusted position size implementing the idea.

---

[4] However, within such a conceptual framework there is not necessarily any universal consensus on what actually corresponds to 'market' beta. For example, would it just be the main market indices like the S&P 500, or would we view it at a more segmented level, e.g. S&P 500 industry sectors? This highlights that 'alpha' can come not just within a given asset class but also by successful timing of allocation between such classes, however granular is the definition of 'asset class'.

[5] Readers interested in understanding more about liability driven investment are directed towards Kemp (2005).

(b) If a portfolio is optimally constructed then we can, in principle, assign to each position an 'implied alpha', see Section 12.5, which is the alpha generating potential that needs to be assigned to that particular stock for the portfolio as a whole to express an optimal balance between risk and reward.

(c) As the manager's ideas change (e.g. because they come to fruition), these implied alphas will change and hence the ideal individual position sizes to express within the portfolio should also change.

(d) Assuming that the manager possesses skill, we can assume that positions of the same magnitude should on average be rewarded over time in proportion to their implied alphas. If the manager knew which ideas would be better rewarded than this then he or she would presumably ascribe them greater weight, which would result in the implied alphas rising to compensate.

Thus any (active) portfolio construction approach can conceptually be reformulated within the context of the quantitative paradigm of optimisation. Given sufficient flexibility in the underlying risk model implicitly included in this process (and its evolution through time), it is possible to frame any set of decisions taken by a manager as optimal for some particular risk model, whether the manager is a more traditional judgemental (i.e. 'fundamental') manager or a more quantitatively orientated manager.[6]

Such a reformulation does not therefore necessarily support (or discourage) the use of high-powered quantitative techniques within any research or portfolio construction process and thus is equally applicable to both fundamental and quantitative fund managers. Rather, it provides a means of analysing some problems in a quantitative manner irrespective of the style of management being employed. Problems that can be tackled in this way include analysis of the optimal sizes of short books in 130/30 funds, see e.g. Kemp (2007) and Kemp (2008b), efficient construction of global equity portfolios, see e.g. Kemp (2008a), and efficient alpha delivery in socially responsible investment portfolios, see e.g. Kemp (2008c).

12.4   RISK BUDGETING

12.4.1   Introduction

A challenge that arises whether or not a quantitative approach to portfolio construction is being followed is to decide how much risk to adopt. There is no right answer here. It depends on the client's *risk appetite*. Mathematically, we see that this is the case because the results of any optimisation exercise depend on the investor's risk aversion, i.e. the λ introduced in Section 12.2.2. This parameter cannot be specified a priori but is instead defined by the investor's 'risk budget'.

Risk budgeting involves:

(a) Identifying the total risk that we are prepared to run;
(b) Identifying its decomposition between different parts of the investment process; and
(c) Altering this decomposition to maximize expected value-added for a given level of risk.

---

[6] We thus see the broad truth of the view expressed at the start of Scherer (2007) that 'the theory of mean–variance-based portfolio selection is a cornerstone of modern asset management'. However, it would perhaps be more strictly correct to argue that it is the theory of risk–return optimisation more generally that is a cornerstone, to cater for the possible impact of fat tails.

Risk budgeting has wide applicability and as a concept is difficult to fault. It can be applied to asset-liability management, asset allocation, manager selection, stock selection, etc. and to practically any other element of the investment or business management process. Indeed, if we apply the concept more generally then it involves framing in a mathematical fashion the fundamentals underlying rational economic behaviour, which is generally taken to be the underpin to all economic activity (although see Section 9.4 regarding 'bounded rational behaviour). As Scherer (2007) points out, the 'merit of risk budgeting does not come from any increase in intellectual insight but rather from the more accessible way it provides of decomposing and presenting investment risks'. In this sense, it is akin to budgeting more generally. It is not strictly speaking intrinsically necessary for countries, companies or individuals to prepare budgets in order to plan for the future, but it is a very helpful discipline, particularly if resources are constrained, as they nearly always are.

Scherer (2007) defines risk budgeting as 'a process that reviews any assumption that is critical for the successful meeting of pre-specified investment targets and thereby decides on the trade-off between the risks and returns associated with investment decisions'. He notes that in a mean–variance world risk budgeting defaults to Markowitz portfolio optimisation, but with results being not only shown in terms of weights and monetary amounts but also in terms of risk contributions.

All other things being equal, the principles of risk budgeting mean that we should focus our investments on those areas where there is the highest expected level of manager skill or 'alpha'. By 'skill' we mean, ultimately, the ability to outperform the market other than merely by luck. In a multivariate Normal world this implies the presence of an underlying mean drift (albeit one that might be time-varying). Typically, those who use such language do so with the implicit understanding that the mean drift is positive. It is rude in polite (active management) circles to disclaim other people's possibly negative mean drifts, even though the average manager must, by definition, be average, and hence (unless everyone is equal) there must be some with below average skill if there are to be others with above average skill.[7]

12.4.2 Information ratios

In a multivariate (log) Normal world, 'skill' can be equated with a fund's information ratio. By this we mean that statistical tests of presence or absence of skill based on historical data will in general focus on the observed values of the fund's information ratio, see e.g. Kemp (2009). To the extent that it is possible to estimate what a fund's (or fund manager's) information ratio might be in the future, then it is also how you would most naturally characterise the extent to which you might expect to benefit from the manager's supposed 'skill' going forwards.

We can see this by re-expressing the definition of the information ratio as follows. An advantage of this re-expression is that tracking error can in essence be thought of as principally deriving from portfolio construction disciplines and information ratio principally from the skill

---

[7] A possible flaw in this reasoning is that the average as a whole may 'add value'. For example, one can argue that the scrutiny that financial analysts apply when assessing a company's prospects and hence share price should ultimately lead to more efficient allocation of capital across the economy as a whole. One then gets led into arguments about whether it is possible/right to 'free-load' off such activities merely by investing in index funds, and how value becomes apportioned between different elements of the capital structure or across different companies in capital raising situations.

that the manager exhibits.[8]

$$Information\ Ratio\ (IR) = \frac{Outperformance\ (\alpha)}{Tracking\ Error\ (\sigma)}$$

$$\Rightarrow \alpha = IR \times \sigma \tag{12.3}$$

The problem that we find in practice is that the results of any asset allocation based on different managers' skill levels are hugely sensitive to our assumptions about these future levels of skill, i.e. future likely observed information ratios. In particular, if we adopt the usual risk management starting assumption that the information ratio is zero then the answers to the optimisation exercise become ill defined. So, to make good use of risk budgeting in this context we need to believe that we have some skill at choosing 'good' managers (i.e. ones with an expected information ratio versus the underlying benchmark greater than zero) as opposed to 'poor' ones (i.e. ones with an expected information ratio less than zero).

Risk budgeting theory can also be used to help define appropriate portfolio construction discipline rules. For example, a fund management house might a priori believe that it has an upper quartile level of skill (e.g. because of the way it selects staff, researches securities, etc.). If it then adopts the working assumption that all *other* managers will behave randomly (which to first order does not seem unreasonable if we analyse many different peer groups) then to target an upper quartile level of skill it should be aiming to deliver approximately a 0.7 information ratio over 1 year (if both return and risk are annualised), a 0.4 information ratio over 3 years or a 0.3 information ratio over 5 years, see Kemp (2009). These are close to the rule of thumb of an information ratio of 0.5 that is often used by investment consultants to define a 'good' manager. Once we have defined an appropriate information ratio target, we can identify what level of risk needs to be taken to stand a reasonable chance of achieving a given client's desired level of relative return. Once this is done, we can use simulation techniques (or other approaches) to identify the sorts of portfolio construction parameters that might typically result in us running approximately this level of risk through time.

Risk budgeting logic also in theory implies that for the same fixed target outperformance level, a fund manager should alter average position sizes as general levels of riskiness of securities change, even if he or she has unchanged intrinsic views on any of the securities in question. This is arguably an appropriate approach if a short-term change really is a harbinger of a longer-term structural shift in the market. But what if it just reflects a temporary market phenomenon?

During the dot-com boom and bust during the late 1990s and early 2000s, average position sizes in many equity peer groups did not change much. Fund managers' ex-ante tracking errors derived from leading third-party risk system vendors thus typically rose (and then fell again). This suggests that fund managers often use more pragmatic portfolio construction disciplines (e.g. applying maximum exposure limits to a single name and changing these limits only infrequently) and view with some scepticism what might arise were risk budgeting theory to be rigorously applied.

---

[8] However, tracking error and information ratio will not be fully independent of each other. For example, alpha might be added by timing of increases or reductions in tracking error. For long-only portfolios, the expected information ratio of a skilled manager might also be expected to decrease as tracking error increased, as the best short ideas are preferentially used up first. With such a portfolio it is not possible to go shorter than the benchmark weight in any particular stock.

12.4.3   Sensitivity to the input assumptions

The results of most sorts of portfolio optimisation exercises are very sensitive to small perturbations in the input assumptions. For a mean–variance optimiser these input assumptions include:

(a) Expected future returns;
(b) Expected future covariance matrix;
(c) Constraints; and
(d) Deemed minimum risk portfolio.

Dependency on the constraints is relatively obvious and easy to explain to lay-people. If the unconstrained result implied a 50 % weighting to a particular asset category, and a constraint imposes an upper limit on that weighting of only 10 % then the 'optimal' weight for that asset category changes by 40 %. Dependency on the minimum risk portfolio is also fairly obvious, at least for less risky portfolios.

Dependency on the other parameters may be less obvious but is no less significant. Mathematically, the optimum (in the absence of constraints) lies at a point where all the partial derivatives of the utility function are zero, i.e. if one were to visualise the utility function in multi-dimensional space then the optimum lies at a point where the utility function is absolutely flat.

The situation is reminiscent of 'Labyrinth', a children's game in which you attempt to navigate marbles around a flat maze board with holes in it by tipping the edges of the board slightly up or down. It requires significant manual dexterity.

A more mathematical analysis of the same point is contained in Scherer (2007). He notes that the solution to the 'unconstrained' portfolio optimisation problem[9] is $\mathbf{a} = \mathbf{b} + \lambda \mathbf{V}^{-1}\mathbf{r}$ (using the notation of Section 12.2.3). The larger the number of dimensions, i.e. the larger the number of securities or asset classes under consideration, the more sensitive the matrix inversion becomes to perturbations in any single element of the original uninverted matrix, so this problem can become more and more acute the more assets there are. In particular, the optimisation will look very favourably on assets (or asset bundles) that are as similar as possible to all other assets as long as they have even a very small return advantage. This can lead to implausible results when estimation errors are taken into account.

The results can also be very sensitive to even relatively modest perturbations in return assumptions. Suppose, for example, we derive return assumptions in part from observed historic returns. We shouldn't really do this, given that what we are actually interested in is the future not the past. Merely because something has performed well in the past doesn't mean that it will necessarily perform well in the future. Indeed, if we believe in mean reversion then we might believe that the two should if anything be negatively correlated! But it is very difficult to get anywhere without at least some reference back to the past. It is the only history we have! Historic returns can be thought of as samples drawn from some underlying 'true' (historic) distribution of returns. But it takes many observations for the average of such draws to converge to the underlying population mean (to the extent that it actually exists[10]).

---

[9] By the 'unconstrained' portfolio optimisation problem, Scherer (2007) means a problem in which the only constraint is that the weights sum to unity, i.e. there are no *other* constraints, such as short-selling constraints.

[10] For such an underlying mean to exist we need the returns to be coming from a stationary distribution and we have noted elsewhere that this can be a questionable assumption.

Normally, we do not have enough past history to infer accurately either the covariance matrix characteristics or the return characteristics of the likely future return distribution. If we merely have 120 observations (say 10 years' worth of monthly data), the observed mean will have a standard error approximately equal to $\sigma/11$, where σ is the volatility of the relevant asset category in isolation. Such errors are typically enough to move the precise composition of the efficient frontier by very significant amounts.

12.4.4   Sensitivity to the universe from which ideas are drawn

A point not always well covered in standard texts on portfolio optimisation and risk budgeting is the sensitivity of the results to the universe from which we are drawing our ideas. This sensitivity is rather obvious when the universes are wildly different – an optimal portfolio will obviously look rather different if it can only contain bonds compared to the situation where it can only contain equities. But even when the universe is more subtly constrained, the answers can be quite heavily affected by universe choice.

In essence, we can think of choice of universe as corresponding to use of some 'super' universe of investment prospects, and then constraining any holdings that do not appear in the particular sub-universe that we are focusing on to be zero weighted. If such holdings are perceived by the corresponding implicit 'super' risk model to have characteristics close to those in the sub-universe of opportunities that are allowed to be included in the portfolio then including or excluding them from this sub-universe may have a significant impact on what then ultimately appears within optimal portfolios.

A way of decomposing such a 'super' universe of possible investment opportunities into broad market areas that appear to move in tandem is to use clustering techniques, see e.g. Scherer (2007) or Kemp (2009).

12.5   REVERSE OPTIMISATION AND IMPLIED VIEW ANALYSIS

12.5.1   Implied alphas

Given the sensitivity to input assumptions described in Section 12.4, it is not surprising that investment managers who are less quantitatively orientated may be sceptical about the merits of explicitly quantitative portfolio optimisation techniques (even though, as we saw in Section 12.3, what they are doing is formally equivalent to such an exercise, whether or not they think it is!). Portfolio optimisation can easily introduce unwanted biases or come up with implausible-looking results if it is not carried out carefully.

A related technique that such fund managers might use is *reverse optimisation*, i.e. the use of *implied alphas*. In this, we work out what views we need to have on the alphas that different positions will deliver, if we assume that the portfolio finally chosen optimally trades off risk versus return.

Even if portfolio construction does not involve an explicit portfolio optimisation step, implied alphas can be used to provide an additional sense check to ensure that no positions in the portfolio are obviously inappropriate in risk budgeting terms. If any positions stand out as anomalous then the manager may explore further whether they really should have the place that they do have within the portfolio. If carried out more formally this sort of activity might be described as *view optimisation*, see e.g. Scherer (2007). This is perhaps not really optimisation per se. Instead, it involves an iterative process of trial and error in which an investor changes allocations (and sometimes forecasts) until implied and expected returns (when appropriately scaled) show a 'reasonable' overlap.

Implied alphas also potentially provide convenient ways of combining views of different teams or contributors within a wider investment process. Given actual (or specimen) portfolios (and benchmarks), we can derive the views that their creators need to hold for them to be optimal. We can then combine these views in a suitable way, perhaps giving most weight to views from individuals or teams in which we have most confidence. The resultant combined views can then be used to formulate how portfolios that are expected to take views across multiple disciplines should ideally be positioned.

Care is needed when combining views in this manner. Implied alphas are usually derived from actual portfolio positions. However, in general they only characterise actual underlying investment views if the portfolio in question is *unconstrained* (which often it isn't). For example, if an investor is not allowed to hold more than 5 % in any one security then it is difficult to work out just how positive is the manager's view on that security if the position is already at the 5 % level. This issue is particularly acute for the vast majority of benchmark constituents that in a long-only portfolio are zero weighted because of the long-only constraint. It is impossible to infer from such information how negatively the manager views such securities.

12.5.2 Consistent implementation of investment ideas across portfolios

Implied alphas may also be used in so-called 'portfolio factories'. Investment managers often have nearly as many benchmarks for their client portfolios as they have (segregated) clients. Each such client may want some (often only relatively slight) permutation within their benchmark. To complicate matters further, clients' investment guidelines may vary (e.g. they may impose different portfolio constraints or involve different target return levels). How can an asset manager ensure in a cost-effective manner that all client portfolios are treated fairly and express the same underlying investment views?

One way of doing so is to characterise these views in the form of implied alphas, and then to reapply the same implied alphas across different portfolios using optimisation techniques using the same underlying risk model. The results will then only differ to the extent that the portfolios have different benchmarks or guidelines. We can recover the original portfolio by reapplying these implied alphas to the benchmark/guideline context from which they were originally sourced. This after all is the essence of reversing any process. Very similar benchmarks/guidelines should result in very similar end portfolios, but greater differences may arise with less similar benchmarks/guidelines.

12.6 CALIBRATING PORTFOLIO CONSTRUCTION TECHNIQUES TO THE MARKET

There are four main ways in which we can better calibrate portfolio optimisation and reverse optimisation techniques to the market. These are:

(1) *We can endeavour to characterise better the distributional form from which we expect future returns to come and then adjust our optimisation approaches accordingly*

This loosely corresponds to the topics we discussed in Chapter 9. We explore this topic further in Section 12.7. We focus only on the single period situation (even though we saw in Chapter 9 that extent of deviation from Normality might depend on period length), because the multi-period (i.e. dynamic) case is typically catered for via a decomposition akin to that described in Section 12.2.

It should be noted that estimation of covariance matrices from past data is subject to the sorts of data limitations referred to in Chapter 7. Moreover, some of the tools that might be prescribed there to de-noise the covariance matrix (and then to reinsert idiosyncratic variability back into the matrix) can materially influence the nature of optimal portfolios derived using the de-noised matrix. Such methodologies can make different securities appear more independent than they might really be, which can result in greater uniformity of position sizes than might be ideal.

(2) *We can better reflect current market implied data in our assessment of the distributional form of future returns*

We might do this either because we think that the past may be a less good guide to the future than current market implied information or because we have bought into the fuller relevance of such information for risk management purposes as implied by the proposed risk management paradigm shift described in Chapter 11. Essentially, the same techniques as arise in (1) apply here too, except that we derive the distributional form differently, so we do not explore this type of application of market consistency further in this chapter.

(3) *We can attempt to incorporate more directly into portfolio optimisation algorithms 'what the market has to say' about what might be plausible return assumptions to adopt for different assets*

Refinements relating to (1) and (2) in essence relate to the 'risk' element of the risk–return optimisation. We should also expect 'what the market has to say' to have some relevance to the 'return' element. This forms the backdrop to many of the forms of robust optimisation that have been developed to reduce the extreme sensitivity that optimisers typically have to their input assumptions. We explore these topics further in Section 12.8. Most of these techniques in some sense dampen non-market consensus views, so care is needed not to dampen out entirely our own views. Taking market consistency to an extreme in portfolio construction activities and assuming that the market is the sole arbiter of knowledge is not the right answer if we are being paid to express conviction about how the market might be wrong!

(4) *We can refine (3) further to take into account not only 'what the market has to say' but also who it is who forms the 'market' when it is saying these things*

This is a somewhat more subtle but perhaps no less important element of market consistency. We explore it further in Section 12.9.

Principle P52: When applying market consistency to (active) portfolio construction, practitioners should remember the importance that *non*-market consistent thinking also plays in such activities, given the importance accorded in these activities to practitioner views about how markets might be 'incorrectly' assessing the future worth of different investments.

12.7   CATERING BETTER FOR NON-NORMALITY IN RETURN DISTRIBUTIONS

12.7.1   Re-normalising historic return distributions

We have seen in Chapter 8 that fat tails are very commonly observed features of investment return series, whether considered singly or in tandem. We might decide that catering for fat tails was 'too difficult'. We might therefore abandon portfolio optimisation techniques and use 'human judgement' instead (perhaps supplemented by reverse optimisation). However, some investment management approaches necessarily require some sort of automated approach to portfolio construction. Moreover, even if 'human judgement' is used, what is the right way to 'train' or foster such judgement?

We may note that:

(a) If all return opportunities (and combinations of them) are in a suitable sense 'equally' (jointly) fat-tailed then the optimal portfolios are the same as those arising using traditional mean–variance optimisation approaches (as long as the risk budget is adjusted appropriately). If different combinations exhibit differential fat-tailed behaviour then portfolio construction ought in principle to be adjusted to compensate, but only if we can reliably estimate these differentials and their impact.

(b) The most important predictable single contributor to fat tails (at least for series that we might otherwise intrinsically expect to be approximately Normal) is time-varying volatility.

Hence, one suggestion, if it is practical, is to:

(i) Calculate the covariance matrix between return series after stripping out the effect of time-varying volatility (and any other fat-tail contributors we can identify, the aim being to get the adjusted return series to be as close to multivariate (log) Normal as possible);

(ii) Then optimise as we think most appropriate (using e.g. standard mean–variance, 'robust', Bayesian, Black-Litterman, . . . , see Section 12.8), using the covariance matrix adjusted as per (a) and with the risk budget accordingly. Implicitly, this involves assuming that the adjusted return series all then exhibit the same degree of fat-tailed behaviour; and

(iii) Identify 'adjusted' optimal portfolios by reversing away the adjustments made in (i) from the optimal portfolios identified in (ii), see e.g. Kemp (2009) for more practical details.

If the focus is on reverse optimisation, i.e. implied alphas, then the same sort of approach can also be adopted. However, if the implied alphas are being principally used to provide a sense check then the gain in doing so may not be particularly large.

12.7.2   Using co-skew, co-kurtosis and other co-moments

Some other possible approaches are summarised in Scherer (2007). These include:

(1) *Modelling non-normality via a mixture of Normal distributions*

This is how we originally alighted on the idea of adjusting for time-varying volatility. A major challenge, if we allow complete flexibility in the choice of Normal distributions which might be mixed together, is the number of additional parameters that might then need to be estimated when doing so. Even a mixture of just two multivariate Normal distributions has twice as many covariance terms and therefore parameters to estimate. The results of optimisation exercises are already notoriously sensitive to input assumptions even when we only have one distribution to estimate!

(2) *Use of lower partial moments, such as co-skew and co-kurtosis or symmetric alternatives*

A description of how to calculate such statistics is given in Scherer (2007). Unfortunately, these again require estimation of substantially increased numbers of parameters, so may again major on error maximisation rather than return maximisation. Moreover, in Section 9.5

we concluded that skewness and kurtosis were not necessarily good ways of describing or characterising fat-tailed behaviour even for individual return series (because they could give inappropriate weights to different data points). Their multi-dimensional analogues, co-skew (also called co-skewness) and co-kurtosis, may be even less effective ways of characterising fat-tailed behaviour in multiple return series.

Scherer (2007) suggests that 'best practice' if this sort of approach is used is to specify the candidate distributional form type using a small number of parameters, to find the form within this candidate type that best fits the data, and then to calculate lower partial moments and thence optimal portfolios from these best fit distributional forms rather than directly from the observed return data. The approach suggested in Sections 9.5 and 9.6 for rectifying some of the weaknesses evident in skew and kurtosis as descriptors of fat-tailed behaviour can be recast to fit within this framework.

12.8   ROBUST OPTIMISATION

12.8.1   Black-Litterman

Within mathematics more generally, the term 'robust' in, say, *robust regression* typically applies to an approach that tries to reduce the sensitivity of the answers to outliers in the input data. Whether this is necessarily a good thing to strive for within finance is questionable. Any 'real' outliers contribute to financial outcomes just as much as other data points. Exclusion of outliers is thus only intrinsically sound if we think that their 'outlier' status is most probably because they have been recorded incorrectly or the like, rather than because they are extreme draws from the underlying probability distribution.

Within finance, therefore, robust optimisation usually has a subtly different meaning, referring to approaches which try to reduce the sensitivity of the answers to inaccuracies in input assumptions (rather than inaccuracies in the data per se).

Perhaps the most important *robust optimisation* approach in mathematical finance is the so-called Black-Litterman approach, see e.g. Litterman (2003) or Cheung (2007a). Originally it was developed as a framework in which we assume, in the absence of differentiating views on individual securities, that we should adopt a portfolio structured in line with CAPM, i.e. some linear mixture of the low-risk portfolio (typically assumed to be cash, but this strictly speaking requires us to view the liabilities to which the assets relate as cash-like in nature) and 'the market'.

One way of interpreting the Black-Litterman approach is to think of it as introducing an *anchor* that constrains the optimisation problem not just at one point (the minimum risk portfolio) but at a second point some way along the efficient frontier, the characteristics of which are derived from general reasoning.

A natural choice for this second point is the *market portfolio*. As we have noted earlier, the mean–variance efficient frontier is effectively piecewise linear, each line segment finishing when some new constraint starts to bite. Portfolio weights are piecewise linear in the risk-tracking error space, again with each line segment finishing when a new constraint bites. So, normally, in the absence of differentiating views on individual securities we recover optimal portfolios being some mix of the minimum risk portfolio and the market portfolio, i.e. the CAPM formulation.

In the presence of differentiating views, optimal portfolios will deviate from the CAPM market line. Ignoring constraints, the result is mathematically equivalent to adopting a Bayesian approach in which we give partial weight to our own assumptions and partial weight to assumptions that correspond to ones that make the market efficient. Cheung (2007b) explains how to adapt the basic theory to situations where we are using a factor type risk model as per Chapter 7.

We note a link with other types of calibrations that we have come across elsewhere within this book. We are, as before, identifying a deemed 'right' answer for a given situation and then extrapolating from it to 'nearby' alternative situations. In this case the alternatives are ones where we are expressing differential market views on different instruments, and the calibration point is the market portfolio.

However, this interpretation then highlights an ambiguity in the approach. How do we define the 'market' portfolio? We might think that its definition is not contentious for, say, a US equity portfolio. But consider the wider universe of investment opportunities. Does the 'market' portfolio then include cash, bonds and property as well as the equities with which it is more normally associated? And if we include asset classes like cash (or derivatives) where the two parties involved strictly speaking have equal and opposite positions, how much weight should we give to each side?

12.8.2 Re-sampling

Another common robust optimisation technique is *re-sampling* (otherwise called *bootstrapping*[11]). This methodology aims to reduce dependency on the sample of the underlying population from which we might have derived our input assumptions. It involves sampling the input data repeatedly only using part of the observed data set, working out the efficient portfolios based on each sample and then averaging the results. Less clear is the exact mathematical problem for which these average 're-sampled optimal' portfolios are then optimal, see e.g. Kemp (2009).

12.9 TAKING DUE ACCOUNT OF OTHER INVESTORS' RISK PREFERENCES

The efficient frontier approach described above places some positive 'value' on the expected future outperformance of some asset categories over others. Indeed, any forward-looking stochastic modelling approach does, if it involves differential return assumptions. The very act of expressing the results in a risk–return space implicitly involves assigning some positive benefit to strategies where the additional return is perceived to more than compensate for perceived additional risk.

However, in a market consistent world, values of different instruments are driven by risk-neutral probability distributions not the 'real world' distributions that typically form the basis of optimisation exercises. For the hypothetical marginal market participant, the future returns on a security should balance the risks. Otherwise the participant wouldn't buy or sell at that price. In short, in such a risk-neutral world, the future returns on different asset categories are effectively equal, i.e. the efficient frontier is no longer upwardly sloping but flat.[12] Using 'real

---

[11] This use of the term 'bootstrapping' is not to be confused with the technique of the same name used to calculate deterministically a yield curve from the prices of a series of bonds of sequentially increasing terms.

[12] However, see comments in Section 4.3.2 regarding the existence of a market price of risk vector.

world' return assumptions will typically give insufficient weight to the greater disutility that investors normally place on downside outcomes.

So a key element in portfolio positioning ought to be incorporation of views about how *our* appetite for the risks being expressed within the portfolio differs from the appetite of the relevant marginal market participant who sets the market price of the relevant asset or liability.

Some of these differences in risk appetite can be accommodated via the use of different minimum risk portfolios for different clients, and so can still be fitted into the above framework. This is perhaps more applicable to bond-land. For example, some investors will prefer fixed interest assets and some will prefer inflation-linked assets because of the different natures of their liabilities. Likewise different investors may prefer exposures to different parts of the yield curve.

However, some of the differences in risk appetite cannot properly be handled merely via adjustments to the minimum risk portfolio. Instead they may depend on the differential appetite investors have for different levels of risk. We cannot necessarily conclude that we should overweight investment A in that market relative to investment B merely because we believe that investment A should on average outperform investment B. Instead, we need to validate how our assumptions compare with those of other market participants. If they too hold a similar belief then they should have reflected such views in their own portfolios. In a risk-neutral sense there is no risk-adjusted outperformance available merely from taking a market consistent view. So key is that we understand how *both* our own risk appetite and our investment views differ from those of other market participants, for all the different types of risk to which we might be exposed.

Calibrating Valuations to the Market

13.1 INTRODUCTION

In Chapters 2 to 6 we focused on the theory and principles underlying market consistent valuations. It had been my original intention to include some practical guidance on how to implement these principles in a chapter positioned immediately after these chapters. However, it became clear as the book developed that such case studies should ideally also come after sections covering the theory behind solvency capital computations. As we noted in Section 2.8, there is no single 'right' way to identify the market consistent value of a firm's liabilities. Instead, such values ultimately depend on the purpose behind the valuation, which often (although not always) relates to solvency assessment.

In this chapter we first focus on the practicalities of actually observing market prices, how such prices form in the first place and how to interpolate or extrapolate from prices ruling for liquid instruments to ones that might apply to less well traded assets and liabilities.

We then consider case study examples designed to illustrate how to value a range of different assets and liabilities in a market consistent fashion. We first consider derivation of 'base' market consistent asset and liability valuations for solvency purposes. We also consider other types of market consistent valuations, e.g. market consistent embedded values. We then consider market consistent equivalents for solvency add-ons, i.e. additional capital requirements akin to those referred to in Chapter 8 such as the SCR for Solvency II. Towards the end of this chapter we explore specialist types of valuation, including pension fund valuations and valuations of unitised vehicles.

Throughout this chapter it is assumed that the reader is bearing in mind materiality. If uncertainty in the value of an instrument has little impact on the end answer (we here implicitly include consideration of the purpose to which the valuation will be put) then excessive sophistication in derivation of that value may be of little relevance.

13.2 PRICE FORMATION AND PRICE DISCOVERY

13.2.1 The price formation process

Before focusing on how we might locate suitable market observables to use in deriving market consistent valuations, it is helpful to describe in broad terms how prices in markets come into being, i.e. the *price formation* process.

A market might be said to exist whenever buyers and sellers come together to trade particular types of goods or services. As explained in Chapter 2, markets can operate on a barter basis but it is more common nowadays for them to involve one party purchasing a good or service in return for some monetary consideration, which the seller of the good or service will use to buy some other good or service at some possibly later point in time.

Market participants will generally have a strong interest in identifying the prices at which other market participants would be willing to buy or sell goods or services in which they are interested, or close substitutes to these goods or services. They will also be interested in the prices at which recent transactions, if any, have actually taken place. If rationally used, such information should strengthen their own negotiating hands as and when they themselves want to carry out corresponding transactions. They may be less interested in equivalent information about their own actual or potential trades being provided to *other* market participants.

However, if there are sufficient market participants operating (or expecting to operate) regularly in the market in question then one might expect the aggregate desire for price visibility to overcome the desire market participants might have to hide their own hands, at least for smaller trades less likely by themselves to move market prices. Even if this desire is not particularly strong, price transparency may be promoted by government or regulation, on the grounds that efficient markets lead to efficient allocation of capital, which is generally considered to be beneficial to society as a whole.

How price transparency is achieved in practice (and how much of it there is!) will differ by market.

The market may have a formal recognised structure like a stock exchange, in which transactions will typically need to be reported to a centralised body within specified time limits. This data would then typically be disseminated in specified ways to other market participants. In the past, stock exchanges were often mutual organisations owned by their members but nowadays they are often joint stock organisations owned mainly by shareholders not directly involved in the activities happening on the exchange.

Alternatively, markets may be less formally structured without a central exchange. These sorts of markets are called over-the-counter (OTC). An OTC market may be no less vibrant than an exchange traded market. For example, the foreign exchange market is the most actively traded market in the world (by notional volume traded). Nearly all deals in this market are bilateral and hence OTC in nature. Conduct of business requirements that regulators place on market participants may apply irrespective of whether trades are carried out on exchange or OTC.

Some exposures can be traded in either format. The format used in the majority of cases may then depend on many factors, particularly commercial aspects like fees and clearing charges. Now that exchanges are often profit-making enterprises, their major customers including market makers may have a commercial incentive to try to disintermediate them by dealing directly with each other in a corresponding OTC market or by setting up competing alternative trading mechanisms or venues through which trades can also be executed. Conversely, centralisation and use of a centralised clearing house can reduce counterparty exposures, which may be viewed as more beneficial than trying to bypass the exchange. Regulators may encourage such centralisation to mitigate systemic risk. Market makers' customers, including end investors, may also have views on the most appropriate way for a market to operate.

Different markets sometimes arise in essentially the same types of exposures in different geographical locations. However, it is rarely the case nowadays that prices in one such market do not strongly interact with prices ruling in equivalent markets elsewhere. Modern communication and the presence of arbitrageurs typically see to that.

One might intrinsically expect pricing data to be easier to come by if transactions are passing through a central agency such as an exchange. However, this is not always the case. It is important to bear in mind where and how the bulk of the trading activity in any particular financial exposure occurs, and in some cases exactly how in practice transactions take place. For example, some derivatives exchanges may offer such a wide range of equity index futures contracts that some of the less actively traded ones may only trade 'by appointment'. The parties to the trade (e.g. an institutional investor and a market maker) may be keen to enter into such a futures transaction rather than, say, buying outright a basket containing a large number of individual equity positions. The futures contract may be more easily handled by the investor's internal systems, or may require less upfront capital outlay. However, the price of such a trade may still be set based explicitly on how much it would cost to transact the underlying basket.

Price formation is not necessarily nowadays driven principally by the market in which a particular instrument trades. It may be driven primarily by a corresponding derivatives market. Perhaps the most obvious example of this is how overall equity market levels typically first respond to changing economic or financial conditions via the equity index futures market, with the effects then cascading to individual equities. For many worldwide equity markets, typical daily volumes of market exposure traded on the main index futures contracts exceed the combined daily volumes of all corresponding individual equities on the underlying stock markets. More recently, index exchange traded funds (ETFs) have seen significant growth in trading volumes although they are still relatively modest compared with futures volumes. These vehicles may be traded on the underlying physical exchanges but they are in many ways more akin to index derivatives than to single stock positions.

Even at, say, the individual equity level, it is also possible for price formation to be driven more by derivatives markets than by the underlying equity markets. Liodakis *et al.* (2008) when commenting on Cremers and Weinbaum (2007) make the comment that (quantitative) equity analysts may often have viewed derivatives as a separate asset class, disregarding the possibility that price discovery might occur first in the derivatives market. They question this assumption, given the leverage possible via derivatives and note increasing interest in extracting and interpreting the information content of option prices when seeking to formulate successful investment strategies. For example, they note that portfolios biased towards stocks with relatively high put–call parity deviations appear to provide noticeable abnormal returns. The larger the deviation from put–call parity, the greater was the apparent concentration of informed traders they identified as relating to these options.

The efficiency and speed of price formation and hence potential accuracy achievable in price discovery other than by actually transacting a deal is also influenced by the typical nature of market participants, particularly the most active ones. As we noted in Section 6.3.3, active managers, particularly very active ones, provide liquidity to markets. The extent of their presence affects the time that it takes market makers to hedge exposures and thus the amount of risk capital needed for market making activities and hence bid–offer spreads, etc. Conversely, if market maker risk capital is in short supply then bid–offer spreads may rise causing liquidity to fall. This is another way in which liquidity stresses can be transmitted across markets.

Bid and offer prices around mid-market prices may also need some investigation. Some exchanges operate an order matching process, with buys and sells matched. Even if they do not do this all the time they may still use such a mechanism at market close and hence for prices most likely to be used by third parties seeking to prepare market consistent valuations. In these cases bid and offer prices may be the same, but this does not mean that there is no effective bid–offer spread in practice, merely that it is hidden from the data that is most easily accessible to the valuer.

13.2.2 Price discovery

Price discovery, as we define it, relates to the process by which a participant identifies the price at which an actual trade may or actually does take place. Some people use the term 'price discovery' to mean the process by which new information leads to new prices applying to an instrument, which we define as 'price formation' as above (part but not all of which is driven by price discovery as described below).

As explained above, there is typically strong demand from regular participants in any market, whether on exchange or OTC, to obtain timely market price data. Data vendors exist who offer systems that provide access to market price data (as well as analytics, news feeds, etc. that may help in the comparative analysis of such price data through time or across instruments). These data vendors have a commercial interest in sourcing timely, relevant and reliable data on market prices whenever the market in question is sufficiently active for it to be practical to collate such data.

The main data vendors may have less good price feed coverage for markets in less mainstream or more nascent types of exposures. In these situations there may be more specialist data vendors focusing just on these niche markets. Alternatively, market participants may need to approach market makers directly to provide them with indicative prices. A problem is that unless the relationship between an investor and a market maker is strong or provision of such data is likely to lead to trades, market makers may have little incentive to provide 'reliable' indicative prices that might correspond reasonably closely with the prices at which such trades might actually take place.

Even when a specialist data provider appears to have access to price data on a given instrument, this data may only come from a single source, if the instrument is relatively illiquid. Moreover, even when there are several underlying price sources, the prices may have come from the relevant market makers' back offices and so may not correspond with where the instrument might trade in practice. In some situations, large parts of the market may no longer be actively trading. Prices from any source can then be suspect. Ideally, you would want some trades to be occurring, in which case you can benchmark the prices you are receiving from the different sources against actual trades. If the two diverge then you can potentially adjust, i.e. calibrate, other data coming from the same source to compensate for this divergence.

Typically, market participants seek to discover as much as they can about the prices at which they might trade, ideally anonymously. They then try to get one or more market makers to make as firm a price as possible, before finally committing to a trade. However, the mere process of seeking such information may itself supply information about a likely trade to the market maker(s) in question. The market maker(s) may also be able to guess from the enquiry the likely direction of the proposed trade. It is not therefore always appropriate to seek competitive quotes from multiple market makers. This may increase the costs each market maker thinks it might incur when subsequently hedging its positions, i.e. the so-called winner's curse, see e.g. Kemp (1997).

In most markets, an important part of price discovery is live[1] price feeds carried by major data vendors such as Bloomberg or Reuters. Because live prices contain much more informational value than delayed prices, market participants may have to pay much more to access them.

It helps to understand exactly what any price feed actually means. For example, some 'live' options' bid and offer price feeds may merely be indicative whilst others may be truly 'live' in the sense that you are guaranteed to be able to trade at the prices shown, if you catch them quickly enough. But if the spread on the latter is narrower than the spread on the former this

---

[1] For some markets, such as physical real estate, where trades can take many days from start to finish, the benefits of 'live' pricing may be reduced. Knowing how other market participants are thinking is still valuable, but their views do not change so rapidly.

does not necessarily mean that the latter is a cheaper market on which to trade, even if the same underlying exposure is being traded. Instead it may merely mean that the 'indicative live' price quotes for the former are being quoted with wider bid–offer spreads than would actually apply were you to trade intelligently on the relevant market.

This reminds us that the way in which a transaction is executed can materially influence the price actually paid. For example, if a large transaction is sliced up into several tranches then earlier parts of the transaction may be expected to have a market impact that influences prices achieved on later parts of the transaction. This might appear to favour trying to do any transaction you want to do all at once. However, this may not be feasible in practice, or may be costly, because you are requiring the market maker with whom you deal to put up risk capital against the possibility that prices might move against it when it is hedging the exposures it has acquired. Such risk capital is not always in ready supply.

13.3   MARKET CONSISTENT ASSET VALUATIONS

13.3.1   Introduction

We set out below illustrations of how to apply the principles developed earlier in this book to a range of asset types. The focus throughout this section is principally on mid-prices for reasons set out in Section 13.4.5.

The examples covered in this section are subdivided into the following categories:

(a) Relatively simple assets (e.g. mainstream equities, currencies and bonds) independent of the firm itself;
(b) More complex assets independent of the firm itself (e.g. more complex derivatives or similar structures where the underlyings or other exposures are not linked to the firm seeking the market consistent value); and
(c) Assets that include risk exposures linked to the firm itself.

13.3.2   Relatively simple assets independent of the firm

(1) *Exchange-traded instruments, e.g. equity assets (other than the firm's own equity) or diversified market index futures contracts*[2]

In general, exchanges go to considerable trouble to ensure that the prices at which things trade on them are realistic market prices, since this is an important part of their rationale for existence and hence for their sound functioning. So if an instrument is traded on an exchange and it is sufficiently frequently traded then just lifting the exchange-derived price would be the normal way to identify its mid-market price at some given point in time.

If the instrument trades less frequently but still on an exchange, then it is worth identifying whether the price feed available from the exchange relates to a 'last traded' price or whether it relates to some fair interpolation or extrapolation of the price at which the instrument would have traded had a trade taken place at the valuation point.

---

[2] Strictly speaking, the market consistent value placed on an index futures contract should include an adjustment as per Section 13.3.4 if the firm is a material constituent of the underlying market index (i.e. analysed on a look-through basis).

If it is the latter (which would rarely be the case for physical securities) then it should be a suitable price to use for a market consistent valuation, assuming that the logic underlying the interpolation or extrapolation is sound.

If it is the former, i.e. a last traded price, then in principle it becomes necessary to identify how far in the past was the relevant trade and whether at the time it occurred it was representative of the market in question. If the last traded price was a firesale trade then it may not have been representative of actual 'fair' market levels at the time, i.e. it may have been at one or other end of a (possibly widened) bid–offer spectrum, rather than providing a guide to the mid-price then ruling. If it is too far into the past then the price may be 'stale'.[3] We may then need to extrapolate from the last (reliable) price to a more reliable estimate of where the instrument 'should' have traded at the valuation point. This, in effect, always involves a marking-to-model.

For, say, an equity, this extrapolation might merely involve application of a multiplier based on the movement in the price of some more easily observed market parameter, e.g. the movement in a corresponding market index (or a future on that index). If you have a comparator index $I(t)$ observable at time t and t_0 (where usually $t \geq t_0$) and you wish to identify the price of an instrument at time $V(t)$ at time t only knowing $V(t_0)$, the natural extrapolation is to assume that $V(t) \approx V(t_0) \times I(t)/I(t_0)$. If additional value, such as a dividend payment, accrues during the extrapolation period to either the comparator or the underlying instrument (i.e. value that is not captured in the price movement but would appear in the total return) then the above formula should ideally be adjusted to strip away the distorting influence that this value accrual would otherwise have on the extrapolation exercise.

The last traded price may potentially be so stale that reliable trades shortly after the valuation point are much 'closer' in time to the valuation point than reliable ones preceding it.[4] In these circumstances it may be best to extrapolate backwards in time, or to use interpolation between prices straddling the valuation point. This works as follows. If (for an instrument being assumed to behave linearly) you know $V(t_1)$ as well as $V(t_0)$ and $t_0 < t < t_1$ then it may be best to estimate $Z(t) = V(t)/I(t)$ by interpolation from its values at t_0 and t_1 and then to back out the modelled price using $V(t) = Z(t)/I(t)$. However, prices often jump overnight, so interpolation using pricing data from after the valuation data is not often used in practice. In this sense the time period between now and tomorrow morning is typically deemed to be far 'longer' than between earlier today and now.

For less linear instruments the same methodological principles apply, but instead of interpolation or extrapolation of price itself, we may need to create a more accurate pricing model for the instrument in question and instead interpolate or extrapolate the inputs into this pricing model. By this we mean having a pricing algorithm $V(\mathbf{m}(t))$ dependent on a set of more readily available market observables, $\mathbf{m}$. We then extrapolate or interpolate each component of $\mathbf{m}$ and feed these values into the pricing algorithm instead. The poorer the probable explanatory power of the pricing model, the less reliability can be placed on the extrapolated price derived from it. We see an immediate analogy with the need when designing risk models capable of handling more complex instruments to include pricing models.

---

[3] The term 'stale' price also refers to prices that seem to show no movement through time. These may be indicative of flaws in the IT systems used to collect price data, rather than a lack of trades going through the market per se. For example, prices of zero (or prices that seem not to have changed for a long time) are also typically questioned whenever they appear in valuations.

[4] The mileage options introduced in Chapter 4 indicate that we should ideally measure 'elapsed time' in this context by reference to the cumulative quadratic variation in prices.

What happens if there are several possible interpolation or extrapolation approaches that come up with materially different answers? We here revert to the definition of market consistency given in Section 1.5 as a reasoned best estimate of where the valuer thinks the instrument would have traded had a market actually been in existence at the time for the asset or liability in question. So, valuers need to apply judgement in such circumstances.[5]

Principle P53: In general, exchanges go to considerable trouble to ensure that the prices at which instruments trade on them are realistic market prices, since this is an important part of their rationale for existence and hence for their sound functioning. It would therefore be normal to use prices directly derived from exchange feeds when valuing these assets and liabilities in a market consistent manner, unless the quoted prices are 'stale', correspond to distressed transactions or express an inappropriate level of 'own' credit risk for the purpose in hand.

---

(2) *Corresponding instruments not traded on-exchange (and which are not issued by or guaranteed by the firm itself), but for which 'live' standardised prices are still available, e.g. currencies, (liquid) corporate bonds, liquid derivative instruments*

The general principles involved are similar to those where the asset is traded on-exchange, except that we may need to delve more deeply to find suitable market observables, and there may be a greater range of plausible pricing models and hence interpolated or extrapolated prices derived from inputting readily available market observables into such pricing models. It is worth bearing in mind that off-exchange trading covers a very wide range of instrument types. Some are very liquid in almost all circumstances (e.g. mainstream currencies), some are liquid in normal times (e.g. leading corporate bonds), some are not so liquid and some trade very rarely. In some markets, exposures may be able to be traded on-exchange, but the bulk of the activity may be off-exchange, e.g. volumes traded in currency futures (on-exchange) are currently much smaller than volumes traded in the equivalent currency forward market (off-exchange).

In an ideal world, all of the hard work involved in collating, interpolating and extrapolating such data for market consistent pricing purposes would be done centrally, to avoid unnecessary duplication of effort. De facto, this does indeed happen for the most important market observables, e.g. key yield curves and the like, which are usually derived from actually observed market prices by leading data vendors or central banks or the like.

For more bespoke exposures, the commercial incentive may be too weak to facilitate centralisation of such activities, although even here specialist data providers often spring up to consolidate whatever pricing data is available from different market participants, see Section 13.2. If firms do not have access to such data feeds (or such data feeds do not exist) then firms will need to carry out the same sorts of analyses themselves when preparing market consistent valuations. Firms in this position are likely to find it helpful to review the techniques that more mainstream data providers might use if faced with the same problem.

13.3.3 More complex assets independent of the firm

It is not easy to come up with clear rules on how to differentiate between 'simple' and 'complex' instruments. Readers are encouraged to refer to whatever sources appear to them likely, with

---

[5] However, such uncertainties may need to be reflected in any additional solvency capital add-ons, see Section 13.6.

the benefit of hindsight, to be considered authoritative in this context. These might include guidelines from accountancy bodies or learned industry-wide bodies such as CRMPG-III.

Usually, but not always, these types of exposures will be traded off-exchange. Although counterparties may be willing to provide valuations, these may not be robust enough for the purpose to which the valuation is put. Even if they eventually prove to be robust enough, it will often be necessary to validate these valuations more carefully.

For more bespoke exposure types there may be no exactly equivalent instruments that actually trade in practice. This cannot by itself be a bar to deriving a market consistent valuation. We happily accept the validity of, say, government bond yield curves for discounting purposes, even though there aren't an infinite number of such bonds. At most only a finite number of points along such a yield 'curve' come *directly* from market observables. Derivation of the rest of the curve involves extrapolation or interpolation from these more basic market observables.

So, our task is to interpolate or extrapolate from the observable prices of *other* instruments, ideally as close as possible in nature to the asset or liability we are attempting to value. We note an immediate link with Section 4.4. If we derive some piece of market implied data, such as an implied volatility or an implied correlation, from a particular instrument then we expect prices of closely similar instruments to trade at closely similar market implieds.

To come up with a market consistent valuation for a specific instrument we therefore need to:

(a) Identify a selection of more readily observable instruments which in aggregate express the same types of risks as are expressed by the instrument in question. We need to be able to observe market prices for these reference instruments (perhaps interpolated or extrapolated through time as per Section 13.3.2);

(b) Identify a range of (no arbitrage) pricing models that we believe are applicable both to the instrument to be valued and to the reference instruments identified in (a);

(c) Calibrate relevant market implieds from the instruments identified in (a) using the models in (b), and insert these market implieds back into the models in (b) to identify plausible market consistent valuations for the original instrument in question; and

(d) Superimpose on (a)–(c) a mindset that asks whether, if we were buying or selling the instrument in question, we would be happy to do so for the sorts of prices our modelling is identifying.

Hopefully, the range of valuations identified in (c) will be small, or if not then this is merely due to numerical limitations relating to how the pricing algorithms are being implemented (which we can resolve by refining the algorithm implementation). For example, if pricing differences seem to be due to use of a finite sample size in a Monte Carlo simulation then the sample size can be increased.

However, if we do come up with a wide 'true' range of valuations then this may be indicative that there are few instruments we have identified in (a) actually similar to the one we are trying to value, or, even if they are similar, their prices are subject to significant uncertainties. We may need to reflect these uncertainties in wider assumed bid–offer spreads or the equivalent.

By the mindset override in (d) we mean a mindset that questions whether the pricing model being used is likely to reflect how traders and investors might actually view the instrument in question. For example, the instrument in question may have a specific characteristic that it shares with none of the deemed 'closely equivalent' instruments in (a). It might have some unusual type of embedded option. If that characteristic has a material impact on the value we might expect others to place on the instrument then no amount of interpolation or extrapolation purely from the instruments originally chosen in (a) will help quantify this part of its market consistent value. We must instead include within the set of instruments used for calibration purposes ones that do express these risks.

How does such an approach correspond with the hedgeable/non-hedgeable divide discussed in Chapter 2? We aim to deem *all* risks to be to some extent hedgeable using instruments for which market observable prices exist. To the extent that such hedging is imperfect we will come up with different answers due to differences in the 'prior' pricing models we might choose. The approach is again conceptually similar to the derivative pricing calibration approaches we considered in Sections 4.12 and 4.13. The valuer is forced to identify some underlying plausible ways of valuing the instrument in question. To the extent that there are market observables available that might guide in the selection of inputs into the pricing model, we calibrate the inputs to match such market observables. This leaves hopefully only a relatively modest contribution from the valuer's prior intrinsic beliefs about how the instrument 'ought' to be priced.

Thus the valuation is *as market consistent as is possible*. We accept that for some more exotic asset types it may not be as market consistent as we might like.

13.3.4   Assets that include risk exposures linked to the firm

Although relatively uncommon, it is possible for a firm to own assets that include exposure to itself, e.g. its own equity held in treasury. Such exposures will typically offset the protection that equity capital provides in relation to customer liabilities. Their market consistent valuations should therefore be calculated as the inverse of the market consistent value placed on a corresponding liability of the firm (e.g. its equity capital base), see Section 13.4. It should thus often be taken as nil in a solvency calculation.

13.3.5   Further comments

Implications for some of the more complicated instrument types that might be held in practice include the following:

(1) *Property or units in property (i.e. real estate) funds*

We do not typically think of property as particularly 'complex', even if it is widely understood to be illiquid, with each individual property having unique characteristics. Property is a very long established asset category whose vagaries are generally well understood.

These vagaries make valuation of property an art as well as a science. This does not diminish the importance or reliance that in practice we need to place on property valuations. Such assets can form significant elements of some institutional portfolios. However, it does mean that these valuations are typically treated with a healthy degree of caution. Investors understand that it can take a long time to sell any particular property, and that the realisation value may not necessarily then bear too much resemblance to the valuation a valuer may have placed on the property.

(2) *Private equity*

Financial firms may hold stakes in unquoted companies or in private equity or venture capital funds. Exposures such as these can often be difficult to value objectively. Nevertheless, current internationally recognised valuation guidelines, i.e. AFIC, BVCA and EVCA (2006), still mandate that investments 'should be reported at Fair Value at the reporting date', where Fair Value is defined as the 'amount for which an asset could be exchanged between knowledgeable, willing parties in an arm's length transaction'. These guidelines note that estimation of fair value doesn't assume that the underlying business could actually be sold, but instead aims to estimate the price at which hypothetical market participants would agree to transact. In the absence of an active market for an instrument, the guidelines require the valuer to apply a methodology that is appropriate in light of the nature, facts and circumstances of the investment and its materiality in the context of the total portfolio, using reasonable data and market inputs, assumptions and estimates.

We see that relative paucity of market data is not necessarily a bar to attempting to identify fair (i.e. market consistent) valuations. However, AFIC, BVCA and EVCA (2006) does contain a 'get-out'. It recognises that there may be situations where the range of reasonable fair value estimates could be significant, the probability and financial impact of achieving a key milestone cannot reasonably be predicted and there have been no recent transactions in the business. It recognises that in these situations the valuer may conclude that fair value cannot be reliably measured. In such situations, it indicates that the valuer may reasonably conclude that the most recent fair value estimate (the carrying value) remains the current best estimate, unless there is evidence that the investment has since then been impaired. In the case of impairment, the valuer is required to reduce the carrying value to reflect the estimated extent of impairment. But since in these circumstances fair value is deemed not capable of being reliably measured, estimation of the impact of the impairment will 'generally be an intuitive (rather than analytical) process and may involve reference to broad indicators of value change (such as relevant stock market indices)'. This is very much akin to the interpolation or extrapolation approaches referred to in Section 13.3.2.

It is also worth noting that specialist private equity companies and funds called 'secondaries' do now exist whose business model involves purchasing private equity exposures from other private equity investors. The prices at which they are prepared to transact may provide a further guide to the market consistent value to place on a private equity exposure.

(3) *Collateralised debt obligations (CDOs)*

The market consistent price of a tranche of a CDO depends on, amongst other things, the level of subordination of the tranche in question, the underlying credits themselves, how exposure to these credits is accessed (e.g. physical versus cash plus CDS) and how the underlying credits might change through time (and the impact of such changes on subordination in the structure). It also depends on factors such as the level of charges included in the structure. All other things being equal, if costs are $x\%$ pa rather than $y\%$ pa then the differential accumulated across the structure as a whole will end up being apportioned in some fashion across the overall ownership structure of the CDO.

The most common CDO pricing model involves the LHP pricing model, see Chapter 4. Inputs into this pricing model include risk-free rates, the term (i.e. tenor) of the structure, spreads on the underlying credits and so-called base correlations, which drive the apportionment of value across the capital structure, i.e. across the tranches.

We can derive market implied base correlations for tranches with different subordinations applicable to leading credit market indices, because tranches on these indices are also actively traded. However, the relevant CDS indices and CDS index tranches may have characteristics that are not shared by the particular CDO tranche we want to value, e.g. liquidity, mix of underlying names, means of access to these names, etc. If the CDO tranche we want to value is not itself actively traded then we should ideally seek to identify market prices for a range of other CDOs closer in nature to the one that we want to value and ideally define a pricing model (or at least a conceptual pricing framework) that includes aspects dependent on these characteristics.

The practical importance of such refinements would be lessened if traded market prices for CDOs in general seemed close to those derived merely from index tranche data. In practice, during the 2007–09 credit crisis, CDOs became less actively traded and there was considerable uncertainty in what might be their fair, i.e. market consistent, values.

(4) *Structured Investment Vehicles (SIVs)*

If valuing CDOs proved challenging during the 2007–09 credit crisis then some of the more complex mortgage-backed SIVs proved even more problematic. Conceptually, the same methodology can often be used as for CDOs except that their underlyings are not potentially tradable bonds or CDS but less tradable mortgages with individual borrowers. A very wide range of plausible correlation assumptions of the sort that need to be inserted into, say, an LHP pricing model can be justified on intrinsic criteria. To value these sorts of instruments in a market consistent fashion it is therefore particularly important to identify reference market prices for other SIVs or other similar instruments to identify suitable market implied assumptions to adopt.

Also problematic is identifying the right way to take account of the liquidity characteristics of such vehicles, particularly where they have funded longer-term loans to borrowers using shorter-term debt from investors (even when both have been floating rate in nature). Market implied valuations of such structures in principle need as an input a market implied view as to the 'value' of the 'liquidity' they are consuming. During the 2007–09 credit crisis liquidity was extremely expensive to access, as precipitous declines in some bank equity valuations (if not their subsequent rescues or outright defaults) demonstrated.

Perhaps investors (and the banking community more generally) placed undue confidence in the reliability of pricing models that had previously been developed to price CDOs and SIVs, and did not fully appreciate the inherent uncertainties involved in such valuations (or the importance of liquidity). Perhaps if these asset classes had been better established, like property and private equity, a more appropriately cautious view on the reliability of such valuations would have been more prevalent.

(5) *Strategic investments and subsidiaries*

Holding company balance sheets will typically include holdings in subsidiary companies or strategic investments in other companies. Wholly or mainly owned unquoted operating subsidiaries are usually consolidated into the overall group (although there may be additional capital that needs to be held within the subsidiary to meet local regulatory requirements). Both Basel II and Solvency II contain guidelines on how and when to consolidate such exposures.

It is less obvious what to do with subsidiaries where there is less clear ownership or control. In extreme cases firms have set up special purpose vehicles (SPVs) specifically to move exposures off-balance sheet. They may have then potentially limited their own power to control the SPV, to avoid the SPV meeting accounting rules that would then require them to be consolidated back onto the originating firm's balance sheet. However, such SPVs may not be quite so distant in practice from the originating firm. For example, the firm may have offered contingent liquidity lines or maintained reputational exposures. In stressed scenarios such SPV exposures can return onto the originating firm's own balance sheet (as indeed happened during the 2007–09 credit crisis).

In a fully market consistent world, such accounting-driven behaviours ought to be largely pointless, since the firm would need to include such contingent exposures whether such subsidiaries or SPV vehicles were or were not consolidated.[6]

Sometimes such investments are themselves quoted, in which case quoted prices might be used for accounting purposes. However, it is then worth bearing in mind the comments in Section 13.3.4. If partially owned subsidiaries are themselves regulated financial entities then presumably the market consistent valuations placed on these assets for solvency purposes should again mirror the corresponding treatment of the capital itself on the liability side of the balance sheet.

(6) Loans

Loans are very common types of asset for some types of financial services entities including banks. Some loans may be fixed term loans, conceptually similar to the issuance of debt by the borrower. Interest payments on such loans may be either fixed or floating in nature (and if floating can use various interest bases, e.g. Libor 3 month, Libor 6 month, OIS, . . .). Other loans may in theory be subject to instant recall and subject to variable interest rates (e.g. many types of overdraft). However, it may be reputationally impractical (and economically inefficient) for a firm to seek to recall most such loans at nil notice. Still others may be loan facilities, i.e. commitments to provide a loan on specified terms should the borrower so wish, in return for a specified premium.

The natural way to value any such instrument in a market consistent fashion is to discount the expected future cash flow (interest and principal), suitably adjusting for the market implied risk of default, for any options open to either the firm or the borrower and for (market implied) expense levels.

Most of the complications arise because of the wide range of options potentially open to both firm and borrower. For example, with traditional instant recall floating rate loans, the firm may have scope to increase the interest rate charged within wide limits, but the customer may also have the option to repay the loan. Whilst over the longer term we might expect banks to make money by advancing such loans (otherwise why would they be in that business?), this requires repeated non-exercise of the option to repay the loan by the borrower. It would be natural to require market consistent valuations for solvency purposes to assume rational exercise of options by borrowers, with deviation from such behaviour then accruing as profit over time.

Increasingly, it is also possible to trade loans in the secondary market.[7] If the economic value of the loan really has been transferred to someone else (and not merely settled into an

---

[6] According to Bank of England (2008c), contingent liquidity lines consumed no risk capital under Basel II, highlighting another weakness of Basel II.

[7] There are some subtleties in relation to trading of loans that are beyond the scope of this book, e.g. the typical need to ring-fence receipt of 'inside' information to avoid constraining what a fund management house responsible for managing the loan portfolio can legally do in other portfolios it manages (e.g. portfolios that might invest in the same name's equities or bonds). Investors in the secondary loan market also need to appreciate the potentially increased exposure to moral hazard since the originating bank may then have less incentive to vet loan origination carefully.

SPV from where it may return to the originating bank in stressed scenarios) then it would seem appropriate to crystallize the realised value of the loan on disposal.

(7) *Constant Proportional Portfolio Insurance (CPPI) and Constant Proportional Debt Obligation (CPDO) structures*

CPPI structures have been commonplace for many asset types for many years, although it is only more recently that they have become more common in the credit area. CPDOs are a more recent innovation principally used in the credit arena. In either case, part of the invested capital is in effect put into a 'risk-free' bond (which may actually be a zero coupon bond issued by a bank, so not free of that bank's credit risk). The remainder is then invested (normally in a leveraged fashion) in 'risky' assets. In the credit space the 'risky' portfolio might involve use of CDS, in the equity space it might involve exposure to market indices or to actively managed funds. With an actively managed CPPI structure, the aim is for the principal to be guaranteed at maturity with the goal being to maximise portfolio value at maturity. With a CPDO the target is excess return over the risk-free rate, subject to structure maintaining a suitably high credit rating (and implicitly therefore not actually defaulting).

Both structures include *gap risk* exposure, which in some cases may be retained by the structure itself but in other cases may be hedged by buying suitable gap risk protection from a bank or an insurer. This is because if the risky assets fall too far too rapidly the 'risky' pot can be completely exhausted. This is called a 'cash-out' event. Garcia *et al.* (2008) explain how the magnitude of the gap risk exposure is heavily dependent on the severity and possible frequency of 'large' jumps, i.e. price movements that occur too quickly to be effectively dynamically hedged against as per the Brownian motion stochastic calculus theory described in Chapter 4. This can also be seen from the cost of capital pricing model referred to in Section 4.5.2.

There are important differences between the gap risk exposures implicit in CPPIs and CPDOs. With a CPPI structure, typically if the 'risky' portfolio performs poorly then the floor becomes closer and the structure deleverages. Conversely, the aim of a CPDO strategy is to obtain a fixed prescribed return over the whole investment horizon. If the assets within the 'risky' component perform well then a CPDO can experience a 'cash-in' event, with risky positions being closed and the return to maturity becoming guaranteed (or the investment being returned to the investor). The structure deleverages as it approaches such an event. However, if the risky positions perform poorly then a CPDO becomes more and more leveraged, so it becomes more and more exposed to gap risk. If it falls too much then the structure suffers a cash-out event and its (now large) risky position is forcibly unwound, even if this occurs on disadvantageous terms. In such circumstances the structure may have ended up heavily exposed to forced unwind risk as described in Section 6.6.

Taking due account of gap risk, and, for CPDOs, forced unwind risk is therefore very important for such structures.

Principle P54: Where instruments do not trade on well-regulated and well-organised exchanges, and particularly where any OTC market in them is also limited, then greater usage of modelling and hence dependency on calibration may be necessary when preparing market consistent valuations. For more exotic instrument types it is particularly important to understand fully the risks being expressed by the instrument, since these risks may not be shared by more accessible market observables.

13.4 MARKET CONSISTENT LIABILITY VALUATIONS

13.4.1 Introduction

Market consistent *liability* valuations naturally need to reflect the nature of the liabilities in question, including their term to payment and any option-like elements. The term of the liabilities is naturally catered for via discounting using a suitable yield curve, as discussed in Chapters 4 and 5. Chapter 4 also explains how in principle to extend such valuations to include option-like features within the liabilities (e.g. for debt issued by a firm, any callability or putability elements, for insurance liabilities written by an insurer, any options available to the policyholder and/or the firm).

But what about *other* characteristics of the liabilities? Indeed, are there any other characteristics that ought to be taken into account? What do we mean by the 'nature' of any particular liability?

Perhaps the two most important additional characteristics that might be relevant here are the *credit risk* (i.e. the credit quality of the firm itself[8]) and the *liquidity risk* characteristics of the liability. The analysis of liquidity in Chapter 6 suggested that liquidity premia ought in principle to apply to liabilities as well as assets. But it was less obvious exactly what form (and of what magnitude) these premia might take, and how (if at all) they might correspond to liquidity premia applicable to assets that the entity might also hold.

The classic example of this in the context of insurance liabilities is the question of how to place a market consistent value on a life insurer's book of annuity liabilities. Annuity liabilities are typically viewed as highly illiquid (both in the sense that there is currently only a limited market for such books of business and because normally individual contracts once in payment cannot be unwound other than by reason of death of the policyholder). Even small differences in the discount rates used to value such liabilities will typically mount up given the relatively long-term nature of such liabilities.[9] Self-interest may then influence the choice of (and justification offered for) the particular approach a firm might wish to adopt, since the higher the yield curve used for this purpose, the lower will be the calculated liability value.

13.4.2 Sure promises from infinitely well-capitalised entities

Although we concluded in Section 2.8 that there was no single 'right' way to identify the market consistent value of a firm's liabilities, we also noted that a natural *special case* we might reasonably want to focus on was the situation where the liability was being incurred by an infinitely well-capitalised company, i.e. the special case where $s = 0$, where s is the market implied spread (versus risk-free) on the customer's liabilities.

---

[8] Some of the liabilities may come packaged with credit protection or other credit enhancement elements, e.g. explicit guarantees from third parties against the risk of default of the firm in question. It would seem appropriate to include these in the liability valuation. Conversely, regulation itself provides implicit guarantees from the state or from industry-wide investor protection schemes. Regulators are generally at pains to point out that firms should *not* assume in their business planning that they will be bailed out by such bodies (even if this might be what we might expect to happen in practice). Presumably, these types of 'guarantees' should *not* be included in liability valuations (for solvency purposes).

[9] This is, of course, only true if we do not also make a compensating adjustment to the probabilities that we assign to the different pay-offs that the liability might generate (away from risk-neutral probabilities).

We may further subdivide this special case into two separate sub-cases:

(1) *The customer liability may be 'illiquid'*

Consider first the situation where the customer liability is fully deterministic in nature (e.g. a known payment of 1 in a given currency in, say, 15 years' time). A sure promise to pay such a liability from an infinitely well-capitalised company would seem to be economically equivalent to a sure promise to pay the same liability from the body responsible for issuing that currency (typically, the government of the country in which the currency is legal tender), as long as the latter is also of undoubted creditworthiness. Any bid–offer spread and other liquidity characteristics might then be expected to mirror those of the corresponding (government) debt.

However, in Chapters 5 and 6 we noted that different government debt issues could potentially offer different yields, with on-the-run issues being more attractive for collateral purposes and therefore yielding less than off-the-run or non-benchmark issues that were less liquid. We characterised the differential in the form of a 'convenience' yield.

We should therefore expect such customer liabilities also to differentiate according to liquidity. In the case of an *illiquid* liability such as a deterministic set of annuity-like cash flows, and if government debt is deemed by the market to be of undoubted creditworthiness, then it would seem natural to value these using the best yield available from investing in government debt but foregoing its liquidity, which in Chapter 4 we argued was best identified with the (government debt) GC repo yield curve. For longer durations we argued that this might be best proxied in practice by reference to OIS rates, e.g. Sonia or Eonia, incorporating an adjustment if necessary if there were sound reasons for believing that OIS rates should diverge from GC repo rates or government bond yields more generally.[10] If government debt is not of undoubted creditworthiness then OIS rates would seem applicable even if they were below (assumed) GC repo rates, because the latter might then include a market implied allowance for sovereign default risk.

Customer liabilities are rarely so deterministic. For example, annuity liabilities in practice generally depend on the length of time that the policyholders in question might live for, i.e. they express longevity risk. Were longevity or mortality risk to be actively traded, we would expect the values of instruments expressing these risks to depend in part on views about uncertain future longevity or mortality rates. They would therefore in general be subject to bid–offer spreads, e.g. because there would be uncertainty in such levels which market makers trading in such markets would need to be recompensed for carrying (and costs involved in setting up, monitoring and trading such instruments, etc.). Annuity liability valuations also include an expense element related to the costs of administering the annuities, which again includes uncertainties.

In these circumstances, the way in which observed spreads depend on liquidity, as discussed in Section 6.5, takes centre stage. If we accept the proposition there that the 'correct' approach includes liquidity risk in a largely multiplicative fashion, via a relationship along the lines of $c_s = c_y + (c_d + c_u) \times (1 + l_m)$, then the correct discount rate to use is the same as in the deterministic case, as long as the longevity and expense elements are incorporated in the valuation in a risk-neutral fashion. The reason is simple. In the special case where $s = 0$, both c_d, the 'pure' credit default risk element, and c_u, the credit risk uncertainty element, are zero, so whatever value we choose to put on l_m it still has zero impact on the end answer.

---

[10] OIS might be above GC repo in the presence of strong systematic stresses that resulted in even overnight bank deposits being perceived to carry significant non-previsible default risk.

(2) *The customer liability may be 'liquid'*

Not all liabilities are illiquid like annuities, not even all insurance liabilities. Consider, for example, an investment in a pooled (i.e. unitised) fund or unit-linked life insurance contract in which the underlying assets are invested in relevant (liquid) government bonds, and customers can redeem on demand in all situations (other than when the government itself bars trading in its own bonds!). As far as the customer is concerned, liquidity of units in the pooled fund mirrors liquidity in the underlying government bonds themselves.

In such a situation, as we saw in Section 6.6, the natural way to value the fund's *liabilities* (to customers) in a market consistent manner is for the 'unit reserve' element of the liability valuation to mirror the asset valuation. It therefore involves *not* including a convenience yield uplift, on the grounds that the investment strategy being followed is *not* attempting to access this uplift (and thus *not* depleting the portfolio's liquidity) in relation to the customers in question.

Somewhat more challenging is the situation where the fund invests in less liquid instruments but units in the fund are still held out to customers as being liquid in nature. There can then be a mismatch between the liquidity characteristics of the customer liability (i.e. the units in the fund) and the liquidity characteristics of the underlying assets. Pooled funds may give the appearance of 'facilitating' or 'generating' additional liquidity, because unit holders may in normal circumstances be able to buy and sell units in the fund on demand even if it takes the fund longer to invest or liquidate corresponding underlying investments. However, in severe enough scenarios (e.g. large numbers of unit holders want to liquidate simultaneously), we cannot 'manufacture' liquidity merely via a pooling mechanism.

It is then important to understand whether the firm is in effect 'guaranteeing' liquidity, even when it cannot rely on the assets within the fund to provide this liquidity. Usually, firms limit their own exposure to such risks by including within policy or other governing documentation flexibility to defer redemptions, sometimes for very considerable periods of time. But if this flexibility is not present (or if reputationally it is not practical to exercise) then firms should arguably *increase* the magnitude of the customer liability they show within their balance sheet, to reflect the extra liquidity burden to which they themselves are then potentially exposed.

13.4.3   Uncertain promises from finitely capitalised entities

More complex is the finitely capitalised situation that would apply in practice. The spread applicable to the customer tranche will then in general depend both on how well capitalised the firm is and on the risk-neutral probabilities assigned to how different elements of the firm's balance sheet might co-move.

In a highly stylised sense, things simplify somewhat if the customer liability in question is fully deterministic. For a given value of s, the market consistent value of such a customer liability is then independent of the rest of the balance sheet structure. The point is that if we are given the right value to use for s then we do not then care how *other* market participants might view this s as being built up. In particular, we would not differentiate depending on the extent to which they view this spread as representing compensation for credit risk, illiquidity risk or any other sort of risk.

However, this hasn't eliminated the issue, merely moved it elsewhere. Someone still needs to decide what s to target. This might be the regulator (for regulatory solvency purposes) or it might be the business itself when carrying out an individual capital adequacy assessment (see Chapter 8). When doing so, presumably the main focus ought to be on how the *customer* views the liability in question. As far as the customer is concerned, for a fully deterministic pay-off, the spread, s, measures the differential between how valuable the pay-off is to him or her if supplied by the company in question versus how valuable it would be if supplied by an infinitely well-capitalised company.

Even in the fully deterministic case, the market consistent value for a contract with a finitely capitalised firm may also depend in part on the liquidity characteristics of the liabilities, for the same sorts of reasons as were explored in Section 13.4.2, if the way in which s is set exogenously depends in part on the liquidity characteristics of the liabilities. All other things being equal, a contract that a customer can cash in on demand (for a value in line with its market consistent value) ought to be worth 'more' to the customer than one where the customer is locked in with no such possibility of early redemption, because of the greater (liquidity) flexibility it provides. However, firms may in practice have wide flexibility to set *cash-in* (i.e. *surrender*) values as they choose fit. If firms adjust surrender values to reflect illiquidity otherwise implicit in the original liability then any illiquidity premium uplift as far as the customer is concerned is negated, so it should not need to be included in the market consistent value that the firm places on these liabilities.

13.4.4 The solvency put option

The finitely capitalised case described in Section 13.4.3 has the possibly counter-intuitive feature that the market consistent value of the liabilities depends on the assets (and other liabilities) present within the firm's balance sheet. In an insurance context, this appears to fly in the face of modern actuarial thought, which argues that the market consistent value of a liability should not depend on how it is funded, but on what the liability involves. The solution to this paradox is that the value placed on the liability then includes a deduction relating to the so-called solvency put option, see Chapter 2. As we noted there, it is generally unhelpful to include the impact of the solvency put option in regulatory capital computations, because what we are trying to do in a solvency capital computation is to figure out how much capital a firm needs to hold to avoid having to exercise this option. This is simply another way of saying that the natural way to calculate technical reserves for insurance liabilities is to value them in the $s = 0$ manner set out in Section 13.4.2, and for any additional capital add-ons required to demonstrate solvency to be set at levels that deliver whatever the regulator sets as a suitable value for s.

A corollary that does not seem to be well covered in the literature is that the solvency add-on included in capital adequacy calculations on top of the base liability valuation can in principle be negative, if the assets and liabilities are closely enough matched and the risk-neutral likelihood of the customer not receiving his due is low enough. One possible reason in systemically stressed circumstances for not using $s = 0$ when determining the 'base' liability valuation is that explicit appearance of a negative solvency add-on may not facilitate orderly maintenance of customer confidence. Regulators and governments may place a high priority on maintenance of such confidence in systemically stressed scenarios, see Chapter 11.

13.4.5 Bid and offer prices

A corollary of the above is that the market consistent value of an asset or liability should in general be struck at its mid-market value. By mid-market we here mean a notional willing buyer/willing seller 'fair' value (less or plus any applicable taxes or other legally imposed transaction costs). The reason is that an infinitely well-capitalised entity can wait indefinitely until the other side of such a notional transaction materialises.

Whilst this may match some current accounting treatments, it is less obviously consistent with typical current regulatory solvency practices. These often mandate use of entry or exit values depending on whether the exposure is a liability or an asset, i.e. they mandate use of whichever is the prudent side of any applicable bid–offer spread. Current regulatory treatment does, however, typically seem to recognise the relevance of the marginal transaction for valuation purposes, i.e. there is no perceived direct need to be able to offload or hedge *all* the liabilities at the stated price(s).

Of course, transaction costs haven't actually disappeared within this formulation. Instead, they end up in the computation of the solvency capital add-on, see Section 13.6. However, they may perhaps be mitigated there if the firm is very well capitalised and hence really able to wait a while for relatively opportune times to trade.

13.4.6 Annuities

We have already explored the cash flow and liquidity aspects of annuity type liabilities in some detail above. In addition, the market consistent values placed on these liabilities will depend on future mortality behaviour and future expense levels.

A market consistent treatment of mortality would reflect the merits of pooling of mortality experience that can be expected to apply to an entire annuity book. However, annuity books are also exposed to *systemic* changes in longevity (e.g. advances in medical treatment that result in improved longevity for wide swathes of the population, or conversely the possibility of pandemics and the like). There are also well-known selection effects, e.g. the larger the annuity, the wealthier typically is the annuitant, and wealthy individuals typically have longer life expectancies than less wealthy individuals.

There is uncertainty in the future evolution of these systemic exposures. This uncertainty means that whatever forecasting techniques *we* might apply to estimate such outcomes, others may have different views.

The market consistent valuation of such risks should ideally focus on *market implied* estimates of such future systemic factors, not our own subjective assessments. We might identify such market implied views either by reference to longevity swaps or from the cost of transferring away such risks using reinsurance. The reinsurance 'market' does not necessarily operate in exactly the same way as markets in, say, listed equities or bonds (e.g. it may be more bespoke and less transparent) but is still a 'market' within the definition used elsewhere in this book.

If reinsurance market prices are being used to source market implied mortality or longevity data then it should be noted that these prices may partly reflect the credit risk characteristics of the reinsurer (if the reinsurance arrangement does not mitigate these risks through, say, collateralisation mechanisms). They may also include service or expense elements (e.g. the reinsurer might also administer the payments to annuitants). It is necessary to strip out such contributions to premium rates when deriving market implied mortality rates for customer liabilities, unless, for example, the customers themselves somehow carry the exposure to the risk of the reinsurer defaulting.[11]

---

[11] This situation can arise within unit-linked arrangements reinsured into another insurer's fund, but is unlikely to be applicable for annuity business.

However, even if we can extract market implied mortality or longevity data from such markets, we are still likely to need to take into account idiosyncratic characteristics of the firm's own annuity book. For example, price data available from longevity swaps might most readily apply to the longevity of the general populace. But a firm's annuitant book will be skewed away from the general populace (e.g. it may include typically wealthier individuals). We should not merely use the market implied data applicable to the general populace. Instead we should include an adjustment reflecting the differential membership base.

Again, we see that we need to create a 'pricing model' that is dependent partly on market implied data and partly on our own subjective views (the latter here influencing how much lighter we think mortality should be for the annuitants actually present in the firm's annuity book versus those to whom available market implied data relates).

Expenses present another interesting challenge in insurance liability valuations. Annuities present perhaps a relatively straightforward example where the servicing requirements (and timescales involved) may be relatively predictable (at least for the book of business as a whole). However, usually there will be uncertainty in the future cost of delivering such services. Whilst some administration providers might be prepared to provide long-term cost quotes for such activities, we are likely to find identifying truly representative *market implied* data on expense levels challenging at best. As with private equity, etc., valuers are likely to need to fall back onto more general reasoning. Often such expenses relate principally to activities the firm itself undertakes. An advantage of price benchmarking exercises is that they may show whether these costs are likely to be systematically higher or lower than market rates. Such factors might then be incorporated as adjustments on top of any data that might be available on market implied expense levels, to the extent that the firm is locked into cost structures differing from prevailing market levels.

13.4.7   Unit-linked life insurance

We have also covered unit-linked life insurance in some detail previously, including liquidity aspects of such contracts. If such policies carry other sorts of customer options or guarantees (e.g. surrender or maturity guarantees, or in the case of pension contracts, options to convert into an annuity on guaranteed terms) then the impact of these guarantees should be included in a market consistent fashion bearing in mind market observables such as (long-dated) equity or interest rate volatility.[12]

Where such guarantees are not present the bulk of the non-unit element of the market consistent value of the contract is likely to be expense related. In more traditional methods of reserving for unit-linked contracts this shows up as an expense overrun reserve. Again, it is likely to prove challenging to identify suitable market implied estimates of the value of future expenses being borne by such policies. However, one incidental benefit of trying to rise to such a challenge is that it may lead to a better appreciation of the uncertainties and hence risks involved in different types of product design. This may in turn lead to better and more customer focused policy design. For example, Kemp (2005) questions whether customers always really value the enforced 'long-term-ness' of typical life insurance contracts used for DC pension scheme provision in the UK, when in other countries equivalent provision may involve direct

---

[12] When market consistent pricing includes implied volatility inputs then it is worth bearing in mind the potential relevance of the volatility skew on what implied volatility to use, see Section 4.9.

investment in mutual funds (e.g. 401(k) schemes in the USA), which may expose providers to less risk of expense overruns.

13.4.8   With-profits (i.e. participating) business

With-profits business (called 'participating' in some jurisdictions) is a type of contract that is relatively rare outside the insurance industry. With such policies, the customer receives payouts that depend, in part, on the investment performance of the assets backing the customer's liabilities, but not with the direct one-to-one link applicable with a unit-linked contract. Usually, payouts to policyholders are 'smoothed'.

We can characterise such a contract as consisting of a 'contractual' element and a 'discretionary' element.

The 'contractual' element can, at a high level, be represented in either of two equivalent ways:

(a) An asset share element (i.e. what the assets underlying the policy and within the with-profit fund have accumulated to) subject to some minimum sum assured (the 'put option' representation); or
(b) A guaranteed benefit plus some market upside (the 'call option' representation).

The 'discretionary' element relates to the smoothing algorithm by which asset (and potentially other) types of returns are apportioned between policyholders (and between them in aggregate and the firm itself). Traditional forms of with-profits contracts typically implement this smoothing via the declaration through time of bonuses, which increase the guaranteed benefits (or in viewpoint (a) the minimum underpins). More recently, unitised with-profits policy designs have been developed, in which the smoothing is implemented via a mechanism akin to the unit-price used in a unit-linked contract. There are further subtleties in practice, e.g. regular rather than single premiums, exposure to mortality and lapses, and the existence of 'market value adjustments' (MVAs) that might be applied to surrender values but might not be applied on certain policy anniversaries, etc.

As we might expect, the market consistent valuation of the guaranteed element of such liabilities should be independent of the representation adopted, because of put–call parity. Conceptually, the methodology is similar to that used for unit-linked liabilities. However, an important additional complication is how to model appropriately the way in which the firm might exercise its discretions under the policy, in particular its discretion over how to 'smooth' policyholder payouts.

This task is complicated because superimposed on the 'contractual' liabilities described above are those that we might consider arise from the need to *treat customers fairly* (TCF). Several jurisdictions including the UK incorporate this concept as an explicit regulatory principle within their regulatory framework. This issue arises because the market consistent value of the customer liability depends in part on how the insurer might operate the with-profits fund and the bonus smoothing mechanisms.

For example, in the UK, insurers now need to issue statements called their *Principles and Practices of Financial Management* (PPFM) setting out how their with-profits funds are to be managed. They need to appoint a separate *with-profits actuary* to look after the interests of the with-profits policyholders. The with-profits actuary cannot have certain other roles within the insurer deemed likely to lead to potential or actual conflicts of interest. One aim of a PPFM is to define more precisely how an insurer's discretion in computing the asset share algorithm is likely to be exercised and what in practice treating customers fairly might mean. This has obvious attractions to the regulator in an era when transparency is seen to be desirable.

Within such a framework, the shareholder provides a solvency underpin (or policy guarantee), implicitly or explicitly receiving payment for doing so via a future profit stream. This might be wrapped up in a 90:10 type profit subdivision (in which 90 % of profits accrue to policyholders and 10 % to shareholders), or in some cases the firm might levy an explicit charge on the fund to defray part of these costs.[13]

How PPFMs or the like are worded, and hence the extent of discretion a firm has, is thus an important factor in the market consistent valuation of such liabilities. Kemp (2005) notes that a market consistent perspective highlights the lack of commonality of interest between shareholders and policyholders as far as the underpin is concerned. What in this respect is a liability to the shareholder is an equal and opposite asset to policyholders! Shareholders will ideally want the fund to use whatever flexibility is available to minimise the value of this underpin, whilst policyholders will ideally want the fund to do the opposite. New business marketing pressures could create greater commonality of purpose (at least for those with-profits funds that remain open). Greater commonality of interest should also exist within a mutual company where shareholders and with-profits policyholders may be the same individuals (although not necessarily in the same proportions). However, Kemp (2005) still thought it more likely that PPFMs would over time *cease to describe* how funds might exercise discretion and would instead over time come to describe how funds would *not* exercise discretion, defining in ever greater detail exactly how the asset shares would be invested.

In the special case where the business is a mutual, one of the 'assets' backing these liabilities may be the net worth of the business as a going concern (including profits arising on future contracts sold). With a mutual, it is perhaps easiest to subdivide notionally the 'overall' customer liability into two parts. The first would relate to the ownership of the underlying business ascribed to certain policyholders because it is a mutual (i.e. the shareholder perspective). The second would relate to everything else (i.e. the customer perspective that would apply were the firm to be a proprietary company).

13.4.9 Other non-profit non-linked life insurance

There are three main types of life insurance – with-profit (called in some jurisdictions 'participating'), unit-linked and non-profit. Usually, but not always, non-profit life contracts are 'long term', in the sense that they can extend for a considerable length of time.[14] They may include a material savings element, although it is perhaps more common for them to focus on protection, e.g. protection against death or disability. Examples include annuities (which we have covered already), term life assurance and disability cover.

Market consistent valuations for these types of liabilities should proceed in much the same way as for annuities (or for with-profit or unit-linked contracts, but stripping out the dependency such policies have on the behaviour of their backing assets). Incorporation of expenses is again likely to prove problematic. It will again typically be necessary to blend market implied

---

[13] Shareholders can also in some instances receive 'special' profit distributions, e.g. if the fund builds up an 'orphan' estate that is surplus to the needs of existing policyholders and future policyholders and comes to an agreement with existing policyholders over how it should be distributed.

[14] Life insurance is necessarily legally 'long term' in many countries, but this can end up as a tautological definition because 'long-term' insurance may then be defined to mean the types of insurance that life insurers can write.

data with judgement in deciding how applicable any available market implied data is to any particular liability type. Some information on market implied mortality or morbidity rates may be available from the prices of relevant mortality derivatives to the extent that they exist (or from other capital markets instruments that express such risks), or from reinsurance prices.

The theory we have advanced above would indicate that we should assume rational policyholder behaviour, and avoid taking credit for future profit margins which do not relate to contractual obligations on the part of policyholders. Thus for recurrent single premium policies (i.e. where the policyholder can contribute extra to the policy but is not obliged to do so) we should ignore future premiums if it would be prudent to do so.[15] This is not necessarily in accordance with current actuarial practice, which might allow prudent but not nil future contributions if the relevant policyholder seems likely to continue to contribute. The policyholder has presumably not elected to exercise his or her option to stop paying in the past when presumably it would also have been 'rational' to do so. A pragmatic approach might be simply to separate out any value assumed from such non-contractual future premiums. More theoretically elegant, but potentially more complicated, would be for this nicety to be taken into account in the solvency add-on calculation, see Section 13.6.11, since presumably we can expect policyholders to reappraise what constitutes 'rational' behaviour in the sorts of stressed scenarios that might lead them to question the continuing viability of the insurer.

13.4.10   Non-life (i.e. property/casualty) insurance

In principle, market consistent valuation of non-life (i.e. property/casualty) insurance should proceed in a manner similar to that for non-profit life insurance. Sometimes such contracts include an element of premium rating, which in this context can be handled in a manner akin to that described above for with-profits life insurance.

Challenges include the wide range of possible future claims experience that can arise with some types of property/casuality business lines. If the range of possible outcomes is too wide then we may need to fall back on approaches akin to those used for private equity, in the sense of being unable in practice to take much account of market observables. Usually, however, actuaries and other experts can predict within some appropriate confidence interval likely future claims developments using standard reserving techniques, see e.g. Kemp (2009). Early on in the life of the contract there may be too little data for this to be practical and such reserves are then often established principally by reference to premiums charged for the relevant cover.[16]

Some types of non-life business are very short term, and hence excessive focus on exactly what yield curve to use may not be terribly relevant. Others (e.g. medical malpractice) can involve claims emerging over much longer periods of time. Taking due account of the time value of money, i.e. discounting, as well as potential future claims inflation then becomes more important.

---

[15] We would not, for example, expect to value in a market consistent fashion for solvency purposes a bank deposit on the basis that the depositor might in future add extra sums to the account merely because he or she might have done so regularly in the past. The two sets of events would not be considered sufficiently proximate in nature, even if we might find that in practice there is some correlation between past and future behaviour of any specific depositor.

[16] In a limited sense, such reserving techniques are still 'market consistent', because we have referred back to market prices at which the relevant trade occurred. But more market consistent would be to adjust these premium rate derived reserves by any known industry trends between policy inception and valuation point, as per the private equity situation.

Market consistency can (or at least ought) to turn up in a wide variety of contexts within the non-life insurance market. For example, syndicates at Lloyd's of London have traditionally not had the same underlying members across all years.[17] However, to allow an old syndicate year's accounts to be closed after, say, its third year of life, it has been common for its residual liabilities on closure to be sold on to a newer year's open book, in return for a *reinsurance-to-close premium* paid from one syndicate year to another. The amount of this premium needs to be certified by the syndicate actuary. The transfer is between two potentially different groups of individuals. Principle P7 would therefore imply that the premium should be set in a manner that the actuary believes represents a fair, i.e. market consistent, value as far as both parties are concerned.

13.4.11   Bank deposits

Bank deposits are often quite short term in nature, in which case some of the complications arising when identifying long-term discount rates fall away. Conversely, banks can have highly leveraged balance sheets, so even relatively modest differentials can have a significant impact on a bank's net asset position.

The market consistent value placed on an instant access account would normally be its face value plus any accrued interest not yet explicitly credited to the account, given the discretion that the depositor has to withdraw on demand. For pure term deposits involving fixed interest rates, it should reflect the present value of sure payments corresponding to the contractual commitments the bank has entered into with the customer in relation to the deposit. For more complex deposits, e.g. ones paying rates with minimum guarantees, the guarantees should be valued appropriately using option pricing theory as exemplified in Chapter 4, and the liabilities adjusted accordingly.

13.5   MARKET CONSISTENT EMBEDDED VALUES

Whatever their purpose, market consistent valuations involve a blending together of the valuer's 'prior' beliefs about likely future idiosyncratic experience with market implied views about market-wide experience, to the extent that the latter are observable via market prices.

However, there are several ways in which calculations used to derive market consistent *embedded values* are likely to differ from computations that concentrate on regulatory solvency. A key rationale behind companies preparing and publishing market consistent embedded values is to make it more practical for shareholders and analysts to compare and contrast the likely value of future profit margins on existing business across different companies and different management teams. Embedded values are, we might argue, principally shareholder focused rather than regulator/customer focused. This has a number of consequences:

(a) Shareholders value (or ought to value!) the shareholder put option, i.e. the limitation on their downside loss available by arranging for the company to default on its obligations. It is therefore difficult to come up with strong theoretical arguments *if the purpose of the valuation is to derive an embedded value* for placing zero value on this option, and hence to mandate use of yield curves to value customer liabilities that incorporate a zero spread

---

[17] More recently, ownership of Lloyd's syndicates has become more focused on corporates rather than individuals, and there is now less differentiation in ownership across syndicate years.

versus risk-free. Instead, it may be more appropriate to use a *standardised* spread (maybe fixed, maybe driven by the spread expressed by a standard yield benchmark such as Libor swap rates, etc.), perhaps set centrally by relevant accounting or actuarial standards setters.

(b) On the going concern basis implicit in an embedded value computation, it is unlikely to be appropriate to include as strong an emphasis on rational customer behaviour as might be the case for solvency purposes. In a distressed situation, customers may seek to take maximum advantage of whatever options are available to them to mitigate financial consequences to themselves. For example, we might need to take account of the possibility that there might be mass early lapse, or mass selective early lapse by customers best able to broker alternative arrangements, with such customers typically being the ones likely to be most profitable in the future to the firm in question if they did not lapse. In more normal circumstances, other elements of the business relationship may be deemed more important by customers (or they may be governed by other customer attributes like inertia).[18]

An extreme example of (b) would be a customer base where contracts can in principle be terminated or varied at little or no notice by either customers or the firm, e.g. instant access bank accounts, holdings in asset managers' pooled funds and some types of unit-linked life insurance. For regulatory solvency purposes, market consistent values for these liabilities should arguably closely match the market value of the accrued holdings within such accounts, since in a distressed situation customers might very well walk away en masse. But for embedded value rather than solvency purposes, such an approach is likely to be an unduly pessimistic way of valuing the customer relationships involved and the probable persistency of future profit margins arising on such customer accounts. We wouldn't expect all customers in the ordinary course of events to terminate their contracts.

More to the point, it is precisely the value of this discretionary persistency that we are trying to capture within an embedded value computation. If it isn't captured within whatever methodology we adopt for embedded value purposes then shareholders and analysts will presumably still want it assessed somehow or other, since it is a core part of the overall value of the firm.

So we see that market consistent embedded values are necessarily only *partly* market consistent. Full market consistency should ideally apply to any elements outside the control or influence of either the existing customer base or the firm. But there is no obvious way of clearly identifying in an embedded value context exactly what assumptions we should make about discretionary elements that are within the control or influence of the customer base or firm. These assumptions will ultimately need to be mandated by whatever body is promoting the relevant embedded value methodology standards.[19]

---

[18] Kent and Morgan (2008) explore further the significant impact that 'dynamic' policyholder behaviour can have on life insurance liabilities (i.e. behaviour that can reasonably be expected to vary according to underlying market or other factors that have other impacts on the liabilities). For example, they explore the substantial impact that dynamic policyholder lapse behaviour can have on the time value of options and guarantees (TVOG) element of a market consistent embedded value (MCEV) computation for life insurance policies that include guaranteed surrender value elements, if these elements are derived from roll-up of premiums paid at some predefined rate of interest. Policyholders might reasonably on average be expected to lapse such policies more (or less) frequently when prevailing interest rates were higher (or lower) than the guaranteed rate of interest used to calculate these guaranteed surrender values.

[19] Another example of the need for assumptions when calculating embedded values can be seen by exploring the logic behind the common approach of having embedded valuations merely apply to *existing* customer contracts. Implicit in such an assumption is that a customer relationship not yet in existence would only come into existence if it is rational for both the customers and the firm to choose for them to do so, and so should be given a zero value

> **Principle P55: Market consistent liability valuations applicable to embedded value calculations will in general not be the same as those applicable to regulatory solvency computations, because the two purposes differ. In particular, the assumptions we should adopt about customer behaviour in the 'normal' scenarios most appropriate to embedded value computations may not be appropriate to assume in the 'stressed' scenarios more applicable to regulatory solvency computations.**

13.6   SOLVENCY ADD-ONS

13.6.1   Introduction

Current solvency capital computations split the task of working out the size of the asset base that a firm needs to hold into two parts:

(a) A value placed on the liabilities; and
(b) An additional capital requirement on top of these liability valuations.

Solvency II is a good example of this approach. Companies are required to have a (market consistent) value of assets minus liablities at least equal to the SCR, if they are not to have to specify in detail to the regulator how they are going to address an inadequate solvency position. If the value of assets minus liabilities falls below a lower hurdle, the MCR, then the regulator can take control of the firm and force it to address its solvency position (if possible).

However, ultimately, the slicing up of the capital requirements into these two parts is arguably somewhat artificial. We could be more prudent in (a) but unwind this prudence in (b) or vice versa.

13.6.2   Current methodologies

In the less than fully market consistent world in which we currently live, the split between 'base' valuation and solvency add-on may not be quite so irrelevant. This is hinted at in Frankland *et al.* (2008). They indicate that in practice regulatory capital computations (including ICA type computations) typically involve:

(a) Computation of a 'base' value for the firm's assets and liabilities;
(b) Computation of the impact of 'shocking' these base values by applying specified 'stresses' catering for the different ways in which factors influencing the firm might move. For example, one such stress test might involve an equity market decline (or rise, if this was more detrimental) of some specified percentage, perhaps believed to correspond to a movement that might be expected to occur only once in 200 years. Another might refer to an adverse movement in interest rates. Other tests might try to capture adverse outcomes relating to expense or insurance risks, etc.; and
(c) Combination of these stress tests via some assumed non-unitary correlation matrix which assumes that the chosen stress scenarios do not all occur at once.

---

until they do actually come into existence. However, brands have a value, even if, for brand value actually to be realised, customers must of their own volition choose that brand over any other. Hence, there is some arbitrariness in this assumption, since we are assuming favourable discretionary behaviour (from the firm's perspective) by existing customers but not by new customers, even though in some cases they may be the same individuals!

With such a methodology, the subdivision between what is base and what is add-on can have some impact on the overall answer, if the correlation matrix is not adjusted accordingly.

13.6.3   Full market consistency

Astute readers will have spotted that if it is the *sum* of the base valuation and the solvency add-on that is ultimately all important then detailed prescriptions on how to identify market consistent base valuations such as set out in Sections 13.3 and 13.4 may merely have moved all the complicated issues into the problem of how to calculate market consistent solvency add-ons.

In a sense there is some truth in such an observation. For example, in Section 13.4.5 we concluded that we should in principle be using mid prices in the base valuations, but this did not mean that we would ultimately end up ignoring bid–offer spreads, merely that we knew that we would have to tackle them somehow within the solvency add-on component.

But in a sense such pessimism is overdone. The methodologies currently being mandated for deriving solvency add-ons in Solvency II (and, perhaps to a lesser extent, in Basel II) are supposed to be aiming to identify a 'real world' VaR-type risk measure for the firm as a whole incorporating all of the risks to which the firm's (existing) business is exposed. Full market consistency applied to the solvency add-on is no different in principle to the shift from a 'real world' VaR to a 'risk-neutral' expected shortfall that is described in more detail in Section 10.3.

Moreover, as we have stressed before, application of market consistency in practice involves a blend of the valuer's own 'prior' views about what might happen (and the prices he or she would expect to apply to the purchase of protection against such risks) alongside market observed prices for instruments that express the same underlying risks. So, current methodologies as set out in Section 13.6.2, if they adopt appropriate stress tests and correlations, are in an artificial sense 'market consistent' in the limiting case where we have *no* market observables available with which to calibrate our 'prior' intrinsic beliefs about the fair market prices for such risks.[20]

However, there are likely to be subtleties in practice when trying to apply market consistency to the solvency add-on component, some of which we explore further below, following loosely the ordering of risks to which different financial firms might be exposed as set out in Section 1.5.

13.6.4   Correlations

Identifying suitable assumptions to make regarding correlations is one of the major challenges that actuaries and others come across when trying to prepare ICAs or internal models under current regulatory solvency regimes. It can therefore be expected to be a major challenge with the Solvency II ORSA. If we adopt an approach akin to that described in Section 13.6.2 then the 'default' assumption that all risks occur simultaneously can be expected to be overly prudent (if the individual stress levels are set appropriately).[21] What in practice has happened is that

---

[20] We assume here that the valuer's intrinsic belief is that in the absence of any data to the contrary, the (hypothetical market's) risk-neutral probability distributions match his or her own assumed 'real world' probability distributions.

[21] Regulators, when trying to identify suitable 'standardised' regulatory capital computations within current regulatory frameworks, face the same kind of challenge. However, there is less disincentive on them not just to choose an overly prudent default approach. Doing so provides a capital incentive on regulated firms to explore more sophisticated approaches, which one hopes will lead to better risk management overall.

firms have sought to use relatively low levels of correlation, resulting in significant credit for diversification benefits. Regulators have then sought to rebut some of these assumptions, on the grounds that in stressed situations correlations have a habit of being higher than one might like.

Market consistent calibration of such correlation effects arguably supports the regulators here. The correlation assumptions used in, say, the LHP pricing algorithm for CDOs do not have quite the same meaning as is typically placed on correlation in current ICA style computations. However, there is a broad correspondence. During the 2007–09 credit crisis, the market implied (base) correlations applicable to more senior parts of the capital structures of CDOs and SIVs rose to high levels, indicating that their pricing did assume a high degree of correlation between the underlying risks within these portfolios in extreme scenarios. The risks run by such structures are mainly credit risks and are thus not likely to be as well diversified as those run by most banks or insurance companies. However, such data still support the thesis that market-implied correlations tend to trend up strongly in scenarios where there is an overriding loss of risk appetite across multiple markets simultaneously.

13.6.5   Equity market and yield curve movements (market risk)

Market risk can be particularly important for some types of financial service firms, including life insurers and pension funds. Frankland *et al.* (2008) concentrate on methodologies that might be used to identify suitable 99.5 percentile 1 year 'real world' stress tests for such risk exposures.

These can be converted into 'market consistent' stress test levels by reference to equity and interest rate implied volatilities. Longer-term implied volatilities on such factors are materially more stable than those for shorter durations. They are accessible from markets in exchange traded equity index options, variance swaps or longer-dated OTC equity index options (for equity implied volatilities) or from swaptions or interest rate caps, collars or floors (for interest rate implied volatility).

13.6.6   Credit risk

There are two main ways in which a market consistent approach to computation of solvency add-ons is likely to differ from current regulatory capital frameworks:

(a) As we have previously noted, current regulatory capital frameworks place considerable emphasis on credit ratings, which are the subjective views of certain parties about the likely future creditworthiness of a business. Whilst credit ratings are often sourced from third party credit rating agencies, this does not make them truly 'objective'. Rather, they are still subjective, in the sense that they represent someone's opinions; it is just that this subjectivity isn't the firm's own. So, greater focus on market consistency here should, as we noted in Chapter 10, lead to greater focus on credit spreads rather than credit ratings.

(b) Credit risk shares some of the characteristics of mortality risk – indeed, it relates to the 'mortality' of companies, rather than of individuals. By this we mean that pooling of exposures to different credits does achieve diversification, but only so far. There are systemic exposures (to the credit cycle, to the economy at large, to forced unwind risk, to liquidity spirals, etc.) that can be expected to influence many parts of the credit market simultaneously, as the world found to its cost during the 2007–09 credit crisis. Such exposures are far more difficult to diversify away, other than by avoiding them altogether (or going short!). As we have noted above, market implied views on the lack of diversification a credit portfolio may exhibit in the tail of the distribution is accessible through prices of senior CDO tranches and the like, and in distressed times can be very high.

13.6.7   Liquidity risk

Liquidity risk is perhaps the risk type least well catered for within current regulatory solvency capital computations, except maybe more recently in relation to stress testing. This will most probably change as soon as there is greater clarity over how best to cater for it in such computations, particularly for banks who appear to have greater exposure to liquidity risk than many other types of financial firms. A big challenge is that liquidity risk appears to be very closely linked to credit risk for such firms.

It can be argued that in a fully market consistent context we don't much care about how an instrument's credit spread is built up between the premium for, say, pure default risk, the premium for uncertainty in how large this default risk might be at any particular point in time, and the premium relating to the liquidity or lack thereof in the instrument in question. All the components are wrapped up in the spread and that is the only thing that is observable.

However, this ignores the point that for solvency add-ons we are in essence trying to work out the plausible extent to which liquidity might get worse and the corresponding implications on instrument valuation.[22]

The prices of some of the instruments such as SIVs that proved so problematic during the 2007–09 credit crisis could potentially provide market observable data on liquidity risk. The challenge is how to interpret the severe liquidity difficulties and hence the price write-downs faced by these entities in the context of other firms facing other types of liquidity risk. Probably, as with credit risk, there are instrument-specific aspects, where there may be little if any read-over, but experience during the 2007–09 credit crunch also highlighted the existence of more systemic aspects, for which such price data should be more relevant. Valuers will again have to use judgement in assessing how much read-over there is to the task that they themselves are carrying out.

13.6.8   Bid–offer spreads

A specific angle to liquidity risk is that of bid–offer spreads. In practice, firms when dealing in size (but not very large size) will often be able to deal using program trades that may come inside usually quoted bid–offer spreads, but they may also suffer 'hidden' additional bid–offer spreads in the form of market impact and the like.

What is ideally needed here is a model of how and when the firm might need liquidity and of the bid–offer spread conditions that might apply at these times, to which we then apply risk-neutral probabilities to the various trajectories that these (and other aspects of the firm) might take. Exposure to uncertain bid–offer spreads is generic to most or all financial entities, so one would expect some data on this topic to be available from pricing of many different types of instrument.

---

[22] More generally, we are interested in the joint behaviour characterising both changes in liquidity and changes in other factors that might influence portfolios.

13.6.9   Expense risk

We noted in Section 13.4 that it was likely to be tricky to identify market observables that would help us calibrate these elements of liability valuations. The same will be true for equivalent elements of the solvency add-on computation.[23]

13.6.10   Systemic mortality and longevity risks (insurance risk)

Some mortality and longevity trades or reinsurance arrangements are structured as 'excess-of-loss' arrangements. In these arrangements, claim payments occur only if the mortality or longevity experience deteriorates (as far as the ceding company is concerned) by more than a pre-specified amount. These sorts of trades can be viewed as options on an underlying that is linked to a suitable mortality or longevity index. It should therefore be possible to use them to estimate market implied volatilities for mortality or longevity risk.

13.6.11   Other demographic risks

The profitability of many types of financial products, including many types of insurance policies, depends heavily on customer persistency. As explained earlier, for the 'base' liability valuation it would seem appropriate in a market consistent context to assume no future contributions to an insurance policy unless the policyholder was contractually obliged to make such contributions. However, we have also concluded that for embedded value computations such an approach would often be overly prudent, particularly if the policy might reasonably be expected to receive additional contributions in 'normal' circumstances. For example, it might be a DC policy technically structured as a recurrent single premium contract, but most probably going to receive new contributions, at least for some time, whilst the policyholder remains in a given employment.

With any practical solvency add-on, we are not seeking absolute certainty (because we are interested in establishing a value for s which will be greater than 0 for any practical regulatory regime). Thus we will inevitably fall into the grey area between 'infinitely bad' and 'normality'. In such circumstances it may be overly prudent to assume absolutely no new contributions when policy characteristics are strongly suggestive that there will be future contributions. Conversely, the same arguments as we advanced in Sections 13.6.4, 13.6.6 and 13.6.7 would suggest that the market implied view on such matters may be substantially more prudent than we might otherwise expect to be the case. For example, if a major public question mark arose over the solvency of the firm then presumably most policyholders would stop making further contributions to their policies if it would be in their interests to do so (or would be advised to do so by third parties, to the extent that they have such advisors).

13.6.12   Operational risk

Operational risk may be a particularly challenging type of risk to reformulate within a fully market consistent framework. This is because a large fraction of it may be idiosyncratic to

---

[23] Often expenses stresses are only treated in a relatively rudimentary way, if at all, in current solvency computation methodologies, presumably because of the difficulties of estimating with much accuracy how such factors might evolve through time.

the firm in question. It is therefore not obvious that there will be market observables that have much relevance to the market consistent price for such risks.

If a firm has professional indemnity insurance then the price paid for this could provide some guide to the market consistent price for its operational risk exposures. However, a number of challenges would arise if we wished to develop this logic, including:

(a) The professional indemnity cover a firm may have in place will typically have exclusions and be capped. The (remaining) operational risk exposures the firm carries may be quite different to the ones that it has hedged by buying such cover; and
(b) There may be undue moral hazard involved in such methodology. It would mean that if a firm could persuade an insurer that it was low risk then it would be treated as if it really was low risk even if this was not actually the case, potentially favouring form over substance.

Perhaps this is an area that will necessarily remain heavily 'real world' orientated. Perhaps work such as the enterprise risk management assessments that ratings agencies are increasingly carrying out on firms will come more to the fore. Perhaps greater market consistency (in the more limited sense referred to in Chapter 9) could be achieved via better collation of industry-wide data, coupled with greater effort to benchmark the firm in question against others within the same industry segment. This already seems to be happening, to some extent, due to market forces.

13.6.13   Non-life (i.e. property/casualty) insurance risk

Many of the emerging ideas being applied to operational risk are already commonplace within the general (i.e. non-life) insurance marketplace. For example, industry-wide data (including expense inflation data) is already often used to project forward future claims amounts (including claims incurred but not yet reported), often using as a base (at least for earlier years of account) claims already paid out to date.

Nevertheless, a good understanding of the particular dynamics of this type of insurance is also relevant here. For example, we might expect the premium rates at which insurance policies are written to give us *some* indication of a market price for transfer of insurance risk. And in some sense it does. However, the property/casualty insurance business, particularly the natural catastrophe business line, is notoriously exposed to the so-called *underwriting cycle*. If industry aggregate claim payments are high in one year (e.g. there is a major natural catastrophe) then marginal industry players stop providing coverage, and the remaining insurers and reinsurers typically succeed in raising prices for relevant insurance cover in the immediately ensuing years. Eventually, however, new players become attracted by such elevated premium levels, additional premium writing capacity re-enters the market and premium rates decline, until there is another set of events that restarts the cycle.

Thus *commutation rates*, i.e. the rates insurers may need to pay to existing policyholders to cancel future claim payments, may be a better guide to market-clearing prices for such exposures. One reason that the underwriting cycle seems to persist is because of the difficulties firms have in re-establishing business relationships if they have exited the market. Some of the price variation that exists in premium rates is therefore arguably a cost of 'staying in the game' in good years as well as bad.

13.7   DEFINED BENEFIT PENSION LIABILITIES

13.7.1   Introduction

Defined benefit (DB) pension liabilities have many similarities to life insurance annuity liabilities. Indeed, in some countries the norm is for defined benefit pension schemes to be established as insurance companies.

Where this is not the case, pensions actuaries have often come up with fairly different valuation approaches to those followed by life insurance actuaries. Often pension liabilities are valued using discount rates higher than risk-free, reflecting the actual assets in which the pension fund is invested.

It is widely recognised within the pensions industry that some of these valuation practices are influenced by political considerations. Private and public sector pension schemes often provide an important leg in the financial support of the elderly.

At first sight it seems difficult to justify from a theoretical perspective some of the differences that have arisen between these two disciplines, although valid differentiators include:

(a) There is usually a sponsoring employer. The (market consistent) 'value' of the scheme's liabilities can be heavily dependent on the strength of the sponsor covenant (even though pension actuarial practice does not typically present the results in this way), particularly if the scheme is in deficit, see e.g. Kemp (2005).
(b) Long ago (at least in the UK) DB pension funds often had substantial surpluses, and these surpluses were often spent providing discretionary pension improvements to beneficiaries, as part of the social 'contract' underlying pension provision. They thus had some of the characteristics of participating insurance contracts. However, this is less the case nowadays, at least in countries such as the UK where over time previously discretionary pension increase policies have become more mandatory and hence guaranteed.

Analysing the picture more closely, we find that some of the differences in valuation approaches actually observed in practice reflect differences in valuation purpose, as discussed below.

13.7.2   Solvency valuations

In a solvency computation, it is difficult to argue against the premise of 'same risk, same market consistent value'.[24] An obvious starting point for definition of the 'base' element as per Section 13.4 is thus to estimate what it might cost to buy out the (discontinuance) liabilities accrued to date with someone else, e.g. an insurance company. However, buy-out costs include some element of credit risk to the insurer, which we should strip out (thus increasing the liabilities) if we want our market consistent valuations to adhere to the principles set out in Section 13.4.2. The appropriate solvency add-on can then be derived in a manner akin to that set out in Section 13.6.

Within the pension fund community such a valuation would be known as a *discontinuance valuation*, although typically any solvency add-on within such a computation would be set to

---

[24] It might be possible to justify some deviation from 'same risk, same capital' if one thought that for systemic reasons solvency requirements for pension funds should differ from those for insurers, although sustaining such a view for the pension schemes of insurers might be tricky if the pension scheme is structured as an insurance contract with that insurer and ranks pari passu with the insurer's other policyholders.

zero[25] and the discount rate used might not exhibit zero spread versus risk-free. For example, the valuation might use corporate bond yields on the grounds that these are the types of assets that insurers might use to back equivalent insurance liabilities (ignoring the implicit credit risk the pension fund or beneficiaries would then have to the insurer itself which is introduced via this logic). Ignoring the need for any solvency add-on may also make the pension fund less resilient to potential future events such as adverse market movements (unless the fund is adopting a fully matched investment strategy).

If there are not enough assets to provide fully for the discontinuance liabilities then the balance is in effect captured within the sponsor covenant. If the sponsor defaults then the market consistent values of the beneficiaries' accrued entitlements will suffer, i.e. s, using the terminology described above, will rise. If the strength of the sponsor covenant is perceived to be weak or might change (as a result of a merger or acquisition) then those acting on the beneficiaries' behalf (e.g. pension fund trustees, if the pension fund is set up under a trust arrangement) will be interested in protecting themselves against the risk of sponsor default. This might involve seeking collateral, guarantees or extra contributions from the sponsor.

13.7.3   Ongoing valuations

Many pension fund valuations do not focus primarily on solvency valuations but instead focus more on the ongoing contribution rate(s) payable by the employer to fund continuing benefit accrual. This will be particularly true for funds that have a healthy surplus in a solvency computation or are perceived to have a very strong sponsor covenant. The latter can be seen to be akin to the former, if an explicit value is placed on the sponsor covenant within the scheme's balance sheet (although this is not commonly how pension fund valuations are currently presented).

Ongoing valuations aimed at establishing future contribution rate profiles are normally commissioned by the scheme itself or by its employer. They could be confidential to these parties alone apart from the usual requirement to provide beneficiaries with summarised results some time after the valuation is prepared.

It will normally be impossible to identify universally agreed upon 'market consistent' assumptions to use within such valuations. This can be seen from papers such as Cardinale *et al.* (2006). They use the term *background risk* to refer to unhedgeable risks such as uncertain mortality, wage growth and staff turnover experience and regulatory and operational risk. They explore the impact that the existence of such risks can have on UK pension funding and finance.

It can be argued that some of the risks that they classify as background risks are not completely unhedgeable. For example, individual pension funds could, if they so wished, hedge their mortality or longevity exposures by buying appropriate insurance contracts, even if there is probably insufficient insurance capacity to allow large numbers of them to do so all at once. Indeed, the UK bulk annuity buy-out market has increased substantially in size since their paper was written. Nevertheless, most of their background risks are not so easily hedged, e.g. uncertainty in wage inflation relative to price inflation. They describe

---

[25] Sometimes we might also need to differentiate between a buy-out valuation of the sort described here, a wind-up valuation and a closure valuation. The liabilities to which different pension scheme beneficiaries are entitled can differ depending on whether the scheme is formally wound up or merely put into run-off. Either can involve effective transfer of the liabilities to some other organisation, although the term 'buy-out' would more normally be associated with a transfer that legally extinguished any remaining liability as far as the pension fund (or its trustees or ex-trustees) were concerned.

various econometric ways of analysing such exposures and hence estimating the 'real world' probability distributions to which these exposures might be subject. They focus principally on how a pension fund's asset allocation should best be positioned to cater for such risks. Exercises like these most closely accord with the sorts of analyses we discussed in Chapter 12. They nearly always involve significant subjective input, most notably here in relation to the future returns expected from different asset categories and whether over the longer term investors will be rewarded for holding equity risk.

Several of the background risks referred to Cardinale *et al.*, such as uncertainty in future wage growth, are less relevant to solvency computations. They affect only future benefit accrual. The sponsoring employer will normally have discretion to stop such accrual (albeit this might cause employee relations issues). Over the years, pension fund actuaries have developed many different ways of taking account of potential future benefit accrual in ongoing valuations. We can view this as another sign that there is no single 'right' answer to how to do such calculations in a 'market consistent' manner. Such valuations can be thought of as akin to embedded value type computations as described in Section 13.5, but with a unique readership in mind.

Another form of 'ongoing' valuation that is even more akin to an embedded value type computation is the one that may be placed on a pension fund within the sponsor's own report and accounts. These would need to be on a 'going concern' basis to correspond with how other elements of these accounts would normally be drawn up. They should therefore again focus more on what might happen in deemed 'normal' scenarios than in the 'stressed' scenarios more applicable to solvency computations. However, there are advantages to the shareholder community more generally in having standardisation of assumptions adopted within such computations. This explains the involvement of accounting standards bodies in setting frameworks for such assumptions, see e.g. Section 5.2(6).

13.7.4 Transfer values

A final type of valuation that arises with a pension fund is the transfer value placed on an individual member's accrued entitlements when he or she seeks to move these entitlements to a different body (e.g. the pension scheme of a new employer).

These transfer values can typically only be reinvested with another pension arrangement.[26] Usually, schemes have flexibility regarding how such transfer values are set. This can lead to the replaying of arguments that we have explored elsewhere in this book in other contexts. For example, a scheme might argue that an illiquidity premium should be added to the discount rate used to derive these transfer values (irrespective of the nature of the assets in which the scheme is invested), thus making the transfer values smaller, on the grounds that the liabilities in question are illiquid, being akin to annuities. However, such scheme members may be able to transfer the value of their accrued benefits to a personal pension arrangement that is invested in cash or in other highly liquid assets. It is difficult to see why such members should be particularly happy to have this flexibility negated by a lower value placed on the accrued liabilities resulting from the application of a higher discount rate merely because of some supposed illiquidity premium type argument linked to the nature of the liabilities. Conversely, the scheme may actually invest in illiquid assets because it is hoping that the illiquidity premium potentially available on these assets should result in higher benefits payable to members. It would then seem less reasonable to allow scheme members to transfer at no cost to more

---

[26] This is because pension arrangements are usually tax privileged, to encourage individuals to save for their retirement.

liquid assets Moreover, if the scheme is underfunded, then paying out higher transfer values may concentrate the impact of the underfunding onto those members who remain with the scheme. Ideally, the focus should be on what the member is actually getting via the pension arrangement and what is equitable between different members.

13.8 UNIT PRICING

A final valuation type that many financial practitioners will come across in practice at some stage in their career is the valuation of a unitised fund.

In many respects the valuation methodology used is relatively irrelevant, because the assets of such a fund exactly correspond with its liabilities. If one side of the balance sheet is increased or reduced then so, automatically, will be the other side.

However, the valuation methodology adopted does have some important implications. In particular, the valuation is normally the price at which ownership entitlement transfers between different unit holders in the event of a unit holder buying or selling units. On the basis of Principle P7 the valuation therefore needs to be market consistent. Principle P9 warns us that this does not necessarily mean that it needs to be at exactly a mid-market valuation in all circumstances. It may not be 'fair' to price the fund in this manner, because fund transaction costs consequential on unit holders adding to or subtracting from their unit holdings may then be borne by the 'wrong' unit holders. Various mechanisms have been developed by fund providers that seek to balance strict equity in this context with simplicity and perceived fairness as far as investors are concerned, e.g. single pricing, dual pricing, swinging single pricing (in which the pricing basis can move from a bid to an offer basis, even if perhaps most of the time it is on a bid basis) and dilution adjustments (which are similar to swinging single prices, but with the 'swing' element explicitly differentiated in contract notes provided to customers). How a fund's governing documentation describes its approach to unit pricing will also strongly influence actual practice, since it can be argued that any reasonable approach should be acceptable as long as all investors in effect have equal opportunity to gain or lose from any particular way in which unit pricing is implemented.

The regulatory 'promise' to behave fairly in such circumstances, see Section 8.2, is particularly relevant here, since it implies that the firm itself should not take advantage of the unit pricing for its own ends. As a generalisation, firms that were singled out for criticism in the wake of the market timing scandals that affected mutual funds some years ago were ones that had offered certain investors privileged unit pricing approaches (that made market timing easier) not shared by the generality of the unit holder base since this could then be construed as involving the firm potentially lining its own pockets.[27]

---

[27] 'Market timing' here involved certain investors being able to buy units at prices that could reasonably be expected to be 'stale' and hence offered the possibility of these investors profiting at other investors' expense. For example, the firm might allow certain investors to choose whether to invest in the fund *after* the formal dealing point applicable to other investors. The investor in question could then decide whether to take up this opportunity on any particular day depending on whether the 'stale' price at which it would deal would be above or below the actual expected price at the precise point in time that its unit deal was placed, thereby on average gaining at the expense of other investors. The firm would then gain from an increased revenue base. Whether the firm realised that this would be the outcome is less relevant to the argument (although relevant to the compensation demanded). As far as the regulators were concerned such firms ought to have realised that they had a conflict of interest and ought to have managed this conflict more effectively.

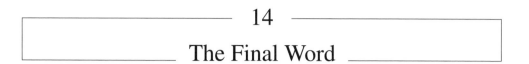

14

The Final Word

14.1 CONCLUSIONS

In this book we have explored from many angles the application of market consistency to a wide range of topics. Throughout, our theme has been to identify how best to reflect 'what the market has to say' in each situation.

In some circumstances, particularly where equity between different parties is concerned, a strong focus on market consistency seems to be very relevant. In others, the linkage is more oblique, although rarely if ever entirely absent given the powerful axioms that underpin market consistency.

In practice, markets rarely exhibit all the qualities we would ideally like them to have to make application of market consistency straightforward. But we reject the notion that we should ditch market consistency merely because it can be tricky to observe all of the market information we might like. Instead, we favour a suitable blending together of market derived information with reasoned human judgement. Even the relative lack of available market information can give us some indication of how a market might operate were it to exist. Markets have a tendency to dry up when what they would otherwise be saying is unpalatable. Adopting a market consistent mindset only when it is easy to do so may therefore introduce inappropriate bias in our own deliberations.

Even when systemic issues are at the fore, and market consistency might be thought possibly undesirable because it might lead to financial instability, we have discovered that it is still highly relevant, but more in terms of relative positioning *between* different market participants. Presumably, we want government actions in such circumstances to be fair and equitable between different economic agents. We should thus aim to take advantage of the strong bias towards equitable treatment that market consistency brings, even if we need to do so in ways that best add value to society as a whole.

14.2 MARKET CONSISTENT PRINCIPLES

We set out for ease of reference each of the market consistency principles we have identified earlier in this book, and the sections in which their derivations may be found.

Chapter 2: When is and when isn't market consistency appropriate?

Principle P1 (2.2.1): 'Value' is a term that has many different meanings. Unless the context makes clear the intended meaning, it should be used with a qualifier.

Principle P2 (2.2.1): When value is expressed in monetary terms and is immediate in nature then people will expect it to correspond to the amount of money that would need to be exchanged to buy or sell the item being valued, because the most important characteristic of money is that it is a medium of exchange.

Principle P3 (2.2.3): Most recipients of advice from financial practitioners will take for granted that monetary value, however measured, adheres to the basic axioms of additivity and scalability unless the context clearly justifies otherwise, because money itself adheres to these axioms.

Principle P4 (2.2.3): Financial practitioners wishing to derive valuations of future cash flows by calculating the expected values of these cash flows using their own (or other people's) 'real world' probabilities of outcomes should carefully consider the risk adjustments that then need to be incorporated in the discount rates used in these computations. In particular, they should bear in mind that the correct 'risk premium' to incorporate in the discounting computation (if they want their valuation framework to adhere to additivity and scalability axioms) may be negative and may bear no obvious link to the degree of uncertainty or 'risk' applicable to the cash flows being valued.

Principle P5 (2.2.4): Whilst a core aim of market consistency is objectivity by being faithful to market prices, market consistent valuations will often still involve subjective input. The more material is this subjectivity the more important it becomes for practitioners preparing these valuations to explain the judgements involved. They should be careful to minimise the impact that their own biases might have in selection of these subjective inputs.

Principle P6 (2.2.5): When a piece of work involves advising just one side of a commercial transaction then undue focus by practitioners on 'market consistency' with any previous ruling market price may not be considered the most desirable sort of advice by the client.

Principle P7 (2.2.6): When a piece of work involves an equitable apportionment of assets or liabilities between different parties then the parties in question are likely to expect the practitioner preparing the apportionment to do so broadly in line with a 'fair' (i.e. 'market consistent') apportionment struck by reference to the prices at which the assets or liabilities in question might trade between a willing buyer and a willing seller.

Principle P8 (2.2.8): One might expect 'market consistent' valuations to be uniquely identifiable if the markets involved are sufficiently deep, liquid and transparent. However, different adjustments in relation to the deemed future creditworthiness of the firm in question may be appropriate depending on the purpose to which the valuation is to be put. The practical impact of these adjustments will depend on the substitute reference rates that are used instead of the firm's own market implied level of creditworthiness.

Principle P9 (2.2.10): Market consistency may not just require a view to be formed about the price at which one might reasonably expect assets or liabilities to trade were markets to exist for them. It may also require assessment of the bid–offer characteristics of these hypothetical markets.

Principle P10 (2.7): Part of the market consistent value of an asset or a liability may relate to how discretion might be exercised in the future. In these cases it is normally helpful to divide the overall market consistent value between the part that relates to the value placed on contractual obligations and the part that relates to the value placed on continued exercise or non-exercise of these discretions. The two have different economic characteristics and hence may react quite differently in different scenarios.

Principle P11 (2.8): Computation of market consistent valuations should not be viewed in isolation. Instead practitioners should bear in mind the wider purpose. In particular, where market consistent liability valuations are being carried out as part of a capital adequacy assessment, practitioners should appreciate that it is the overall balance sheet size and strength of the covenant being provided to customers that is important, rather than how this balance sheet is apportioned between values placed on customer liabilities and on other balance sheet elements.

Chapter 3: Different meanings given to 'market consistent valuations'

Principle P12 (3.5.2): Markets, when they exist, temper the impact that optimistic (or pessimistic) views about the intrinsic 'worth' of an asset or a liability have on its market price. Failure of a market to form (or to continue to exist) may indicate a collective bias in such assessments by practitioners most obviously associated with advising potential market participants. These practitioners may therefore need to temper their own (collective) views when estimating the (market consistent) price at which an asset or liability would trade were such a market to exist.

Principle P13 (3.5.7): It is not correct to assume that there is a clear dividing line between marking-to-market and marking-to-model. Many examples of marking-to-market involve some element of modelling, albeit potentially hidden from the end-user. Even when the market in question appears to be deep, liquid and transparent, inclusion of some modelling element may result in a more accurate market consistent valuation, because the market may not be open continuously around the clock.

Chapter 4: Derivative pricing theory

Principle P14 (4.2.1.2): The term 'arbitrage' has several different meanings. Practitioners using this term should make clear what meaning(s) they are ascribing to this term, particularly if they may be perceived as providing both market consistent and non-market consistent advice at the same time, since the most natural meanings for this term are then inconsistent with each other.

Principle P15 (4.2.1.5): The most important mathematical principle in derivative pricing theory is the so-called 'principle of no arbitrage'. In the absence of market frictions this principle results in market prices adhering to the axioms of additivity and scalability and might better be described as the axiom of 'contemporaneous value continuity' in the light of Principle P14.

Principle P16 (4.2.3.2): In the absence of market frictions, *symmetric* derivatives can be valued by reference only to the principle of no arbitrage, as long as suitable market observables exist to price the underlying building blocks. However, the valuation of *asymmetric* derivatives requires further assumptions, which can be encapsulated in the so-called *risk-neutral probability distribution* ascribed to future outcomes.

Principle P17 (4.3.1.2): In the risk-neutral formulation, the value of a derivative can be calculated by working out the expected value of future outcomes (conditional on where the world is currently), weighting these outcomes by the risk-neutral probability of occurrence and discounting at the risk-free rate.

Principle P18 (4.3.1.6): However sophisticated are the models in question, the reliability of derivative pricing algorithms for deriving market consistent valuations depends heavily on the reliability of the calibration of these algorithms to market prices. This will depend not only on the computational robustness of the calibration process but also on how close in economic terms to the instrument being valued are the instruments whose prices are being used as inputs to the calibration process.

Principle P19: A pricing model that perfectly calibrates to a wide range of observed market prices will not necessarily correctly mimic the future or even current price sensitivities of these instruments or necessarily provide a reliable indication of how to hedge or mitigate the risks incurred with such exposures.

Principle P20 (4.4.2): Market standard pricing models should be seen principally as providing price quotation conventions to make comparative value analysis between similar instruments easier or to facilitate extrapolation from one instrument to others that have similar characteristics. They provide little if any guide as to how any particular market practitioner might actually think markets might behave in the future. Market practitioner views on the applicability or otherwise of these assumptions will, however, influence the practitioner's views on how similar the instruments might need to be for these comparisons or extrapolations to be meaningful.

Principle P21 (4.13): The determination of a market consistent value for an asset or liability not readily traded in a deep, liquid and transparent market will typically involve a calibration exercise incorporating market observable information. It therefore implicitly or explicitly includes subjective views about how relevant different market observables might be for the calibration in question.

Principle P22 (4.13): Even if no market observables closely match the calibration needs in question, it will typically still be appropriate when carrying out market consistent valuations to give *some* weight to available market observables. Including *some* element of reference back to market data, however imperfect, is likely to be more objective than relying solely on the practitioner's own (uncorroborated) views about how a hypothetical market in the asset or liability in question might operate.

Chapter 5: The risk-free rate

Principle P23 (5.2): The term 'risk-free' means different things to different people. As a result there may be a variety of observable rates all of which might be described by some as 'risk-free'. Practitioners should be careful to ensure that they choose the most appropriate rate when carrying out market consistent valuations, depending on the purpose to which the valuation will be put.

Principle P24 (5.2): Debt issued by governments, even ones overseeing well-established and robust economies, are not necessarily free of risk of issuer default. Exactly how this observation should be taken into account by firms within that government's jurisdiction in relation to market consistency poses tricky business and regulatory questions.

Principle P25 (5.3.1): Different market participants may place different interpretations on what should be meant by 'risk-free' rates because they may be interested in rates that exclude some risks but not others. It is important that the underlying logic justifying selective inclusion of certain types of risk is soundly based, because it is often difficult to demarcate precisely between different types of risk.

Principle P26 (5.3.2): Practitioners should not assume that swap rates contain no element of credit risk premium merely because the two parties to a swap may be protected from each other's default via collateralisation techniques. The main way in which swaps incorporate a credit risk element is indirectly, via the way in which the interest payable on their floating leg is defined. If practitioners wish to use swap rates to derive 'risk-free' rates then they should adjust observed swap rates by the market implied credit risk implicit within the underlying floating rates.

Principle P27 (5.3.4): Choice of methodology for determining risk-free rates can have a significant impact on the value placed on long-term liabilities.

Chapter 6: Liquidity theory

Principle P28 (6.2): Liquidity risk tends to show up only in extreme scenarios. But in such scenarios it can grow in severity very rapidly and can then be strongly influenced by the overall liquidity market 'climate' as well as by a firm's own internal liquidity needs.

Principle P29 (6.5.1): Liquidity is a concept that is quite complicated to pin down (and therefore to measure). Emphasising some elements of the concept over others can materially influence how much (il)liquidity premium we might expect different instruments to exhibit.

Principle P30 (6.5.4): It is virtually impossible to measure the price or value that the market places on liquidity in isolation, because most or all market observables that might incorporate that value depend on other risks that also cannot themselves be observed in isolation. Whilst it is tempting to seek to measure proxies and to extrapolate from their behaviour in 'normal' market conditions, the validity of such extrapolations may be limited because liquidity risk manifests itself most in 'stressed' market conditions.

Principle P31 (6.6): Pooled funds may give the appearance of providing customers with additional liquidity, even for intrinsically less liquid assets. However, this appearance can prove ephemeral in stressed circumstances. If a firm offering such funds cannot pass on this illiquidity to its customers in such circumstances then it may need to include in its own balance sheet a (negative) market consistent value relating to this liquidity mismatch.

Principle P32 (6.7): In stressed scenarios, market participants can be chillingly rational towards others in distress. Assumptions by a firm that it can access illiquidity premia on specific assets because it will be a long-term (e.g. a hold-to-maturity) investor in these assets may prove unfounded if the firm gets into distress and cannot then continue to be a long-term holder of the asset. As far as customers are concerned, capital is present to provide protection as and when such stressed scenarios *do* occur. Capital adequacy tests should treat with caution the assumption that a firm will always remain a long-term holder of such assets merely because this is its current stance.

Chapter 7: Risk measurement theory

Principle P33 (7.3.1): Risk can be measured both looking backwards in time and looking forwards in time. The two, whilst related, aim to answer somewhat different questions. We can only influence the future not the past, so most practical risk management focuses on forward-looking risk measurement.

Principle P34 (7.3.2.2): All historic risk measures are only imprecise measures of the 'intrinsic' but ultimately unobservable risk that a portfolio has been running. A portfolio that seems in the past to have run a low level of risk may actually have been exposed to latent risks that just happened not to show up during the period under analysis.

Principle P35 (7.4.4): Practitioners have developed many different forward-looking risk models and ways of estimating them. However, on closer analysis there are fewer variants than may appear at first sight, because most models and ways of estimating them extrapolate, in some way, the past into the future and we only have one past on which to base this extrapolation.

Principle P36 (7.5.1): Forward-looking risk measures that are ultimately derived from extrapolation, in some shape or form, of the past into the future are subject to the inherent limitation that there is relatively little data contained within 'the past' compared to what we would ideally want to have available for risk modelling purposes.

Principle P37 (7.6.2): A feature of modern credit markets is the assignment of credit ratings to different instruments by external credit ratings agencies. However, the existence of such ratings does not by itself ensure that these ratings are directly relevant to whatever activity the practitioner might want to use them for, or even that the ratings ascribed by such an agency to different types of instrument have the same degree of relevance for these activities.

Principle P38 (7.6.4.4): Collateralised debt obligations and other similar structures render theoretically invalid the distinction between market and credit risk because they make it possible to convert one into the other. Their existence therefore also highlights the need for risk measurement and management to be holistic, considering all types of risk simultaneously.

Principle P39 (7.8.2): Important tools in the armoury of practitioners wishing to mitigate against 'model' risk are to think outside the box and to carry out a range of stress tests that consider potentially different scenarios. However, stress testing should not be seen as a perfect panacea when doing so, since the stresses tested will often be constrained by what is considered 'plausible' in relation to past experience.

Chapter 8: Capital adequacy

Principle P40 (8.2): An accepted feature of modern economies is the regulation of firms operating within the financial services industry. The formulation of the different regulatory frameworks applicable to different parts of this industry should bear in mind the different types of roles different players undertake within this industry and how they interact with the fundamental attributes of money, namely how money is a medium of exchange and how it is also a store of value. For practical reasons, harmonisation across different types of firms may also be desirable, to avoid regulatory arbitrage, given that many firms are involved in many different parts of the industry simultaneously.

Chapter 9: Calibrating risk statistics to perceived 'real world' distributions

Principle P41 (9.1): The risk management paradigm currently adopted by most practitioners in the financial community involves assessing risks by reference to their perceived 'real world' likelihood of occurrence. It does not therefore necessarily provide effective estimates of the market costs of hedging against such risks, which are instead driven by their risk-neutral probabilities of occurrence. It is arguably therefore an inappropriate basis to use when formulating economic (or regulatory) capital requirements.

Principle P42 (9.3.2): How well a risk model might have performed had it been applied in the past can be assessed using backtesting. However, practitioners using such techniques should bear in mind that it is tricky in any such backtesting to avoid *look-back* bias, even when the model is tested out-of-sample, i.e. even when any parameter estimates used at a particular point in time within the model are derived from data that would have been historic at that time. This is because look-back bias will creep in via the structure of the risk model itself and not just via the input parameters used in its evaluation at any particular point in time.

Principle P43 (9.5.2): Most financial markets seem to exhibit fat-tailed returns for data sampled over sufficiently short time periods, i.e. extreme outcomes seem to occur more frequently than would be expected were returns to be coming from a (log) Normal distribution. This is true both for asset types that might intrinsically be expected to exhibit fat-tailed behaviour (e.g. some types of bond, given the large market value declines that can be expected to occur if the issuer of the bond defaults) and for asset types, like equities, where there is less intrinsic reason to postulate strong asymmetric return characteristics.

Principle P44 (9.5.2): Not all fat tails are bad. The extent to which a portfolio exhibits fat-tailed behaviour appears to be partly linked to the extent of conviction being expressed within the portfolio. If the manager can arrange for the fat tails to be concentrated on the upside rather than the downside then they will add to performance rather than subtract from it.

Principle P45 (9.5.5): Skewness and kurtosis are tools commonly used to assess the extent of fat-tailed behaviour. However, they are not particularly good tools for doing so when the focus is on behaviour in the distribution extremities, since they do not necessarily give appropriate weight to behaviour there. Modelling distribution extremities using the so-called fourth-moment Cornish-Fisher approach (an approach common in some parts of the financial services industry that explicitly refers to these statistics and arguably provides the intrinsic statistical rationale for their use in modelling fat tails) is therefore also potentially flawed. A more robust approach may be to curve fit the quantile–quantile form more directly.

Principle P46 (9.5.6): For major western (equity) markets, a significant proportion of deviation from (log) Normality in daily (index) return series appears to come from time-varying volatility, particularly in the upside tail. This part of any fat-tailed behaviour may be able to be managed by reference to rises in recent past shorter-term volatility or forward-looking measures such as implied volatility.

Principle P47 (9.6.5): A substantial proportion of 'fat-tailed' behaviour (i.e. deviation from Normality) exhibited by *joint* return series appears to come from time-varying volatility. This part of any fat-tailed behaviour may be able to be managed by reference to rises in recent past shorter-term volatilities and correlations or by reference to forward-looking measures such as implied volatility and implied correlation or implied covariance.

Principle P48 (9.6.5): Conversely, time-varying volatility does not seem to explain all fat-tailed behaviour exhibited by joint (equity) return series. Extreme events can still come 'out of the blue', highlighting the continuing merit of practitioners using risk management tools like stress testing that seek to reflect the existence of such 'unknown unknowns' or 'black swan' events.

Chapter 10: Calibrating risk statistics to 'market implied' distributions

Principle P49 (10.3.1): Fully 'market consistent' risk measurement focuses on market implied, i.e. 'risk-neutral', probabilities of occurrence. It also favours use of coherent risk measures that satisfy additivity and scalability criteria, these being key axioms underlying market consistency more generally.

Principle P50 (10.3.2): Fully 'market consistent' regulatory capital frameworks should focus on how much capital is required to arrange for the market implied risks expressed within customer liabilities to be lower than some pre-specified (but possibly time-varying) level.

Chapter 11: Avoiding undue pro-cyclicality in regulatory frameworks

Principle P51 (11.3): In times of systemic stress, market consistency still has strong relevance, because the public still expects fair and equitable value to accrue from public expenditure, including public expenditure aimed at promoting financial stability.

Chapter 12: Portfolio construction

Principle P52 (12.6): When applying market consistency to (active) portfolio construction practitioners should remember the importance that *non*-market consistent thinking also plays in such activities, given the importance accorded in these activities to practitioner views about how markets might be 'incorrectly' assessing the future worth of different investments.

Chapter 13: Calibrating valuations to the market

Principle P53 (13.3.2): In general, exchanges go to considerable trouble to ensure that the prices at which instruments trade on them are realistic market prices, since this is an important part of their rationale for existence and hence for their sound functioning. It would therefore be normal to use prices directly derived from exchange feeds when valuing these assets and liabilities in a market consistent manner, unless the quoted prices are 'stale', correspond to distressed transactions or express an inappropriate level of 'own' credit risk for the purpose in hand.

Principle P54 (13.3.5): Where instruments do not trade on well-regulated and well-organised exchanges, and particularly where any OTC market in them is also limited, then greater usage of modelling and hence dependency on calibration may be necessary when preparing market consistent valuations. For more exotic instrument types it is particularly important to understand fully the risks being expressed by the instrument, since these risks may not be shared by more accessible market observables.

Principle P55 (13.5): Market consistent liability valuations applicable to embedded value calculations will in general not be the same as those applicable to regulatory solvency computations, because the two purposes differ. In particular, the assumptions we should adopt about customer behaviour in the 'normal' scenarios most appropriate to embedded value computations may not be appropriate to assume in the 'stressed' scenarios more applicable to regulatory solvency computations.

Bibliography

Hyperlinks to many of the references set out below are accessible via www.marketconsistency .com or www.nematrian.com/marketconsistency.aspx.

Abramowitz, M. and Stegun, I.A. (1970). *Handbook of Mathematical Functions*. Dover Publications Inc.

Acharya, V.V. and Pedersen, L.H. (2005). Asset pricing with liquidity risk. *Journal of Financial Economics*, **77**, 375–410

AFIC, BVCA and EVCA (2006). *International Private Equity and Venture Capital Valuation Guidelines, October 2006 edition*. Association Française des Investisseurs en Capital, British Venture Capital Association and European Private Equty and Venture Capital Association

Amato, J. and Furfine, C. (2003). Are credit ratings procyclical? *Bank for International Settlements*, Working Paper No. 129

Arbarbanel, H.D.I. (1993). The analysis of observed chaotic data in physical systems. *Reviews of Modern Physics*, **65**, 4

Artzner, P., Delbaen, F., Eber, J. and Heath, D. (1999). Coherent measures of risk. *Mathematical Finance*, **9**, No. 3, 203–228

ASB (2008). *Discussion Paper: The Financial Reporting of Pensions*. UK Accounting Standards Board

Avellandeda, M., Friedman, C., Buff, R, Granchamp, N., Kruk, L. and Newman, J. (2001). Weighted Monte Carlo: a new technique for calibrating asset-pricing models. *International Journal of Theoretical and Applied Finance* **4**(1), 91–119

Bank of England (2008a). Exceptional fine-tuning OMO. *Bank of England*, 17 March 2008

Bank of England (2008b). Markets and operations. *Bank of England Quarterly Bulletin, Q1 2008*

Bank of England (2008c). *Financial Stability Report, October 2008*. Bank of England

Bank of England (2008d). Markets and operations. *Bank of England Quarterly Bulletin, Q3 2008*

Baxter, M. and Rennie, A. (1996). *Financial Calculus: An Introduction to Derivative Pricing*. Cambridge University Press

BCBS (1988). *Basel Committee: International Convergence of Capital Measurement and Capital Standards*. Basel Committee on Banking Supervision

BCBS (1996). *Amendment to the Capital Accord to Incorporate Market Risks*. Basel Committee on Banking Supervision

BCBS (1998). *Amendment to the Basel Capital Accord of July 1988*. Basel Committee on Banking Supervision

BCBS (2006). *Basel II: International Convergence of Capital Measurement and Capital Standards: A Revised Framework – Comprehensive Version*. Basel Committee on Banking Supervision

BCBS (2008). *Principles for Sound Liquidity Risk Management and Supervision*. Basel Committee on Banking Supervision

Benford, J. and Nier, E. (2008). Monitoring cyclicality of Basel II capital requirements. *Bank of England*, Financial Stability Paper No. 3, December 2007

Billah, M.B., Hyndman, R.J. and Koehler, A.B. (2003). Empirical information criteria for time series forecasting model selection. *Monash University, Australia, Department of Econometrics and Business Statistics*, Working Paper 2/2003, ISSN 1440-771X

Black, F. and Scholes, M. (1973). The pricing of options and corporate liabilities. *Journal of Political Economy*, **81**, 637–654

Bookstaber, R.M. and McDonald, J.B. (1987). A general distribution for describing security price returns. *Journal of Business*, **60**, No. 3, 401–424

Booth, P.M. and Marcato, G. (2004). The measurement and modelling of commercial real estate performance. *British Actuarial Journal*, **10**, No. 1, 5–61

Bouchard, J. (2008). Economics needs a scientific revolution. *Nature*, **435**, 1181

Brunetti, C. and Caldarera, A. (2006). Asset prices and asset correlations in illiquid markets. *Computing in Economics and Finance 2006, Society for Computational Economics*, Paper 331

Brunnermeier, M.K. (2009). Deciphering the Liquidity and Credit Crunch 2007–2008. *Journal of Economic Perspectives*, Vol. 23, No. 1, Winter 2009, 77–100

Campbell, S.D. (2006). A review of backtesting and backtesting procedures. *Journal of Risk*, **9**, No. 2, 1–17

CAQ (2007a). *Measurement of Fair Value in Illiquid (or Less Liquid) Markets*. Center for Audit Quality

CAQ (2007b). *Consolidation of Commercial Paper Conduits*. Center for Audit Quality

CAQ (2007c). *Accounting for Underwriting and Loan Commitments*. Center for Audit Quality

Cardinale, M., Katz, G., Kumar, J. and Orszag, J.M. (2006). Background risk and pensions. *British Actuarial Journal*, **12**, No. 1, 79–134

CEIOPS (2007a). *Solvency II QIS3 Technical Specifications Part 1*. Committee of European Insurance and Occupational Pensions Supervisors

CEIOPS (2007b). *Solvency II QIS4 Technical Specifications (draft)*. Committee of European Insurance and Occupational Pensions Supervisors

CEIOPS (2008). *Technical Specifications QIS4*. Committee of European Insurance and Occupational Pensions Supervisors, 31 March 2008

CESR (2008). *Risk Management Principles for UCITS. Consultation Paper*. The Committee of European Securities Regulators, August 2008

CFO Forum (2008a). *Market Consistent Embedded Value Principles*. CFO Forum

CFO Forum (2008b). *Market Consistent Embedded Values: Basis for Conclusions*. CFO Forum

Cheung, W. (2007a). The Black-Litterman model explained (II). *Lehman Brothers: Equity Quantitative Analytics*, 29 March 2007

Cheung, W. (2007b). The Black-Litterman model (III): augmented for factor-based portfolio construction. *Lehman Brothers: Equity Quantitative Analytics*, 30 August 2007

Christensen, B.J. and Prabhala, N.R. (1998). The relation between implied and realized volatility. *Journal of Financial Economics*, **50**, 125–150

Christoffersen, P. (1998). Evaluating interval forecasts. *International Economic Review*, **39**, 841–862

Christoffersen, P. and Pelletier, D. (2004). Backtesting value-at-risk: a duration-based approach. *Journal of Empirical Finance*, **2**, 84–108

Cowling, C.A., Gordon, T.J. and Speed, C.A. (2004). Funding defined benefit pension schemes. *British Actuarial Journal*, **11**, No. 1, 63–97

Creedon, S., Forrester, I., Jakhria, P., Kemp, M.H.D., Pelsser, A., Smith, A.D. and Wilson, D.C.E. (2008). Choice of discount rate: review of principles and recent developments. *Institute of Actuaries: Finance, Investment and Risk Management Board working paper*

Cremers, M. and Weinbaum, D. (2007). Deviations from put–call parity and stock return predictability. *Social Science Research Network*

CRMPG-III (2008). *Containing Systemic Risk: The Road to Reform*. Report of the Counterparty Risk Management Policy Group III, 6 August 2008

CRO Forum (2008a). Comments on QIS4 Draft Technical Specification. *CRO Forum*, 18 February 2008

CRO Forum (2008b). Addressing the pro-cyclical nature of Solvency II. *CRO Forum*, 25 November 2008

Das, S.R., Ericsson, J. and Kalimipalli, M. (2003). Liquidity and bond markets. *Journal of Investment Management*, **1**, No. 4, 1–9

Davidson, C. (2008). Measuring liquidity risk. *Risk*, September 2008

Davis, M.H.A., Panas, V.G. and Zariphopoulou, T. (1993). European option pricing with transaction costs. *SIAM Journal of Control and Optimisation*, **31**, 470–493

Derman, E. and Kani, I. (1998). Stochastic implied trees: arbitrage pricing with stochastic term and strike structure. *International Journal of Theoretical and Applied Finance*, **1**, 61–110

Deutsche Bank (2007). Volatility Returns. *Deutsche Bank Equity Derivatives Strategy Group Research Paper*, 14 December 2007

Dowd, K. (2006). Backtesting market risk models in a standard normality framework. *Journal of Risk*, **9**, No. 2, 93–111

Duffie, D. (1992). *Dynamic Asset Pricing Theory*. Princeton University Press

Dupire, B. (1994). Pricing with a smile. *Risk Magazine*, January 1994

Dwyer, D.W. (2007). The distribution of defaults and Bayesian model validation. *Journal of Risk Model Validation*, **1**, No. 1, 23–52

Economist, The (2008). Economics focus: same as it ever was. *The Economist*, 12 January 2008

Edelman, A. and Rao, N.R. (2005). Random matrix theory. *Acta Numerica* **14**, 233–297

Elices, A. and Giménez, E. (2006). Weighted Monte Carlo. *Risk*. May 2006

Emrich, S. and Crow, C. (2007). Quant 2.0? *Morgan Stanley Global Quantitative Insights*, 18 December 2007

Escaffre, L., Foulquier, P. and Touron, P. (2008). The fair value controversy: ignoring the real issue. *Edhec Financial Analysis and Accounting Research Centre Working Paper*

European Commission (2007a). *'Solvency II': Frequently Asked Questions (FAQs)*. europa.eu Memo/07/286

European Commission (2007b). *'Solvency II': EU to Take Global Lead in Insurance Regulation*. europa.eu IP/07/1060

Fabozzi, F.J., Focardi, S.M. and Jonas, C. (2008). *Challenges in Quantitative Equity Management*. CFA Research Foundation

Financial News (2008). BarCap backs Libor alternative. *Financial News*, 2 June 2008

Financial Times (2008a). Auditors apply extra scrutiny. *Financial Times*, 2 January 2008

Financial Times (2008b). An unforgiving eye. *Financial Times*, 14 March 2008

Financial Times (2008c). UK banking association looks at boosting Libor dollar products. *Financial Times*, 10 June 2008

Financial Times (2008d). SEC aims to curb ratings dependency. *Financial Times*, 26 June 2008

Financial Times (2008e). Banking regulator calls for clean slate. *Financial Times*, 17 October 2008

Financial Times (2008f). Volkswagen driven to top spot by shock surge in its share price. *Financial Times*, 29 October 2008

Fisher, M. (2002). Special repo rates: an introduction. *Federal Reserve Bank of Atlanta Economic Review*, Second Quarter 2002

Frankland, R., Smith, A.D., Wilkins, T., Varnell, E., Holtham, A., Biffis, E., Eshun, S. and Dullaway, D. (2008). Modelling extreme market events. *Paper presented to Institute of Actuaries Sessional Meeting*, 3 November 2008

FSA (2007). Discussion Paper 07/7: Review of the liquidity requirements for banks and building societies. *UK Financial Services Authority*

FSA (2008a). Discussion Paper 08/4: Insurance risk management: the path to Solvency II. *UK Financial Services Authority*

FSA (2008b). Consultation Paper 08/22: Strengthening liquidity standards. *UK Financial Services Authority*

FSA (2008c). Consultation Paper 08/24: Stress and scenario testing. *UK Financial Services Authority*

Garcia, J., Goossens, S. and Schoutens, W. (2008). Let's jump together: pricing credit derivatives. *Risk*, September 2008

Giamorridis, D. and Ntoula, I. (2007). A comparison of alternative approaches for determining the downside risk of hedge fund strategies. *Edhec Risk and Asset Management Research Centre*

Gordy, M. (2003). A risk-factor foundation for risk-based capital rules. *Journal of Financial Intermediation*, **12**, 199–232

GPPC (2007). Determining fair value of financial instruments under IFRS in current market conditions. *Global Public Policy Committee* (of the large accounting networks)

Hayes, B.T. (2007). August 2007 quantitative equity turbulence: an unkown unknown becomes a known unknown. *Lehman Brothers Alternative Investment Management*, 9 November 2007

Heath, D., Jarrow, R.A. and Morton, A. (1992). Bond pricing and the term structure of interest rates: a new methodology for contingent claims valuation. *Econometrica*, **60**, 77–105

Heywood, G.C., Marsland, J.R. and Morrison, G.M. (2003). Practical risk management for equity portfolio managers. *British Actuarial Journal*, **8**, 1061–1123

Hodges, S.D. and Neuberger, A. (1989). Optimal replication of contingent claims under transaction costs. *Review of Future Markets*, 8

Hosty, G.M., Groves, S.J., Murray, C.A. and Shah, M. (2007). Pricing and risk capital in the equity release market. *Paper presented to the Institute of Actuaries*, October 2007

Hu, Z., Kerkhof, J., McCloud, P. and Wackertapp, J. (2006). Cutting edges using domain integration. *Risk*, November 2006

Hull, J.C. (2003). *Options, Futures and Other Derivatives*, 5th edition. Prentice Hall

Hull, J.C. and White, A. (1998). Incorporating volatility up-dating into the historical simulation method for VaR. *Journal of Risk*, **1**, No. 1, 5–19

Hurlin, C. and Tokpavi, S. (2006). Backtesting value-at-risk accuracy: a simple new test. *Journal of Risk*, **9**, No. 2, 19–37

IAA (2008a). *Measurement of Liabilities for Insurance Contracts: Current Estimate and Risk Margins. Re-exposure draft*. International Actuarial Association ad hoc Risk Margin Working Group, 24 March 2008

IAA (2008b). *A Note on Financial Economics*. International Actuarial Association (Financial Risk Committee)

IASB (2007a). *Discussion Paper: Preliminary Views on Insurance Contracts. Part 1: Invitation to Comment and main text*. International Accounting Standards Board

IASB (2007b). *Discussion Paper: Preliminary Views on Insurance Contracts. Part 2: Appendices*. International Accounting Standards Board

IASB (2008). *Reclassification of Financial Assets. Amendments to IAS Financial Instruments: Recognition and Measurement and IFRS 7 Financial Instruments: Disclosure*. International Accounting Standards Board

IMA (2004). *Market Timing: Guidelines for Managers of Investment Funds*. Investment Management Association

IMA and DATA (2004). *Pricing Guidance for Investment Funds: Fair Value Pricing*. Investment Management Association and the Depositary and Trustee Association

Jarrow, R., Li, L., Mesler, M. and van Deventer, D. (2007). The determinants of corporate credit spreads. *Risk*, September 2007

Jaschke, S.R. (2002). The Cornish-Fisher-expansion in the context of delta-gamma-normal approximations. *Journal of Risk*, **4**, No. 4

Kashyap, A.K., Rajan, R.G. and Stein, J.C. (2008). Rethinking capital regulation. *Federal Reserve Bank of Kansas City symposium on Maintaining Stability in a Changing Financial System*, 21–23 August 2008

Kemp, M.H.D. (1997). Actuaries and derivatives. *British Actuarial Journal*, **3**, 51–162

Kemp, M.H.D., Cumberworth, M., Gardner, D., Johnson, J. and Sandford, C. (2000). *Portfolio Risk Measurement and Reporting: An Overview for Pension Funds*. Institute of Actuaries

Kemp, M.H.D. (2005). Risk management in a fair valuation world. *British Actuarial Journal*, **11**, No. 4, 595–712

Kemp, M.H.D. (2007). 130/30 funds: extending the alpha generating potential of long-only equity portfolios. *Threadneedle Asset Management working paper*

Kemp, M.H.D. (2008a). Efficient implementation of global equity ideas. *Threadneedle Asset Management working paper*

Kemp, M.H.D. (2008b). Enhancing alpha delivery via global equity extended alpha portfolios. *Threadneedle Asset Management working paper*

Kemp, M.H.D. (2008c). Efficient alpha capture in socially responsible investment portfolios. *Threadneedle Asset Management working paper*

Kemp, M.H.D. (2008d). Catering for the fat-tailed behaviour of investment returns: improving on skew, kurtosis and the Cornish-Fisher adjustment. *Threadneedle Asset Management working paper*

Kemp, M.H.D. (2009). Market consistency: tools and studies. www.nematrian.com/marketconsistency. aspx

Kent, J. and Morgan, E. (2008). Dynamic policyholder behaviour. *Paper presented to the Staple Inn Actuarial Society*, 18 November 2008

Kuenzi, D.E. (2005). Variance swaps and non-constant vega. *Risk*, October 2005

Kupiec, P. (1995). Techniques for verifying the accuracy of risk management models. *Journal of Derivatives*, **3**, 73–84

Ledlie, M.C., Corry, D.P., Finkelstein, G.S., Ritchie, A.J., Su, K. and Wilson, D.C.E. (2008). Variable annuities. *Paper presented to the Faculty of Actuaries*, 17 March 2008 *and to the Institute of Actuaries*, 31 March 2008

Lee, C.M.C., Shleifer, A. and Thaler, R.H. (1990). Anomalies – closed-end mutual funds. *Journal of Economic Perspectives*, **4**.

Leippold, M. (2004). Don't rely on VaR. *Euromoney*, November 2004

Liodakis, M., Dupleich-Ulloa, R. and Mesomeris, S. (2008). Academic Research Digest. *Citigroup Global Markets Quantitative Analysis Research Paper*, 15 January 2008

Litterman, R. and the Quantitative Resources Group, Goldman Sachs Asset Management (2003). *Modern Investment Management: An Equilibrium Approach*. John Wiley & Sons, Inc.

Longstaff, F.A. (2005). Asset pricing in markets with illiquid assets. *AFA Boston Meetings Papers or Social Science Research Network*, January 2005

Longuin, F. (1993). Booms and crashes: application of extreme value theory to the U.S. stock market. *Institute of Finance and Accounting, London Business School*, Working Paper No. 179

Lowenstein, R. (2001). *When Genius Failed: The Rise and Fall of Long-Term Capital Management*. Fourth Estate

Mackay, C. (1841). *Extraordinary Popular Delusions and the Madness of Crowds*. Wordsworth Reference

Malz, A. (2003). Liquidity risk: current research and practice. *RiskMetrics Journal*, **4**, No. 1

Markowitz, H. (1952). Portfolio selection. *Journal of Finance*, **7**, No. 1, 77–91

Mehta, S.J.B., Abbot, M.G., Addison, D.T., Dodhia, M., Hitchen, C.J., Oddie, A.J., Poulding, M.R. and Riddington, D.M. (1996). The financial management of unit trust and investment companies. *British Actuarial Journal*, **2**, 1195–1253

Merton, R.C. (1974). On the pricing of corporate debt: the risk structure of interest rates. *Journal of Finance*, **29**, 449–470

Neuberger, A.J. (1990). Option pricing: a non-stochastic approach. *London Business School Institute of Finance and Accounting*. IFA Working Paper 183

Novy-Marx, R. (2004). On the excess returns to illiquidity. *University of Chicago Booth School of Business working paper*

Overhaus, M., Bermúdez, A., Buehler, H., Ferraris, A., Jordinson, C. and Lamnourar, A. (2007). *Equity Hybrid Derivatives*. John Wiley & Sons, Inc.

Palin, J. (2002). Agent based stock-market models: calibration issues and application. *University of Sussex MSc thesis*

Palin, J., Silver, N., Slater, A. and Smith, A.D. (2008). Complexity economics: application and relevance to actuarial work. *Institute of Actuaries FIRM Conference*, June 2008

Patel, C. (2008). Pensions regulation: a bridge too far? *The Actuary*, 1 March 2008

PCAOB (2007). *Staff Audit Practice Alert No. 2: Matters Related to Auditing Fair Value Measurements of Financial Instruments and the Use of Specialists*. Public Company Accounting Oversight Board, 10 December 2007

Peek, J., Reuss, A. and Scheuenstuhl, G. (2008). Evaluating the impact of risk based funding requirements on pension funds. *OECD Working Papers on Insurance and Private Pensions*, No. 16, OECD Publishing

Pena, V.H. de la, Rivera, R. and Ruiz-Mata, J. (2006). Quality control of risk measures: backtesting VAR models. *Journal of Risk*, **9**, No. 2, 39–54

Pengelly, M. (2008). Sunk by correlation. *Risk*, **21**, No. 7, 20–24

Persaud, A. (2007) The right direction for credit ratings agencies. *Financial Times*, 19 October 2007

Press, W.H., Teukolsky, S.A., Vetterling, W.T. and Flannery, B.P. (1992). *Numerical Recipes in C: The Art of Scientific Computing*, 2nd edition. Cambridge University Press

Pykhtin, M. and Dev, A. (2002). Analytical approach to credit risk modelling. *Risk*, **15**, 26–32

Ren, Y., Madan, D. and Qian, M.Q. (2007). Calibrating and pricing with embedded local volatility models. *Risk Magazine*, September 2007

Roach (2008). Add 'financial stability' to the Fed's mandate. *Financial Times*, 28 October 2008

Rockinger, M. and Jondeau, E. (2002). Entropy densities with an application to autoregressive conditional skewness and kurtosis. *Journal of Econometrics*, **106**, 119–142

Rogers, L.C.G. and Williams, D. (1994). *Diffusions, Markov Processes and Martingales Vol I*. John Wiley & Sons

Rogoff, K. and Reinhart, C. (2008). Is the 2007 sub-prime financial crisis so different? An international historical comparison. *American Economic Association*, January 2008

Rösch, D. and Scheule, H. (2007). Stess-testing credit risk parameters: an application to retail loan portfolios. *Journal of Risk Model Validation*, **1**, No. 1, 55–75

Rowe, D. (2005). Whither stress testing? *Risk*, **18**, No. 10

Rubinstein, M. (1996). Implied binomial trees. *Journal of Finance*, July 1994

Rule, D. (2008). Time is nigh to rethink basis of floating rate debt. *Financial Times Insight Column, Financial Times*, 10 April 2008

Scherer, B. (2007). *Portfolio Construction and Risk Budgeting*, 3rd edition. RiskBooks

Schönbucher, P.J. (2003). *Credit Derivatives Pricing Models*. Wiley Finance

Sheldon, T.J. and Smith, A.D. (2004). Market consistent valuation of life assurance business. *British Actuarial Journal*, **10**, 543–626

Smith, A.D. (1995). Recent developments. *Working paper for the Group Consultatif Summer School, March 1995, run by the Institute of Actuaries*

Smith, A.D. (2008). Swap spreads – why have they become negative? *Deloitte Financial Services IMU Team*

Soklakov, A. (2008). Information derivatives. *Risk*, April 2008

Stein, R.M. (2007). Benchmarking default prediction models: pitfalls and remedies in model validation. *Journal of Risk Model Validation*, **1**, No. 1, 77–113

Taleb, N.N. (2004). *Fooled by Randomness*, 2nd edition. Penguin Books

Taleb, N.N. (2007). *The Black Swan*. Penguin Books

Tasche, D. (2007). Shortfall: a tail of two parts. *Risk*, February 2007.

Times, The (2008). Lehman's demise triggers huge default as Fed bailout fears grow. *The Times (UK)*, 11 October 2008

Treacy and Carey (1998). Credit risk rating at large US banks. *Federal Reserve Bulletin*, **84**(11), 897–921

Turner, A. (2009). The financial crisis and the future of financial regulation (Speech given to the Economist's Inaugural City Lecture). *FSA*, 21 January 2009

Vasicek, O. (1977). An equilibrium characterization of the term structure. *Journal of Financial Economics*, **5**, 177–188

Vetzal, K.R. (1994). A survey of stochastic continuous time models of the term structure of interest rates. *Insurance: Mathematics and Economics*, **14**, 139–161

Webber, L. and Churm, R. (2007). Decomposing corporate bond spreads. *Bank of England Quarterly Review*, Q4 2007

Whalley, A.E. and Wilmott, P. (1993). An asymptotic analysis of the Davis, Panas and Zariphopoulou model for option pricing with transaction costs. *Mathematical Institute, Oxford University, Oxford*.

Wilson, D.C.E. (2008). (Il)liquidity premium estimation. *Barrie & Hibbert research quoted at The UK Actuarial Profession Open Forum on Liquidity Premia in the Current Environment*, 6 November 2008

Wood, D. (2008). Correlation: breaking down. *Risk*, September 2008

Wüthrich, M.V., Bühlmann, H. and Furrer, H. (2007). *Market-Consistent Actuarial Valuation*. Springer

Yetis, A. (2008). The capital ratio conundrum. *Risk*, September 2008

Zumbach, G. (2006). Backtesting risk methodologies from one day to one year. *Journal of Risk*, **9**, No. 2, 55–91

Index

Indexed by Terry Halliday (HallidayTerence@aol.com).